Failure to Adjust

Failure to Adjust

How Americans Got Left Behind in the Global Economy

Edward Alden

A COUNCIL ON FOREIGN RELATIONS BOOK

ROWMAN & LITTLEFIELD
Lanham • Boulder • New York • London

Published by Rowman & Littlefield
A wholly owned subsidiary of The Rowman & Littlefield Publishing Group, Inc.
4501 Forbes Boulevard, Suite 200, Lanham, Maryland 20706
www.rowman.com

Unit A, Whitacre Mews, 26-34 Stannary Street, London SE11 4AB

British Library Cataloguing in Publication Information Available

Library of Congress Cataloging-in-Publication Data

The hardback edition of this book was previously cataloged by the Library of Congress as follows:

Names: Alden, Edward H., author.
Title: Failure to adjust : how Americans got left behind in the global
   economy / Edward Alden.
Description: Lanham : Rowman & Littlefield, [2016] | Includes bibliographical
   references and index.
Identifiers: LCCN 2016026357 (print) | LCCN 2016038649 (ebook) |
Subjects: LCSH: United States—Commerce. | United States—Commercial policy.
   | United States—Foreign economic relations. | United States—Economic
   conditions—1945- | United States—Economic policy.
Classification: LCC HF3031 .A598 2016 (print) | LCC HF3031 (ebook) | DDC
   382/.30973—dc23
LC record available at https://lccn.loc.gov/2016026357

ISBN: 978-1-4422-7260-6 (cloth : alk. paper)
ISBN: 978-1-5381-0479-8 (pbk. : alk. paper)
ISBN: 978-1-5381-0909-0 (electronic)

∞™ The paper used in this publication meets the minimum requirements of American National Standard for Information Sciences—Permanence of Paper for Printed Library Materials, ANSI/NISO Z39.48-1992.

Printed in the United States of America

Contents

Foreword   vii

Acknowledgments   xvii

1   The End of the World's Greatest Autarky   1

2   Confronting the Competition: The Limitations of Trade Policy   21

3   Confronting the Competition: How a Strong Dollar Has Hurt   53

4   Investment: The Winners and the Losers from Offshoring   79

5   Helping the Losers: The Tragedy of Trade Adjustment Assistance   107

6   Tiger Moms and Failing Schools: Competitive Challenges at Home   127

7   How to Think about Economic Competitiveness   153

8   A Strategy for Competing in a Globalized World   171

Notes   203

Index   237

About the Author   249

Foreword

Donald J. Trump visited the once-thriving steel town of Monessen, Pennsylvania, on June 28, 2016, during his run for the Republican presidential nomination. It had been a long time since anyone with aspirations to the White House had bothered to remember Monessen, which lies along a bend in the Monongahela River about twenty-five miles south of Pittsburgh. The last had been President John F. Kennedy, more than half a century prior. When he rolled into town on October 13, 1962, Kennedy's crowd was estimated at more than 25,000 people—in a city with an official population of 18,400. It was a typical campaign rally, with Kennedy—who had won some 75 percent of the town's votes when he was elected in 1960—urging residents to turn out even more strongly for the Democrats in that year's congressional and gubernatorial races. To the residents, many hard hit by two recent recessions, growing foreign competition, and the automation of the steel mills that had cut jobs in the town, Kennedy pleaded for a strong majority to tackle problems such as education, medical care, better housing, and "jobs, jobs, jobs." From a stage outside the A&P grocery parking lot in the center of town, Kennedy had exhorted the crowd to support Democrats in the November election. "There isn't any doubt that all of the things that can make a difference to this town and other towns which have been hard hit by all of the technological and industrial changes that have come in this country, all of these measures which are essential to action, must finally depend upon a majority vote of the House of Representatives and the Senate," he said in urging the town's residents to vote.[1] And after just over seven minutes, he stepped down from the stage, shook hands with a few of the local steelworkers, and moved on to the next town down the river to make the pitch again.

By the time Trump arrived nearly fifty-four years later, the population of Monessen had shrunk to less than a third of the size of Kennedy's crowd, just 7,500 people. The slide had begun even before Kennedy's visit: Pittsburgh Steel, by far the town's largest employer, had boomed after the Second World War, but the company's growth had stalled in the late 1950s, burdened by big wage increases, frequent strikes by its workers, and the emergence of lower-cost foreign competition from Europe and Japan. By the mid-1960s, imports had grown to capture nearly half of the market for steel wire rod in the United States, used for making everything from nails to barbed wire fences. Pittsburgh Steel started phasing out its steel wire rod production, and then stopped producing the product completely in 1972. Other closures followed. The Page Steel and Wire Company, the town's second largest employer, also closed in 1972.

Wheeling-Pittsburgh Steel—created by Wheeling's acquisition of Pittsburgh Steel in 1968—had held onto the Monessen plant, even as foreign competition stiffened and new environmental regulations required costly upgrades to the plant. But the final blow was the deep recession of the early 1980s, exacerbated for steelmakers by President Ronald Reagan's budget and tax policies, which had sent the value of the dollar soaring and given a big competitive advantage to steel companies in Japan and Europe. The company's unions made a series of wage concessions, but then balked at additional cuts that management demanded and launched a crippling strike in 1985, even as the company had already declared bankruptcy and was trying to reorganize. It was the final blow.

The next year, Wheeling-Pitt announced that it would close what remained of its Monessen operations.[2] Hollywood producers showed up and paid $10,000 to the Monessen unemployment committee to feed the families of jobless steelworkers in exchange for using one of the shuttered blast furnaces as a setting for the movie *Robocop*.[3]

The demise of the Monessen steel industry also meant the end of many local businesses that had relied on the paychecks of the factory workers—the bowling alleys, the local movie theater, and the restaurants—and by 1990 the town had shrunk to fewer than 10,000 residents, as those who could leave in search of better opportunities did so. In 2016, Monessen's median household income of $35,000 a year was about $17,000 less than the U.S. average. In 2013, just 875 students still attended the town's public schools; academic achievement was ranked 475th out of 500 school districts in Pennsylvania. The town's daily newspaper, the *Valley Independent*, folded in December, 2015, after 113 years of continuous publication. Few of the measures that Kennedy had once promised to help the communities hit by rapid economic change have come to fruition; instead, like many once solid American towns, Monessen has simply faded.

When Trump arrived in the summer of 2016, rather than holding a large outdoor public rally, he spoke indoors against a backdrop of crushed soda cans at the local factory of Alumisource, a recycling company founded on the grounds of one of the defunct steel mills. It was an enthusiastic crowd, but a small one—about 200 attendees including the two dozen or so employed by the company. Pennsylvania's steel industry, Trump told the gathering, had played a central role in building the country, "but our workers' loyalty was repaid—you know it better than anyone—with total betrayal. Globalization has made the financial elite who donate to politicians very wealthy. . . . For years they watched on the sidelines as our jobs vanished and our communities were plunged into Depression-level unemployment."[4]

The speech was by far the most detailed and specific given by Trump during a campaign waged on broad themes and a weak grasp of policy details. It was focused on America's trade policies, a topic that Trump had thought about from the earliest days when he became interested in running for office. In 1987, a then-rising New York real estate developer, Trump had spent nearly $100,000 to take out full-page ads in the *New York Times, Washington Post,* and *Boston Globe* blasting the U.S. government for continuing to pay for the defense of Japan and other allies while they ran up large trade surpluses with the United States.[5] In his 2000 book, *The America We Deserve,* which was written when he was considering a presidential run under the banner of Ross Perot's Reform Party, Trump had said that he would take "personal charge" of the nation's trade negotiations, "Our trading partners would have to sit across from Donald Trump and I guarantee you the rip-off of the United States would end."

In the Monessen speech, Trump promised a series of specific measures to "bring back our jobs." He promised to pull the United States out of the Trans-Pacific Partnership (TPP) trade agreement with Japan and ten other Pacific Rim countries, a deal which had been concluded by the Obama administration in October, 2015, but not yet approved by Congress. He pledged to renegotiate the North American Free Trade Agreement (NAFTA) with Canada and Mexico to "get a better deal for our workers." He promised to enforce trade rules vigorously, both through disputes brought to the World Trade Organization (WTO), and by using "every tool" under American and law. "Under a Trump presidency," he promised, "the American worker will finally have a president who will protect them and fight for them." This, he said, "is how we are going to make America great again." And in Monessen, it was clear what Trump meant by "great"—the Monessen of 1962, not the Monessen of 2016.

When I first conceived of this book some five years ago, it had never occurred to me that a man like Donald Trump might one day occupy the Oval Office, and that public discontent over the response to trade and globalization would be one of the biggest issues that put him there. Since I began covering trade negotiations as a young reporter in 1992, I had recognized that trade was controversial and becoming more so. In 1979, Congress had approved the Tokyo Round global trade agreement by a vote of 90–4 in the Senate and 395–7 in the House, an extraordinary majority. But after a decade of withering competition, especially from Japan, many in Congress and the country had started to sour on trade. This crystallized in the fight over the NAFTA, the first trade agreement linking the United States to a much poorer country. Texas billionaire Ross Perot launched a briefly successful third-party campaign for the presidency in 1992, running against the NAFTA and warning there would be a "giant sucking sound" of American jobs moving to Mexico if Congress approved the deal. Bill Clinton, who would become the Democratic president, had broken with the labor unions to back the NAFTA, and was able to push it through

Congress against the majority opposition of his own party. From there, the fights only got deeper and uglier. I missed the famous "Battle in Seattle" in which anti-globalization rioters clashed with police in 1999 while Clinton was trying to launch a new round of global trade talks, but I managed to get tear-gassed in Quebec City in 2001 at a "Summit of the Americas" where leaders were considering a hemisphere-wide free trade agreement. I watched in Congress as the votes on trade got closer and closer, including the 2005 vote on a free trade agreement with Central America and the Dominican Republic, known as CAFTA, which passed the House by just two votes with only fifteen Democrats in support. And I watched as President Obama, himself a skeptic on trade during the 2008 election, changed direction and embraced the TPP, but was unable to get more than a small minority of his own Democratic Party to support him.

Still, trade had never before had any role in deciding a presidential election. It was conventional wisdom among those of us who reported on trade that the issue was not one that moved voters—it was a subject for debate largely among Washington insiders, with multinational companies and their supporters pushing for continued trade liberalization while labor unions and their allies pushed back. But Trump took the issue to the nation, and won. Although he ended up with nearly three million fewer votes nation-wide than his rival Hillary Clinton, he won the election largely because he swept the Rust Belt states that Democrats had believed would be Clinton's firewall against the Republicans. Wisconsin had not voted for a Republican president candidate since 1984. Pennsylvania and Michigan had not done so since 1988. Add in Ohio, North Carolina, and Indiana, and Trump won all of the most manufacturing-dependent states in the country, and the ones that had been hit hardest by import competition. During the 2000s, when the United States lost about 6 million manufacturing jobs—nearly a third of the country's total—North Carolina saw the biggest hemorrhage, followed closely by Michigan, Ohio, and Pennsylvania. All voted for Donald Trump.[6]

When I started this book, I thought I was writing a story that would warn national policymakers about the growing dangers of ignoring those left behind by global competition, and the need to craft and implement policies to help them move forward. Instead, it turned out I was writing a book about why Donald Trump would become this country's 45th president, and overturn the long-standing, though already seriously eroded, consensus about the benefits of trade and globalization. The subtitle of the book, conceived long before Trump's campaign, is "Why Americans Got Left Behind in the Global Economy." In truth, it was a bit of hyperbole. Many Americans, especially in the big coastal cities that are linked to the global economy, have done tremendously well in the globalization era. It is hard to imagine the United States having built world-champion companies like Google, Intel, Apple, Microsoft, Cisco, and many others without the network of trade rules that give them access to a global supply chain and customer base.

But for the America that Trump spoke to so effectively, the story has been quite different. A post-election analysis by Mark Muro and his colleagues at the Brookings

Institution found that, while Hillary Clinton carried fewer than 500 counties in the election—compared to nearly 2,600 for Trump—Clinton's counties accounted for nearly two-thirds of U.S. economic output.[7] Never before has a losing presidential candidate represented such a large share of the country's economic base. While much of "Trump country" is made up of large, rural counties, the swing districts in the Trump coalition were places like Monessen, which had once been prosperous, thriving, working-class towns, and still dreamed of those better days. While trade was certainly not the only issue dividing the Trump and Clinton counties, it was a big one. Research by the team of economists David Autor, Gordon Hanson, and David Dorn suggests that "trade shocks"—in particular the enormous growth of imports from China during the 2000s—weakened centrist politicians in the places hardest hit by import competition.[8] Vermont Senator Bernie Sanders was the beneficiary of some of that anger in his surprisingly competitive Democratic primary race with Clinton. Like Trump, Sanders was a strong critic of the TPP and trade agreements in general.

The winners from globalization—like America's large and successful companies—failed to respond to a gathering storm of public discontent that had been decades in the making. It has long been conventional wisdom among economists that trade brings broad benefits and concentrated costs—in other words, there are winners and losers. The winners include global corporations, American consumers who enjoy better quality and lower cost goods, and developing countries like China that have integrated themselves into global supply chains, thereby lifting hundreds of millions of their citizens out of poverty. Conventional wisdom in economics suggests that "winners" from trade should compensate the "losers." In the United States, that could have included tax redistribution, concerted efforts to attract investment and promote development in hard-hit towns and cities, generous retraining and relocation assistance for workers who lose their jobs, wage insurance to top up salaries, and similar measures.[9] However, for most of the period I write about in this book, the winners did little or nothing to compensate the losers—indeed, they kept moving further ahead. In November 2016, the losers hit back.

Since this book was published just prior to the election, I have spent a lot of time traveling the country and talking about what happened and why. Working at the Council on Foreign Relations—whose membership encompasses a cross-section of America's business and public policy elite—most of my audiences may be accurately described as globalization's winners. But the conversations today are noticeably different than they were before the election. For many years, the main concern was whether the United States could sustain trade liberalization, through trade deals such as the TPP or the Trans-Atlantic Trade and Investment Partnership (TTIP) with Europe. Since the election, the conversations have quickly turned instead to retraining and education, entrepreneurship, investment promotion, and corporate tax reform—in other words, how to attract more job-creating investments to the United States, and how to better prepare U.S. citizens to fill those jobs. The discussions on how to help those left behind by technological advances and globalization have become more urgent. There appears to be a newfound recognition—because of Trump's electoral victory, the United Kingdom's controversial decision to leave the European Union, and the rise of populism in Europe—that political discontent poses a serious threat to the system of global commercial rules built over the past seventy-five years that has done so much to bolster economic growth around the world. If these challenges are not addressed in a serious way, the gains from globalization will certainly be threatened.

Which brings us back to Donald Trump. He seems, on the surface, an unlikely champion for those left behind by global competition. He is the son of a wealthy real estate developer, he made his fortune in an industry with little international competition, and he then went on to leverage his wealth and media savvy into a successful reality television career. His cabinet appointments were heavily tilted to the fabulously wealthy. Trump has a weak grasp of public policy and his senior White House advisors—with a few notable exceptions—are similarly inexperienced. But Trump understands better than his predecessors that many Americans want a fighter in the Oval Office; they want a president who is seen to be scrapping to defend their interests, not one who seems more worried about treading on the delicate feelings of allies or powerful corporations.

Trump's post-election bullying of the Carrier Corporation, in an effort to force the company to renounce its plans to relocate its Indiana air conditioning plant to Mexico, was Exhibit A. Carrier is far from the first U.S. company to relocate manufacturing work south of the border to take advantage of lower wages, but it had the misfortune of a company manager being captured on a smart phone video telling his Indianapolis-based employees that their jobs would have to be sacrificed "to stay competitive and protect the business for the long-term." Trump used the video to make Carrier the poster child for heartless corporate greed, and launched a Twitter war against the company when he was still president-elect. His vice-president elect, Indiana Governor Mike Pence, then worked with the state government on a modest package of incentives to persuade Carrier to reconsider and keep approximately 800 jobs in-state. Those actions caused enormous hand-wringing among the political establishment. Conservative columnist George Will lamented that in Trump's America, "political coercion shall supplant economic calculation in shaping decisions by companies." Former Democratic Treasury Secretary Larry Summers ominously warned that "we have started down the road towards changing the operating assumptions of our capitalism." But the rest of the country did not agree with them. Going after Carrier was among the most popular things Trump has done since the election—60 percent of Americans, and 87 percent of Republicans, said it improved their opinion of the incoming president.[10]

Trump seems to get that Americans quite reasonably expect their companies to have some obligations to the citizens of the United States and to their employees not just to their shareholders. This should not be a radical idea. Michael Porter of the Harvard Business School—the bastion of capitalism that trains many of the country's top corporate executives—has argued that American companies need to take more responsibility for the "commons." This means, for example, sourcing from local suppliers whenever possible and offering more apprenticeships and job training programs for their employees. In a 2012 interview, Porter—who is widely regarded as the country's leading thinker on economic competitiveness—noted that many U.S. executives now see themselves as running *global* companies, not *American* companies. "The notion in business that this is *our* country and we own its challenges has diminished," Porter said. But he warned that "this corporate perception is ill-advised. It may be true that more of a company's activity is global, but that doesn't diminish the importance of U.S. vitality to its vitality."[11]

Some companies are starting to get this. General Electric Chief Executive Jeff Immelt, speaking six months before Trump's election, delivered a remarkably prescient speech in which he warned: "Protectionism is rising. Globalization is being attacked as never before. For those looking to succeed, the playbook from the past just won't cut it. It's time to pivot, be bold, and not fear criticism." He announced that GE would focus increasingly on producing closer to its final markets—"a local capability inside a global footprint."[12] The company is increasingly focused on demonstrating to the countries where it invests, including the United States, that it is bringing real value in terms of creating good jobs. Another example: AT&T has launched what *Fortune* magazine called "the most ambitious retraining program in corporate American history." With the company moving from its legacy switching systems to modern software-driven systems, it has embarked on massive effort to encourage 100,000 or more of its employees to retrain in the math, science, and computer skills needed to run the new systems. It has partnered with universities and community colleges to offer company paid in-person and online courses, and the initiative has also required huge commitments from the employees themselves to balance work, family, and schooling. Tens of thousands of AT&T's employees are seizing the opportunity.[13] But too few American companies are following these examples. Corporate apprenticeship programs, for example, which provide on-the-job training skills, have been cut by one-third over the past fifteen years.

By reminding U.S. companies of their responsibilities to the United States, Trump has delivered a long overdue message. But it is impossible for a president to turn around an economy one company at a time, however big his following on Twitter. Helping many of the voters who put him in the White House will actually require developing and passing legislation and implementing policies that, in Kennedy's words, do something to help those "hard hit by all of the technological and industrial changes that have come in this country." And here it seems unlikely that Trump can deliver. He leads a Republican Party that remains deeply suspicious of any sort of government policies that would try to give a leg up to those struggling to find better jobs. On health care, for example, most Republicans in Congress favor changes that would reduce the tax burden on companies but increase the number of Americans without health insurance, many of whom would then be forced to take any job that provided some meager health benefits, rather than seeking retraining to develop new skills or launching their own companies. Those already behind would fall farther behind. His first proposed budget, crafted by Office of Management and

Budget (OMB) Director Mick Mulvaney, a former Tea Party stalwart, proposed deep cuts to job training programs that would throw as many as one-third of recipients out of job training and employment service programs.[14] Other targeted cuts would reduce federal economic aid to hard-hit regions in the Rust Belt, Appalachia, and the Mississippi Delta, as well as many other places whose voters supported Trump, and would slash the Job Corps program that provides job training for young people from poorer families. Trump's campaign promises that would actually do something to create new jobs and bolster U.S. competitiveness—such as huge investments in roads, transit, seaports, and broadband communication—seem to have fallen down the priority list.

The other issue is whether Trump's policies on trade will do anything to create the better-paying jobs that Americans desire. I argue in chapter 2 of this book—and in the recommendations at the end—that tough enforcement of trade rules is critical for protecting American industries against predatory competition. The U.S. government did a great deal in the 1980s, for example, to defend the interests of the U.S. semiconductor and aircraft industries against competition from what amounted to government-industry alliances in Japan and South Korea (semiconductors) and Europe (aircraft). Without the active engagement of the U.S. government—including the threat and willingness to impose trade sanctions—it is likely that the United States would have lost significant chunks of two of its most innovative and high-paying sectors. In the early days of his administration, Trump has already shown a willingness to use the full arsenal of U.S. trade weapons more aggressively than any of his predecessors.

There are two dangers, however. The first is that the administration will simply try to fight the last war over again. Wilbur Ross, Trump's commerce secretary, has initiated or promised a series of trade actions aimed at helping the steel, aluminum, shipbuilding, and semiconductor industries, and, in addition to NAFTA, has called for a renegotiation of the U.S.-Korea free trade agreement, largely because of the growing bilateral trade deficit in autos and auto parts. While perhaps these were a random selection of industries that have faced tough trade competition, it is a list that sounds very much like the priorities of the Reagan administration in the U.S. trade battles with Japan in the 1980s. Any tally of America's most competitive industries today would include software, telecommunications, digital services, entertainment, and financial services. These are the industries that are driving a growing trade surplus in "services," and they are industries that pay as well or better than export-intensive manufacturing industries and employ far more workers.[15] All of them face significant trade barriers that impede the growth of job-creating exports, and yet these sectors seem wholly absent from Trump's trade agenda.

The president's decision to pull out of the Trans-Pacific Partnership deal with Asia was a good example of Trump's "back to the future" approach. He simply wrote it off as another deal that, like NAFTA or China's entry into the World Trade Organization, would promote outsourcing and import competition. But the TPP, for anyone who took the time to understand its details, was a far better deal than that. Many of the TPP's provisions—expanding e-commerce and digital trade to help companies like Amazon and eBay, restricting subsidies to state-owned enterprises, toughening labor and environment standards—would have been hugely beneficial to the United States. The TPP would have further opened markets in express delivery for giants like Federal Express and UPS, and would have boosted other service sectors—like accounting, consulting, and wealth management—ignored by Trump. The deal would also have greatly expanded export opportunities in agriculture—in beef, pork, poultry, rice, and dairy—all of which would have helped many of the rural voters who put Trump in office. And perhaps most importantly, by writing a new set of trade rules for the Asia-Pacific region, it would have forced China to the negotiating table on terms more favorable to the United States. The rules on state-owned enterprises were not written to constrain Vietnam, for example, but to provide leverage in future negotiations with China, which by itself accounts for more than half of the big trade deficit that so troubles President Trump. But he walked away from the deal with scarcely a glance at what he was giving away.

The second danger in Trump's approach is that it could lead to trade retaliation from other countries. Columnists and reporters love to warn of a "trade war" any time the United States restricts imports of one product or another. But the reality is that the United States has not faced a genuine trade war since the 1930s. While there have been hundreds of trade disputes that have led the United States to restrict imports, the disputes have all been conducted within the established rules of global trade. A good example is the steep tariffs on imported steel imposed by the Bush administration in 2001. The tariffs were levied under what is known as a Section 201 "safeguard" action, which is a procedure sanctioned by the WTO that permits countries to temporarily protect a domestic industry when it is faced with a flood of imports that is seriously harming the industry. The Europeans, Japan, and others, complained to the WTO that the United States had not followed the proper procedures under WTO rules, and when they won their case before the WTO's Appellate Body, the United States promptly complied and removed the steel tariffs. The United States has complied in other politically sensitive cases as well, including ending a tax break for Boeing and other large exporters, and eliminating country-of-origin labeling on imported meat. But the Trump administration has challenged the legitimacy of these rules. Trump officials have suggested that the dispute settlement processes are rigged against the United States, and hinted that they may not defer to the rulings of foreign judges in trade cases.

If the United States, which, in partnership with Europe, helped to build the modern system of global trade rules, stops complying with those rules, other nations will follow. The result could be a genuine trade war—in which countries raise tariffs to protect themselves against tariff increases by other countries, creating a tit-for-tat cycle of retaliation. A trade war would be enormously costly, and not just in economic terms. Many parts of the country benefit enormously from international trade. U.S. agricultural exports to Mexico, for example, have grown four-fold since NAFTA was enacted, and Mexico is the largest export customer for U.S. corn, poultry, wheat, and dairy products. Mexico has strongly suggested that if Trump pulls the United States out of NAFTA or imposes discriminatory tariffs on Mexican exports, U.S. corn farmers will be the first to suffer. China has made the same veiled threats on purchases of U.S.-made aircraft. U.S. cities that are home to major manufacturing industries—including Seattle, Portland, and Detroit—would be especially vulnerable to trade retaliation.[16] But more than just the economic impact, a trade war would undermine the international rules that govern commerce, smashing the trust built up over decades of painstaking negotiations. An America that thumbs its nose at international rules will free up other nations to act in their own narrow self-interests, driven by their own nationalist political demands. The world tried this in the 1920s and 1930s, and it did not end well.

A final note: one legitimate critique I have heard of the book is that—somewhat like the Trump administration's trade policy—much of it is backward looking. The growth of global trade has slowed dramatically over the past decade. It is highly unlikely that there will be another "trade shock" to the United States of the sort posed to Japan in the 1970s and 1980s and China in the 2000s. The only country with the scale to create that sort of disruption is India, and it has never embraced the export-led development strategies of its Asian counterparts. But the discontent that Trump rode to the White House was not just about trade—it was about economic disruption that had ripped away many stable, decent-paying jobs. And even with the trade slowdown, bigger disruptions are coming. The much-heralded arrival of driverless vehicles, likely within the next decade, will have its biggest impact in the trucking industry, where companies are certain to seize on the opportunity to deploy their fleets around the clock without paying overtime to drivers. Including express delivery drivers, there are more than 3 million truck drivers in the United States; "truck driver" is the single largest occupation in more than half of U.S. states.[17] Looking just at larger trucks, there are nearly two million drivers in the United States who earn a median annual wage of about $42,000, or $20 an hour. Like the manufacturing jobs that disappeared in the 2000s, these jobs will not be replaced easily. The retail sector is equally vulnerable. Grocery stores and drug stores have already begun installing self-checkout machines. Amazon this year launched the first "checkout free" retail store in Seattle, in which customers can simply choose their products, walk out of the store, and be charged through their Amazon accounts. Nearly 5 million Americans currently work in retail sales jobs.

Even if trade growth continues to slow, the problems addressed by this book are almost certain to become more acute. In a fast-changing economy, whether driven by trade or technology, the challenge of adjustment—how a country helps its citizens to prosper in a time of economic disruption—will continue to be among the most pressing issues facing the United States. If the failure to adjust continues, the political disruptions of the future will be larger still.

Acknowledgments

This book was the result of many years of effort to make sense of the growth of global trade and investment and its impact on Americans. It began in classrooms at the University of California, Berkeley, where I was fortunate enough to learn about international institutions from such great scholars as Vinod K. Aggarwal and the late Ernst B. Haas. It continued for the many years I worked as a reporter covering international trade negotiations and disputes. I was fortunate enough to land a job at the newsletter *Inside U.S. Trade*, under the tutelage of editor Jutta Hennig—the grand dame of Washington trade reporters—and got a ringside seat to some of the biggest international economic stories of the past half century. These included the US negotiation of the North American Free Trade Agreement with Mexico and Canada, the conclusion of the Uruguay Round that created the World Trade Organization, and the bruising battles between the United States and Japan over trade in cars and auto parts. Later, as a reporter in Washington for the *Financial Times*, I covered China's admission to the WTO, the Bush administration's controversial tariffs on steel imports, and the launch of the ill-fated Doha Round of global trade talks.

My immersion in the world of trade negotiations left me somewhat torn. My own politics mostly lean to the Democratic Party, and yet as the years went by fewer and fewer Democrats supported these efforts at trade liberalization that I believed, and still do, were largely a good thing for the United States. The United States has moved from an era of strong consensus over the benefits of global economic engagement to one in which many voters in both parties see more harm than good in America's integration into the global economy. This book is my effort to explain how the country arrived at this impasse, to show some of the mistakes made by government, business, and labor along the way, and to suggest how the United States might better move forward in the future.

The Council on Foreign Relations has been an enormously congenial place to carry out this project. I have hosted regular CFR roundtable meetings and workshops for many years on the challenges facing the United States in international economic competition, and I have been privileged to learn from such fine scholars and policymakers as Rob Atkinson, Fred Bergsten, Robert Blecker, Aaron Brickman, Joe Gagnon, Doug Holtz-Eakin, Dan Ikenson, Brad Jensen, Jonathan Kallmer, Clay Lowery, Gary Pisano, Dan Price, Derek Scissors, Stephen Shays, Willy Shih, Shanker Singham, and Andrew Stern.

Richard N. Haass, the president of CFR, and James M. Lindsay, the director of studies, were patient and supportive throughout the research and writing. I would especially like to thank the publications team, led by Editorial Director Patricia Dorff.

The book benefited enormously from the superb research support of Rob Maxim, my former research associate who undertook detailed work on each of the chapters. Jane McMurrey and Shelton Fitch also provided valuable additional research work, as did Rebecca Strauss, formerly the associate director for CFR's Renewing America publications series. Becky's research was particularly helpful for chapter 6 of the book on the efforts to bolster US competitiveness. I am also grateful to several of CFR's interns who contributed as well, including Sebastian Beckman, Fritz Claessens, Valeriya Denisova, Michael Ng, and Sahana Kumar.

The manuscript received a careful reading and extremely valuable feedback from the members of my Council on Foreign Relations study group, composed of CFR members and others who were generous in sharing their expertise and experience: Eric Biel, Nelson Cunningham, I.M. Destler, Ed Gresser, Jennifer Hillman, Gary Horlick, Kevin Nealer, Jason Marczak, Dan O'Flaherty, Bruce Stokes, John Veroneau, Irving Williamson, and John Yochelson. William Reinsch also graciously read and offered feedback on the full manuscript, as did Thomas Alden. I also benefited from the feedback of several CFR colleagues on selected chapters, including Jennifer Harris, Miles Kahler, Rob Kahn, Michael Levi, Sebastian Mallaby, Brad Setser, Benn Steill, and Thomas Bollyky. I received helpful suggestions from CFR national members in Los Angeles, Phoenix, and San Diego during roundtable meetings to discuss my research, and I want to thank Irina Faskianos, director of CFR's national and outreach program, for arranging those meetings. Any mistakes and omissions, of course, are my own.

The book was also influenced very much by my work as the co-project director for the 2011 CFR Independent Task Force on U.S. Trade and Investment Policy, which was chaired by Andrew Card and Thomas Daschle. My co-director Matthew Slaughter, now the dean of the Tuck Business School at Dartmouth, played a critical role in the conception and writing of that report and greatly influenced my own thinking on these issues, especially regarding the labor market impacts of international investment.

Thanks as well to my agent Andrew Wylie, and to the team at Rowman & Littlefield, including Jon Sisk, Christopher Utter, and Laura Reiter.

This work was generously funded throughout by the Bernard and Irene Schwartz Foundation, and I would like to extend my deepest appreciation to Bernard for his support over the years for my work on US economic competitiveness and CFR's Renewing America initiative.

1

The End of the
World's Greatest Autarky

I was born into the most prosperous autarky in the history of mankind. Wikipedia, which has replaced Webster's as our go-to source for definitions, says that "autarky" is derived from the Greek αὐτάρκεια, which means self-sufficiency. "Autarky exists whenever an entity can survive or continue its activities without external assistance or international trade." The listing cites several recent examples, including Albania under Communist Party leader Enver Hoxha in the 1970s and 1980s, Burma from 1962 to 1988 under dictator Ne Win, and North Korea to this day. What sets the autarky into which I was born apart from those cited by Wikipedia is that its people were generally well-off and growing wealthier. In the other great autarkies of the day—the Soviet Union and China—most people were poor, and opportunities for economic advancement were few. My autarky, in contrast, was one in which a large middle class bought houses, drove cars, took vacations, and saved for retirement. A lucky and ambitious few even became rich.

Unlike the countries in the Wikipedia examples, the United States had not become self-sufficient out of ideological conviction; indeed, its leaders had for some years believed strongly in trade with the world and encouraged it. It was just that it had no particular need to buy much of anything from anywhere else and plenty of customers at home to purchase the things it made. The "Survey of Current Business" for April 1961, the month I was born, made only passing reference to imports and exports and instead focused on the state of internal demand for domestically produced manufactured goods such as steel, automobiles, textiles, television sets, radios, and vacuum cleaners. In the first two months of that year, overall steel production averaged 151,000 short tons daily—about enough to build two Golden Gate Bridges—of which just 6,000 tons were exported. Of the nearly $6 billion in cars and car parts made in those two months, less than $200 million worth, or just 3 percent of total output, was exported. There were almost no imports of cars and trucks. Gross national product for the previous year had been just over $500 billion, and all exports and imports combined had amounted to less than $50 billion, or just under 10 percent of the size of the total economy.

Economists will probably object that a trade-to-GDP (gross domestic product) ratio of nearly 10 percent does not constitute a true autarky, and that is certainly true. But it was pretty close. Trade-to-GDP is the standard measure of an economy's openness to trade. China, which was then pursuing autarky as a matter of national policy, had a trade-to-GDP ratio of about 5 percent. In the Soviet Union, which also had a policy of self-sufficiency, it was about 4 percent. No other wealthy country of the time traded so little as did the United States. In France, trade was equal to more than 25 percent of GDP; in Canada it was more than 35 percent; in the United Kingdom it was 41 percent.[1] Smaller countries depended even more on trade. In the United States of the early 1960s, foreign markets mattered only at the margins. All of the big economic questions—employment, incomes, inflation, and profits—depended on conditions at home. Foreign economic policy was primarily a matter of diplomacy and defense, of encouraging trade as a means of strengthening overseas alliances and bolstering the economies of allies.

Autarky has acquired a bad name because authoritarian political leaders have used it to increase their control over society. Keeping out foreign goods also helps dictators keep out unwanted foreign ideas and influences. But high self-sufficiency in a large country with relatively free markets and a liberal political system is not a bad thing. Such a market can still be highly competitive internally, and its size allows for economies of scale that generate improvements in productivity—making more with less—which is how a country's wealth grows. International trade allows smaller countries to replicate the advantages of size, but it comes at a cost. Competition within a single country permits adjustments that are not possible with competition across borders. Historically, for example, the northern US states were more industrialized than those in the South, and the need for employees was stronger. The result was an enormous internal migration that raised overall living standards by relocating people from poorer regions with few jobs to richer ones where labor demand was strong. By the 1960s, the flow had shifted and was going in the other direction, with jobs moving from a higher-wage North to the lower-wage but more rapidly growing southern states. In contrast, Europe today has faced repeated economic turmoil in part because it has both freed up trade and created a common currency, but labor mobility remains limited due to language and skill barriers. In any given year, just 0.2 percent of Europeans move to another country, compared with nearly 3 percent who move each year to another US state.[2] Greece and Spain have endured crippling unemployment rates for years, and while there has been some movement of their peoples north, it has not been nearly enough to compensate for their weak domestic economies.

Such mobility tended to level wages within the United States as well since industry was just as mobile as labor—though, very importantly, not more so. While people could move to take advantage of higher wages, companies could also move to take advantage of lower labor costs. Labor-intensive industries such as clothing and shoe making, for instance, were already heading to the southern states in the 1950s and 1960s. Between 1959 and 1970, the northern states lost more than 200,000 jobs in textile and apparel manufacturing, while the southern states added nearly 250,000 jobs in those same industries.[3] While such jobs were not high paying, they offered a decent income in many smaller cities and towns where the cost of living was much lower than in the big cities. As with labor migration, the effect of this capital mobility within a single national territory was to smooth out economic adjustments. Those who lost their jobs in the inevitable churn of a competitive market generally found other jobs, even if they had to move to do so. Wages had risen steadily as well. Real average hourly earnings rose by some 75 percent between 1947 and 1973, an extraordinarily rapid gain. Productivity growth was similarly strong, indicating that a highly competitive internal market was driving both efficiency and innovation.[4]

By the time I went off to college in the fall of 1979, however, the conditions that had produced this self-sufficiency had largely disappeared. In the decade from 1970 to 1980, international trade as a share of the US economy had nearly doubled to more than 20 percent. In 1982, one of the country's most respected economic analysts wrote, "Job growth, price stability and economic security . . . all depend substantially on events abroad and the interaction with them of internal economic developments and policies," a claim that would have seemed ludicrous just fifteen or twenty years earlier.[5] Two big things had changed. First, the other large industrial economies that were still recovering from World War II had again become producers of such core industrial goods as steel and cars. US steel imports, for example, began to rise sharply beginning in the mid-1960s and by the end of the 1970s accounted for about 20 percent of steel consumption; steel exports, in contrast, remained very small.[6] Imports of automobiles followed a similar pattern. In 1955, imports were less than 1 percent of all registered cars; by 1978, however, that number had grown to nearly 20 percent.[7] A similar story was taking place for simpler goods like textiles, clothing, radios, and televisions, with imports rising from close to zero in the early 1960s to capture a significant market share by the end of the 1970s.

Second, companies began moving across borders as well. In 1960, all American direct investment overseas was less than $34 billion, about 6 percent of GDP. Over the next two decades, it rose steadily, reaching $216 billion by 1980; by the mid-2000s US foreign investment was worth more than 20 percent of GDP annually.

Unlike with the earlier moves from north to south, however, when companies moved to other countries, their employees could not follow. While all Americans benefited from the lower-cost and often higher-quality consumer goods that were increasingly imported, those who lost their jobs to import competition had a harder time finding new jobs at similar wages. Real wages stopped growing and even began to fall for many, especially men, who comprised most of the manufacturing labor force. The job and wage effects could possibly have been coincidental. Growing integration into the global economy coincided with two recessions and a spike in energy costs that slowed overall growth. But the shift from a full-employment economy with few economic links to the rest of the world to a volatile economy that was more integrated with the world touched off an inevitable public debate over whether such growing integration was a good thing. By the late 1970s, one of the country's largest carmakers, Chrysler, teetered on the verge of bankruptcy and had to be bailed out by the government to avoid a collapse that would have thrown hundreds of thousands out of work. Other major industries were facing cutthroat competition from imports. The governor of California warned that these were "signs that the basis of our industrial prosperity—sustained economic growth that has allowed for a certain liberal politics in this country—is seriously eroding."[8]

The debate was often cast as a struggle between proponents of "free trade" and "protectionism," but that was always misleading. The nearly self-sufficient United States of the early 1960s was not a "protectionist" country; by the standards of the time, it was one of the more open economies in the world. It simply had few competitors. As competition grew, presidents and Congress continued to favor open trade, even as some beleaguered industries demanded and occasionally received government protection from imports. The problem, rather, was how best to adjust to the new economic competition. In a relatively closed economy, the concept of national "competitiveness" is meaningless. If an economy produces most of the goods and services needed by its people, competition is something that concerns individuals and companies but not the entire country. Like other young people, I had gone to college to learn a skill (journalism) that would allow me to compete with other young people for jobs in my field. My employers (mostly newspapers) were competing with other newspapers and magazines, as well as television and radio stations, for the market share and advertising revenue that would allow them to pay salaries and turn a profit. The question of whether the country was "competitive" in journalism, however, was nonsensical, because there was virtually no foreign competition. If one newspaper went out of business, I could always go work for another or branch out into radio or television, as long as my skills were attractive to employers. If they weren't, then I was the one with the competitiveness problem, not my country.

Two decades previously, that had been true for nearly every sector of the economy; by the end of the 1970s, it was not. For those who earned their livings making steel or stitching clothing or assembling TV sets, the nature of competition had changed profoundly. If one domestic car company gained market share at the expense of another, it had little impact on those who made cars; the employees let go by one company would likely be hired by another. But if the competitor was in another country, the impact was not so benign. Given the tight immigration restrictions in place in most countries, not to mention generally insurmountable cultural and linguistic barriers, laid-off auto workers could not simply pick up and move to another country where carmakers were hiring. The "adjustment costs," in the antiseptic language of economists, were much higher than in a closed economy.

Technology was in theory equally disruptive—and would greatly disrupt my chosen profession when the Internet undermined the advertising model for many newspapers. If companies invested in machinery that required fewer workers, or if new technologies made some jobs obsolete, then those workers would not likely find jobs doing the same type of work they had done previously. But if the companies reinvested their profits domestically, other sorts of jobs would be created that would at least partly compensate. Technology would also improve the productivity of the workers who remained in those industries, thereby increasing their earnings. When those earnings were spent on consumer goods or services, this would create additional domestic employment. In a more global market, however, the circle could be less virtuous. If corporate profits were invested in other countries, or if the additional earnings of workers were spent largely on imported goods, or if competition from lower-paid workers abroad held down wages, the jobs lost from technology were less likely to be offset by jobs created elsewhere in the economy. Recent economic research suggests that import competition and technology have quite different impacts on the US workforce; while technology and trade are both disruptive, import competition has a much bigger impact on labor markets. Those who lose their jobs to computers are likely to find new ones, while those who lose their jobs to imports are much less likely to do so.[9]

For several decades now, these challenges created by America's growing integration into the world economy have been at the center of a highly divisive debate. The United States has faced increased import competition in a growing number of economic sectors that once employed millions of people at generally higher wages than they could earn at other jobs. And the competition is not just over trade but over investment as well. The ease with which companies can move across international borders has given them enormous leverage over their workforces; capital is far freer to move in search of investment opportunities, but labor cannot follow. That has given business far more power than it had enjoyed in the more self-sufficient economy of a generation ago. Finally, the scale of the disruption has called into question many of the country's institutions. Education, science, universities, and government itself are now all judged in good part by whether they strengthen or weaken the country's international competitive position. The question of how best to adjust to the competitive pressures of a global economy has moved from irrelevance to the center of a debate over the performance and prospects of the United States that still rages today.

FAILURE TO ADJUST: THE COMPETITIVENESS CHALLENGE

For most of my life, the United States has faced a deep schism over how to respond to the competitive pressures of the global economy. As a reporter, I covered the negotiations that concluded in the North American Free Trade Agreement (NAFTA) in 1993 and the bitter fight that followed over its ratification in Congress. I spent many sleepless nights in hotels in Geneva reporting on the talks that led to the creation of the World Trade Organization (WTO) in 1995. I watched the wrenching debate that finally led Congress to support China's admission to the WTO in 2001. And that same year I got tear-gassed in Quebec City at a "Summit of the Americas," where leaders were talking about expanding NAFTA across the Western Hemisphere, and those locked outside the old city walls were protesting. Today these issues have become, if anything, even more divisive, with some leaders in both the Democratic and Republican parties calling for a halt to further trade liberalization and even a reversion to protectionist tariffs on imports from big developing countries like China and Mexico. The same fears that turned so many Americans against NAFTA were on full display as President Barack Obama tried to persuade Congress—and in particular the skeptical members of his own Democratic Party—to support the Trans-Pacific Partnership (TPP) trade agreement with Japan and ten other countries. The debates have a depressing similarity. Supporters of the trade agreements promise more jobs, higher wages from exports, and a consumer cornucopia, while opponents warn that trade will send away jobs, drive down wages, and increase inequality.

Americans can't quite make up their minds about which side to believe. When asked by pollsters whether America's integration into the global economy over the past two decades "is good because it has opened up new markets for American products and resulted in more jobs, or bad because it has subjected American companies and employees to unfair competition and cheap labor," about half have responded each way. Other poll questions about trade produce similarly mixed results.[10] The pessimists gained a bit of ground during the deep recession that followed the 2008 financial crisis, and the optimists later recovered along with the economy, but there has been no clear trend up or down over time. It's almost like Americans are telling the pollsters to ask a different question. The right question is not whether trade is good or bad for the United States; a better question is whether the United States has used the new opportunities created by international trade to boost American living standards while minimizing the costs for those who lose out to import competition or outsourcing. Trade remains highly contentious because the United States has done rather poorly at both.

How poorly? In 1983, at a time when rising imports of cars and consumer electronics from Japan had created a deep pessimism about the US ability to compete globally, President Ronald Reagan appointed the chief executive of one of the country's most successful technology companies, John Young of Hewlett-Packard, to lead a national commission to examine the problem. The commission came up with a definition of "competitiveness" that remains the standard one today. "Competitiveness," Young's team wrote, "is the degree to which a nation can, under free and fair market conditions, produce goods and services that meet the test of international markets while simultaneously maintaining or expanding the real income of its citizens." In other words, a competitive economy is one whose companies do very well in global markets *and* whose people also do very well and reap the benefits both of rising wages and falling real prices. By that definition, the US economy is, as Michael Porter and his Harvard Business School colleagues have said, doing only half its job. Porter, the country's most respected authority on US competitiveness and a member of the Young commission, argues, "America's leading companies are thriving, but the prosperity they are producing is not being shared broadly among U.S. citizens."[11]

US corporate profits have been at or near record highs for several years, though they weakened slightly in the first half of 2016. US companies like Apple, Google, Amazon, and Facebook account for more than half of the top one hundred companies in the world by market value, and US firms have gained ground over the past five years. But for Americans, the picture has been far more mixed. Even as the price of many consumer goods has fallen, the real income of the median American household (which takes into account falling prices) has scarcely budged in the past four decades. Since 1970 the real, inflation-adjusted income for families in the middle fifth—a decent definition of the middle class—has risen from about $48,000 (in 2014 dollars) to just over $53,000, an increase of 13 percent.[12] And even that small increase was primarily the result of longer working hours, mostly because many more women have entered the workforce and two-income households are more common (though offset to some degree by a growing number of single-parent households). Even before the Great Recession hit in 2008 and further eroded incomes, men in their thirties were earning significantly less in real terms than their fathers had earned a generation before.[13] The only strong wage gains came in the late 1990s, and those proved fleeting. Over the last decade, even with the recovery from the Great Recession finally kicking in, median family income has fallen back to where it was in the late 1980s.

While weaker overall growth is part of the story, US growth has been stronger than that of most other advanced economies in recent years, and the United States overall remains one of a handful of the wealthiest countries in the world. But US workers and their families have nonetheless lost ground, even compared to economies whose overall economic performance has been weaker. From 2000 to 2014, the median income in Canada and Great Britain grew by nearly 20 percent, with Ireland and the Netherlands not far behind. In the United States, median incomes were up just 0.3 percent. "The idea that the median American has so much more income than the middle class in all other parts of the world is not true these days," Harvard economist Lawrence Katz told the *New York Times*. "In 1960, we were massively richer than anyone else. In 1980, we were richer. In the 1990s, we were still richer."[14] But today, he said, the US edge has disappeared. Since the mid-1980s, income inequality in the United States has also risen faster than in any other major advanced economy, and the level of inequality today is higher than in any other country in the Organization for Economic Cooperation and Development (OECD) except for Chile, Mexico, and Turkey.[15] And since the mid-1980s, the percentage of those living in poverty has risen more in the United States than in any other advanced economy in the OECD, with the sole exception of Israel.[16] A recent study from Stanford University put the United States at the back of the pack among the larger wealthy economies in terms of spreading wealth to citizens. While much of that was a reflection of growing income inequality and the weak US social safety net, the United States was near last even in economic mobility and the percentage of working-age individuals who have jobs.[17]

Cause and effect are notoriously difficult to sort out in economics, of course, and there is a robust business in trying to explain that uncertainty. The coincidence between the stagnation of median incomes over the past four decades and America's growing integration into the global economy in no way means that one necessarily caused the other. There are simply too many other things going on in the economy to have any certainty. But what is clear is that the gap between promise and performance has been enormous. Americans have been told by a succession of presidents—including a once skeptical President Barack Obama—that the liberalization of trade and investment would produce big economic gains for most Americans. That has not happened. The price of many goods has certainly fallen as a result of global competition. The average American household now spends just over 3 percent of its annual budget on clothing, shoes, and linens, compared to more than 7 percent in the early 1970s. The real costs of other household goods are down as well, and the variety of goods available is certainly far larger.[18] But those gains have been offset by international competitive pressures that have held down wages and limited the number of better-paying middle-class jobs. The US Commerce Department notes that jobs in exporting industries pay on average nearly 20 percent more than jobs in purely domestic industries. But the number of those jobs has remained flat.

The failure of the United States to nurture its competitiveness as a business location and to help more of its citizens build the skills to continue to prosper in a more competitive world has come with a big cost. As Harvard Business School professors Gary Pisano and Willy Shih have put it, "The competitiveness of a place matters most to the people who work and live there because, unlike investors, they cannot readily redeploy their [human] capital." Changes in competitive advantage, both within a country and across nations, can have big effects on prosperity, they argue. The expansion of software engineering in the Indian cities of Hyderabad and Bangalore, they note, has produced a rising middle class of engineers and managers and made those two of the most livable cities in India. In contrast, when Michigan and other upper midwestern states became less attractive places to make automobiles, "unemployment soared, real estate prices fell, buildings deteriorated, public services eroded, and life became terribly difficult for many people."[19] In his provocative book *Our Kids: The American Dream in Crisis*, Harvard sociologist Robert Putnam tells the story of his hometown of Port Clinton, Ohio, where manufacturing employment fell from 55 percent of all jobs in 1965 to 25 percent by 1995 and to just 16 percent in 2012. Incomes fell from slightly above the national average in the mid-1970s to 25 percent below by 2012. Divorce rates, unwed births, and child poverty all climbed precipitously.[20]

Responding to a more competitive global economy has been one of the great challenges facing political leaders in the United States for the past half century. While there are many critics of globalization, the problem is not globalization itself; indeed, given technological advances and the aspirations of poorer countries across the world, growing global trade and investment were both inevitable and desirable. US leadership in building the rules for global commerce is one of the great success stories of the past fifty years. The problem has been the domestic political response to globalization, which in too many ways has been deeply irresponsible. A central task of any government is to provide the tools to help people to adjust and succeed in the face of economic change, but the story of the last half century has instead been the failure by governments to ease that adjustment. America's political leadership, weighted down by the habits of a country that had been nearly self-sufficient and highly competitive in the few things it did trade, has done far too little to help Americans make the adjustment. Rather than thinking carefully about the competitive implications of growing trade and the freer flow of investment dollars—trying to maximize the benefits and minimize the costs—Washington has left most Americans to fend for themselves. Some have flourished in the more competitive global economy, but far too many have not.

THE PETERSON MEMO

In February 1971, the United States was facing the first big economic crisis of the modern era of globalization. The postwar Bretton Woods economic system, named for the New Hampshire resort town where the agreement was reached by the major Allied powers in 1944, was crumbling. In an effort to end the "beggar-thy-neighbor" currency devaluations of the Great Depression, the agreement had fixed the value of major currencies to the US dollar, while the dollar was made fully convertible to gold at a price of $35 per ounce. That stability, coupled with American foresight in spending generously to rebuild war-damaged Europe and Asia, had helped trade and investment flourish in the years that followed. But by the late 1960s, the arrangement had become increasingly untenable for the United States. The costs of the Vietnam War, rising overseas investment by US multinational corporations, and growing currency speculation had created a chronic balance-of-payments deficit. The link to gold also meant that foreign holders could freely exchange dollars for gold at the fixed price, draining US gold reserves. One consequence was an increasingly overvalued US dollar as productivity soared in countries like Japan and Germany but currency values did not adjust, hurting American companies competing with rivals selling their products in discounted currencies. A working group on monetary policy led by Paul Volcker, President Richard Nixon's undersecretary of Treasury for international monetary affairs, had warned nearly two years before that the United States was likely to face repeated crises that could force Washington to end gold convertibility unless allies like Germany and Japan let their currencies rise in value against the dollar.[21]

As the economic pressures continued to grow, Nixon asked his newly appointed White House advisor for international economics to prepare "a review and analysis of the changing world economy" to help set future directions for US foreign economic policy. The resulting 133-page memo, titled *The United States in a Changing World Economy*, set out to persuade the president that the United States was at the end of one economic era and on the cusp of a new one that required a radical change in direction to ensure its future prosperity. The memo would be well received by the president, and it would contribute to Nixon's decision on August 15, 1971, to stop gold convertibility, slap a temporary tariff on imports, and begin the move toward floating currencies—steps that brought an end to the Bretton Woods system. It was lauded in the press when it was published later in the year and brought some small measure of fame to its author, who would go on to a highly lucrative Wall Street career (and a prominent role in supporting many research institutions, including the Council on Foreign Relations, where I work). But its warnings about the competitive challenges facing the United States would be largely ignored and the problems it raised poorly addressed. Indeed, much of the memo could still be written today with only modest amendments.

The author was a forty-four-year-old business executive named Peter George Peterson, who was appointed January 19, 1971, by Nixon as the first-ever White House assistant to the president for international economic affairs. Peterson, born in Kearney, Nebraska, was the son of Greek parents. His father had changed his name from Petropoulos when he immigrated to the United States as a young man. After graduating at the top of his high school class, Peterson earned admission to the Massachusetts Institute of Technology and later graduated from Northwestern University in 1947, finally going on to receive an MBA from the University of Chicago. He went to work in advertising at the McCann-Erickson agency in Chicago and was recruited to the number three executive slot at Bell & Howell, then one of the biggest US makers of professional and consumer movie cameras. Just three years later, at age thirty-eight, he became chief executive and chairman of the board. While Nixon would introduce him as "the greatest CEO of his generation," Peterson later gave himself only a B for his time with the company. He had cut costs, introduced popular new consumer products, and maintained the company's market share. But he had failed, he admitted, to recognize the fast-arriving future of digital cameras and recorders that would transform the consumer video industry. Within a decade, that business would be dominated by Japanese companies such as Sony, Samsung, and Panasonic, while Bell & Howell was left struggling in a series of modestly profitable enterprises.[22]

Peterson was recommended to Nixon by George Shultz, director of the Office of Management and Budget and an old friend from their University of Chicago days. As assistant to the president, Peterson directed the newly created cabinet-level White House Council on International Economic Policy (CIEP). Like the National Economic Council formed by President Bill Clinton two decades later, the CIEP was charged with ensuring that economic concerns would have a stronger voice in the foreign policy–making process. Nixon and his national security advisor, Henry Kissinger, were largely uninterested in international economics, their hands full with the Vietnam War and the secret negotiations to reopen diplomatic ties with China. Nixon told Peterson, "Henry doesn't know a damn thing about economics. What's worse, he doesn't know what he doesn't know."[23] And one of Kissinger's top aides would later conclude that Kissinger's record on economic issues was "dismal," writing that "on most issues he has totally abstained," and when he did reluctantly get involved, "he usually bungled badly."[24]

Peterson's memo was aimed at ending that neglect. For too long, he warned the president, Americans had lived with the comfortable belief that "the international competitive superiority of the U.S. was an unalterable fact of life." In 1971 the United States was still producing almost a third of the world's output, but Peterson argued that the era of singular American economic dominance had already come to an end. "The central fact of the past twenty-five years had been the conviction—ours as much as that of other countries—that the U.S. was dominant, both in size and competitiveness, in the international economy," he wrote. "The practices, institutions and rules governing international trade and payments were structured to fit that fact. We as a nation and the world as a whole were too slow to realize that basic structural and competitive changes were occurring."

That was a message that few American leaders wanted to hear then—and to a surprising degree, they do not wish to hear it even today. The assumption of US competitive dominance makes both foreign and domestic policy much easier for presidents to manage. It means that trade negotiations can focus on shoring up alliances or strengthening the economies of potential allies rather than on squeezing out maximum advantage for the US economy. It means that Treasury officials need not be especially concerned with the value of the dollar, assuming that US companies can prosper even when an overvalued currency offers price advantages to foreign competitors. It means that US corporate tax policies can be structured in ways that encourage companies to invest overseas rather than favoring investment at home. And it means that the US government's role is limited to setting the rules for international competition, assuming that more liberal trade and open competition will mostly favor American companies and workers. There is little need for anyone in the government to think strategically about how to help some sector or other of the economy respond to foreign competition. And it absolves the government from thinking about adjustment issues—if US companies and workers are almost always winners in global economic competition, why worry about how to help the losers?

Peterson's memo tried to turn those assumptions on their head. First, he argued that the weakening competitive position of the United States meant that other countries simply had to carry more of the burden for international growth by opening their markets to imports and maintaining appropriately valued currencies. Second, he asserted that the government needed to promote the United States as a business location, using tax policies and other tools to encourage investment and bolster exports. Third, while open trade would create many winners, he maintained, there would also be losers, and policies were needed to help workers retrain and find new jobs. And finally, he argued that the United States needed an ambitious, sustained effort to strengthen its own competitiveness through education, investment, and new scientific research.

The first cause of America's weakening competitive position—the "rise of the rest," as it later came to be called—took up much of the memo. While the same story could have been told in the 2000s about China, Peterson's worry at the time was Japan and, to a lesser extent, Europe. Over the previous two decades, Japan's economy had been growing at 10 percent per year on the strength of rising exports, "the most dramatic rate of economic progress in the world" and more than twice the US growth rate. A decade before scholars like Ezra Vogel and Chalmers Johnson would explain the "Japanese miracle" to a broader audience, Peterson had grasped its essential characteristics. Japan's economy, he noted, was "consciously shaped to meet long-range objectives" under the guidance of powerful bureaucracies. International trade was not an end in itself but rather an instrument to promote domestic production and employment. The Japanese bureaucracy was not, as in the United States, an "umpire of private business"; rather it was a partner in advancing economic goals. That partnership had already brought Japan the largest steel mills in the world and a dominant role in shipbuilding, and future targets included computers, petrochemicals, aluminum, and aircraft. Japan had also exported its model to less developed countries in East Asia, leading Peterson to foresee the rise of the "East Asian rim" as an economic competitor to the United States. In Europe, the creation of the European Economic Community—which was supported by the United States as a bulwark against the advance of Soviet communism—had left US companies at a competitive disadvantage. Trade preferences within Europe meant that companies producing outside the European economic zone faced higher tariffs than those inside the zone, encouraging US companies to invest directly in Europe rather than exporting from the United States. And Europe had in 1967 implemented a value-added tax, a production tax that is rebated to producers for exports and added to the price of imports, further hurting US companies trying to export to the European market.[25]

Peterson did not bemoan European or Japanese success. US foreign policy had been aimed at achieving exactly that result. Nor did he predict, as later commentators would do with both Japan and China, that the United States would be overtaken economically by any of its competitors. Instead, what worried him was the impact on the economic well-being of many Americans. The United States had also been disappointed, he wrote, by the failure of those countries to accept their new economic strength. Instead of opening up to imports from the United States, "it seemed to many Americans that the interests of those countries which had benefitted most from American policies were increasingly concentrating on regional or nationalistic arrangements, which were too often either restrictive or discriminatory or both." These countries had also provided "a wide variety of aids to producers and exporters over the years to help them compete against external pressures" and had negotiated more firmly for their own interests in trade talks. In moderation, such practices could be tolerated by the United States. But carried to the extreme, he warned in language that could be used today to describe the gyrations of the Chinese economy, the "internal preoccupations of any developed world power center can become externally provocative and ultimately self-destructive." Peterson argued for a more robust US posture to promote and defend its economic interests. He rejected the view that "our competitive advantage was so great that we could easily afford concessions here and there, in an ad hoc fashion, in the interest of maintaining flexible and friendly relations with our international partners and developing a prospering world market."

Instead, he predicted that the new era was "likely to be an era of great competition among countries." In order to respond to those new realities, "not only our policies but our methods of diplomacy will have to be changed. Our international negotiating stance will have to meet its trading partners with a clearer, more assertive version of new national interest. This will make us more predictable in the eyes of our trading partners. I believe we must dispel any 'Marshall Plan psychology' or relatively unconstrained generosity that may remain. . . . [T]his is not just a matter of choice but of necessity."

Peterson worried as well about overseas investment by American corporations and what this would mean for the US economy and American workers. By 1971, foreign sales by affiliates of US companies were twice as large as US exports. Scholars had only just begun to explore the significance of the new multinational business models. Most saw the companies bringing significant gains both to the United States and to other countries by lowering consumer prices and spreading technology and industrial knowledge. But labor unions feared that the ability of these companies to invest anywhere in the world would not be in the interests of the world's highest-paid industrial workers, those in the United States. The labor movement, which had supported free trade well into the 1960s, had done an about-face as the US trade surplus eroded. The shift in labor's stance was not due to cyclical economic factors. Unemployment had fallen from nearly 7 percent in 1961, when the unions were in favor of freer trade, to just 3.5 percent by 1969, when unions were leading the charge for Congress to block imports. Instead, the unions saw a fundamental threat to their members from growing offshore investment. The American Federation of Labor and Congress of Industrial Organizations, the umbrella labor organization, warned that the new global production models would harm US workers. "A U.S.-based multinational corporate can produce components in widely separated plants in Korea, Taiwan and the United States, assemble the product in a plant on the Mexican side of the border and sell the goods in the United States at American prices—perhaps with a U.S. brand name."[26] The companies in question—household names like IBM and Xerox, along with chemical, oil, and mining companies—had mounted a fierce rebuttal, commissioning their own studies that concluded that expansion overseas actually boosted growth and job creation at home. The newly formed Emergency Committee for American Trade, a lobbying group for the multinationals that was founded with President Lyndon Johnson's encouragement in 1967 as protectionist pressures began to rise, asserted, "American multinational companies do not export jobs. They outperform other companies in making jobs." Peterson was skeptical of the union claims but acknowledged that "little is publicly known about the interlocking effects of these corporations on U.S. jobs, trade and the balance of payments, and the effects on the economies of other countries." Refusing to draw any firm conclusions about the multinationals, he suggested, "The sheer volume of their activities requires us to take a new look."

He was much less equivocal in arguing for a generous program of "adjustment assistance" for those Americans harmed by rising imports and overseas investment.

While trade would generally benefit most Americans, he believed, there would be some sectors and industries that would lose out in the face of rising import competition, hurting employees and their communities. He told the president, "A program to build on America's strengths by enhancing its international competitiveness cannot be indifferent to the fate of those industries, and especially those groups of workers, which are not meeting the demands of a truly competitive world economy. It is unreasonable to say that a liberal trade policy is in the interest of the entire country and then allow particular industries, workers, and communities to pay the whole price." Congress had tackled this problem in 1962 when it created the first "trade adjustment assistance" program as part of President John F. Kennedy's Trade Expansion Act, which was critical to winning labor support for the bill. But the unions came to feel they had been sold a bill of goods instead. The act required that workers prove they had been harmed by import competition that was explicitly the result of a trade concession made by the United States. From 1962 to 1969, though twenty-five petitions were filed with the Labor Department, not a single American worker received help through the program.[27] Peterson urged a far more ambitious scheme of adjustment assistance that would "facilitate the processes of economic and social change brought about by foreign competition." That would require temporary income support and job retraining for workers and might even require broader federal assistance to affected communities. Certain industries might need temporary protection from imports or other trade restrictions to help them adjust rather than permitting huge job losses to occur. And greater efforts to promote exports would be needed to help offset the jobs lost from imports. He called for a program "which can be accepted by unions" and would persuade them that "their workers will enjoy real benefits" even if they had to be retrained for new occupations.

While the rising economies of Europe and Japan needed to import more and the multinational companies needed to be closely watched, the major sources of America's economic challenges, Peterson told Nixon, were homegrown. Prosperity in the new era of global competition "depends mainly *on our own efforts* rather than on the actions of other countries," he wrote. The United States must undertake a concerted effort "to increase our competitiveness, our productivity and, in general, enlarge the areas of comparative advantage vis-a-vis the rest of the world. The way to do this is to concentrate on the things we do best. This in turn will increase our international competitiveness." Higher productivity would come from greater investments in plant and equipment and public infrastructure. It would require greater focus on research and development, including a more active federal government role in identifying and nurturing promising technologies. And it would require better educating and training Americans in the skills that the emerging industrial and services economy required, a "fundamental reorientation" to ensure that the American workforce was prepared for the coming, highly competitive global economy.

Nixon was delighted with the memo. Peterson presented his findings to the cabinet in a color slide show, and the president asked him to share the report with business, labor unions, the press, and congressional leaders. He ended up on the cover of *Businessweek*, and the *New York Times* called him "an economic Kissinger." The report, which was published later in 1971, sold over ten thousand copies.[28] But those inside the administration, who better understood its implications, were far less persuaded by his arguments. Peterson was the leading figure in the Nixon White House calling for a more assertive foreign economic policy. "The view more people are taking is you shouldn't abandon vital economic interests merely to improve your relations with another government," a senior National Security Council official told the *National Journal*. "We are willing now to push harder on economic interests," he said, adding that for too long "we bent over backwards" to accommodate the economic interests of Europe and Japan. But the State Department in particular saw the memo as far too nationalistic and worried that its aggressive tone would jeopardize political relations with close allies. Others feared its publication would encourage Congress to pass protectionist legislation to block imports. One high-level State Department official said there were "sharp differences of opinion on [the] substantive issues" raised by Peterson and that he lacked understanding of the implications for US foreign policy.[29] Fred Bergsten, a young economist who was Kissinger's advisor on international economic issues, cautioned his boss that while US trade and other foreign economic policies had long been used to serve broader foreign policy goals, "there is now great and increasing pressure to change this relationship." While a degree of rebalancing made sense, Bergsten wrote to Kissinger, "some go so far as to say that foreign policy should now become the handmaiden of foreign economic policy, that we should use our political and military muscle to pursue basically economic objectives. Pete himself believes that a trend in this direction is inevitable. There is certainly widespread support for it in Congress." He urged Kissinger to resist and to make clear to Peterson that "you are not prepared to see economic issues dominate foreign policy in areas where our political interests are sufficiently important."[30]

Peterson himself would prove unable to see the fight through. A year after he came to Washington, Nixon "promoted" him to secretary of commerce, removing him from a White House in which a handful of the president's most loyal aides jealously controlled all major policy matters. Following Nixon's 1972 reelection, with the president increasingly distracted by the growing Watergate scandal, Peterson was not reappointed as secretary and turned down an offer to take the newly created post of ambassador to Europe, headquartered in Brussels. Five years later, the White House Council on International Economic Policy was abolished by President Jimmy Carter. Nothing similar would exist until President Bill Clinton created the National Economic Council in 1993, promising that it would finally develop a coordinated response to America's competitive challenges.

LESSONS NOT LEARNED

Peterson's memo to Nixon had urged the president to see trade in a broader context. While he was a strong supporter of trade liberalization and better international trade rules, he did not assume that growing trade alone would automatically benefit most Americans. Instead, the gains would come only if the United States was vigilant in ensuring that the new rules were followed and that the playing field was a level one for American companies and workers. They would come only if the United States invested in its own future by building better infrastructure, educating its young people, and leading in technological breakthroughs. The federal government would need to adjust its tax policies and take other steps to boost exports, attract more investment, and ensure that Americans got their share of the growing global pie. It would need a strategy for rising to meet the competition. In short, along with international trade and financial policies, the United States needed a competitiveness policy.

The idea of competitiveness is an elusive one. Indeed, many economists insist that only companies, not countries, compete economically. They point out, quite rightly, that international trade and investment are not zero-sum and that a well-functioning global economy can raise prosperity for all. Indeed, over the past two decades, global trade has helped lift more people out of poverty worldwide than at any time in human history. But saying that international economic competition is not "win-lose" is quite different from saying there is no competition at all. Even as trade and investment have been freed up across much of the world over the past half century, countries are competing aggressively for a bigger share—for investment, for exports, and for the jobs they create. Sometimes the tools they use are trade-distorting ones such as subsidies or currency manipulation or regulations that discourage imports; in effect, these are "beggar-thy-neighbor" policies that serve to boost a country's share of global trade and investment beyond what the market would otherwise allocate. Left unchecked, these practices are not only harmful to other countries but produce lopsided economies that are overly dependent on investment and exports, eventually harming the countries that are doing the distorting. But competition can also be an incentive for countries to raise their game—by investing in education, in world-class infrastructure, and in cutting-edge research and development. It can force countries to think carefully about the competitive implications of their tax policies and their monetary and fiscal policies. Trade and investment liberalization, while necessary, are only the first step, one that sets the rules for international economic competition. Equally—perhaps more—important is what governments do next, how they try to ensure that both their companies and their citizens are prepared to prosper in the more competitive world that the new rules have helped to create.

For decades now the United States has been a remarkably successful leader in building rules to free up trade and investment globally. From the end of World War II through the mid-1990s, it led successive rounds of global trade liberalization, culminating in the creation of the WTO in 1995. More recently, as global trade liberalization has stalled, it has led the completion of the TPP in Asia and the negotiations for a Transatlantic Trade and Investment Partnership with the European Union. The TPP is designed as an open agreement, one that could be joined later by countries like Korea, Indonesia, the Philippines, and perhaps eventually China. And despite the stalemate in the WTO, the United States has pursued other avenues for liberalization, including services negotiations with a willing group of countries and the negotiation of an investment treaty with China.

But the United States has done much less to shape trade rules, to encourage public and private investment, and to support its own workforce in order to help Americans secure a bigger share of the gains. On trade and international investment, it has too often looked the other way while competitors manipulated currency values, subsidized their companies, or blocked imports to gain a competitive advantage. At home, the quality of the roads, bridges, and ports that bring US products to overseas markets has badly deteriorated; today the United States ranks sixteenth in the world in the quality of its infrastructure, behind even countries like Spain and Portugal.[31] Americans between the ages of fifty-five and sixty-four are better educated than their counterparts anywhere in the world, but Americans aged twenty-five to thirty-four have slipped to thirteenth.[32] The United States has been a laggard in exports, losing more ground to new competitors like China than have the Europeans or most other advanced economies. And the United States has done much less than almost any of its competitors to help out citizens who find themselves getting the short end of the stick with regard to global competition, those who have lost their jobs to cheap imports or whose factories have relocated to Mexico or China. For example, the United States today spends far, far less on retraining workers than any other advanced economy, even as employers complain of a skills shortage that makes it hard to find employees with the abilities they need.

To caricature only slightly, the US approach to the global economy for the last half century has been "Build it, and we will succeed." In other words, if trade and investment rules are liberalized, then competition alone will lift up Americans. Few other countries behave that way. China, Korea, Japan, and most other Asian countries subsidize their companies or protect their markets through discriminatory regulations to gain an edge in global competition. Germany nurtures its competitive manufacturing industries, trains its workforce, and heavily promotes its exports around the world. Denmark and the Nordic economies have generous schemes for upgrading the skills and education of their employees to help them move to new careers. For some Americans—those with the right mixture of education, ambition, and connections—the lack of support doesn't matter very much. Highly educated Americans have been enormously successful in the more open global economy, building and staffing some of the world's most innovative and dynamic companies. And the United States, largely because of its unmatched universities, continues to attract the lion's share of the brightest, most ambitious immigrants. But far too many Americans are simply unprepared for the competition they are now in. They are like overmatched boxers who keep getting knocked down, only to be told by their corner that they just have to get back in the ring and keep taking the punches in the hope that eventually they will become better fighters. It would make more sense to pull them out of the ring for a year of training and conditioning before sending them back again.

Peterson had warned that the consequences of failing to respond to the new competitive challenges would be severe. With capital moving more freely and transportation costs falling, the pressures for adjustment would "come faster and harder than anything experienced in earlier years," he wrote. "The rising pace of change poses adjustment policy problems which simply cannot be ignored." Failure to adjust, he warned, would be "paid for in abnormal unemployment and wasted opportunity." Today, even with the strong job growth of recent years, fewer Americans are working than at any time since the mid-1970s, and wage growth continues to be anemic. For more Americans to prosper in the hypercompetitive global economy, governments need to recognize that they are in a competition. Peterson had hoped that Washington would take the lead. For the most part it has not, but fortunately there are signs that state and local governments are recognizing and responding to at least some of the challenges. With greater support from Washington, they have the potential to build the sort of competitiveness strategies that the United States has been lacking for far too long.

FACING THE COMPETITIVE CHALLENGE

In early 2015, Sweden's flagship car producer Volvo (now owned by a Chinese billionaire) announced that it would build its first North American plant just outside Charleston, South Carolina. The $500 million plant is scheduled to open in 2018 and employ about two thousand people. It comes at the same time that Germany's BMW has announced plans to expand in the state and create its largest production facility in the world in nearby Spartanburg. The state government of South Carolina has established permanent foreign offices in Shanghai, Tokyo, and Munich. Exports have doubled as a percentage of the state's output over the past decade, and the state has a higher percentage than any other of employees working for foreign-owned companies.[33] Nearby, Daimler, the maker of Mercedes, has its largest SUV production facility in Alabama. Tennessee lured the South Korean tire maker Hankook Tire in 2014, and the company is expected to invest $800 million and create nearly two thousand jobs. Chattanooga is already home to Germany's Volkswagen, which chose the state based on a package of expensive incentives that included the creation of a new job-training program tailored to the factory's needs. For decades now the US share of global investment has been shrinking in the face of competition from Asia. But led by the states and many cities, America is fighting back.

More than two dozen American cities, from large ones like San Diego and Los Angeles to mid-size ones like Portland and Columbus, have developed their own strategies to boost exports, attract investment, and gain jobs in the traded sectors. The most successful ones are busily promoting businesses in which they are already world leaders—medical devices in Minneapolis–St. Paul, aircraft and parts in Wichita, life sciences in San Diego. Portland, which has long been a hub for exports because of chipmaker Intel, has launched a new initiative for boosting exports of clean technology and has undertaken trade missions to promote its athletic and outdoor industry, built around Nike. The athletic footwear company, which became the poster child for outsourcing to low-wage countries like Vietnam, has recently announced that it could create as many as ten thousand new jobs in the United States based on new advanced manufacturing techniques like 3-D printing that could revolutionize how the soles of athletic shoes are made.

These are some of the encouraging signs that at least some American political leaders are finally waking up to what it will take to prosper in the competitive global economy that the United States itself did so much to create. Some of the response is coming from Washington. The federal government, for the first time since the late 1980s, when the semiconductor industry was facing crippling competition, has become serious about boosting advanced manufacturing in the United States. The Obama administration expanded the first real national effort to attract foreign investment in US history. And the government has become more aggressive in demanding that other countries adhere to negotiated trade rules. But for the most part Washington remains mired in foundational disputes over the proper role of government that have prevented an effective response. Once noncontroversial policies—like incremental increases in the gas tax to pay for roads, bridges, and rail lines—have become impossible to enact. Even as other countries are aggressively promoting their exports on global markets, the US Congress shut down for nearly six months the US Export-Import Bank, which helps American companies sell in developing-country markets, and refused to make a needed appointment to the bank's board of directors, which blocked it from making any new large loans. And even as other countries are trying to educate their citizens for the jobs of the future, US public education is hostage to constant skirmishes over national versus local control. In a competitive world, such ideological battles are a luxury that the United States can ill afford.

The real progress has been not in Washington—where the idea of an active government role in promoting economic competitiveness remains suspect—but in the states and the largest cities. More and more local governments have taken the lead in developing competitiveness strategies that start from the premise that local prosperity depends in good part on success in international economic competition. Nearly every state—from the biggest, like Texas and California, to smaller ones, like Tennessee and Nevada—is now competing aggressively for job-creating investments, promoting exports, and trying to build a stronger foundation for future job growth. Too often this is a competition only with other states that does little to benefit the US economy as a whole and instead simply diverts business from one state to another. And too often as well, governments dole out costly tax breaks and other incentives only to discover that the promised benefits fall short. But despite some blunders, more and more states are going global in their search for both investment and new markets, especially for advanced manufacturing that creates higher-paying jobs with a range of spin-off benefits for the local economy. The most successful states and regions are boosting their competitiveness not just, and sometimes not even, by cutting business costs through low taxation or subsidies but instead by investing in infrastructure to help get products to market, by encouraging the commercialization of university research, and by working with companies to ensure they will have the trained workforce they need.

Washington should follow their lead. For the past half century, the federal government has seen its role almost solely as the champion of rules that allow large corporations to invest and move goods freely around the globe. Successive trade agreements—under terms devised largely by the United States—have eliminated quotas and import taxes on most imported goods and offered unprecedented protection for the investments that companies make almost anywhere in the world. But the federal government has done little to help the United States actually compete for those investments and for export market share. Washington needs to follow the lead of the states and cities, standing behind them to help build, attract, and retain businesses in the internationally competitive sectors that provide many of the best jobs in our economy. The timing is right—with its lead in innovation, the falling price of energy, and labor costs that are highly competitive compared to Europe or Japan, the United States is becoming one of the most attractive places to invest in the world.

The federal government needs to go further, however, by negotiating with other countries to create better rules for international economic competition and enforcing those rules vigorously. The trade and investment agreements of the past have made it easier for goods and capital to move around the world, which has brought gains in productivity and efficiency. But those same rules have too often made it easier for large corporations to simply play one country off against another. Companies have enormous leverage to demand government subsidies, tax cuts, or a compliant, low-wage workforce as a condition for investment. Even as it competes fiercely for investment, the United States must lead a new international effort to curb the destructive effects of unbridled competition. New rules should be put in place to set higher standards for business around the world, to discourage corporations from racing to the lowest tax jurisdictions, and to create the conditions for fairer global economic competition. And those rules must be enforced with a vigor that has too often been lacking. The United States needs to launch a new effort to negotiate and enforce rules that will bring the benefits of a global economy to the many rather than the few.

Americans have been told too often by their political leaders that the global economy is something beyond control, that the United States has no choice but to bow to the creative destruction of the market. In his memo to Nixon, Pete Peterson roundly rejected that view. The United States, he argued, must "meet head-on the essential—if demanding—task of improving our productivity and competitiveness in an increasingly competitive world, to seize the initiative in designing a new, comprehensive program designed to build on America's strengths, and to encourage a competitive world trading system that comes from having a sense of our future." In short, he wrote, the United States must lead "a conscious effort to shape our own future rather than resign ourselves to whatever it may bring." That same challenge remains today.

2

Confronting the Competition

The Limitations of Trade Policy

On May 16, 1995, US Trade Representative (USTR) Mickey Kantor walked into the White House conference room, a short stroll from his 17th Avenue office in the Winder Building, and announced that the United States would slap $5.9 billion in tariffs on imports of Japanese automobiles, the largest single trade retaliation ever considered by the US or any other government. A punitive tax of 100 percent would be imposed, he said, in retaliation for Japan's refusal to open its doors to US-made cars. A $35,000 Lexus would overnight become a $70,000 Lexus for American buyers. Among the targets were thirteen fast-growing brands of Japanese luxury cars, including Nissan's Infiniti and Honda's Acura as well as vehicles made by Mazda and Mitsubishi. It was nothing short of a direct threat to a who's who of Japan's most important companies, a move that would have blocked Japanese sales of high-end cars in the world's largest market. Newspaper editorials called the administration's action "bullying" and warned that it could destabilize the world's trading system and weaken the US security alliance with Japan.[1]

The threat was the culmination of a twenty-five-year struggle in which the United States had seen one dominant company after another wilt in the face of Japanese rivals that had figured out how to make competing products that were cheaper, better, or both. Zenith and RCA, the American companies that had introduced and dominated the sales of black-and-white and color televisions in the 1950s and 1960s, had been decimated in the 1970s and 1980s by Japanese competitors such as Matsushita, Sanyo, Sony, Toshiba, and Hitachi.[2] US steel giants such as Bethlehem Steel and US Steel had shrunk, firing hundreds of thousands of workers as a global supply glut, their own failure to invest in new technologies, and rising wage, health-care, and pension obligations reduced their profitability; steel imports had grown from just 5 percent of the US market in the 1950s to nearly one-quarter in the 1980s. The same year, 1995, that Mickey Kantor was threatening tariffs on Japanese car imports,

21

Bethlehem, which had produced most of the steel for the Golden Gate Bridge and once been the largest shipbuilder in the United States, closed its mills in the Pennsylvania town that bears its name, leaving the rusting ruins of five football-field-size blast furnaces along the Lehigh River that runs through the heart of the city. Even in fast-growing new sectors like semiconductors—a technology invented and first commercialized in the United States—Japan had captured half of the total US market by the mid-1980s. Republican president Ronald Reagan had dismayed the free traders in his party in 1987 by slapping 100 percent tariffs on Japanese semiconductor imports for unfair trading practices—a penalty worth about $300 million each year and up to that time the largest US trade retaliation since the Great Depression.[3]

For the Democrats, Japan was an even harder problem. President Bill Clinton had come to the White House in January 1993 trying to paper over deep fissures in his party over how the US government should respond to the country's increasingly precarious position in global trade. A committed internationalist, Clinton was determined to win congressional assent for the North American Free Trade Agreement (NAFTA) with Canada and Mexico, which had been concluded under Republican president George H. W. Bush. In his first major speech on trade, at Washington, DC's American University in February 1993, he had insisted that the United States must "compete, not retreat" and that "open and competitive markets will enrich us as a nation."[4] His own party, heavily concentrated in the industrial Northeast and Midwest, was largely against him; more than half the House Democratic caucus voted against NAFTA later that year, and the treaty was approved thanks only to strong Republican backing. In an effort to appease internal critics, Clinton had promised to do more to help US manufacturing workers and others facing growing import competition. He had insisted that Mexico accept side agreements to NAFTA pledging to uphold stronger labor and environmental standards, an effort to raise business costs in Mexico and reduce the competitive pressures on American workers. And he had promised to take a far tougher line in trade negotiations, in particular by forcing Japan to open its market to US exports, so that new export sales could help offset the losses to some industries from imports. "We cannot stop global change," Clinton said when he signed NAFTA. "We cannot repeal the international economic competition that is everywhere. We can only harness the energy to our benefit. Now we must recognize that the only way for a wealthy nation to grow richer is to export, to simply find new customers for the products and services it makes."[5]

The Japanese were obvious customers. By the mid-1990s, Japan had become the world's second-largest economy and was selling millions of cars in the United States. Toyota's midsize Camry and Honda's Accord were among the best-selling vehicles in 1995, while the Toyota Corolla would go on to become the top-selling car in US history. But the United States, while it still made more cars than any other country, rarely sold any in Japan; foreign companies, most of them Japanese, sold one-third of all the cars in the United States by the mid-1990s, but non-Japanese automakers captured less than 5 percent of Japan's market. Nor did the United States sell many auto parts, despite having a large and sophisticated network of parts companies to support the "Big Three" US automakers—Ford, General Motors (GM), and Chrysler. Less than 3 percent of all auto parts sold in Japan were made by foreign companies. The previous year, Japan had run a $37 billion trade surplus with the United States in autos and auto parts, nearly 60 percent of the total US trade deficit with Japan.[6]

Opening Japan to US cars and car parts was symbolically important for the Clinton administration. "Our market is open to Japanese products. Their market should be open to our products. It's a fundamental question of fairness," Kantor said in announcing the tariff threat. By supporting NAFTA, President Clinton had rejected protectionist solutions. Unlike President Reagan for much of the 1980s, he was not even asking Japan to restrain its sales of cars in the United States; indeed, his administration had agreed to outlaw so-called voluntary export restraints as part of the global trade talks that led to the creation of the WTO in 1995. In order to appease critics in his own party, however, Clinton had to deliver something in return, and that something was greater export opportunities for US companies and the high-paying jobs that such exports would support at home. It was one thing for a Democratic president to plant the flag firmly on the side of free trade and another thing to keep it there if other countries refused to play by the same rules.

But the Japanese were formidable negotiating rivals, even for Mickey Kantor, a lawyer who had honed his craft representing the tobacco giant Philip Morris. The Japanese had become increasingly frustrated with what they saw as America's bullying and hectoring over trade, believing that the United States' own failure to respond to the new competition was at the heart of the problem, and they were determined to resist. Kantor's opposite, then Japanese trade minister and later prime minister Ryutaro Hashimoto, compared negotiating with Kantor to the Japanese sport of kendo, in which two contestants dressed in Darth Vader–like attire duel with bamboo swords; Hashimoto was a sixth-degree black belt in kendo. Kendo is as much about evading and deflecting blows as about landing them, and the Japanese were masters at using America's strengths against its own negotiators. Rejecting charges of protectionism, the Japanese would point out that their tariffs on most imports were actually lower than those of the United States and Europe. When the United States complained about informal barriers—such as the reluctance of many Japanese auto dealers to sell foreign cars—the Japanese government would issue statements urging the dealers to offer American cars; when nothing changed, the Japanese would suggest that their discriminating buyers were not interested in inferior American cars. And when, in frustration, the Clinton administration demanded numerical targets for foreign imports—in effect a guaranteed US share of the Japanese market—Tokyo chastised the Americans for seeking "managed trade" rather than a free market. The two negotiators did not conceal their mutual dislike. Following a particularly difficult session, Hashimoto told an audience full of reporters that "negotiating with Mickey Kantor is scarier than facing my wife when I come home drunk"; not one to shy from a fight, Kantor shot back, "I'd like to hear your wife's side of the story."[7]

The talks broke down on May 12, 1995. Four days later, Kantor threatened massive retaliation. "We recognize today's announcement represents strong action," he said. "The gap between one automotive market that is open and one automotive market that is closed has existed for 35 years. This imbalance has benefited Japanese manufacturers at the expense of American workers and American companies. This must end."[8]

GETTING OTHERS TO HELP

The crisis with Japan marked a breakdown in the US government's preferred response to growing economic competition: getting other countries to help. In his 1971 memo to President Richard Nixon, Pete Peterson had called for "an acceptance of more responsibility by the countries which have made the most significant economic progress in recent decades." At the time, this meant that countries, like Japan and Germany, that were enjoying a growing trade surplus needed to buy a bit more from the United States and other countries and sell a bit less. Peterson urged the president to press these allies for "a system which distributes the burdens of responsibility for preserving economic order equitably among the economically stronger countries."

In the aftermath of World War II, the United States had been the engine of the world economy, but by the late 1960s it was becoming clear that America was running out of steam. Its large and open market served as a kind of global public good. By absorbing manufactured goods from Asia and Europe, the United States had allowed those regions to grow more rapidly than they could have otherwise. As part of a Cold War strategy, such generosity made sense; stronger, more prosperous allies would be better able to resist the blandishments of Soviet and Chinese communism. As former Federal Reserve chairman Paul Volcker has put it, "Despite the direct costs to the United States, budgetary and otherwise, there was never much question about the balance of advantages, either in terms of the world order or to the United States itself."[9] But as the United States moved from trade surplus into trade deficit, that role became less tenable. What made sense in the 1950s and 1960s was by the 1970s imposing too great a burden—fewer jobs, falling production—in sectors of the economy that employed millions of people in reasonably high-paying jobs. Other countries, Peterson argued, would need to step up by opening their markets more widely to US goods, boosting the value of their own currencies to lower the price of imports, and encouraging their consumers to spend more rather than save. While the United States would need to do many things at home to ensure it could be competitive in the world's markets, if those markets were closed or the prices were distorted through undervalued currencies, then the competition could never be a fair one.

The United States must, Peterson argued, persuade these countries to share the burdens of adjustment. Over time, it was probably inevitable that the United States would lose much of its labor-intensive industry to countries where wages were lower than American levels. The United States would make fewer clothes, fewer shoes, and less furniture, and it would also have to share the market for sophisticated goods like autos, aircraft, and computers. But if foreign markets were open to these and other US exports—medical devices or computer software, say, or Hollywood movies—and their consumers were encouraged to buy rather than just to save, then the growth generated by those exports would at least ease the transition for the United States. A faster-growing US economy fueled in part by rising exports would generate new opportunities for those displaced in the older manufacturing sectors and offer new career paths for young Americans.

In his memo to Nixon, no issue concerned Peterson more than the question of how to get other countries to help the United States manage what he feared would be a wrenching transition to the more competitive global economy. The economic crisis in 1971 arose, he argued, from the inability of the US government and its trade competitors to recognize the new reality. The world still believed that the United States remained the sole economic superpower—but even worse, Americans believed it too. Both sides needed a wake-up call. For the United States, that meant a new focus on improving education, increasing business and public investment, retraining its workforce, and supporting cutting-edge research and development that would strengthen US economic competitiveness. For other countries that were advancing rapidly, it meant acknowledging their own success and agreeing to do more to support global economic growth.

There were, broadly speaking, two ways in which other countries could have helped. The first was through trade. The United States has long been a fairly easy place for the rest of the world to sell its goods. If other countries were to emulate the United States by removing more of their import restrictions, implementing clearer and nondiscriminatory regulations, reducing government subsidies for exporters, and encouraging consumers to spend more, that would likely reduce the US trade deficit and ease the adjustment for American workers. The second, the subject of the next chapter, was by allowing and even encouraging their currencies to rise against the dollar. A weak currency, all other things being equal, is an advantage in competitive international markets; having a strong currency is like paying a steep sales tax when selling to your overseas customers, while your competitors get rebates selling in your home market. These measures would certainly not have eliminated the growing competitive pressures facing the United States but could have eased them considerably.

Peterson was far from being a protectionist and indeed had a conventional economist's take on the value of trade. The purpose of trade was to enable consumers to "obtain abroad goods and services which are either unobtainable or more expensive at home." Exports were simply the means to pay for such imports. He was a firm believer in the classical notion of comparative advantage: "If all countries produce those things which they are most efficient at producing, then the world's wealth will be maximized by the international specialization of labor which results." Protecting uncompetitive industries was a pointless exercise that robbed consumers of the benefits of lower prices. And he acknowledged that the US record on trade protection was far from spotless, noting, "The catalogue of American restrictive practices is also long and growing." At the time of his memo, Congress was considering the biggest list of protectionist measures since the Depression, including bills to slap quotas on steel, textile, footwear, and dairy imports.[10] "To go down that road signaled by these proposals," he warned, "is to guarantee that in the long run the American economy will become less and less competitive and less and less productive. This is a prescription for defeat and an admission of failure."

Instead he proposed an ambitious, outward-looking agenda that would "take the offensive against the defects in the present international system, and in our own economy." He urged Nixon to lead an effort to create "a new, open and fair world trading system" in which there was "more responsibility by the countries which have made the most significant economic progress in recent decades." The goal of US trade policy, in other words, should be not just to write new rules for trade but to bring greater balance to the world economy and to ensure that America's openness to imports was matched by new export opportunities. The new system for trade relations must be "a more open, outward-looking, multilateral, prosperous, increasingly symmetrical and well-balanced world—in which a commonly accepted system of rules and behavior patterns will ensure the continuing prosperity of each and all."

THE TRADE DILEMMA

In the more than four decades since Peterson's memo, the United States has done a great deal to build a commonly accepted system of global rules for trade. But it has done far less to induce changes in the behavior of other countries that he feared would do economic harm to Americans. His memo captured the dilemma that has bedeviled US trade policy for the past half century. On the one hand, as the world's largest economy, the United States carried the biggest burden for making the international trading system work. It tried to champion a set of shared rules for global commerce that would keep countries from going their own way, as they had done with such disastrous consequences in the 1930s. On the other hand, if those rules did not also benefit most Americans, public support for trade openness would wane, threatening a return to the very protectionist policies that the new rules had been meant to prevent. That debate over the benefits and costs of trade for Americans continues to be a highly divisive one today, with the country deeply split over the impacts of past trade agreements and proposed deals with Asia and Europe that would result in nearly two-thirds of all US trade being carried out under the rules of free trade agreements. Too many Americans, whether accurately or not, see themselves as losers in an increasingly competitive world and are blaming trade agreements for those losses. In the 2016 presidential election, for the first time in modern history, none of the leading candidates campaigned in favor of further trade liberalization.

At the heart of the trade dilemma is the question of "adjustment costs." As trade was freed up, all countries would have some winners and some losers, sectors in which they could outcompete the rest of the world and sectors in which they could not. While underlying comparative advantages such as natural resources and skilled labor obviously play a role in sorting out which countries thrive in which sectors, the outcome is in no way preordained. Instead, all countries have tried to ensure, through government actions of different sorts, that they have more winners and fewer losers. As political scientist Robert Keohane has written, "The politics of foreign economic policy center around the question of which states will bear the major costs of adjusting to change. . . . Each state seeks to impose unwanted costs on others rather than inflicting them on its own citizens."[11] Countries whose prosperity depends heavily on exports—Japan, Germany, and, more recently, China and many of the other emerging market economies—quite naturally have wanted to keep their export advantages to provide more jobs and higher incomes for their citizens, bigger profits for their companies, and a more robust tax base for government. As former commerce undersecretary Jeffrey Garten has written, these countries have maintained "a single-minded preoccupation with international competitiveness."[12] To varying degrees, they have protected their home markets, channeled resources to investment rather than consumer spending, trained their workers to serve the needs of export-oriented companies, managed their currencies, and subsidized their companies with the goal of capturing a growing share of both domestic and global markets.

But for the United States, the calculus has long been more complicated. In the years after World War II, a generous, asymmetric trade policy—in which the United States opened more to the world than the world did to the United States—made both economic and strategic sense. Even as the US competitive lead had shrunk by the end of the 1960s, strategic goals usually continued to outweigh economic ones for US policymakers. The pushback that Peterson's ideas got from State Department and other US officials responsible for diplomacy showed that foreign policy and security interests would continue to trump economic interests even in a more competitive international environment. It is no coincidence that the first US bilateral free trade agreement, in 1985, was with Israel, America's most important security ally in the Middle East but one that last year accounted for about 1 percent of total US trade. US trade policy has continued to be shaped by many things other than the economic returns to Americans. China was brought into the WTO largely for strategic reasons, to give that country's Communist regime a stake in maintaining the rules of the global economy rather than challenging them. The TPP is seen by US officials as a vehicle for maintaining US influence in the region against an increasingly assertive China. The free trade talks with Europe are intended in part to strengthen the Western alliance against efforts by Russian president Vladimir Putin to divide the West. Sometimes American economic and security interests overlap fairly neatly, which makes it easier for American officials to set clear priorities; it is no coincidence, for example, that the two industries that have enjoyed the most support from the US government in trade fights are the aerospace and semiconductor industries, which have extremely valuable commercial applications but are also vital for building advanced weaponry. But unlike the policies of most of the United States' trading partners, which have focused narrowly on economic advantage, US trade policy has long had multiple goals—strengthening military alliances, developing the economies of allies, encouraging foreign investment in developing countries, expanding the international rule of law, and, if all goes well, increasing the competitiveness of the American economy.

Even in purely economic terms, the United States has faced a dilemma between recognizing mutual benefits and asserting its national interests. The challenge with trade, as Keohane and his coauthor Joseph Nye have observed, is how to "generate a mutually beneficial pattern of cooperation" among countries that are all trying to "manipulate the system to their own benefit."[13] Too much manipulation to serve narrow national interests, and the trade system will fall apart because countries will decide they are better off going it alone; too little, however, and domestic support for an open trade system will weaken.

LEVELING THE PLAYING FIELD

For the United States, the response to the trade dilemma has been to champion ever more elaborate international rules to govern trade, with the hope that these rules will maintain international cooperation and keep other countries on board while bringing greater economic benefits to Americans. This is the philosophy of the "level playing field," a metaphor that is ubiquitous in American discussions of trade policy. In his 2012 State of the Union address, to use one of hundreds of similar examples, President Barack Obama said, "Our workers are the most productive on Earth, and if the playing field is level, I promise you: America will always win." If international trade rules can be written so that they are "fair," the argument goes, then the United States will come out on top more often than not. And as long as the rules have been agreed to by other countries, then any outcomes resulting from market competition will have greater legitimacy.

The creation of such trade rules has been the project of American trade policy for the past half century. Under both Republican and Democratic presidents, the United States has led the farthest-reaching efforts at trade liberalization in history. The Kennedy Round of the General Agreement on Tariffs and Trade (GATT), completed in 1967, lowered tariffs on traded goods by roughly 35 percent in the advanced economies. The Tokyo Round, completed in 1979, cut tariffs by another 35 percent in developed countries and for the first time included rules aimed at curbing government subsidies to industry and opening government purchases to foreign suppliers. The still more ambitious Uruguay Round, concluded in 1993, furthered lowered tariffs in both advanced and developing countries and eliminated quotas on food imports (though food quotas were often replaced by very high tariffs). It created the WTO with its binding procedures for settling trade disputes, partially freed up trade in services such as banking, insurance, and telecommunications, phased out quotas on textiles and apparel, and created new rules for protecting intellectual property such as drug patents, movies, and computer software. Nearly every country in the world today is a member of the WTO. The United States has pursued regional and bilateral deals as well. US trade agreements with Canada in 1989 and Mexico in 1994 created the second-largest free trade area in the world after the European Union and pioneered new rules for trade in financial services, automobiles, and textiles. Other US free trade agreements with Korea, Singapore, Australia, and Central America have extended NAFTA-type rules to other countries.

By many measures, the US record on trade has been an enormous success. Trade with Western Europe and East Asia during the Cold War helped those regions build or rebuild wealthy democracies, a sharp contrast to the economic stagnation and political repression on the other side of the Iron Curtain. Trade has been an engine of prosperity for many developing countries; participation in the global economy has been the only successful way for poor countries to become richer.[14] Economist Branko Milanovic of the World Bank has shown that over the past two decades, in no small part because of growing trade, the poorer countries closed the income gap with the richer ones for the first time since the Industrial Revolution.[15] Since World War II, trade has grown faster than during any other comparable period in human history, though with some notable slowing in recent years. While much of this growth was driven by technological changes that have shrunk the world, such as air travel, containerized shipping, and the Internet, trade policy has also contributed enormously. Rules negotiated over the past half century have helped to prevent, even during the Great Recession, a return to the catastrophic "beggar-thy-neighbor" trade policies of the 1930s in which countries engaged in a self-defeating effort to boost their own economies by blocking imports. Indeed, there is no area of "global governance"—not climate change, not the oceans, not monetary policy, not peacekeeping—in which the world's countries have agreed to cooperate more closely and relinquish more sovereignty than in international trade.

Trade has also brought to Americans an unprecedented array of consumer goods, many at prices that have been falling steadily year after year. The costs of toys and clothing, for example, in real terms are barely a third of what they were several decades ago. In the mid-1980s, clothes purchases ate up about 5.5 percent of personal consumer spending; three decades later they amounted to just 3 percent.[16] A 32-inch high-definition color television (which used to be considered large) can be bought today for about one-tenth the price of the far inferior models of two decades ago. And competition from imports, while sometimes highly disruptive, has forced US companies to boost their productivity and quality to remain in business. Anyone who drove, say, a Ford Pinto or the AMC Pacer in the 1970s knows that the quality of American-made cars has improved vastly in response to foreign competition.

But for all those successes, US trade policy has done little to promote the more balanced trade outcomes that Peterson believed were critical for successful US adjustment to the global economy; indeed, there is a case to be made that US-led trade agreements have made the problem worse. US goods trade with Japan, which had been balanced in the early 1960s, fell into deficit in 1965 and deteriorated steadily from there. By the mid-1980s the annual US trade deficit with Japan exceeded $50 billion, and even after Japan's economy weakened in the 1990s, its surplus with the United States continued to increase. Today it remains nearly $70 billion annually. Trade with the smaller Asian "tigers" such as Taiwan and Korea followed a similar pattern, with the United States running successively larger trade deficits with those countries; indeed, the US trade deficit with Korea has nearly doubled since the 2012 implementation of a bilateral free trade agreement that was supposed to do more to open Korea's market to US goods and services. So did trade with Germany, where the United States moved from surplus to deficit in the mid-1960s and was running deficits of nearly $75 billion by 2015. US trade with Mexico, which was balanced when NAFTA was signed in 1994, has been in deficit ever since, though many Mexican exports at least use a high proportion of American-made inputs. The story has been the same with China. Over two decades, China did more than any country in history to lift its people out of poverty, moving millions out of marginal rural livelihoods to factory work. But US trade with China went from a rough balance in the early 1990s to a deficit of more than $250 billion by the late 2000s, following China's accession to the WTO, and had reached more than $350 billion by 2015—the largest bilateral trade imbalance between any two countries in history.

Of greater concern than the raw numbers is the sectors in which many of those countries have succeeded. Japan first became competitive in high-employment sectors like textiles and shoes; then it came to dominate the auto and consumer electronics industries and briefly became the world's largest producer of semiconductors before US companies rebounded. Germany has long enjoyed a huge surplus in such pillar industries as trucks and cars, pharmaceuticals, machine tools, and power-generating stations. And when China's export growth hit full stride in the 1990s and 2000s, it wasn't confined only to cheap consumer goods like toys and clothing; China, along with its Asian neighbors like Taiwan and Korea, became the global supply hub for such products as smartphones, solar panels, LED lighting, liquid crystal displays, and rechargeable batteries. These are sophisticated, capital-intensive, and high-skilled industries that should be a comparative advantage for a wealthy, highly educated country like the United States.[17] Most of these technologies, indeed, were invented in the United States. Up until 2001, America ran a large trade surplus in advanced technology products such as aerospace, biotechnology, and information technology; since 2002 that has turned into a growing deficit that is now well over $100 billion, mostly as a result of China's growing dominance in information technology industries.[18] As a percentage of its total exports, the United States has lost considerably more ground in high-technology trade than the largest economies of Europe like France and Germany.

American workers in these and other internationally competitive industries have paid a heavy price for the US failure to maintain more balanced trading relationships. There are big disagreements among economists over how to measure the domestic impacts of trade on employment and wages. And the discussion has been further distorted by both advocates and opponents of freer trade. The US Commerce

Department, for example, uses the rule of thumb that every $1 billion in exports creates about six thousand US jobs to claim that exports therefore supported 11.7 million US jobs in 2014.[19] And such jobs, on average, pay nearly 20 percent more than jobs at US companies that don't export. That is good news to be sure. But by that same rule of thumb, there would have been an additional 3 million well-paying US jobs in 2014 if trade had been balanced rather than over $500 billion in the red. On the other side, opponents of NAFTA claim that the rising US trade deficit with Mexico has cost nearly seven hundred thousand jobs in the United States, and this proves that trade agreements like NAFTA have hurt US workers.[20] But that calculation assumes that without NAFTA the goods being imported from Mexico would instead have been made in the United States. More likely they would simply have been imported from Asia or somewhere else instead.

Economic analysis that has looked at US regions facing the greatest import competition suggests that the huge growth in imports from China between 1999 and 2011 was likely responsible for the loss of somewhere between 1 million and 2.5 million jobs during a decade in which overall US manufacturing employment fell by nearly 6 million jobs.[21] That figure alone does not say anything definitive about the US-Chinese trade relationship. US exports to China also grew over the same period, increasing at more than twice the rate of US exports to the rest of the world. And the surge in Chinese imports created new jobs for dockworkers, truckers, rail workers, and retailers in the United States, certainly compensating for some of the lost manufacturing jobs. While there is no consensus on how to balance these losses and gains, recent research suggests that trade competition has had at least a modestly negative impact on the number of jobs in the United States.[22] Robert Lawrence of Harvard, who has long argued that trade is responsible for few lost jobs and that technology is more to blame, recently estimated that Chinese import competition likely accounted for about one hundred thousand US job losses in manufacturing each year from 2000 to 2007, though he noted this was still just 20 percent of the overall manufacturing jobs lost in that period.[23] Research for the Council on Foreign Relations by Nobel Prize–winning economist Michael Spence and Sandile Hlatshwayo showed that from 1990 to 2008 nearly all of the 27 million new jobs in the United States were created in sectors not facing international competition, particularly government and health care.[24]

Assessing the impact of trade on wages for Americans is even harder. Wages have generally been stagnant for most Americans for several decades now, though there have been some recent signs of improvement. During the 2008–2010 recession, the job losses were concentrated in higher-wage industries facing international competition (with the exception of construction), while the job gains coming out of the recession came mostly in lower-wage industries, such as nursing homes and food services, that do not face international competition.[25] Even during the recovery, which has been the longest since the 1980s and has added nearly 6 million jobs, wage growth has generally been weak across the board.[26] But there is disagreement over how much these wage trends have to do with import competition as opposed to other factors like new technology, weaker labor unions, and huge pay packets for chief executives. Pitting American workers against hundreds of millions of additional workers in countries that have opened to trade, like Mexico, Korea, China, and Vietnam, has likely had a depressing effect on US wages. Many economists conclude this is exactly what has happened, but others insist that trade is still too small a share of the overall US economy to explain much of the wage stagnation.[27] One conclusion, which we return to in chapter 5, is undisputed: workers who lose their jobs to import competition, particularly in higher-paid manufacturing industries, suffer huge income losses that last for the remainder of their working lives.[28]

The US response to these competitive pressures has been to double down on negotiation of still better rules, hoping that—if the playing field finally becomes level enough—those trends will be reversed. President Obama has promised that the next generation of trade agreements, led by the "gold standard" Trans-Pacific Partnership, will finally provide that long-promised export boost to the United States. "We have the best workers in the world, the most innovative companies in the world, the best products in the world, the most productive agricultural sector in the world," he told the *Wall Street Journal*. "And we want to make sure that we are not being impeded by a bunch of unfair rules outside of the United States."[29] While acknowledging that trade had hurt some Americans, especially in the manufacturing sectors, he argued, "That's not a reason for us not to enter into trade agreements anymore, it's a reason for us to strengthen the trade agreements that we do enter into."

Yet, while trade deals are very effective at getting rid of overt barriers to trade such as quotas and tariffs, they have proved far less successful at eliminating the myriad of clever ways in which governments promote exports and discriminate against imports. With most of the overt barriers now abolished, the covert ones have become far more important in shaping the trade and investment decisions of companies. Neither the WTO nor the growing web of bilateral and regional trade deals has done very much to tear down the vast web of regulations, government subsidies, and informal directives—mostly, but not exclusively, among developing countries in Asia—that have the effect of protecting those markets from imports and boosting exports. Shanker Singham, a US trade and antitrust lawyer, has called these practices "anticompetitive market distortions"—government actions that give certain favored companies and sectors an artificial competitive advantage over their rivals. These can include licensing restrictions, regulations, local content requirements, limitations on access to telecommunications networks, below-market government-backed loans, energy and land subsidies, and a myriad of other means by which governments can help chosen industries gain a competitive advantage over rivals. Traditional trade rules have largely been unable to tackle the problem. As Singham argues, "WTO rules are written in such a way that broad regulatory measures are generally allowed, even if their effect is to block new competitors."[30] Recent US trade deals such as the TPP have tried to address some of these market-distorting measures and may begin to chip away at more of these informal trade barriers. And the United States has tried to tackle these problems through bilateral negotiations with China and other countries. But progress has been slow and difficult.

Even where the trade rules have more bite, enforcing them has proved tremendously difficult. Enforcement has become a game of "whack-a-mole." Through often painstaking research, the US government has identified practices that violate trade rules—from intellectual property theft to discriminatory tax breaks to standards that favor domestic companies—and then tried to use bilateral negotiations or the binding dispute-settlement rules of the WTO to force governments to eliminate those practices. While the United States wins far more often than it loses before the WTO's dispute-settlement panels, the practical effects are often limited. America's competitors have become extremely adept at substituting one set of market-distorting practices for another, meaning that victory at the WTO has too often proved Pyrrhic. The United States won its first WTO cases against China in 2005, for example, when China agreed to end discriminatory taxes that favored domestic semiconductor companies over foreign competitors; since then, however, China has used a mix of procurement policies, licensing and standards, and regulatory delays under the rubric of "indigenous innovation" in order to boost domestic chip companies at the expense of foreign competitors, measures that are far harder to challenge under trade rules. And even the clearest victories can take two, three, four, or more years to work their way through the WTO legal process, by which time the damage is often impossible to undo. In auto parts, for example, the United States won a 2006 WTO challenge against a discriminatory import tax imposed by China, but by the time the case was resolved, US automakers had shifted to buying from local Chinese suppliers instead.

FROM JAPAN TO CHINA: WHY THE UNITED STATES KEEPS LOSING ON TRADE

The Japan that so frustrated Mickey Kantor was a good example of the challenges that have bedeviled US trade policy. Today, after years of anemic Japanese growth, it is easy to forget the enormous impact that Japanese trade competition had on the US economy—and on the US national psyche. In the early 1980s, a survey of US business leaders found that "the problem of the Japanese challenge to American industry arouses more concern among America's leaders than any other social or economic issue . . . in over 20 years."[31] There is "a subtle hint of defeatism about the prospects for success—and this from many of the men and women who are and will be the architects of America's response to Japan." Two decades later, many of the internal problems in Japan have been laid bare. Its cleverly closed economy and cozy relations between corporate leaders and government bureaucrats produced a highly successful model that concealed a slow rot. Domestic competition was stifled, the exclusion of foreign investment and low levels of immigration discouraged innovation, bid rigging on huge construction projects increasingly impoverished the government, and banks made billions in bad loans to related companies that invested them poorly.

Japan's overreliance on exports also made it far too vulnerable to economic fluctuations elsewhere in the world. Except for occasional strong quarters, Japanese economic growth has been weak for more than two decades now, and living standards have fallen below the OECD average. Yet even a diminished Japan still maintains some of the world's most competitive firms, from auto companies like Toyota and Honda to the medical imaging company Fujifilm to Nippon Steel, the world's second-largest steelmaker. And Japan still runs a sizeable trade surplus with the United States.

Japan established the model, since followed by most of the successful Asian economies, including China, of growing through investment and exports. It started with a high national savings rate, encouraged by government tax incentives—the Japanese still save about a fifth of their disposable income, four times the rate in the United States—which provided a huge pool of capital for investment. Japanese companies, to a greater extent than their US rivals, invested for the long term, focusing on revenue and market-share growth and accepting lower profit margins. That allowed them to sell more cheaply than American companies that needed to produce greater returns for shareholders.[32] And Japanese management practices were in many ways revolutionary, at least in their export-oriented sectors; entire business school curricula were rewritten to try to understand the "Toyota Way" and other forms of flexible manufacturing that proved more adept than US mass production at producing higher-quality goods and meeting changing consumer tastes. Japan's industrial success also depended heavily on what scholars would come to call the "developmental state"—a government that is focused above all else on competitive success in international markets. Japan used the tools of state power, in close cooperation with private companies, to move its economy from the production of labor-intensive goods such as clothing and shoes into more advanced sectors such as steel, cars, televisions, and computers.[33] Chalmers Johnson, in his classic study *MITI and the Japanese Miracle*, wrote that the Japanese government's main concern was "with the structure of domestic industry and with promoting the structure that enhances the nation's international competitiveness." At home, that meant insulating its companies wherever possible from foreign competition, allowing those firms to charge higher prices and earn greater profits that could be invested to boost their export competitiveness.

By US standards, this was not playing by the rules. Japan joined the GATT just five years after its founding and had signed all the agreements; its formal barriers to imports such as tariffs and quotas were as low or lower than those in the United States. But Japan used a variety of subtle tools—none of them expressly prohibited by GATT rules—to ensure that US companies rarely made significant sales in Japan. These included restrictions on foreign investment that made it difficult to establish subsidiaries, opaque regulations that made it extraordinarily hard to win government permission to sell foreign goods in Japan, close ties among Japanese companies that preferred to give their business to each other rather than to foreign competitors, and cultural pressures that encouraged consumers to steer clear of foreign products. It was all but impossible for the United States to prove, however, that the failure of US companies to sell more in Japan was entirely, or even largely, due to these informal barriers. The Japanese could always retort, with some justification, that Americans were either making inferior products or were simply not trying hard enough to sell in Japan. The defect rate in US-made cars in the 1980s, for example, was twice that of American carmakers' Japanese rivals, and it took them much longer to introduce new designs to the market.[34] And none of the "Big Three" US auto companies actually built a small, right-hand-drive car designed especially for the Japanese market until 1995.[35]

Former US trade negotiator Clyde Prestowitz gave a simple but compelling illustration in his 1988 book *Trading Places*. He told the story of how Rawlings and Easton, two US makers of aluminum baseball bats, tried for years with little success to sell their bats in Japan. Youth baseball is big business in Japan, which has more than three hundred local leagues, the largest participation of any country outside the United States; in 1967, a Japanese team became the first non-American team to win the Little League World Series, and Japan has captured the title eight times since. Aluminum is among the most energy hungry of all manufactured products, and lower US electricity costs meant that US-made bats were much cheaper. Japan has no quota on imports of foreign bats, tariffs are very low, and there was every reason to believe the US companies would be successful. But first they needed the Japanese government's approval to sell their bats. In the early 1980s Rawlings and Easton sought help from the US consulate. Any company selling bats to the Japanese Little League required a seal of approval from the league, which was effectively an arm of Japan's Ministry of Education. Foreign bats had never before been sold in Japan because no foreign company had ever been granted the seal. As a result of the 1979 Tokyo Round GATT negotiations (so named because that round of global talks began in Tokyo in 1973, not because they were especially focused on Japan), the United States had persuaded Japan to make the seals available to qualifying foreign companies. But when Rawlings and Easton sought approval, they were flatly rejected. Japanese baseball, they were told, was a unique game (the league uses a softer, rubberized ball) for which only Japanese-made bats were suited. And in any case, there were already ten Japanese companies awaiting approval—a good example of Shanker Singham's point that restrictive regulations harm new domestic competitors as well as foreign ones. What followed was a three-year saga in which the US government tried to pressure Japan to live up to its GATT commitment. At one point, the Japanese-speaking US official trying to pursue the case was told bluntly by a representative of the Japanese sporting goods companies that "those international trade agreements are one thing, and doing business in Japan is another." Even after Japan finally relaxed its restrictions under US pressure, few of the US-made bats were ever sold. As recently as 2012, Rawlings was launching yet another push to expand its still meager sales in Japan.[36]

The United States was not alone in its struggles to open the Japanese market. While European companies made better small and luxury cars and had a bit more success in Japan, European complaints were largely the same. In 1983, the European Community launched a sweeping challenge before a dispute-settlement panel set up under the GATT, charging that "the benefits of successive GATT negotiations with Japan have not been realized owing to a series of factors particular to the Japanese economy which have resulted in a lower level of imports, especially of manufactured products, as compared with those of other industrialized countries." Under the pre-WTO rules, both countries had to agree for such a case to proceed; Japan blocked this one.[37]

The absence of GATT or later WTO remedies left only second-best options for tackling the problem. Prior to the creation of the WTO, which outlawed such practices, Washington periodically demanded that Japan "voluntarily" restrain its exports of cars or steel or televisions to the United States. Those requests were often backed up by threats to unilaterally slap tariffs or quotas on imports from Japan, which was possible under pre-WTO trade rules. The two sides also engaged in endless negotiations. In an effort to boost US sales in Japan, President Jimmy Carter formed a bilateral United States–Japan Trade Facilitation Committee to identify Japanese practices that restricted US exports. President George H. W. Bush pursued bilateral talks aimed at making it easier to do business in Japan by reforming regulatory procedures or opening up distribution networks, the co-called Structural Impediments Initiative. Other presidents favored industry-specific negotiations aimed at boosting exports of a particular good by removing regulatory barriers such as standards and testing and licensing restrictions. President Reagan's market-oriented sector-specific talks targeted the electronics, medical equipment, pharmaceuticals, and telecommunications industries. President Clinton's "Framework" negotiations were focused on autos and auto parts, telecommunications, and insurance. None was particularly successful in boosting US sales; the United States continues to complain about limited access to Japan's huge insurance market, for example, while exports of US telecoms equipment to Japan have fallen in each of the past three years.[38]

In the automotive sector, Mickey Kantor's blunt threats to the Japanese over autos in the mid-1990s proved to be empty ones. As soon as he threatened to slap tariffs on imports of Japanese luxury cars, Japan quickly sought protection under the umbrella of the WTO, which was established on January 1, 1995, just months before the United States–Japan trade showdown. The new WTO rules explicitly forbade such unilateral trade sanctions; the Japanese complaint, if allowed to proceed, would certainly have been upheld by a WTO dispute-settlement panel. The Clinton administration also began to get cold feet, worried about negative market reactions that could damage the US economy and scared that continued escalation might get out of hand and even harm US-Japanese cooperation on security issues.[39] Following all-night talks in Geneva in June 1995 with his counterpart, Japanese trade minister Hashimoto, Kantor settled for a series of "voluntary commitments" by Japan promising that imports of US-made autos and auto parts would grow by some unspecified amount.[40]

Nearly two decades later, just 6 percent of cars on the roads in Japan are made outside the country, by far the smallest share of any advanced economy. The US share of all vehicles sold in Japan, which was a miniscule 1.4 percent in 1995, has fallen to an almost unnoticeable 0.3 percent today.[41] In autos and auto parts alone, the US trade deficit with Japan remains more than $50 billion. Ford Motor Company, which first set up operations in Japan in 1974, pulled out of the market in early 2016, saying the company saw "no reasonable path to achieve sales growth or sustained profitability."[42] Opening the Japanese auto market was again among the top US priorities in the TPP trade negotiations,[43] but veteran critics are skeptical. Sander Levin, a Democratic congressman who has represented a suburban Detroit district for more than three decades, says, "Japan's automotive market is the most closed automotive market in the industrialized world, and past agreements to open it have repeatedly failed."[44]

The legacy of Japanese economic competition for the United States is not that Japan discovered a superior economic model; indeed, the distorted nature of its economy—a heavy reliance on exports, low imports, limited foreign investment and immigration—all conspired to produce a lasting economic slump that the country has been unable to escape. Japan would have been far better off heeding US demands in the 1970s and 1980s that it open more to foreign investment and imports. But the failure to build a more balanced trading relationship also harmed US companies and US workers, limiting opportunities for exports of US-made goods and services into what was long the world's second-largest consumer market, and which today remains the third largest despite two decades of slow growth. The failure to open Japan's market also weakened domestic support in the United States for open trade, calling into question whether US trade policy could actually create the "level playing field" that had so long been promised. Skepticism among the public and political leaders in both parties today poses a huge hurdle to the successful implementation of the TPP, which probably has the best chance of any trade agreement ever written to improve the US-Japanese trading relationship. The history of failed US efforts to open Japan's market has deepened public cynicism about whether a more balanced economic relationship remains possible. As former deputy US trade representative Alan Wolff has put it, "U.S. policy was largely unequal to coming to grips with Japan's highly perfected mercantilism. And from the Japanese point of view, this was the natural order of things, part of an unspoken deal—a one-way flow of goods across the Pacific was the price America paid for having a loyal foreign policy ally in the East."[45]

THE CHINA SYNDROME

The failure to open Japan's market to more imported goods also set a precedent that has been difficult for the United States to shake. Edward Lincoln, a former economic adviser to US ambassador to Japan Walter Mondale in the early 1990s, has argued that Japan's ability to resist US pressure encouraged other Asian economies to follow suit. "If a more open global market is a goal of the U.S. government," he wrote, "then letting the Japanese government maintain barriers is the wrong signal to send."[46]

And indeed a largely similar trade story has played out with Korea, Taiwan, Malaysia, and many other smaller Asian nations, with the United States running chronic trade deficits and showing little success in closing them. The big test, however, was China. Through the end of the 1980s, the very small volume of US imports from China was roughly matched by the very small volume of US exports. By the time China first asked to join the WTO, in 1995, the United States was running a $30 billion bilateral trade deficit, second only to Japan. With China's economy growing by nearly 10 percent annually throughout the 1990s, it was clear that the trade challenge to the United States would be at least as large as that posed by Japan. It turned out to be far larger.

Like much of US postwar trade policy, the decision to welcome China into the WTO in 2001 was driven more by geopolitical concerns than by economic ones. China was a rising power with a population of more than 1 billion. Since loosening the reins of Communist central planning in the 1980s and allowing a market economy to emerge, China had grown at double-digit rates year after year. Bringing China under the umbrella of the WTO would, the United States hoped, help ensure that it was integrated peacefully into the established global economic order. President Bill Clinton's treasury secretary, Larry Summers, told Congress in 2000, "The reality is that rising economic powers that are insecure, that confront a sense of being excluded from the global economy have, since Assyria and Sparta, been sources of global conflict."[47] Robert Zoellick, the first trade representative in the George W. Bush administration, said that a central goal of WTO membership was to make China a "responsible stakeholder" in the global community.[48]

But Congress and the broader public were also assured repeatedly by top administration officials that persuading China to adhere to WTO rules would be a boon for the American economy and help to balance trade with China. Clinton's second trade representative, Charlene Barshefsky, said that the deal "secures broad-ranging, comprehensive, one-way concessions on China's part."[49] In order to join the WTO, she said, China would have to make a vast range of concessions by reducing tariffs, lifting quotas, and ending discriminatory regulations; the United States for its part would be required to do nothing other than promise "normal trade relations" in which imports from China would be treated the same as all other imports. President Clinton called it "a hundred-to-nothing deal for America when it comes to the economic consequences." The president of the US-China Business Council, a coalition of American companies doing business with China, went so far as to predict that "opening China's markets to U.S. products and services under this agreement is the biggest single step we can take to reduce America's growing trade deficit with China, a problem we have faced for a decade."[50]

Rarely in the history of trade policy has a prediction been quite so wrong. US exports to China have indeed grown strongly, but they have been dwarfed by the unprecedented surge in imports. The trade deficit with China, which stood at $83 billion the year before China joined the WTO, now exceeds $350 billion annually. And the imports are mostly not the low-wage, low-skilled products that comparative advantage would have predicted. Instead, the largest categories of the US trade deficit with China include such high-technology industries as telecommunications equipment, computers, smartphones, and solar panels. More than half of all Chinese exports today are in high-technology sectors, compared with just 15 percent in labor-intensive sectors like clothing and shoes.[51] The trade data is somewhat misleading, since a good portion of Chinese high-technology exports comprise components made in other countries and then assembled into finished products in China. But China is trying hard in most of these sectors to develop indigenous capabilities and gradually replace imported components with Chinese-made goods. While China's WTO accession did indeed create a new market for exports of US-made goods, the bigger impact was to make China an enormously attractive location for foreign companies to invest as a platform for exporting to the United States and other countries. China in 2015 attracted a record $126 billion in direct foreign investment despite a slowing economy; foreign-owned companies, most in joint ventures with Chinese partners, account for nearly half of all Chinese exports.[52] The WTO deal further encouraged the Chinese government to pursue rapid export growth, confident that the United States and other countries now had few ways to block or discourage Chinese imports. Having promised to give China "permanent normal trade relations," the United States could not suddenly close its market. And the new rules of the WTO, which required countries to settle their trade disputes through impartial tribunals in Geneva, barred the US government from making the sorts of unilateral threats that were at least partially effective against Japan.

While China has indeed implemented many of its WTO commitments, especially by lowering tariffs and quotas, it is far from fully abiding by the rules. The US Trade Representative's own annual report to Congress on China's WTO compliance is the most detailed repudiation of the claims that the USTR itself made at the time of China's WTO accession. Over the past decade, according to the 2014 report, China's government has "pursued new and more expansive industrial policies, often designed to limit market access for imported goods, foreign manufacturers and foreign service suppliers, while offering substantial government guidance, resources and regulatory support to Chinese industries, particularly ones dominated by state-owned enterprises. This heavy state role in the economy, reinforced by unchecked discretionary actions of Chinese government regulators, generated serious trade frictions with China's many trade partners, including the United States."

The list of complaints is long and touches many of the most competitive US sectors. Chinese regulators, for example, often require US companies to share proprietary technologies "even though Chinese law does not—and cannot under China's WTO commitments—require technology transfer."[53] More than half of the US companies in a recent Commerce Department survey said that technology transfers are required to do business in China.[54] In its development of high-speed rail, for example, the Chinese government in 2009 required foreign bidders to enter into joint ventures with Chinese state-owned companies, to manufacture 70 percent of the systems in China, and to offer up their latest designs. The winning bidder, Kawasaki of Japan, agreed to train a new generation of Chinese engineers and to develop a local supply chain for components. As a consequence, the two Chinese partners, CSR and CNR, now dominate the Chinese market and are building railways in developing countries such as Turkey and Venezuela, aided by Chinese government subsidies. The Chinese even bid to win contracts for high-speed rail from Los Angeles to San Francisco.[55]

The effects of such policies are not limited to the Chinese market. China, to a far greater extent than Japan, Europe, or any other major US competitor, heavily subsidizes most of its internationally competitive industries. As the USTR report puts it, "The Chinese government's provision of preferences and financial support to state-owned enterprises and domestic national champions continue[s] to skew the commercial playing field in many sectors, both in China's market and abroad." The most detailed investigation of the topic suggests that China's government subsidies of its major industrial sectors exceed 30 percent of its total industrial output, an astonishing figure.[56] In many heavy industries such as steel and aluminum, such subsidies have helped China become the world's largest exporter, even in sectors where it holds no obvious competitive advantage. Most of the subsidies go to companies that are directly owned or controlled by the Chinese government. State entities have effective monopolies in aviation, oil, coal, petrochemicals, power generation, shipping, and telecommunications. State-owned enterprises also have leading roles in information technology, construction, autos, insurance, railways, and media.[57]

In solar energy, China's top five solar panel makers receive more than $30 billion in low-interest loans annually from state banks and other government agencies; in comparison, the Obama administration was pilloried for its failed $535 million loan to Solyndra and smaller loans to a handful of US solar companies. Since 2000, the US share of the global solar panel market has fallen from 30 to 7 percent, while China's share has leaped from just 2 to nearly 60 percent.[58] In 2011, Evergreen Solar, the third-largest US maker of solar panels, shuttered its Massachusetts factory and laid off eight hundred employees. By the standards of most American companies, Evergreen had enjoyed generous government support, including some $43 million in aid from the state of Massachusetts, the biggest such grant ever offered by the state. But that was dwarfed by the subsidies to Chinese competitors. Instead of continuing to fight, Evergreen abandoned its Massachusetts plant and moved the operation to China, lured by a partnership with the Wuhan municipal government and the Hubei state government in central China that allowed it to borrow two-thirds of the cost of building the new factory at minimal interest rates. "Therein lies the hidden advantage of being in China," said Evergreen's chief executive.[59] Despite the move, Evergreen was forced into bankruptcy in 2011 and sold its remaining assets to competitors in China; there were no buyers for its US plant.

No sector shows the challenges more clearly than autos and auto parts, where China is today the largest single market in the world. When China's entry into the WTO was being debated in the US Congress, US Trade Representative Charlene Barshefsky predicted a windfall in exports of US-made cars and parts. The new rules would guarantee, she said, that dealerships in China could directly import US cars and that auto plants could buy American-made parts. Industrial policies designed "to draw auto investment, jobs and technology to China" would be abolished; China would be forbidden from instituting local purchasing requirements or forcing transfers of technology. It is true that, unlike Japan, the Chinese market is far from closed to US auto exports, and the Chinese government has encouraged foreign investment in its auto and auto parts sectors. Yet the result—a large and growing US trade deficit in an important sector—has been identical. In practice, China has systematically evaded or skirted many of the WTO requirements in order to achieve its explicitly stated goal of building an internationally competitive auto industry.

China has at times also deliberately violated its WTO commitments in order to give advantages to Chinese producers. Prior to its WTO accession, for example, China maintained prohibitive tariffs on imports of cars and parts; as part of the WTO deal, the tariff rate on imported vehicles was dropped to 25 percent, and on parts it fell to 10 percent. But the Chinese government moved quickly to offset the impact of those tariff cuts. Fearing that foreign carmakers would bypass the higher vehicle tariffs by importing foreign parts and building finished cars in China, the government in 2005 slapped an arbitrary 15 percent tax on parts imports unless the companies were also using a high proportion of Chinese-made parts. The discriminatory tax was a clear violation of WTO rules, and in 2006 the United States challenged it, joined by the European Union and Canada. Two years later, the WTO panel ruled in favor of the United States; in 2009 the decision was upheld after China appealed, and China complied by eliminating the tax. But the victory came too late. During the four years that the tax was in place, the biggest foreign automakers, led by General Motors, had largely stopped using imported auto parts in their Chinese-made vehicles and had replaced them with lower-priced Chinese-made versions. As the *New York Times* wrote after the final decision, "General Motors, the automaker that accounts for three-quarters of American-brand vehicle sales in China, now manufactures or purchases in China so many of its auto parts for vehicles sold in China that the government decision to comply with the WTO rules makes little difference."[60] By 2009, all of the major North American parts producers—Delphi, TRW, Visteon, Magna, and others—had built factories in China. With costs being lower in China, the big automakers are increasingly requiring their parts suppliers to locate there. And given the economies of scale, many of these companies are not only producing parts for vehicles made in China but exporting parts as well. A 2011 report by the US Department of Commerce said that the "Big Three" US carmakers have "advocated that U.S.-based suppliers move production to lower cost countries or risk losing future contracts."[61]

China also heavily subsidizes its own auto parts producers, which are quickly learning from foreign producers. The best estimates suggest that Chinese parts makers received nearly $28 billion in government subsidies from 2001 to 2011 and have been promised another $11 billion through 2020.[62] The subsidies are showered on thousands of smaller producers—some of them owned directly by local or provincial governments—that would otherwise enjoy no competitive advantage. Chinese companies have also been making acquisitions of US parts firms to move up the value chain; Beijing West Industries bought Delphi's suspension and brake unit for $100 million in 2009, and Pacific Century Motors bought Nexteer, which makes steering assemblies for GM pickups and SUVs, for $450 million in 2010.[63] In 2012 the United States brought another WTO case, arguing that the subsidies from municipal governments to Chinese auto and auto parts makers violate WTO rules.

The result has been that while US auto sales to China have indeed grown rapidly, particularly since 2009, they have been dwarfed by the exports of Chinese-made parts back to the United States. Sales of imported cars are largely in the luxury segment, where German and Japanese companies have a greater range of offerings than US companies. And China's consumption tax—though probably not a violation of WTO rules—falls most heavily on the American-made vehicles with the biggest engines. Even so, China has been the fastest-growing export market for US cars, and by 2014 China was the second-largest vehicle export market for the United States, with exports of more than three hundred thousand vehicles, worth nearly $10 billion.[64] But the United States imported more than $18 billion in Chinese-made parts in 2014; in contrast, exports of US-made parts to China totaled just $2.2 billion.[65] There was no reason to predict that China would emerge as a powerhouse in auto parts production, a capital-intensive industry in which labor accounts for just 5 percent of the total costs of a typical Chinese producer.[66] And China's parts industry remains highly fragmented, with few economies of scale. Yet, as a consequence largely of government intervention, China has built a highly competitive industry.

Such practices are common across major industries, particularly those deemed "strategic" by the Chinese government. Chinese exporters enjoy a range of subsidies that are conditional on exports, even though such "export-contingent subsidies" are mostly against WTO rules. The benefits include lower tariffs on intermediate inputs and tax rebates and, prior to 2008, a 50 percent reduction in the corporate income tax for companies that exported more than 70 percent of their output. That preference was removed only after a US challenge in the WTO. Yet many Chinese companies still exist almost solely to export. A typical US or European multinational company even today mostly sells in its home market. In China, more than one-third of multinational manufacturing companies sell more than 90 percent of their production abroad. Just 2 percent of French exporters and a mere 0.7 percent of US exporters have such high export intensity.[67] The difference is huge Chinese government subsidies tied to exports, which, in theory at least, are a clear violation of WTO rules.

Such heavy subsidies have two big consequences. The first is massive oversupply in many industries, which drives down prices and makes it difficult for US-based production to compete. In steel, for example, China alone accounted for nearly all of the global increase in steelmaking between 2000 and 2015, and its capacity now exceeds that of the United States, the European Union, Japan, and Russia combined. USTR notes, "China has no comparative advantage with regard to the energy and raw material inputs for steelmaking, yet China's capacity has continued to grow exponentially."[68] Steel is an energy-intensive industry, and the Chinese steel industry is much less energy efficient than its Western competitors, using 20 to 40 percent more energy per ton of output. But government subsidies mean that energy costs for Chinese firms are one-third to one-half of the world average.[69] The story is similar in other heavy industrial sectors like glass, paper, plastics, and chemicals. In none of these sectors does China enjoy an apparent advantage; these are capital-intensive industries in which labor costs are largely irrelevant and scale matters, while Chinese production is fragmented across the country. But Chinese firms enjoy tens of billions of dollars in subsidies for energy and land, as well as low-cost loans that allow them to undersell Western competitors. The second consequence of heavy subsidies, as Derek Scissors of the American Enterprise Institute points out, is to suppress Chinese consumer demand, reducing export opportunities in China for the United States and other countries.[70] Subsidies have to come from somewhere; in China's case, they come from government-controlled banks paying savers low interest rates on deposits and from protected industries charging monopoly prices for consumer goods. The subsidies are, in effect, a direct transfer from ordinary Chinese to the country's wealthiest companies. And that leaves consumers with much less to spend on goods and services, including imports.

While such practices are clearly harmful to the United States and to China's other trading partners, they are harmful to China as well. Much like Japan in the 1980s, China has built an economy that is too heavily dependent on export growth, is fueled by large investments at low interest rates that may not pay off for the companies or their bankers, and is thus vulnerable to oversupply and asset bubbles. China's recent economic slowdown and stock market fluctuations are symptoms of that imbalance. Of the world's largest economies, no other comes close to China's dependence on investment and exports for growth. While China has been promising a rebalancing toward greater consumer spending, consumption still accounts for just 30 percent of Chinese GDP, and it is predicted to remain at roughly that level for the next decade.[71] In the United States, that figure is 76 percent, while in India it is 52 percent, a level more typical of emerging markets in the throes of industrialization.

And much as with Japan, the competitive challenge from China is not that it has discovered a new economic model worthy of emulation; indeed the limitations of the Chinese economy are likely to become more apparent as its population ages and its workforce shrinks. But the US failure to discourage China from using such trade-distorting policies has had serious domestic consequences, reducing employment and holding down wages for too many American workers, especially in manufacturing. China's growing trade surplus in high-technology goods and its role as the manufacturing hub for a range of information technology industries could also threaten the US edge in innovation, which remains the biggest source of American competitive advantage. The failure has also deepened US public distrust over international trade. Radical ideas like slapping WTO-illegal tariffs on Chinese imports are getting a far more serious hearing in political debates than ever before. The promise of the last half century of trade negotiations was that better rules would discourage such behavior and allow the logic of comparative advantage to drive trade. But even as the rules have improved on paper, the means for enforcing them have fallen well short of the challenge.

ENFORCING THE RULES

The US government has long promised that better enforcement of trade rules could stop, or at least do far more to discourage, such trade-distorting practices. Every president has pledged to take enforcement more seriously—most recently, President Obama created a new Interagency Trade Enforcement Center, promising "robust monitoring and enforcement of U.S. rights under international trade agreements, and enforcement of domestic trade laws." Over the past decade, the United States has brought more than two dozen WTO cases against China and won most of them. These wins have at times produced real gains for the United States. China, for instance, is now by far the world's largest consumer of semiconductors; in 2013, driven by the growth in production of smartphones and tablets for Apple, Google, Samsung, and others, China consumed 55 percent of the world's output.[72] Chinese semiconductor makers for years enjoyed a big tax rebate from the government that was not available to foreign companies, a clearly discriminatory policy. China eliminated the rebate following a WTO challenge in 2004 brought by the United States and joined by the European Union, Taiwan, Japan, and Mexico. While China is still trying to ramp up its domestic production by offering large incentives to big foreign firms like Intel and favoring indigenous companies, China today imports about $160 billion worth of chips annually, some 90 percent of its total demand.[73] Direct exports from the United States remain modest—while Intel still makes most of its chips in the United States, as do other smaller companies like Micron, "fabless" firms like Qualcomm do most of the actual chip assembly in Taiwan and other offshore locations. But these profits support an array of well-paid design and engineering jobs in the United States. Other WTO decisions, like the auto parts case, came too late to make much difference. And in other cases China has dragged its heels on implementation. At the behest of US banks, for instance, the United States in 2010 filed suit with the WTO to open up China's electronic payments system. Financial services is an area of US competitive advantage and one that has been growing. Yet the Chinese government currently allows only a single Chinese company, China Union Pay (CUP), to process all credit card transactions denominated in renminbi. American companies like MasterCard and American Express have to negotiate deals with CUP in order to offer credit cards to Chinese consumers. While the WTO's 2012 ruling largely favored the United States, China continued to block entry by foreign credit card companies and maintained the CUP monopoly for three more years. China finally lifted the restrictions in the middle of 2015, but it has imposed other regulatory hurdles that will make it hard for Visa, MasterCard, and other competitors to break into the market.

Trade enforcement has been most effective when the US government's commitment has been focused and sustained, which has too rarely been the case. Two industries stand out as notable exceptions: semiconductors and aerospace. Both were rare cases in which US defense and commercial interests overlapped so strongly that the US government felt compelled to act. Semiconductors were first developed in the United States for military uses; today not only are they the building blocks for computers, smartphones, and the rest of the information technology industry, but they are increasingly being built into almost every imaginable consumer product, from cars to refrigerators. US chip companies account for more than half of all global sales. Intel is the largest semiconductor company in the world, and US companies hold five of the top ten spots. Intel earns about 85 percent of its revenue overseas but employs half of its global workforce of more than one hundred thousand in the United States. Boeing, the world's biggest maker of commercial jets, started out building planes for the military and did not branch out into commercial aviation until the 1950s. Boeing today is the largest single US exporter and also remains the second-largest defense company in the world.

Those histories could have been quite different if the US government had looked the other way in the face of growing international competition. While US companies invented and commercialized the integrated circuit, in the 1980s the United States nearly lost its semiconductor industry; for much of that decade the US share of even its own domestic market was a mere 30 percent, while Japan controlled most of the rest. US dominance in aerospace, led by Seattle-based Boeing, was never threatened to the same extent, but the rise of the European Airbus consortium in the 1980s posed a similar challenge. By the early 2000s, Airbus had overtaken Boeing to become the largest builder of commercial aircraft in the world. But unlike many of the other industries facing import competition in the 1980s, the potential demise of the semiconductor and aircraft industries set off alarm bells in the US government. The turnarounds in the semiconductor and aircraft industries are the result of a successful competitiveness strategy based on close cooperation between the US government and industry. But they are rare examples.

While textiles and shoes or steel and televisions all received some form of US government trade protection from time to time, the goal was more to manage the decline of US-based production than to preserve a strong competitive position. But chips and aircraft were both seen as industries of the future. Semiconductors are the building block for nearly every other advanced manufacturing sector. As three analysts wrote in the early 1980s when US companies began to lose market share to Japanese rivals, "For the foreseeable future, the relative economic strength of all advanced industrial economies will rest in part on their capacity to develop and apply semiconductor technology to product design and production processes. Thus the loss of leadership in this one industry would mean the loss of international competitiveness in many of the advanced technology sectors that have been the basis of a U.S. advantage since World War II."[74] Semiconductors were also critical for the US military, and the Defense Department had heavily subsidized the research that produced the major breakthroughs. Following the development of the integrated circuit in the research labs of Texas Instruments and Fairchild in 1958, the main buyer of semiconductors was the US government. Fairchild's primary customer was the US Air Force and its missile guidance system for the Minuteman II nuclear ballistic missile; for Texas Instruments, it was NASA and the guidance computer for the Apollo spacecraft.[75] The US commercial aircraft industry similarly benefited enormously from Pentagon support. Boeing began as a military contractor and was the most important maker of bomber aircraft during World War II, including the B-17 Flying Fortress and the B-29 Super Fortress. The B-52 was at the heart of the US nuclear deterrent force for much of the Cold War, and the plane remains in operation today. The company based its first long-range commercial jets on designs for long-range bomber aircraft and remains one of the largest contractors for the Pentagon.

Semiconductors

The importance of semiconductors was obvious to Japan as well, and the government had nurtured its own domestic industry to catch up with the United States. In the 1960s, the Japanese government used the full range of tools—investment restrictions, licensing, high tariffs and quotas—to keep out US competition. The only way for foreign companies to enter the Japanese market was through joint ventures in which they were minority shareholders, which required sharing of their technologies with their Japanese partners. It was not until 1971, after a decade of effort backed by US government pressure, that Texas Instruments became the first US chip company to establish a wholly owned subsidiary in Japan. Despite these import barriers, by the early 1970s US semiconductors were so much better and cheaper than their Japanese rivals that the big Japanese electronics companies had little choice but to import them for use in everything from computers to calculators. The US market share in Japan hit 35 percent in 1971.[76]

The Japanese response was to double down on the development of its own domestic industry and drive out the American competition. The chief executive of Sharp, one of the biggest buyers of US chips for its calculators, was accused in the Japanese press of being "a traitor who would waste Japan's precious foreign currency." Japan's powerful Ministry of International Trade and Industry (MITI) then singled out the company by denying it licenses to import the American-made chips. At the same time, the Japanese government launched, subsidized, and promoted a huge cooperative research-and-development effort among its companies with the explicit goal of overtaking the United States.[77] A MITI vision paper spelled out that "possession of her own technology will help Japan to maintain and develop her industries' international superiority and to form a foundation for the long-term development of the economy and society."[78] US sales to Japan began to fall even as Japan lowered its tariffs, lifted quotas, and removed other formal barriers to imports.

While Japan could not compete directly in the most advanced products, the government-backed research initiatives and huge capital investments allowed its companies to master memory chips, where price and quality control were the keys to competitiveness. Semiconductor manufacturing is enormously capital intensive, and the economies of scale are so large that, once the initial investments have been made, the incremental cost of making additional chips is minimal. At the same time, product cycles are so short that heavy investments must be made months and even years in advance of the anticipated demand. The result is a boom-and-bust cycle that favors companies that can ride out the downturns. The close relationships between the Japanese companies and Japanese banks meant a lower cost of capital that allowed them to continue investing during the inevitable cyclical downturns in demand, positioning the Japanese to seize market share whenever demand recovered. By the late 1970s, Japanese producers had captured 40 percent of the US market for the 16K DRAM chip, the chip used by Steve Jobs and Steve Wozniak to build their breakthrough Apple II computer. And the Japanese beat their American rivals in development of the 64K chip, controlling 70 percent of the US market by 1981.[79] DRAMs were less than one-fifth of the total US market for semiconductors, but they were critical to the emerging computer industry. And in contrast to US openness to imports, the Japanese market was largely closed to the products in which US companies remained the world leaders. While US companies such as Intel and Motorola sold more than half of all the chips used in Europe, their market share in Japan never rose above 12 percent.

For many years, US companies flailed in their efforts to break back into Japan, despite some help from the US government. Years of negotiations between the United States and Japan produced no noticeable changes. Finally, in 1984, the companies begged the Reagan administration for tougher action, arguing that their inability to sell in Japan could undermine the industry at home.[80] In contrast to the US government's tepid response to growing competition in televisions, steel, autos, and nearly every other sector, the fear of losing the semiconductor industry galvanized Washington. The collapse in chip prices in the summer of 1985 in one of the industry's cyclical downturns was a further spur. The companies filed two antidumping cases, one against 64K DRAMs and another against erasable memory chips. And fearing that Japan was on the verge of dominating the next-generation 256K chips as well, the Reagan administration took the highly unusual step of "self-initiating" an antidumping case against the Japanese producers (normally the government is merely a passive recipient of cases launched by private companies).

In the face of three simultaneous trade actions that threatened large import tariffs, Japan agreed in 1986 to an unprecedented bilateral deal with the Reagan administration that for the first time set what amounted to market share targets for foreign companies selling in Japan. The language, written down in a secret side agreement, was vague on exactly how the share was to be realized. It said, "The Government of Japan recognizes the U.S. industry's expectation" that foreign sales would "rise slightly above 20 percent."[81] In the aftermath of the agreement, Japan denied that it had accepted any government commitment to ensure that its companies hit that target. Frustrated by what it saw as slow compliance, the Reagan administration in

1987 imposed 100 percent tariffs on $300 million worth of Japanese imports of computers, color televisions, and machine tools. It was the first time in the postwar era that the United States had directly slapped Japan with trade sanctions. Trade historian Douglas Irwin has called it "among the most dramatic events of postwar U.S. trade policy."[82]

The market share deal was backed by a series of other measures that added up to perhaps the most extensive US government intervention in a major traded industry in the postwar era. Following the sanctions, Japan agreed to set minimum prices for many chips, and the Japanese government pressured its companies to cut back investment and restrain production to ensure that prices stayed high.[83] For its part, the US government emulated the Japanese by relaxing antitrust laws to encourage research cooperation among the companies, resulting in a new research consortium of fourteen chip companies called Sematech to improve chip-making technology; the consortium continued to operate even after government funding was halted in 1996.[84] Intel became a particular success story, coming to dominate the market for computer microprocessors to run the emerging generations of faster computers and becoming the first chip maker to develop a distinct public brand; by the end of the 1990s, it had captured an astonishing 82 percent of the microprocessor market. And the Japanese themselves—in part because of the higher prices forced on them by the deal with the United States—were increasingly squeezed out of the memory market by lower-cost Korean competitors, such as Samsung and Hynix, whose strategies emulated the Japanese.

To trade purists, the US-Japanese semiconductor trade agreement was one of the cruder efforts in US history to force open a foreign market. It had some unintended consequences. US computer companies and other users of semiconductors howled at the price increases that followed the 1986 agreement. While the deal referred to increasing "foreign" sales in Japan rather than just US sales, the European Union complained to the GATT that its companies were harmed by their exclusion and then signed its own deal with Japan. But it was also a rare US win in opening the Japanese market, one that actually helped change the structure of trade in an industry critical to US competitiveness. By the end of 1991, foreign producers, both US and European, had achieved nearly a 30 percent market share in Japan.[85] Following the agreement, MITI shifted its stance from actively discouraging imported chips to actively promoting them. The US share of the world market also increased. In 2015, the US semiconductor industry sold more than one in every three chips used in Japan. By creating an opening to Japanese buyers that had long shunned American products, the deal helped to build much deeper ties between US and Japanese firms that remain to this day. The US Semiconductor Industry Association says that the two industries today enjoy "a close working relationship."[86]

There are certainly competitive threats on the horizon, especially from China, which is investing heavily to increase domestic chip production and pursuing foreign acquisitions, including a failed bid by state-owned Tsinghua Unigroup for Micron in 2015. But the US semiconductor industry today is an American success story.

Semiconductors are the third-largest manufactured US export, and sales by American companies totaled just over half the global market, far ahead of their nearest competitors in Korea and Japan. Nine of the top twenty semiconductor companies are American, and the explosive growth in smartphones, tablets, and the "Internet of things" offers a fast-growing market for the foreseeable future and promises growing exports to China, Germany, Japan, and Korea. The United States is also a big producer of semiconductor manufacturing equipment, behind only Japan.[87] With the growth of fabless companies, like Qualcomm, that focus on chip design rather than manufacturing, much of the final production of chips takes place in countries like Taiwan, Korea, and China, in part because of generous government tax incentives that reduce the high cost of building new foundries. Those distortions should be tackled through new investment rules. But the United States is far from left out even in fabrication, and overall the industry does more than half its manufacturing in the United States. Foreign companies are also investing in the United States; Samsung, the Korean DRAM maker, recently expanded its foundry in Austin, Texas. Today, the chip industry directly employs some 250,000 American workers at salaries more than twice the national average and spins off nearly 1 million other jobs.[88]

Aircraft

The European Union in the 1960s identified and targeted commercial aircraft as a sector of strategic economic importance in which it aspired to achieve a strong market position. Much as with Japan and semiconductors, the US government looked the other way until the challenge became impossible to ignore. And much as with semiconductors, the US government and the industry finally began to work closely together to try to maintain and even strengthen the US industry's market position by aggressively disputing alleged violations of the trade rules. Since 2005, the United States and the European Union have been embroiled in a bitter WTO dispute following US charges that the latter subsidized its aerospace industry in violation of global trade rules, which triggered a series of EU counterclaims.

The commercial dispute has played out over many decades. While the cycle times are much longer for aircraft than they are for semiconductors, the economics are similar—both require enormous up-front investments in the development of new products. US commercial aircraft companies, led by McDonnell-Douglas and Boeing, had long dominated the commercial market and had become complacent in assuming that no other company could afford the costs of challenging their dominance. But the Europeans found a way. Airbus was created in 1970 as a consortium of four national aircraft corporations—from France, Germany, the United Kingdom, and Spain—and it solved the problem of entry barriers by relying largely on government funding for research and development of its fleet of aircraft. The European scheme was royalty based—if Airbus made profits on the sales, the governments would be repaid and perhaps even turn a profit. If not, the governments would lose their initial investments. It was, in effect, an interest-free loan with no obligation for repayment.

Throughout the 1980s, the US companies grumbled but did little in response. The economics of the industry favor continuing to build and sell established designs as long as possible rather than investing billions in new, unproven models. Boeing in the mid-1980s was making record profits on the sales of its long-haul 747 and other designs. This complacency had been slightly rattled as early as 1977, the year that Airbus made its first big sale in the United States of its new A300 to a longtime Boeing customer, Eastern Airlines. Subsidies were only part of the Airbus story, to be sure. The company was the first to use cutting-edge technologies like "fly by wire," and it was extremely well managed for much of the 1980s and 1990s at a time when Boeing had lost direction and was doing little to develop new competitive models.[89] It was not until the mid-1980s, when Airbus signed big contracts with PanAm, American, and Northwest Airlines, that the US industry finally turned to the government for help. The US government brought two cases before the GATT, in 1990 and 1991, and threatened unilateral trade action that could have led to high tariffs being slapped on Airbus exports to the United States. Then, in just the second month of his presidency in February 1993, President Bill Clinton raised the temperature further when he visited the Boeing 747 plant in Everett, Washington. Just before his visit, nearly thirty thousand of the company's workers had received letters warning that they could be facing layoffs because of weak aircraft sales. In a speech to the factory's workers, Clinton made it clear whom he blamed. "A lot of these layoffs would not have been announced if it had not been for the $26 billion the United States sat by and allowed the Europeans to plough into Airbus," he declared.[90] While Boeing was reluctant to pull the trigger of US trade sanctions and possibly jeopardize its sales to European airlines, the US pressure was enough to persuade the European Union to accept a negotiated compromise in 1992. Under the bilateral agreement, the European governments agreed to end production subsidies, limit government development support to no more than one-third of the total costs of any new plane, and require repayment of the loans over seventeen years at interest rates that reflected the governments' borrowing costs.[91] The United States in turn agreed to limit the so-called indirect subsidies that Boeing enjoyed from its defense-related work.

Like the semiconductor agreement, the 1992 aircraft agreement involved heavy government interference in trade, but again with the purpose of reducing market distortions. It was at least partially successful. Airbus's early designs, like the A300 and the A320, were developed with nearly 100 percent government funding, but when Airbus announced plans to develop its new A380 jumbo following the 1992 agreement, it adhered to the one-third ceiling. The restrictions also had a small impact in raising production costs for Airbus.[92] In the longer run, the deal proved inadequate, however. To the European Union, the deal had legitimized subsidies up to the agreed levels, but to the United States it was intended only as a first step toward further reductions in subsidies. The European Union's determination to offer launch aid for the jumbo A380 and the newer A350, a lightweight aircraft, triggered a broad US challenge in the WTO in 2005 alleging that support for Airbus was in violation of the subsidies rules in the Uruguay Round agreement. No doubt Boeing's willingness to launch the dispute was influenced by its losing its top spot in new aircraft deliveries to Airbus for the first time in 2003. In its WTO complaint, the United States alleged that Airbus had benefited from more than $17 billion in trade-distorting launch loans during the life of the company. The European Union filed a countercomplaint alleging that Boeing had benefits from more than $23 billion in trade-distorting subsidies in the form of Pentagon and other US government support for research and development and production tax breaks from Washington State and Kansas.

More than a decade later, the WTO disputes remain unresolved. Both sides have won many of their arguments on the merits, but the dispute has dragged out; neither side is prepared to come into full compliance or to impose billions of dollars in trade sanctions in retaliation. It is too soon to say what the ultimate effects of the trade dispute will be on the shape of the industry. But the US government's determination to press the fight seems at least to have kept Airbus and the European governments off balance. Boeing made a big leap in developing the first of a new generation of fuel-efficient, composite aircraft, the Boeing 787, which, despite delays and launch problems, has become the fastest-selling airplane in the world. The Airbus A350, which made its first commercial flight in 2015, is a formidable competitor in the same category, but its launch was slowed by intra-European disputes over government funding for the project, allowing Boeing to gain an edge. Both companies today have order books that are overflowing, but there are new challengers on the horizon. Bombardier of Canada and Embraer of Brazil, both makers of smaller regional jets, are moving into the low end of the large civil aircraft market. And China's government-owned Commercial Aircraft Corporation of China, Comac, is also set to compete directly with Boeing and Airbus in the low end of the market. Both the United States and the European Union could soon find common ground in trying to limit government subsidies to these new competitors. The trade fight had one other benefit for the United States as well. In 2012, in the midst of the WTO dispute, Airbus announced plans to erect its first assembly plant in the United States, in Mobile, Alabama, to build narrow-body jets. Much like the Japanese car companies that began investing heavily in the United States in the 1980s, Airbus is hoping that its $600 million investment and the one thousand jobs it will bring will help ease trade tensions with the United States and encourage new US airline customers.[93]

Counterfactuals are difficult, to be sure. There is no way of knowing for certain what would have happened to the semiconductor industry without intervention by the US government, though the fates of so many other industries facing Japanese competition in the 1980s suggest it would not have been good. Boeing's revival is largely a story about the company's again assuming the technological lead with its 787 after years of resting on established designs. But the US government's action succeeded at least in placing some real limits on European subsidies. In both cases, assisting the industries required sustained, aggressive action by Washington, something that has been rare in the history of US efforts to enforce trade rules.

THE LIMITATIONS OF TRADE RULES

Over the past half century, the United States has been a leader in building the rules for global economic competition. The benefits have been enormous in increasing trade flows, lowering the cost of goods, bringing up living standards in developing countries, and discouraging protectionist measures that would jeopardize these gains. But the US experience with trade negotiations also suggests that better rules alone will not be enough to alter in fundamental ways the behavior of at least some important US trading partners. That is not to say that rules don't matter—indeed, the only real alternative to weak international trading rules is better ones. The TPP agreement, for example, contains the first serious effort to reduce subsidies and market-distorting incentives to state-owned enterprises, addressing a problem that has challenged many US companies doing business in Asia. And it goes farther than any previous trade agreement to eliminate barriers to digital trade, in which US companies like Google, Facebook, and eBay are world leaders. The Transatlantic Trade and Investment Partnership negotiations with Europe, if concluded successfully, would do more than any previous agreement to reduce regulatory barriers—making it easier, for example, for a car built to US specifications to be sold in Europe, and vice versa, without requiring elaborate additional testing. But if the last half century teaches us anything, it is that creating even somewhat reciprocal openings in trade demands constant attention and pressure by the US government. As in the case of the semiconductor and aircraft industries, persuading other countries to help the United States by importing a little more and supporting their exporters a little less requires not just a US government commitment to better rules but a commitment to better results.

In a hypercompetitive world, all countries are looking to gain advantages in export markets. If they play by the rules, this can encourage an upward spiral of innovation, efficiency, and higher productivity that leaves both the United States and other countries better off than they would be otherwise. Good rules, properly enforced, can encourage countries to invest in building their own competitive advantages, giving them greater confidence that those investments will not be rendered worthless by the actions of other countries. But if those rules are skirted, the spiral can be less virtuous, with countries competing instead on the basis of subsidies, protectionist restrictions, or other artificial forms of advantage. For all the limitations of global trade rules, however, they are still the most robust and successful example of international economic cooperation that exists today. Efforts to build similar cooperation on rules for currency, which can have at least as big an impact as trade rules on the flow of goods and investment, have been far less successful.

3

Confronting the Competition

How a Strong Dollar Has Hurt

Much like the candidates in the 2016 election, President Barack Obama was more than a bit skeptical about the direction of US trade policy when he campaigned for the presidency in 2008. He had called for a renegotiation of NAFTA, charging that the deal with Canada and Mexico had been "a mistake." In a primary debate in heavily industrial Ohio, Obama said, "If you travel through Youngstown and you travel through communities in my home state of Illinois, you will see entire cities that have been devastated as a consequence of trade agreements that were not adequately structured to make sure that U.S. workers had a fair deal." Challenging his rival Hillary Clinton, whose husband had supported NAFTA despite strong opposition in his own party, Obama argued, "The net costs of many of these trade agreements, if they're not properly structured, can be devastating."[1] While later admitting that his rhetoric was perhaps "overheated and amplified," Obama showed little more enthusiasm for free trade negotiations after taking office in 2009. He delayed for several years the ratification of three free trade deals negotiated by the George W. Bush administration—with Korea, Colombia, and Panama—demanding changes to each before he would submit them to Congress for approval. It wasn't until after his reelection in 2012 that the president changed direction. He threw his support behind a huge regional trade agreement, the Trans-Pacific Partnership (TPP), to free up trade between the United States, Japan, and ten other Asia-Pacific countries. The TPP, his officials hoped, would be the first step toward the long-standing US goal of creating a region-wide free trade area that could eventually include China and perhaps even India, allowing the United States "to write the rules of the road in the 21st century."[2] At the same time, Obama agreed with European leaders to launch the similarly ambitious Transatlantic Trade and Investment Partnership to eliminate the remaining trade barriers between the United States and Europe. If successful, the two deals would mean that nearly two-thirds of all US trade would be covered by free trade agreements.

To move ahead, Obama needed the support of Congress. Under the so-called fast-track mechanism first created in 1974, Congress had agreed to give presidents the authority to negotiate trade deals and then to vote on those agreements without amendment. The procedure was intended to allay the fears of America's trading partners that they would make difficult concessions to American negotiators to secure a deal, only to have Congress amend that agreement and force the US president to come back for more. For many years, trade-negotiating authority was routinely granted to presidents. But in the wake of the bruising congressional battle over NAFTA, Congress had pulled back. It denied fast-track authority to President Bill Clinton twice in 1997 and 1998 and gave it to President George W. Bush by the narrowest of margins, a single vote in the House, in 2001. In 2015, even with both the House and the Senate controlled by Republicans who largely favored free trade, President Obama faced a bruising fight in winning congressional support for new fast-track authority. Few of his fellow Democrats stood with him, and the labor unions were unanimously opposed.

But the biggest threat to Obama's trade vision came from an unexpected place. Rob Portman, a Republican senator from Ohio, had long been an ardent champion of freer trade. He had served for two years as President George W. Bush's US trade representative and had led the successful congressional fight for passage of the Central American Free Trade Agreement in the face of almost solid Democratic opposition, including from then senator Barack Obama of Illinois. But Portman, facing a tough reelection fight in his home state, had sided with most Democrats and the unions on an increasingly contentious issue: whether trade agreements should somehow try to prevent countries from manipulating the value of their currency to gain a trade advantage. The issue had simmered in Congress for more than a decade. In 2005, in the face of surging exports from China, the Senate had passed a bill that would have slapped tariffs on all Chinese imports unless China agreed to boost the value of its currency. In 2011 the Senate had again passed, on a 65–35 bipartisan vote, a bill to punish nations that maintain "fundamentally misaligned" currencies. The bill, a watered-down version of the 2005 measure, would have visited an array of penalties on countries deemed to be using artificial means to depress their currencies and pump up exports. It would have barred the US government from buying any goods and services from such a country, prevented the government from insuring investments in that country, and made it easier for companies to win high countervailing duty tariff penalties on imports from that country. Neither bill was taken up by the House, but it seemed only a matter of time.

With the fast-track vote coming in the spring of 2015, Portman had seized the moment. He had teamed up with Democrat Debbie Stabenow of Michigan—representing Detroit automakers, which had long complained that Japan was deliberately undervaluing the yen and Korea was intervening to depress the won—on an amendment that would have made it a "principle negotiating objective" of the United States to end "unfair currency exchange practices." These were defined, mirroring language already used by the International Monetary Fund (IMF), as "protracted large-scale intervention in one direction in the exchange markets . . . to gain an unfair advantage in trade." The new element was that, by being included in a trade deal, such provisions would become subject to the same dispute-settlement provisions that govern tariffs, intellectual property, and every other provision of a trade agreement. A country found to be manipulating its currency, in other words, could for the first time find itself facing trade sanctions. In a speech on the Senate floor, Portman urged his colleagues, "The last thing we want to do is complete an agreement called the Trans-Pacific Partnership and then find out after the fact that, guess what, all these tariffs have been reduced, all these non-tariff barriers got knocked down, but it didn't matter much because these same countries decided they were going to manipulate their currencies, which undoes so many of the benefits of a trade agreement."[3] Democrats like his fellow Ohio senator Sherrod Brown had made similar arguments in the past; indeed, President Obama himself had argued when he was a senator that any trade agreement brought before Congress should include "protection from unfair trade practices, including currency manipulation." But with Portman, a solidly pro-trade Republican, championing the cause, the chances for passage seemed far better than at any time before.

But rather than embracing Portman's proposal, the Obama administration turned hard against it. With the TPP negotiations nearing their final stages in the early summer of 2015, the administration saw in the amendment a dangerous threat to the deal. Treasury Secretary Jacob Lew wrote senators a letter warning, "Our trading partners have made it clear that they will not join a trade agreement that includes enforceable currency provisions." Japan, in particular, was said to be prepared to walk away from the table rather than accept binding currency language. Business groups, led by the Business Roundtable, similarly worked with friendly Republicans to try to kill the amendment. And while the Portman-Stabenow language had clearly stated that it would in no way "restrict the exercise of domestic monetary policy," Secretary Lew said that such language "could give our trading partners the power to challenge legitimate U.S. monetary policies needed to ensure strong employment and a healthy robust economy, an outcome we would find unacceptable." He warned that if Congress passed the Portman amendment as part of the trade bill, he would recommend that the president veto the entire bill. The Senate did not take that chance—the amendment was defeated, falling short of the sixty votes it needed.

CURRENCIES AND TRADE

Alongside the obstacles that have faced US exports in many of the world's largest markets, the problem of an often overvalued dollar has chipped away at US competitiveness for nearly half a century, contributing to the large, sustained trade deficit that has held back growth and reduced employment, especially in manufacturing.

The United States has been both perpetrator and victim; its own domestic economic policies have too often been implemented with little regard for their impact on the value of the dollar and the traded sectors of the economy. And the United States has too often looked the other way as its trading partners intervened to depress the value of their currencies and gain a competitive advantage. Currency manipulation, roughly defined as government measures aimed at keeping the value of a nation's currency lower than market forces would dictate, is supposed to be outlawed by international rules. The IMF, the organization created after World War II to foster international cooperation on financial stability, says clearly that its member countries should "avoid manipulating exchange rates or the international monetary system in order to prevent effective balance-of-payments adjustment or to gain unfair competitive advantage over other member countries." The World Trade Organization (WTO), which is responsible for managing the rules of global trade, has largely avoided addressing the currency issue. But WTO rules do say clearly that member countries "shall not, by exchange action, frustrate the provisions of this agreement." The theory underlying both is that currency values should, broadly speaking, reflect market forces. Countries with globally competitive sectors that produce steady trade surpluses should, over time, have currencies that appreciate. This will help their consumers by lowering the cost of imported goods and making it cheaper to travel abroad, but it will also reduce the competitive edge for traded sectors. Conversely, countries that run chronic deficits over time should see a weakening of their currencies, which makes imports more costly and foreign travel more expensive but boosts the competitiveness of their exporting industries.

In practice, however, neither organization has been able to exercise any real discipline over currency values. Fred Bergsten has called it "a gaping hole in the international economic architecture."[4] The single biggest flaw in that system, he said in 2013, "is its failure to effectively sanction surplus countries, especially to counter and deter competitive currency policies. Indeed, this systemic failure almost assures that the problem will continue because the manipulators get away with it and thus are presented a policy option, especially attractive in tough economic times, through which they can subsidize exports, import substitutes and jobs without budget costs domestically or effective restraint internationally." In theory, the IMF is supposed to "exercise firm surveillance" over the currency practices of member countries, but it lacks any authority to force surplus countries to change their practices and has failed to exercise the little authority it does have. No country, for example, has ever been cited under the IMF's exchange-manipulation rules.[5] And in any case, unlike the WTO, the IMF has no formal dispute-settlement mechanism and no real ability to levy sanctions against offending countries unless they are in need of an IMF loan, which surplus countries by definition do not need.[6] Under WTO rules, countries are restricted from imposing new import tariffs or using export subsidies to help the competitiveness of their industries; yet there are no effective international restraints on currency manipulation, which has roughly the same impact on trade.

The economic consequences of this failure have been enormous because the effects of currency movements on trade are so large. Following half a century of successive global rounds of trade liberalization, as well as an array of bilateral and regional trade deals, the tariffs charged by most countries on imported goods now are very low, generally in the single digits or zero for all but a few highly price sensitive items like shoes, clothing, and some agricultural products. The trade effects of tariff cuts, however, can be undermined very quickly by currency fluctuations. From 1980 to 1985, for example, the value of the US dollar rose nearly 60 percent against the currencies of its major trading partners; then it gave back all of those gains over the next two years. The undervalued Chinese renminbi helped fuel the unprecedented surge in Chinese exports to the United States following China's accession to the WTO in 2001. And more recently, the US dollar has risen strongly against the currencies of many of the United States' major trading partners.

While the US dollar has fluctuated enormously over the past half century, economists are generally in agreement that it has too often been overvalued. And there have been periods, especially in the first half of the 1980s and again in the late 1990s and early 2000s, when the dollar was greatly overvalued compared with some of the United States' largest trading partners. Bergsten and others have argued that, while other countries have sometimes been hurt as well, the United States has been the biggest economic loser from an overvalued currency; Europe is a distant second.[7] The reasons for the overvalued dollar are many and not always clearly understood, even by the legions of economists and currency traders who make their livings trying to explain and predict currency movements. In a textbook world with floating currencies, trade imbalances are not supposed to be a chronic problem. As Harvard's Robert Lawrence has put it, there are "automatic adjustment mechanisms that tend to keep the trade balance in goods and services within fairly narrow bounds."[8] If global demand shifts away from US products, for instance—perhaps because the Germans and Japanese are right, and they really do make things better—then the price of American-made goods should begin to fall until a rough trade balance is restored. The ready mechanism for lowering these prices is a fall in the US dollar. While short-term imbalances would happen even in a smoothly functioning system, over time no country should be running either chronic surpluses or deficits. But in practice, the United States has run chronically large deficits since the early 1970s.

Several explanations have been offered. First, as it has been the primary global reserve currency for the past seventy years, most international transactions are carried out in US dollars.[9] Virtually all purchases of oil internationally, to take the most prominent example, are made in US dollars regardless of whether the United States is involved in the transaction. As a result, demand for US currency is higher than it would otherwise be because countries need American dollars to make such purchases. Second, countries that have historically run large trade surpluses with the United States, especially Japan and China, have invested a significant portion of their export earnings in safe US Treasury bills, further increasing the demand for dollars and giving these countries a strong incentive to resist devaluation of the dollar, which would reduce not only their trade surpluses but also the value of those dollar holdings. Finally, while the central banks of many other countries often influence their currency values directly by buying or selling US dollars, the United States has in recent years largely avoided intervening in currency markets, fearing that intervention would be ineffective and could call into question the stability of the dollar and weaken the global financial system. All of this helps the United States in some ways, because large foreign purchases of US Treasury securities tend to keep interest rates a bit lower than they would otherwise be. This keeps down borrowing costs for housing, cars, and other goods. It also allows the federal government, for better or worse, to continue spending more than it collects in tax dollars and to issue low-interest IOUs to make up the difference. The strong US dollar further helps consumers by keeping the price of imported goods lower. It benefits the financial services sector in the United States by encouraging international investors to purchase and hold US dollars. And it helps the United States geopolitically, making it easier to finance military and other operations overseas. But it imposes significant costs directly on the sectors of the US economy facing international competition, particularly manufacturing, but also tourism, agriculture, moviemaking, technology services, and a host of other sectors that are seeing growing competitive pressures. As a consequence, the strong dollar has certainly been a factor in holding down employment and wages in the traded sectors of the economy that historically have provided some of the country's best jobs. The attractiveness of the United States as a location for the production of traded goods and services has been harmed by the failure to keep the dollar at a more competitive level.

RESTORING A GLOBAL BALANCE

Pete Peterson, in his memo to Richard Nixon, had little patience for such theorizing. "Most of the problems that have arisen in the world economy are not problems of theory," he wrote. "They are problems of national attitudes and practices which thwart the operations of the international adjustment process." He argued that all countries agreed in theory that "simple arithmetic should have made it obvious that one could not have countries in large and perennial surplus without having perennial deficit countries." But in practice, despite periodic urging from the IMF and summit meetings of finance ministers or leaders, surplus countries "resisted this advice because the fiscal adjustments were politically painful." All countries had an interest in maintaining the profits and jobs that came from exporting, he wrote, and the political muscle of exporting interests in industry, agriculture, and labor far outweighed the voices of consumers who would benefit from lower-priced imports. Governments too had an interest in generating surpluses, both for traditional mercantilist reasons of national power and to protect their countries from debt crises that could leave them at the mercy of creditors. The easiest solution to global imbalances was for those nations running surpluses to let their currencies rise in value until a rough trade balance was again achieved, Peterson wrote. Without government meddling, indeed, market forces should naturally have produced such an outcome. But those countries "resisted because their successful and obviously important exporters wished to keep their markets and jobs." In other words, if some of the biggest trading countries were determined for reasons of their own national growth strategies to maintain cheap currencies, they had many tools available to thwart what was supposed to be the proper workings of currency markets. As Peterson noted, "In the real world, almost no level of reserves has seemed too high to the governments of surplus countries, and there has been no means of forcing surplus countries to take action."

The US position, Peterson noted, was a special one. The dollar was the anchor of the global trading system, and the US willingness to run balance-of-payments deficits "provided the liquidity which the system needed." But by the time of his memo in 1971, that role had become an increasingly costly one for the United States. Its willingness to run rising balance-of-payments deficits under the fixed Bretton Woods currency regime had kept the system afloat, but at a growing cost to domestic US producers and their employees, who found themselves increasingly priced out of world markets by the strong dollar and less able to compete with imports at home. And the effects were escalating. With the growing mobility of capital and technology and falling transportation costs, "many nations now have greatly increased capacity to invade markets rapidly, and we find that pressures for adjustment in particular industries come faster and harder than anything experienced in earlier years. . . . The rising pace of change poses adjustment policy problems which simply cannot be ignored."

The right solution, Peterson believed, was an "effective overall monetary and exchange rate institutional system," a set of international arrangements or understandings that would limit the scale of the disruption caused by such competitive adjustments. He called for "a new regime under which there is a presumption that exchange rates will change when needed rather than a presumption that they will remain fixed and inflexible for long periods." The regime, he said, should create incentives for both surplus and deficit countries to adjust their economies as needed and to reduce the dependence of the global economy on US trade deficits. Such measures, Peterson hoped, while they would in no way solve the US competitive challenge, would at least insulate US companies and workers from needless disruptions caused by misvalued currencies.

While these ideas briefly received serious attention across Nixon's administration in 1971, the United States has only rarely attempted the sort of hands-on management of currency values that Peterson recommended. Instead, the federal government has lurched between long periods of inattention and short bursts of activity only after the dollar has risen so high that complaints from industry and Congress have become irresistible. And unlike in more export-dependent economies such as Japan, Germany, and more recently China, US monetary and fiscal policies have generally been set with little attention to their effects on the value of the US dollar. In his overview of the exchange rate policies of Japan, Germany, and the United States through the end of the 1980s, Randall Henning argued that the United States "often neglected the impact of exchange rates on the competitiveness of its traded goods sectors altogether," while its biggest competitors "maintained competitively valued currencies, using the full panoply of instruments available to manage the exchange rate directly."[10] The same could be said of China throughout the 2000s, which managed the value of the yuan to maintain its competitive edge while allowing just enough appreciation to avoid a protectionist US backlash.

The US government has long been reluctant to push the issue more forcefully. There are certainly good reasons for that reluctance. Any country's fiscal and monetary policies affect the value of its currency, as do the fiscal and monetary policies of other countries. But fiscal and monetary policies have a broad range of objectives, be it reducing unemployment or curbing inflation. For the United States, which continues to be less dependent on trade than any other major economy, the effects of these policies on the value of the dollar and the trade balance have usually been seen as second-order effects. Treasury Secretary Lew's opposition to the Portman amendment reflected that thinking—in this view, maintaining complete flexibility to establish "U.S. monetary policies needed to ensure strong employment and a healthy robust economy" is far more consequential than the negative impacts of an overvalued dollar. The independent Federal Reserve, which sets monetary policy, has in most cases been only modestly interested in the impact of its interest rate decisions on the dollar's value. Alan Greenspan, the Fed chairman from 1987 through the end of 2006, candidly wrote in his 2007 memoirs, following the biggest increase in the current account deficit in US history, "There are a lot of imbalances, especially our potential federal deficit, to worry about in the years ahead. I would place the U.S. current account far down the list."[11]

While such priorities can certainly be defended, the costs of this neglect for US competitiveness in the traded sectors have been considerable. Research by Joe Gagnon and Fred Bergsten at the Peterson Institute for International Economics in 2013 suggested that currency market interventions by at least twenty countries had worsened the US trade deficit by $200 billion to $500 billion annually, resulting in a loss of between 1 million and 5 million jobs in the United States. While it is difficult to disentangle the currency effects from the trade policy effects discussed in the previous chapter, they argued that roughly half of excess US unemployment—that is, unemployment beyond the rate that represents full employment—is a consequence of currency manipulation by foreign governments. These market distortions, Bergsten wrote in a separate article, have "artificially impeded the ability to export, and accelerated imports, in the United States and other victimized countries in ways that have contributed significantly to their continuing high unemployment."[12] Research by Kenneth Austin of the US Treasury put the number of jobs lost even higher at as many as 6 million.[13] He argued that the huge accumulation of US dollar reserves by countries like China, which is necessary for these countries to hold down the value of their currencies and maintain a competitive advantage, is "a classic beggar-thy-neighbor policy." Such estimates are hard to prove of course. The jobs lost in traded industries may have been replaced in part by jobs in other industries, such as construction or home remodeling, that generally benefit from lower interest rates. But many of those jobs were fueled by unsustainable consumer borrowing that ultimately led to the 2009 financial crisis. And as the Obama administration repeatedly reminded members of Congress in 2015 and 2016 in the debate over the TPP, jobs in the traded sectors are generally better ones—higher paying, usually full-time with benefits. The neglect of those sectors has played no small role in the hollowing out of the American middle class.

As with trade rules, the US government's efforts to do something about the problem have been sporadic. On occasion—usually in the face of a surging trade deficit and threats from Congress to block imports—US administrations have tried to persuade or force other countries to revalue their currencies and ease the competitive pressure on the United States; more rarely they have taken steps to adjust US economic policies to encourage a weaker dollar. President Nixon moved unilaterally in 1971 by renouncing the convertibility of dollars into gold and imposing a temporary import surcharge. President Ronald Reagan, after ignoring the biggest surge in the dollar's value in the postwar era, changed course and was able to win support from the world's biggest economies in 1985 to engineer a steep decline. And President George W. Bush tried through bilateral negotiations with China in the 2000s to persuade Beijing to relax its peg to the dollar, which produced notable appreciation in the yuan, but only after the bilateral US trade deficit with China had soared to record levels and Congress was threatening retaliation. While these actions succeeded temporarily in bringing the dollar back to a more reasonable level, none has produced a lasting solution to the problem. Indeed, conscious policies to depress their currencies to gain an export advantage continue to be central to the development strategies of some Asian countries in particular.[14] The US response has generally been tepid at best, in part because successive US governments have had other priorities and have often paid little attention to the dollar, in part because there has never been consistent pressure from US business to tackle the problem, and in part because belief in the virtues of a "strong dollar" is so deeply ingrained in US political leaders.

The Nixon Shocks

If a single event could be said to mark America's awakening to the growing competitive pressures of the modern global economy, it occurred on a mid-August weekend in 1971. On Friday the 13th, President Nixon's closest economic and political advisors—including Pete Peterson—were quietly ordered to fly in secret to the presidential retreat in Camp David, Maryland. Even Treasury Secretary John Connally received no advance notice and had to turn right around after arriving at his Texas ranch for a summer vacation. Notably absent were Secretary of State William Rogers and Nixon's national security advisor, Henry Kissinger, who were reportedly unaware that the meeting was even taking place. Over the next three days, they hammered out what *Time* magazine called "the most sweeping changes since the Hundred Days of the New Deal in 1933." On Sunday night, in a broadcast to the nation from the White House that preempted the popular Western TV series *Bonanza*, Nixon announced that the United States would no longer exchange dollars for gold at the internationally agreed price of $35 an ounce, unilaterally renouncing the fixed currency regime that had been in place for the past quarter century. And in a further effort to right the declining US balance of payments, he immediately slapped a 10 percent import surcharge on all foreign goods that were not otherwise limited by quotas. The tariff, while legal under international trade rules that allow for such measures in the face of a balance-of-payments crisis, was the most protectionist action by a US government since the Smoot-Hawley tariff of 1930. The next day, the Dow Jones average surged, and overseas markets plunged. President Nixon's decisions that weekend were, Peterson wrote, an "effort to force the pace of adjustment."

Nixon's actions were the most serious—some would say aggressive and unilateral—effort in modern US history to force other countries to help the United States adjust to growing global competition. The United States had agreed in 1944 to establish the dollar as the world's reserve currency, backed by American gold, with other currencies exchangeable for US dollars or for gold at an agreed exchange rate. For the system to work properly, one country had to be passive and make no effort to influence the value of its currency; as Nixon's treasury undersecretary for monetary affairs, Paul Volcker, later put it, under Bretton Woods exchange rates against the dollar were effectively set by other countries.[15] The US goal was to build a foundation for a more stable postwar global economy and speed postwar reconstruction in Europe and Asia. In practice, this system had resulted in a significant outflow of US dollars in the 1950s that helped in the rebuilding of Europe and Asia, balanced by a US trade surplus and growing earnings on those foreign investments. Bretton Woods was hugely successful in achieving those goals, but by the mid-1960s, it was already becoming shaky. Foreign holdings of US dollars were by then about five times as large as US gold reserves, threatening the ability of the United States to honor its commitment to redeem dollars for gold. During the 1960s, imports to the United States had been growing about 25 percent faster than exports, and overseas investment by US companies had been growing rapidly, finally pushing the trade balance into the red in 1971.

Nixon's action is often presented as a precipitous move to force the burden of adjustment onto US trading partners in order to preserve the United States' ability to stimulate its domestic economy, pursue its foreign policy objectives, and, not coincidentally, help the president's reelection campaign.[16] And indeed, it is quite possible that the United States at the time could have pursued more cooperative strategies with its trading partners and achieved similar results.[17] But it was far from an overnight decision. Pressure had been building throughout the 1960s, as rising productivity in Europe and Japan made those economies more competitive against the United States, but the constraints of the fixed-rate regime made it difficult to adjust currency values to reflect the new competitive realities. In late 1970, Volcker had quietly commissioned an internal study that suggested a dollar devaluation of 10 to 15 percent was needed to restore equilibrium. He wrote a memo for Connally arguing that the prospects of negotiating such a change were unlikely without strong unilateral action, in particular suspending the convertibility of dollars into gold. Volcker later wrote that Peterson's report to President Nixon, while it stayed away from specific recommendations on international monetary policy, "helped explain and dramatize our weakening trade and competitive position."[18]

Events may well have forced Nixon's hand regardless of the recommendations from his advisors. By the summer of 1971, currency speculators were betting heavily that the United States would be forced to devalue; in the first week of August alone, foreign central banks had bought nearly $4 billion to shore up the dollar and prevent their currencies from appreciating.[19] Facing a potential run on US gold reserves, a deteriorating balance of payments, and a brewing revolt in Congress—not to mention a weakening economy in the year before he was up for reelection—Nixon took his dramatic steps in an effort to force other countries, particularly Japan, to come to the rescue.[20] After strong initial resistance, Japan agreed to a significant appreciation of the yen, while Germany and other major US trading partners accepted smaller adjustments. The break with the postwar norm, in which the United States had subordinated its own domestic competitiveness for the sake of global stability and faster growth in its alliance partners in Europe and Asia, was striking. Said Nixon's treasury secretary Connally, "No longer can considerations of friendship, or need, or capacity justify the United States carrying so heavy a share of the common burdens. And, to be perfectly frank, no longer will the American people permit their government to engage in international actions in which the true long-run interests of the U.S. are not just as clearly recognized as those of the nations with which we deal."[21]

Peterson had hoped that Nixon's actions would only be a first step, encouraging the major powers to work together to try to manage currency values so that chronic current account surpluses and deficits would be avoided. Instead, efforts to coordinate monetary and fiscal policies internationally have consistently fallen short, and maintaining a competitively priced dollar has rarely been a top priority for the US government. The United States continued on the path to becoming a chronic current account deficit country; while the weaker dollar of the late 1970s briefly brought the current account close to balance, in only a single year since the mid-1970s has the United States run a current account surplus, a small one in 1991. Its major trade competitors, first Japan and Germany and later China and many of the smaller Asian economies, became chronic surplus countries. US presidents have rarely paid much, if any, attention to the impact of the dollar on US competitiveness. As Volcker later wrote, "To any president, economic advantage was a bargaining chip for political concession."[22] The result was to force much of the costs of adjusting to international competition onto American-based companies and their workers, which too often have been unable to raise their productivity fast enough to overcome the handicap of an overvalued dollar.

While there have certainly been periods of dollar weakness, far more often a strong dollar has put tremendous pressure on US industries competing in international markets. A 1984 report by the consultancy DRI, which looked at unit labor costs in the United States and its major competitors, concluded that "the most fundamental cause" of the deteriorating US competitive position "was a foreign exchange rate which overvalued the dollar for much of the past 34 years."[23] Even though productivity in Germany had surpassed that in the United States by the end of the 1970s and Italy, Japan, France, and Canada were nearly as productive, the strong dollar meant that each of those countries enjoyed a significant cost advantage over the United States. The Japanese advantage was especially large in the 1980s. In real terms of purchasing power, adjusting for inflation and productivity improvements, the US dollar was as strong against the yen in the mid-1980s as it had been in the 1960s. In the late 1980s and 1990s, following the active intervention by the Reagan administration that resulted in the Plaza Accord, the yen strengthened considerably, and the US position became temporarily more favorable, though the currencies of newly emerging competitors such as Korea, Taiwan, and Singapore remained undervalued. In the early 2000s, while the US dollar had risen sharply against all the major currencies, the most serious misalignment was with China. China pegged the renminbi to the dollar in the mid-1990s and was praised by the United States as "an island of stability" for maintaining the peg rather than devaluing during the Asian financial crisis in order to sustain its competitive advantage over its neighbors. But then China continued to defend that peg for nearly a decade, even as its trade surplus with the United States soared and its productivity surged—both of which should have resulted in appreciation of the yuan.

The overvalued dollar has had real effects on trade. Even controlling for a variety of other factors, the level of US exports remains highly sensitive to the value of the dollar;[24] since the early 1970s, US export growth has fluctuated roughly in line with the dollar's value against major US trading partners. From 1980 to 1985, when the dollar was hitting record highs, the total volume of US exports actually fell by 16 percent—a decline not seen since the Great Depression—while German and Japanese export volumes rose by 29 and 46 percent, respectively. Over the next decade, however, with the exchange rate at a more favorable level, US export growth far exceeded that of either Germany or Japan.[25] Then the trade deficit soared again beginning in the mid-1990s as the dollar strengthened, reaching a record level of more than $800 billion from 2006 to 2008, before falling back as a result of the US recession and a weakening dollar. US exports saw record growth for several years coming out of the 2009 recession, but then flattened again with weaker growth in Europe and China and a rapidly rising dollar. US exports declined in value in 2015, the first year-on-year decline since 2009.[26]

The failure to manage currency values in a more effective way has been a big handicap as the United States has tried to adjust to its growing integration in the global economy. The system of international currency management set up after World War II was one in which the United States deliberately put itself at a competitive disadvantage in order to encourage the rapid rebuilding of Europe and Japan. It agreed to make a strong dollar the anchor of the global financial system and to tie its own hands tightly, even as other countries retained some freedom to manage the value of their currencies. The system was a security and foreign policy triumph, and given the small share of US trade compared to the overall size of its economy at the time, the economic costs to the country were insignificant. Yet, as those economic conditions changed and the war-damaged countries became formidable economic competitors, the basic US stance did not change. The US government continued to tie its own hands in all but the most extreme circumstances, while its major competitors—first Japan and later China, Korea, and others—have often pursued policies designed to hold down currency values and gain export advantage. And the United States further harmed its own competitiveness through fiscal and monetary policies devised with little, if any, attention paid to their impacts on the value of the US dollar. US political leaders became wedded to the idea of a "strong dollar," even at times when the dollar was clearly overvalued and was clearly harming US competitiveness. Two periods in particular highlight this failure: the run-up in the dollar under the Reagan administration in the early 1980s and the slow response to China's currency manipulation beginning in the mid-1990s.

THE REAGAN DOLLAR

The first years of the Reagan administration were a period of enormous pressure on internationally competitive US companies, especially in manufacturing. The deep recession of 1980–1981 pushed unemployment up to nearly 11 percent; by 1983 US manufacturers had shed more than 10 percent of their workforce, nearly 2 million employees, and profits were down by a third.[27] In an effort to stop the double-digit inflation of the late 1970s, Federal Reserve chairman Paul Volcker, the former Nixon treasury official, had raised short-term interest rates to nearly 20 percent by early 1981. At the same time, the new administration's economic program of tax cuts and higher defense spending created a large federal budget deficit, further pushing up interest rates as the government's borrowing needs rose. Investors, attracted by the high and safe returns, flooded into US dollars. From 1980 to 1984, the dollar rose by 40 percent against the UK pound, gained 50 percent against the mark, and doubled against the French franc.[28] Overall, the dollar appreciated nearly 60 percent against the currencies of its major trading partners, while the yen and the mark fell back to their 1973 levels or below.[29] The real-world impact was even larger than that—adjusting for the composition of the traded goods, the Federal Reserve calculated that between 1979 and the first quarter of 1985, the dollar's value rose 73 percent against its ten largest competitors.[30]

In the early 1980s it was the United States' own monetary and fiscal policies, not the policies of its trading partners, that led to the surging dollar. The Reagan administration, pursuing its election promises of tax cuts and military spending increases but unable to persuade Congress to cut domestic spending in tandem, allowed the federal budget deficit to grow from $41 billion in 1979 to $221 billion by 1986. At the same time the Federal Reserve, determined to stamp out what had become chronic inflation, curbed the money supply and pushed short-term interest rates to record levels. Both measures boosted the dollar, the first by depleting domestic savings and requiring an inflow of capital to finance investments and the second by offering higher returns to international investors. The Reagan administration also deliberately abandoned the other tools at its disposal to help tamp down the dollar's appreciation. In 1981, the Treasury Department announced that, consistent with the administration's philosophy of limiting government interference with markets, it would no longer intervene in currency markets to stabilize the value of the dollar by buying or selling foreign currencies except in extraordinary circumstances. Such interventions had become routine in the late years of Jimmy Carter's presidency.[31] With the economy facing dangerously high levels of inflation, the Carter administration had cooperated closely with Japan and the Europeans, intervening frequently— sometimes on a daily basis—to boost the dollar's value in an effort to lower the cost of imports and curb inflation. While market interventions by the Treasury and the Federal Reserve can do little to counter long-run shifts in the dollar's value, they have been effective at tempering excessive increases or declines.[32] Yet from 1981 to 1984, even as the dollar rose precipitously, the Reagan administration only intervened once, and then to keep the dollar from falling when markets panicked after President Reagan was shot in March 1981.

Japan, for the most part, went along for the ride. The weakening yen, further encouraged by domestic interest rate cuts in Japan, helped make Japan the only G-7 country to avoid the deep recession of the early 1980s. Japan did intervene in currency markets regularly to try to slow the fall of the yen, and the Bank of Japan called for "international concerted action" to try to stabilize exchange rates. But without coordinated action by the United States, the interventions made little difference.[33] And continued strong economic growth driven by exports meant Japan had little incentive to try harder. The Europeans were less sanguine. The rising dollar had forced them to raise their own interest rates and intervene repeatedly to protect the value of their currencies and keep a lid on inflation.[34] But even as the dollar surged in 1983 to levels that had European governments pleading with the United States to intervene, Reagan's treasury secretary, Donald Regan, refused. "We would like to see a somewhat weaker dollar to help our exports," he told the *New York Times* in March 1983. "But that doesn't mean we're going to do anything about it."[35] In 1984, the president's own Council of Economic Advisers (CEA) estimated in its annual report that the dollar was overvalued by 30 percent, in part as a result of the rising federal budget deficit, and that this was the major cause of the rising trade deficit; asked about the estimate, Regan told a Senate committee to toss the CEA report in the waste basket.[36] He said that any claim that the US dollar was overvalued was based on "confused thinking."[37]

There is little evidence that the president or his senior economic advisors were much concerned with the impact the strong dollar was having on the competitiveness of US manufacturing. The few who did understand and worried about competitiveness, like Martin Feldstein, chairman of the CEA, nonetheless told the president that the costs were acceptable. In a memo to the cabinet in 1983, he wrote that while the strong dollar was damaging America's competitive industries, the huge inflow of foreign capital and low-cost imports was good for consumers and for home construction and, given the high federal budget deficit, was likely helping to keep interest rates from rising even higher. Given the trade-offs, he wrote, "it is better to reduce exports and increase imports."[38] Indeed, the few concrete administration actions in response to the growing imbalance actually worsened the problem. In order to encourage foreign capital inflows to help finance the growing budget deficit, for example, the administration persuaded Congress to end the 30 percent withholding tax then levied on foreign holders of US Treasury securities and corporate bonds, immediately making them far more attractive to foreign investors. Treasury also created a special new issue of government bonds for foreign buyers, with senior officials traveling to Europe and Japan to peddle them.[39] And in his 1985 State of the Union address, just as the dollar was reaching its peak, President Reagan called for making the United States "the investment capital of the world," speaking with what two observers called "complete disregard for the impact of this sort of declaration on the exchange markets, the worsening trade balance, and the burgeoning pressures for trade protectionism."[40]

Predictably imports surged and exports fell as the dollar strengthened.[41] As Feldstein later put it, "Economists recognized from the start that the deteriorating trade balance in the early 1980s was a natural reaction to the rising value of the dollar."[42] But the scale was unprecedented. Arthur Burns, who had been Nixon's Federal Reserve chairman, wrote in 1984, "[Prior] to last year, the biggest current account deficit that any country had ever experienced in a single year was about $15 billion. The $70 to $80 billion shortfall that the United States is headed for this year is awesomely different from anything experienced in the past."[43] The deficit would hit $122 billion in 1985. Combined with the deep recession of 1981–1982, the effect on US manufacturing was devastating. Imports of manufactured goods—cars and semiconductors from Japan, consumer electronics from Taiwan, machine tools from Germany—rose at more than three times the rate of overall economic growth. In just five years, from 1981 to 1986, imports rose from the equivalent of 21 percent of all US manufacturing output to 34 percent, while exports fell more sharply than at any time since the Great Depression.[44]

Congress finally forced the administration's hand. US business, which was generally supportive of President Reagan, had rarely voiced an opinion on the value of the dollar. But by the mid-1980s, the consequences had become too large to ignore. Caterpillar, the US tractor maker, lost more than $700 million between 1982 and 1984 as sales fell by more than 40 percent due to rising competition, mostly from

Japan's Komatsu.[45] Three-quarters of the twenty thousand jobs cut by the company in a desperate effort to reduce costs were a result of falling exports. "We think the number one problem is the strong dollar," said CEO Lee Morgan.[46] He warned that unless the dollar weakened, the company would have little choice but to expand in Europe and Asia and reduce its US production to serve only the US market. Using his perch as chairman of the International Trade and Investment Task Force of the Business Roundtable, the lobbying organization of US chief executives, Morgan recruited US companies that were facing unprecedented price competition from overseas—including Ford, US Steel, Honeywell, Pfizer, IBM, General Motors, and Kodak. It was the first time in the postwar era that US business had seriously engaged on the issue of the dollar's value. In 1984 the National Association of Manufacturers passed a resolution calling for "an explicit U.S. exchange rate policy supportive of U.S. trade performance."[47] Anthony Solomon, president of the New York Federal Reserve, acknowledged that the strong dollar was "decimating our export industries," though neither he nor his boss, Paul Volcker, favored lowering US interest rates to weaken the dollar, fearing that doing so would simply encourage the Reagan administration to run still higher budget deficits. And it was not just manufacturers who suffered; American grain farmers lost a third of their global market share between 1981 and 1983 as the export price of wheat and corn nearly doubled with the rising dollar.[48]

Morgan and his corporate colleagues urged the Reagan administration to follow the Nixon model and impose a surtax on Japanese imports to offset the currency disadvantage, but that was flatly rejected. Rebuffed by the administration, the companies turned to Congress and found a more sympathetic ear. In early 1985, the House and Senate each passed a raft of bills meant as warning shots to the administration, threatening to slap import tariffs on Japanese goods or to block the administration from launching a new round of global trade negotiations. The House twice passed bills that would have added a 25 percent import surcharge on countries that were running large trade surpluses with the United States, including Japan, Korea, Taiwan, and Brazil—the same remedy the Senate would try to pursue against China two decades later.[49] Senators even flirted with the idea of restricting the independence of the Federal Reserve and Treasury on exchange rate policy and mandating intervention when the current account deficit grew too large.[50] In 1985 alone, more than one hundred protectionist bills were introduced.

James Baker, who was named by Reagan to succeed Donald Regan at the Treasury Department in 1985 (with Regan in turn replacing Baker as White House chief of staff), said that this growing political pressure and the threat of a protectionist backlash finally caused the administration to change course. In his memoirs written three decades later, Baker wrote, "The disparity between the strong dollar and weak foreign currencies gave foreign competitors a big advantage over companies in the United States. This contributed to our growing trade deficit and sparked demands for high tariffs, import quotas and other protectionist measures."[51] He persuaded Reagan that it was critical to change course in order "to beat back the protectionist sentiment in Congress."[52]

Much like the Nixon shock, the about-face was done in secret. The Treasury quietly contacted finance ministries in Japan, Germany, France, and the United Kingdom, telling them that the Reagan administration was finally serious about devaluation. Baker later wrote, "Our leverage with them was that if we didn't act first, the protectionists in Congress would throw up trade barriers." On September 22, 1985, the finance ministers met in the Gold Room of New York's Plaza Hotel and emerged with a statement noting that "some further orderly appreciation of the main non-dollar currencies against the dollar is desirable." The ministers added that "exchange rates should play a role in adjusting external imbalances." In a secret side agreement, all five countries agreed to sell dollars and buy other currencies to help bring the dollar down.[53] The next day, the United States launched its first intervention in five years, selling dollars and buying yen and marks. The yen, which had already risen nearly 10 percent in the first six months of 1985 in anticipation of a dollar devaluation, rose another 18 percent by the end of the year. Appreciation of the mark was similarly steep. Indeed, the pace of appreciation was so fast that G-5 finance ministers met again in early 1987 and agreed to intervene to halt the dollar's decline.[54] More importantly, in what was known as the Louvre Accord, they established mechanisms for ongoing cooperation to try, as Baker put it, "to stabilize world currencies within an agreed, but unpublished, set of ranges."[55] Following the deal, he wrote, there were serious efforts by the key countries to address some of the underlying causes of the imbalances. The Japanese pledged to stimulate domestic demand, the Germans promised to cut regulations, and the United States promised to reduce its budget deficit. The Plaza Accord and its immediate aftermath were as close as the United States has ever come to Pete Peterson's call for effective international coordination on exchange rates. Baker acknowledged that the performance fell short of the promises due to domestic political constraints, but the effort to better coordinate economic policies was a serious one.

There are debates to this day about how much the large devaluation that followed Plaza was a result of government action and how much had to do with the market finally responding to the overvalued dollar.[56] Certainly by the time of the Plaza agreement, the dollar had already passed its peak and was on a downward trajectory. But the effect was dramatic regardless. The trade deficit, which had reached a record $152 billion in 1987 (more than 3 percent of GDP), was nearly gone by 1991 as exports surged and import growth slowed. The falling dollar was key to the turnaround of Caterpillar's fortunes. By 1992, Ford's Taurus had overtaken the Honda Accord as the highest selling car in the United States. Japanese automakers, looking for relief from the strong yen, began to invest heavily in building new plants in the United States. US semiconductor makers like Intel and Texas Instruments, which had been reeling from Japanese competition, were able to regain a significant share of the US market and then overtake their Japanese rivals as world leaders (Korea, which resisted US pressure for revaluation, also began to take market share from Japan in basic memory chips). After falling sharply in the early 1980s, US manufacturing employment remained largely stable over the next decade at between 17 and 18 million jobs.

Overall, the decade that followed the Reagan administration's about-face on currency policy would be the most successful in the post-1971 period for American industries facing international competition. A reasonably priced currency was not all of that story, but it was a big part.

But the focus did not last. As the urgency of bringing down the overvalued dollar receded, efforts at international coordination fell to the side, returning to the neglect that had characterized the early Reagan administration. Congress, hoping to lock in the gains from the Plaza Accord, in 1988 directed the administration to prepare an annual report that would "consider whether countries manipulate the rate of exchange between their currency and the United States dollar for purposes of preventing effective balance of payments adjustments or gaining unfair competitive advantage in international trade." If a country was deemed to be manipulating its currency, the administration was required to initiate bilateral negotiations ensuring that such countries regularly and promptly adjust the rate of exchange in order to "eliminate the unfair advantage."[57] The early Treasury Department reports actually cited currency manipulators—Korea, China, and Taiwan were named several times on the grounds that these countries were building up excessive foreign exchange reserves and/or intervening in currency markets. But since 1994, the Treasury Department has refused to single out any country as a currency manipulator, even as many countries have built up surpluses and foreign exchange reserves far bigger than those of the early 1990s and engaged in far larger interventions in currency markets.

A REPLAY WITH CHINA

After soaring in the early 1980s, the US trade deficit had fallen sharply by the early 1990s. Over the fifteen years following the Plaza agreement, from 1985 to 2000, the US share of global trade would rise faster than that of any other large nation except for China, which was starting from a far smaller base.[58] With similar good news domestically, including low and stable inflation and strong productivity growth, by the late 1990s the US economy was in its strongest position since the 1960s. In the last quarter of 1999, the unemployment rate fell to just 4.1 percent, the lowest since 1969, inflation was low and stable at about 2.5 percent, and the federal budget deficit had turned to a surplus. But once again, as in the early 1980s, the US government was slow to react when the dollar began to rise against its biggest competitors. Ironically, this time the inaction occurred first during an administration that, unlike the Reagan administration, was acutely concerned about the competitive pressures facing the US economy. Unlike in the Reagan years, Clinton's domestic economic policies did not drive the dollar to unreasonable levels. Clinton inherited a budget deficit in 1993 and handed off a large surplus in 2000, and inflation remained under control throughout the decade, allowing for more stable monetary policies. Instead, the Clinton administration and the George W. Bush administration that followed were both slow to recognize the changing composition of US trade and the rise of developing-country competitors, such as China, that were adept at using weak currencies to drive rising exports.

Belief in the virtue of a strong dollar was widely shared among Clinton's top economic officials. Christina Romer, who became President Obama's first chair of the CEA in 2009, tells a story about sharing a cab with former Clinton treasury secretary, Larry Summers, in November 2008, just after Obama's election. To prepare her for congressional confirmation, Summers asked for her views on the proper exchange rate for the dollar. She responded, "The exchange rate is a price much like any other price, and is determined by market forces." The voluble Summers cut her off. "Wrong!" he boomed. "The exchange rate is the purview of Treasury. The United States is in favor of a strong dollar."[59] The Clinton administration's "strong dollar" policy was always, as Summers's predecessor Robert Rubin explained, as much rhetorical as substantive. The intention was to maintain a consistent public stance that would avoid moving exchange markets unintentionally.[60] But Rubin also believed that a stronger currency was very much in the interests of the US economy. He told the *New York Times* in 1995, "It is the height of unsound policy to devalue yourself into competitiveness."[61] He later wrote, "A strong currency means that American consumers and businesses can buy imported goods and services more cheaply and that inflation and interest rates will tend to be lower. It puts pressure on American industry to increase productivity and competitiveness. Those benefits can feed on themselves as foreign capital flows in more readily because of greater confidence in our currency."[62]

But such confidence is a double-edged sword. Foreign capital flows tend to further increase the dollar's value, which makes it more difficult for US manufacturers and other traded industries to compete either at home or in global markets. The Clinton administration's aggressive trade stance toward Japan was an effort to alter the terms of competition in favor of the United States. Currency traders understood this, and the dollar had fallen sharply against the yen in 1993 and 1994 amid the rising trade frictions between the two countries. The administration indeed chose to intervene in currency markets several times to support the dollar, including in the spring of 1993 when it feared the dollar was falling too fast because of investor concern over the fallout from US-Japanese trade friction.[63] Yet when the dollar began to rise sharply against most other major currencies starting in 1995, driven in part by the growing strength of the US economy, the administration did little to discourage it. From 1995 through 2002, the dollar rose by roughly 40 percent against the currencies of the major industrialized countries,[64] including Japan, Germany, and later the newly formed Eurozone. Much of that increase was certainly justified by the strong US economy, which experienced a burst in productivity driven by the information technology industries and saw unemployment fall to historic lows. Robust US economic growth, which averaged nearly 4 percent from 1992 to 1999, attracted rising direct foreign investment, and the surging stock market drew in shorter-term investors. The Mexican peso crisis of 1994 and the 1997–1998 Asian financial crisis further triggered a "flight to quality," with investors seeking a safe haven in US dollars. The

Clinton administration's approach was certainly not as hands-off as the Reagan first-term administration's; nor was it rigidly ideological. The Treasury intervened to slow the dollar's rise in 1998 and 2000, the first time to stop a slide in the yen and the second to boost a falling euro. Nonetheless, the trade impact was similar to the early 1980s. As the dollar strengthened, the US trade deficit ballooned from less than $100 billion in 1995 to more than $400 billion by 2002.

The biggest impact, however, came not from traditional exporters like Japan and Germany but from the new rising export powerhouses in Asia, especially China, which carefully managed the value of their currencies in order to maintain an export advantage. The dollar's strong run-up in the late 1990s against the currencies of other advanced economies was largely a response to market forces; indeed, when the US economy went into recession in 2002, the dollar began to fall against the euro, the yen, and the British pound. But even as the economy weakened, the dollar continued to rise against the currencies of most of the developing economies, which by the early 2000s accounted for more than half of the US trade deficit in goods.[65] China was the biggest challenge. Exercising its option under IMF guidelines, in 1994 China had pegged the value of its currency, the renminbi or yuan, at 8.28 to the US dollar. Maintaining that peg required China's central bank to buy as many dollar-denominated assets as were needed to eliminate any excess demand for newly printed yuan. At the time, that action received little attention; total US imports from China in 1994 were less than $40 billion, and exports to China were less than $10 billion. But over the next decade, as Chinese exports surged, the result was a huge buildup of Chinese foreign exchange reserves as China's central bank bought up dollars to hold down the value of the renminbi. China's foreign exchange reserves quadrupled between 1995 and 2002 to nearly $300 billion, then surged to $400 billion at the end of 2003, to nearly $950 billion by the end of 2006, and to more than $3 trillion by the end of 2011. The purchases were financed in large part by a soaring Chinese trade surplus with the United States, which rose from $35 billion in 1995 to $83 billion in 2001, the year China joined the WTO, to a record of more than $350 billion by 2015. The rapid deterioration of the US trade balance with China was unprecedented. As Randall Henning wrote, "Chinese policy is far outside the range of experience since the Second World War for systemically important countries."[66]

China has had sound reasons to try to maintain a weak currency, but the consequences were harmful to both the United States and China. The Asian financial crisis, which saw the collapse of currencies in Thailand and Indonesia in the face of large dollar debts and speculative attacks, taught many countries, China among them, the importance of holding large reserves of dollars. And unlike Japan, which exports many high-value products that are less price sensitive, emerging markets depend more on "low-technology products with razor-thin profit margins," says Eswar Prasad, former head of the IMF's China division.[67] China's policy in the 2000s, Prasad argues, was to intervene not to further devalue the renminbi but to keep it from rising in order to avoid losing market share to other developing economies. But the results were clearly damaging to the United States: the high dollar further eroded the competitiveness of its traded industries and, by helping to keep interest rates low, encouraged unsustainable levels of consumer borrowing and consumption that fueled the subprime mortgage crisis and the ensuing recession. And because many other Asian countries followed China's lead in holding down the value of their currencies, the US trade deficit soared to record levels. As Fred Bergsten told Congress in 2007, "China's currency policy has taken much of Asia out of the international adjustment process."[68] And in the longer run, the weak yuan was not in China's interests either. China's reliance on investment and exports discouraged the shift toward greater domestic consumption that would have provided a firmer base for future Chinese growth. Instead, China is now facing a sharp slowdown in its economic growth because domestic demand is too weak to fill the gap left by slowing export growth, while investment is being propped up by unsustainable low-cost financing from state-run banks.

The US Congress had tried to prevent a rerun of the early 1980s. Reacting to the failure of the Reagan administration to manage the dollar effectively in its first term, Congress had, in the Omnibus Trade and Competitiveness Act of 1988, directed the administration to tackle the problem of currency manipulation and to take actions against those countries at fault. The language was far milder than some in Congress had wanted, in part because the sharp fall of the dollar after the Plaza Accord had placated many of the critics. But the act stated clearly that currency values "have a major role in determining the patterns of production and trade in the world economy" and that efforts by some countries to hold down the value of their currencies "continue to create serious competitive problems for U.S. industries." It said that the US government and other industrialized countries should continue the process of coordination begun with the Plaza agreement, with the objective of "producing more orderly adjustment of foreign exchange markets" and encouraging more balanced trade. Congress called for the United States to work with other countries both to intervene in currency markets and to adjust domestic economic policies as needed to achieve that outcome. "A more stable exchange rate for the dollar at a level consistent with a more appropriate and sustainable balance in the United States current account should be a major focus of national economic policy," the act read.

The means for achieving those ends were limited, however. Congress, not wanting to tie the administration's hands too tightly on an issue with significant implications for domestic economic and monetary policy, left the means entirely up to the executive branch. It directed the Treasury to prepare a twice-yearly report identifying countries that were manipulating their exchange rates in ways that produced both a global current account surplus and a significant trade surplus with the United States. In such cases, the administration was required to "initiate negotiations with such foreign countries on an expedited basis," working multilaterally through the IMF and bilaterally to ensure that the targeted country adjusted its exchange rate to eliminate any unfair advantage.[69] Congress did not spell out any sanctions for noncompliance, but the intent was clear. As Henning wrote, Congress "wanted to make it more difficult for Treasury to neglect a strong dollar and undervalued foreign currencies," as it had done with such damaging consequences for traded US industries during the first term of the Reagan administration.

For several years, the act worked more or less as its congressional authors had intended; indeed, President George H. W. Bush's treasury secretary, Nicholas Brady, called it "an enormously useful vehicle."[70] In the very first report, in October 1988, the Treasury cited Korea and Taiwan, both of which had intervened heavily to keep their currencies from rising significantly following the Plaza deal. Under US pressure, both countries agreed to a modest boost in their currencies, and both saw their trade surpluses with the United States shrink.[71] But the provision fell into disuse during the 1990s, and when the first truly big test came, with China, the Treasury balked. China had been cited once, in 1994, which led to some modest reforms in the country's foreign exchange regime. Yet, in the face of far more egregious distortions in the early and mid-2000s, the George W. Bush administration Treasury Department looked the other way. There was little question that China's actions were exactly the sort that the 1988 act intended to target. Henning wrote that intervention by "Chinese authorities" had kept the renminbi substantially undervalued, prevented a desirable adjustment of current account imbalances, and constituted "'manipulation' as that term was meant to be interpreted by Congress."[72] Yet, as Chinese intervention increased, the Treasury repeatedly refused to cite China for currency manipulation. Some in the George W. Bush administration simply did not want to pick a fight with China on the issue, fearing that it would damage the relationship; others were persuaded that the evidence against China was not sufficiently compelling; and within the Treasury many officials believed that quiet diplomacy would be more effective than publicly embarrassing Beijing with the "manipulation" label. The Treasury did make a belated effort, starting in 2006, to persuade the IMF to put pressure on China, encouraging member countries to designate the renminbi as "fundamentally misaligned" and launch consultations with China to correct the problem. But China was able to delay any IMF decision until 2008, when the collapse of Lehman Brothers and the onset of the financial crisis pushed the currency issue off the US agenda.

As with the Plaza Accord, it was only the threat of congressional action that finally produced some results. In March 2005, Democratic senator Charles Schumer of New York and Republican senator Lindsay Graham of South Carolina introduced legislation that would have slapped 27.5 percent tariffs on all Chinese imports unless China moved quickly to revalue the renminbi. The measure got sixty-seven votes in the Senate on a procedural motion related to the bill, and while it did not pass the House, the vote nonetheless sent a powerful signal to the Bush administration that Congress was running out of patience on the issue. In its report to Congress that spring, while still refusing to name China as a manipulator, the Treasury finally warned, "If current trends continue without alteration, China's policies will likely meet the statute's technical requirements for designation. . . . It is now widely accepted that China is now ready and should move without delay in a manner and magnitude that is sufficiently reflective of underlying market conditions."[73] In July

2005, facing growing US pressure, China abandoned the peg and began to allow upward movement in the value of the renminbi, slowly at first but gradually more aggressively, until it reach roughly six per dollar in 2014, more than a 25 percent appreciation. Globally, China's current account surplus fell from a record high of more than 10 percent of its GDP in 2008 to just over 2 percent by 2014. In part because the yuan has risen even more against other currencies as the dollar has strengthened, the IMF recently declared that the renminbi was no longer undervalued.[74]

The failure of the United States to move sooner and more forcefully to deal with the undervalued yuan was a mistake with consequences nearly as severe as the overvalued dollar of the early 1980s. In the first eight years of the 2000s, even prior to the financial crisis and the recession that followed, more than 5 million manufacturing jobs disappeared in the United States. Some were certainly victims of technology and productivity growth, but others were the result of import competition that was more intense than it should have been due in no small part to the undervalued yuan. And as China's recent economic volatility demonstrates, neglecting the imbalance was no favor to China either. It reinforced an economic growth model that depends far too heavily on business investment and exports and not nearly enough on increasing domestic consumption. The consumption share of China's economy fell steadily for five decades and is at best predicted to remain flat over the next decade at roughly 30 percent of the economy—a consumption level far lower than any other similar economy and less than half the US level.[75] There are some encouraging signs of rebalancing; China's consumption-to-GDP ratio has recently risen slightly, and the service-sector share of the economy is growing. China's leaders say they are committed to future growth that is less reliant on exports.[76] And while the renminbi has fallen slightly in the face of weaker Chinese growth and growing capital outflow, Beijing has backed up that claim by intervening to keep the renminbi from falling even faster. These are encouraging developments, but they have come far too late. By permitting China to increase its exports beyond what its underlying competitiveness would have produced, the United States harmed its own manufacturing economy and encouraged the development of a distorted economy in China that is now hurting China as well. As with Japan, the failure by the United States to insist on more balanced outcomes was helpful to neither.

INTENSIFYING AMERICA'S PROBLEMS

In October 2013, the Treasury Department shocked Germany by singling the country out with an unusually harsh critique. Unlike Japan or China, Germany in recent years has not been a particularly large exporter to the United States, with most of its goods going to neighboring European countries. But with exports surging due in part to a euro that was too weak for Germany given its underlying competitiveness, Germany's current account surplus had reached more than 7 percent of GDP in the first half of 2013. The Treasury said that Germany's robust exports and weak domestic demand were retarding growth in other European economies and in the world economy as well. Exports are vital for German economic growth, with net exports—which are exports minus imports—accounting for roughly one-third of Germany's total growth (in the United States, in contrast, the large trade deficit subtracts significantly from overall GDP growth). To the United States, that export performance was in effect stealing growth from other countries, particularly other European countries that were part of the eurozone, but also from those outside. "Germany's anemic pace of domestic demand growth and dependence on exports have hampered rebalancing at a time when many other euro-area countries have been under severe pressure to curb demand and compress imports in order to promote adjustment," the Treasury said. The Germans were not amused. The day after the report's release, Germany's Economic Ministry issued a blistering statement that called the conclusions "incomprehensible" and urged the United States "to analyze its own situation." Echoing Japan in the 1980s, the German ministry said that, rather than a problem to be solved, Germany's surplus was "a sign of the competitiveness of the German economy and global demand for quality products from Germany."[77]

The response was not unusual. As Pete Peterson had told President Nixon, surplus countries will do everything in their power to resist the costs of adjustment. In this they have been aided by US policies that have too often neglected exchange rate effects in the name of preserving greater flexibility for monetary and fiscal policy. The Obama administration's opposition to including any sort of binding provisions against currency manipulation in the TPP—on the grounds that it might "give our trading partners the power to challenge legitimate U.S. monetary policies"—reflects a long-standing set of priorities that has too often harmed the US ability to compete globally. Martin Feldstein, Reagan's former economic adviser, has argued that there is no need for such a stark trade-off—that the United States can maintain a "competitive dollar" without hurting the ability of the Federal Reserve to use monetary tools to control inflation. The United States, he argued, should strive for "an exchange rate that will make American goods more attractive to foreign buyers and that will cause American consumers and firms to choose American made goods and services."[78] That would mean a greater willingness by administrations and by Congress to consider more seriously the exchange rate effects of monetary and fiscal policies and to adjust them accordingly. And it would require a far more determined effort to respond to countries that are engaged in currency manipulation.

In 2013 Fred Bergsten, by then director emeritus at the influential Institute of International Economics, which was later renamed for Pete Peterson, delivered a lecture summarizing the previous half century of mostly failed efforts by the United States to deal with currency misalignment.[79] The problem, he warned, was still big and likely to get bigger. Virtually every major country was seeking depreciation, he said, or at least blocking market-driven appreciation, in order to boost exports and create jobs. They were doing so by using central bank reserves to buy dollars or euros and push up those currencies. Such currency manipulation, he said, "is very large and very widespread." Chinese currency manipulation, he argued, had played no small role in triggering the 2008 financial crisis and the deep recession that followed. Chinese competition had slowed US growth in the 2000s, leading the Federal Reserve to keep interest rates low to support employment, and Chinese purchases of Treasury bills had further lowered long-term interest rates. Although this in no way absolves the United States from its own mistakes in the run-up to the crisis, there is no question that such easy money helped to fuel the housing bubble that collapsed with such devastating consequences. He lamented the continued failure of countries to develop an international monetary system that would do what Peterson had hoped for and create incentives for both surplus and deficit countries to adjust their economic policies as needed to maintain a rough balance. Instead, he said, "from its very inception, the system has been unable to bring effective pressure on surplus countries. This is particularly true with respect to currency undervaluations, whether of the Germans in the 1960s or the Japanese in the 1970s or the newly industrializing economies (mainly Korea and Taiwan) in the late 1980s or the Chinese over the past decade."

Bergsten spelled out a series of measures that, he said, might finally tackle the problem effectively. IMF members, he argued, should give some teeth to long-standing rules that admonish countries for repeatedly intervening to hold down currency values. In cases where the IMF determined that a currency was significantly undervalued, countries hurt by the action would be authorized by the IMF to launch a counterintervention to offset the effects. The WTO should spell out that deliberate currency undervaluation amounts to a prohibited export subsidy, authorizing countries to slap countervailing duty tariffs on the imports. Even more broadly, in extreme cases the WTO could authorize across-the-board retaliation in the form of a Nixon-style import surcharge, the same remedy contained in the Schumer-Graham legislation. The purpose of such big sticks would be to deter currency manipulation. "Countries contemplating competitive undervaluation should be placed on clear notice that such policies would trigger prompt and forceful reactions by their trading partners under agreed rules and procedures."

None of these measures would be in any way easy to implement; most require international agreements of a sort that may be impossible to achieve. Though a committed internationalist, Bergsten argued that the United States may have little choice but to "break some crockery to galvanize serious consideration of the issue and launch a multilateral reform process." The model, he said—acknowledging his own, quite different view four decades ago—was the Nixon shocks of 1971. "The U.S. 'unilateralism' of the time, which was then almost universally excoriated (including by Bergsten), turned out to be essential to achieve systemic reform and produce a better world economy."

Finally, Bergsten stated, currency manipulation by others in no way excused the United States for the myriad failures in its own response to global economic competition. "The United States," he said, "must of course put its own house in order." It must reduce its federal budget deficits to sustainable levels. It must "strengthen fundamental components of its national competitive position, ranging from its shockingly poor K–12 education to its antiquated infrastructure." It needed to unleash rather than impede the huge creative potential of the American private sector by overhauling tax policies that discourage investment and immigration policies that drive away too many of the best and brightest. "But it must also," he said, "insist that other countries stop intensifying its problems."

4

Investment

The Winners and the Losers from Offshoring

In 1952, President Dwight D. Eisenhower nominated the chief executive of General Motors (GM), Charles E. Wilson, to be his secretary of defense. Wilson had been president of GM since 1941, overseeing the company's wartime production of tanks, aircraft, and armaments and its transition back to cars and trucks in peacetime. In the 1950s, GM was the country's largest employer, with more than six hundred thousand Americans on its payroll, and it was the first company to earn more than $1 billion in a single year. One in every two vehicles sold in the United States that decade was made by General Motors. When Wilson came before the Senate Armed Services Committee in January 1953 for his confirmation hearing to lead the Pentagon, the biggest question for the senators was what he would do with his $2.5 million worth of GM stock and other holdings while he served in the government. Republican senator Robert Hendrickson of New Jersey asked him, "If a situation did arise where you had to make a decision which was extremely adverse to the interests of your stock and General Motors Corp. or any of these other companies, or extremely adverse to the company, in the interests of the United States government, could you make that decision?" In his famous, though often misquoted, reply, Wilson said, "Yes, sir, I could." But he added, "I cannot conceive of one because for years I thought what was good for our country was good for General Motors, and vice versa. The difference did not exist."

That assumption—that the economic interests of large American companies were indistinguishable from the economic interests of Americans—was one of the reasons that American business and labor had walked hand in hand in opening the United States to greater foreign trade. If the United States was the world's most competitive economy, which seemed self-evident in the 1950s, then expanded trade would clearly benefit both US companies and their employees. Exports would grow at least as much as imports, creating more jobs and higher wages for American workers and more profits for US companies. Indeed of the two, the labor unions were the more enthusiastic and less fearful of global competition. The American Federation of Labor and Congress of Industrial Organizations (AFL-CIO) had supported President John F. Kennedy's Trade Expansion Act of 1962, which led to the Kennedy Round of global trade talks, slashing tariffs on goods by some 35 percent in more than fifty countries. "Foreign trade policy should be a liberal one, aimed at more trade, not less, on the grounds that more trade means more prosperity, more opportunity, more jobs," said AFL-CIO president George Meany in a 1962 address.[1] The labor movement's support for freer trade, as the union organization later put it, was "based on the expectation that such expansion would contribute to the growth of employment and improvement of living standards at home and abroad."[2] While most business groups came around to support Kennedy, it was far tougher to sell the idea of freer trade to the traditionally insular American business community. The National Association of Manufacturers, the voice of large companies, took no stand on the trade bill, and the Chamber of Commerce, which represented smaller companies, reluctantly backed it despite some strong internal opposition.[3]

By the middle of the 1960s, however, the marriage between business and labor was fraying. Import competition was growing much faster than either had anticipated. In almost every large manufacturing sector—textiles, machine tools, footwear, consumer electronics, cars, and steel—imports had gone from being a negligible part of the US market in 1960 to a significant competitive threat by the early 1970s. Faced with markets abroad that were generally less open to US exports and a US business culture that had rarely pursued export opportunities, American sales abroad had failed to keep pace with rising imports. The US trade balance moved from a $3.3 billion surplus in 1962 to a $1.3 billion deficit by 1971. Growing foreign competition from Japan and Germany was driving down corporate profit rates, with core manufacturing industries such as steel, automobiles, machine tools, textiles, chemicals, and shipbuilding hit especially hard.[4] In virtually every major manufacturing sector exposed to global competition, average pretax corporate profits in the 1969–1975 period were less than 6 percent, half of what they had been in the previous five-year period.[5]

Falling profits had two consequences, both of them bad for the employees of large American companies. First, the cost pressures led US companies to start looking overseas in search of lower wages or less competitive markets where profit margins would be higher. From 1960 to 1969, US direct investment abroad doubled, mostly in Europe, Canada, and Latin America, and most of the growth was in manufacturing investments, like consumer electronics, which competed directly with US production, rather than in extractive industries, like mining or oil drilling, which had accounted for most outward US investments in the 1950s.[6] RCA, for example, long the biggest maker of radios and TV sets, had moved its operations from Camden, New Jersey, to Bloomington, Indiana, in the 1950s and 1960s following a series of strikes in Camden. Then, in the 1960s, in the face of rising import competition, it jumped the border and built its largest factory in Juarez, Mexico, encouraged by

Mexico's new Border Industrialization Program, which allowed for duty-free imports of parts if the final product was exported back to the United States.[7] RCA was not atypical; between 1960 and 1975, the share of US manufacturing corporate profits earned abroad tripled, from less than 5 percent to more than 15 percent, and growth outside the United States outpaced growth at home.[8] While hiring continued in the United States, new jobs were being created much faster overseas. From 1966 to 1970, according to data gathered by AFL-CIO economist Elizabeth Jager, foreign employment in US multinational corporations grew by more than 25 percent, compared to just 7.6 percent inside the United States.[9] In manufacturing, there was no US job growth at all. Import competition also forced many companies to cut costs at home, which meant resisting union demands for higher wages and more generous benefits. Companies that had once acceded to union wishes, confident that higher costs could be passed on to consumers, began to fight back; those without unions fought harder to keep them out. In 1965, 42 percent of US companies immediately complied with union petitions to the National Labor Relations Board for recognition; by 1973, only 16 percent did.[10]

Under growing pressure from the companies, whose mobility gave them leverage the unions could not match, the labor movement filed for divorce. By the late 1960s, the major unions—with a handful of exceptions like the United Auto Workers union, which had close ties with its Canadian counterparts, and the International Longshoreman's Association, whose members benefited from handling the rising volume of imports—had concluded that the growing overseas investments of American business posed a fundamental threat to their interests, one that required a frontal challenge to the emerging global strategies of large US companies. In a formal resolution in December 1967, the AFL-CIO called for "direct restrictions on U.S. investment" overseas and for higher corporate taxes on their overseas investments.[11] "Large corporations—with increasing investments, plants and sales offices in different countries—juggle production schedules, exports and imports to their own profit advantage with little regard to national interests, employment, labor standards or the American consumer," Andrew Biemiller, the AFL-CIO's legislative director, told the House Ways and Means Committee in 1968. "The U.S. worker cannot effectively bargain for higher wages, better health standards, better work rules—and all of these are cost factors—while the investment and trade policies of private firms operate to escape these costs. The advantage is only to those firms. This does not necessarily benefit the United States."[12] Stanley Ruttenberg, an economist hired by the unions to help flesh out their analysis, warned that the result of this trend would be an economy divided between highly trained and well-paid professionals and low-skilled service and clerical workers, which would "destroy the great strength of the middle class on which democracy rests."[13]

It would take business longer to react. Not until the unions succeeded in getting their ideas into legislation and mounted a fierce effort to push the bill through Congress did business finally fight back. But when it did so, its response was the economic equivalent of massive retaliation—a huge lobbying and public relations campaign that not only quashed the union-backed trade legislation but set US trade and investment policy in a direction that, to this day, remains anathema to the labor unions.

The union-business conflicts over foreign investment during the late 1960s and early 1970s were reprised in the 1990s as part of the North American Free Trade Agreement (NAFTA) debate—when presidential hopeful Ross Perot famously warned of the "giant sucking sound" of jobs moving to Mexico—and again in the early 2000s in the fight over China's admission to the World Trade Organization (WTO). Both times, the unions lost badly in Congress despite mounting all-out lobbying campaigns and despite having a Democratic president in office. The issues are every bit as divisive today over the Trans-Pacific Partnership (TPP) agreement with Asia. During the debate in 2015 over whether to give President Barack Obama the fast-track congressional authority he needed to complete the negotiations, the AFL-CIO threatened to cut off campaign funding to and encourage primary challenges against any Democrat who dared to support the president on trade. The union president, Richard Trumka, charged that the TPP would simply send more American jobs offshore to Asia and further drive down the wages of working Americans. "There is no middle ground," he warned.[14]

THE GLOBAL CORPORATION

The split between Democratic presidents and the labor unions arises from a fundamental dilemma created by an increasingly competitive global economy. To be competitive, the United States (or any other country) needs to welcome and encourage the large corporations that do most of the world's trading and investment. But the success of those corporations is not enough in itself; if they are profiting by investing more overseas and less in the United States, their success will do little to create jobs or raise wages for Americans. Nearly all American employees outside a small mobile elite of managers and professionals benefit only when companies invest and create jobs and pay higher wages inside the physical territory of the United States. That is where most of us live, after all. But as US companies have pursued global business strategies, their ties to the physical territory of the United States have become weaker and weaker. At the height of the congressional debate over investment restrictions in 1972, Carl Gerstacker, the former chief executive of Dow Chemical, mused, "I have long dreamed of buying an island owned by no nation, and of establishing the world headquarters of the Dow company on the truly neutral ground of such an island, beholden to no nation or society."[15] Many of his fellow CEOs would nod in agreement today. Modern multinational companies have found more prosaic ways to achieve the same end, by setting up operations in dozens of countries, breaking up supply chains, and shifting investments, or sometimes just paper profits, to the most welcoming and profitable jurisdictions.

While it is difficult to generalize across sectors, the strategy has largely been a successful one for America's companies. The adjustment did not happen overnight; US corporate profits were weak throughout much of the 1970s and the first half of the 1980s, and as the United States was losing ground to Japan, American companies were frequently blamed for complacent and ineffective leadership.[16] Corporate leaders, the argument went, had been lulled by decades of American dominance and were ill equipped to raise their performance to match the new foreign competitors.[17] After decades of producing almost solely for a huge domestic market, the Commission on Industrial Productivity of the Massachusetts Institute of Technology (MIT) reported in 1989, US companies were paralyzed by their own parochialism. "The legacy of these years of self-sufficiency is an economy ill-equipped to compete for worldwide markets or exploit foreign innovations," the study concluded.[18]

But while American-headquartered companies may have been slow to respond to the new competitive challenges, once they did, they proved highly creative and adaptable. By the mid-2000s, the same MIT commission later reported, American companies had led a global move toward fragmentation, what project director Suzanne Berger called "the Lego model of production."[19] Manufacturing was increasingly broken into its component parts to maximize cost-efficiency and quality along each link in the production chain. That made it possible for companies to outsource—either across the street or across the world—work that had once been done solely in-house. Improvements in technology, logistics, and transportation made it possible in the 2000s for a company like Hewlett-Packard to outsource most of its computer manufacturing and engineering design to independent contract manufacturers in Asia. The high-value components for an Apple iPhone are mostly built in Taiwan, Korea, and Japan and assembled in China by a Taiwanese-owned contract manufacturer, Foxconn. Apparel companies like Liz Claiborne and Ralph Lauren rely almost entirely on contract producers overseas, primarily in China but also in Vietnam, Bangladesh, and Indonesia. Most of Nike's athletic shoes are designed in the United States but made in Korean- and Taiwanese-owned factories in Vietnam. The United States pioneered "fabless" semiconductor manufacturing, in which US-headquartered firms like Qualcomm and AMD handled all the design and marketing but outsourced actual production to foundries in Taiwan and China. Such fragmentation allowed for significant cost savings that would not have been possible otherwise. American companies today are by most measures the most productive in the world, and their global strategies are critical to that success.[20]

These strategies have been highly profitable as well. US corporate profits hit record levels in 2013 and 2014, and as a share of national income, corporate profits were the highest recorded since 1929.[21] A steadily larger share of those profits is now earned overseas. Nearly half the revenue for companies on the S&P 500 now comes from outside the United States, and some 60 percent of their cash is held outside the United States.[22] US-headquartered multinational companies have pioneered global strategies of splitting up the production process and outsourcing noncore features so that work is done in whatever countries and regions are most profitable for the corporation. The large, integrated companies of the 1950s and 1960s have been replaced by smaller, nimbler enterprises that employ fewer people and focus on fewer lines of business. The research suggests that companies operating in multiple countries tend to be more productive than purely domestic companies, in part because they have no choice but to compete with the best firms in the world. As economists Robert Solow and Martin Baily have written, "When an industry is exposed to the world's best practice, it is forced to increase its own productivity."[23] Many American companies have responded successfully to that challenge.

But the union fears of the late 1960s were far from misplaced. The successful competitive strategies of US companies have produced, at best, mixed results for their American employees. As Michael Porter of Harvard Business School has put it, "U.S. companies are okay, but the U.S. location is not."[24] The multinational companies still provide some of the best jobs in the United States, but there are fewer of those jobs than there used to be. Over the past two decades, the number of jobs created at US-headquartered multinational companies in the United States grew more slowly than in the rest of the economy, by about 17 percent from 1990 through 2011 compared to overall private-sector job growth of about 22 percent. And all of that employment growth at US multinationals came during the boom of the 1990s; since 2000, these companies have shed nearly 1 million jobs in the United States. In contrast, employment has continued to surge at their overseas affiliates, doubling over the past two decades. The share of their total employment in the United States fell from 79 to 66 percent over those two decades.[25] These numbers almost certainly understate the trend, since employees for contract manufacturers like Foxconn do not count as employees of the multinationals, even though almost all of the work is being done for big American, European, or Japanese companies.[26] The weak job performance of the big US companies has been offset partially by growing foreign investment in the United States, though here too, following strong growth in the 1990s, US employment at foreign-owned multinationals has been flat for the past decade.

Those numbers do not prove, in any direct way, that the big companies are "outsourcing" jobs from the United States or that the job gains overseas are coming directly at the expense of domestic jobs. The economic research, while far from definitive, suggests that most US companies investing overseas do so primarily to expand in new markets, not to displace US production. Many markets are hard to serve through exports, and a local presence is either essential or very helpful. While about half of the jobs in overseas affiliates of US companies are in manufacturing, most of the growth over the past decade has been in the service sector—from Walmart and McDonalds to banks and law firms—with jobs going to workers who do not compete directly with US workers.[27] Less than 10 percent of the goods and services produced abroad by these firms are directly exported back to the United States, a share that has actually dropped slightly over the past decade.[28] And America's biggest overseas direct investors are also its largest exporting companies. As Robert Lipsey has summarized the economic research, "A country's most competent and successful firms tend to export and to invest in production abroad, and the same is generally true of the most successful industries."[29]

Despite vigorous assertions from both sides, there is no clear answer to the question of whether foreign investment by US companies creates or destroys jobs in the United States, because the claims depend on essentially unprovable assumptions.[30] Unions argue that millions of jobs have been lost from outsourcing, but that claim rests on the assumption that, had the companies not invested abroad, they would have maintained or expanded US production instead to meet consumer demand. On the other hand, when the companies claim that US jobs are created by their foreign investments, they assume instead that if American companies had not made those overseas investments, other multinational companies from Germany or Japan or Britain would have done so instead. General Motors, for example, today builds and sells more cars in China than it does in the United States, more than 3 million annually, and the company has plans to exceed 5 million in a few years. If even some small fraction of that number of finished vehicles were exported from the United States rather than assembled in China, GM would create thousands of good American jobs that it is instead creating in China. So in that sense, GM's investments in China are "outsourcing American jobs." On the other hand, the company could quite reasonably argue, if GM were not building those cars in China, some other competitor—Volkswagen, BMW, Toyota, Honda—would probably do so instead and capture most of the Chinese market growth. With GM investing in China, there is at least some small increase in the export of some US-made parts to be included in the vehicles assembled in China, parts that would otherwise likely be made in Germany or Japan. And Chinese-consumers may acquire a taste for American-designed cars, allowing GM or other US companies to increase exports of higher-end vehicles rather than letting Germany capture the lion's share of that market. So are GM's investments in China destroying or creating US jobs? The answer depends entirely on the assumptions.

But whether overseas production is directly displacing American jobs or not, there is no question that American multinational companies today are no longer creating many American jobs. In some industries, like consumer electronics, companies no longer make much of anything in the United States. Apple, which is the iconic US company of today in the way General Motors was in the 1950s, directly employs about fifty thousand people in the United States—one-twelfth as many as GM at its peak—and more than half of those are in its retail stores rather than in higher-wage engineering and design jobs. In comparison, the Asian subcontractors that assemble its iPads, iPhones, and computers employ hundreds of thousands of workers in China, Taiwan, and elsewhere.[31]

The picture on wages has been similarly mixed. When multinationals do create jobs in the United States, they are pretty good ones. Total compensation, including benefits, for US workers at American-owned multinationals is about 25 percent higher than the private-sector average, or more than $76,000 a year. Here, the evidence suggests that the growth overseas may have helped slightly, in the sense that as less well-paid work moves offshore, what remains behind are the higher-skilled and better-paid jobs.[32] Indeed, average compensation for employees in these companies is up nearly 20 percent since 2000.[33] But even the best-paid workers have received a smaller share of the growing corporate returns. In the overall economy, labor's share of total US income, which was largely stable from the end of World War II through the early 1980s, has been falling steadily. The decline is especially steep in manufacturing, the most globalized sector of the economy, and in other trade-exposed sectors. In 2013, payments to employees as a percentage of total GDP, including benefits, fell to their lowest level since 1948. And the steepest drop in the wage share over the past quarter century was in those sectors and industries most exposed to global competition.[34]

For the unions themselves, the global mobility of capital has been devastating. As they became global enterprises, US companies also became increasingly effective at using the threat of moving jobs overseas to keep out unions and to hold down wages and benefits in their US operations. A study of union organizing drives in the 1990s illustrated the effectiveness of that threat. When unions tried to organize in mobile industries such as manufacturing and communications, in more than two-thirds of the cases companies threatened to close their plants if the unions succeeded. By and large, their employees heeded the warning; in only one-third of those cases did the unions succeed, much lower than the success rate of nearly 60 percent in industries, like health care, that could not credibly threaten to pick up and leave.[35] Perhaps more important than the fate of the union workers themselves has been the loss of an effective counterweight to business interests in the debate over the best strategies for enhancing US competitiveness. While global economic competition is only one of several factors that have weakened unions in the United States, private-sector union membership today is below 7 percent, half the rate of the mid-1980s, and the lowest since 1932. With the waning of union power, there is no longer a strong organized voice advocating for the interests of wage earners rather than the owners of capital. Private-sector union membership is now so small that unions can quite accurately be portrayed as advocates for only a tiny, and not particularly representative, slice of the American workforce. But the rest of that workforce, much of which is still working in competitive, traded sectors, now has no organized voice at all. By changing course in the late-1960s and challenging the largest American companies head-on over their foreign investments, the unions knew they had picked the fight of their lives. They could not have predicted just how badly they would lose.

AN OPPORTUNITY LOST: THE BURKE-HARTKE BILL

Pete Peterson, in his memo to Richard Nixon, was certain that multinational corporations would matter enormously in the new economic reality that he was sketching out for the president. He just wasn't quite sure how. In contrast to his clear recommendations on currency, trade, and adjustment assistance for workers, which are the subject of the next chapter, he was far more tentative about what, if anything, should be done about the growing overseas investments of American business. Multinational companies would, he wrote, "pose both new challenges and new opportunities. There has been a tendency to say more than is known about these new and extraordinarily important enterprises."[36] He called for more study and "fresh thinking" before any firm conclusions were drawn. Among the issues that he said would need to be addressed were taxation, investment controls, expropriation and the treatment of investors, the promotion of foreign investment in the United States, and the effects on US employment. Peterson was skeptical of the labor union claims that these companies were "job exporters," noting that US exports from the same companies that were investing abroad were also growing rapidly, creating jobs in the United States. But he was concerned over the "enormous disparity between American investment abroad and foreign investment in the United States." And he worried about the "artificial inducements to operate in one place rather than another" and whether some "burden sharing of pollution costs" was needed to discourage companies from fleeing the costs of environmental regulation. Indeed, in a few brief paragraphs, he summarized the major issues of the debates that continue today over outsourcing, offshoring, international labor and environmental standards, and foreign anticompetitive practices. He just wasn't certain what to do about them: "These broad types of questions have not had sufficient attention in the past in our policy planning process, but they must now be addressed in the context of the new realities discussed in this paper," he wrote.

Such a considered analysis never occurred, however. Instead, the unions went to war. The Burke-Hartke bill—named for its cosponsors, Massachusetts Democratic representative James Burke and Indiana Democratic senator Vance Hartke—is the most important trade bill that never passed the US Congress. First introduced in 1971, it was, as John Judis has put it, "based on the premise that the public had a right to regulate what an American corporation did internationally when American jobs were at stake." To large American businesses, that idea was so threatening—not just to their narrow economic interests but to their beliefs about the way the economy should be organized—that it sparked a backlash that, more than any other single trigger, created the huge, powerful business lobby that exists today in Washington. Before the labor push that led to Burke-Hartke, most large US companies—with the exception of defense contractors and oil companies—were politically disorganized and not terribly interested in what went on in Washington. But as labor rallied behind the Burke-Hartke bill and other trade- and investment-restricting measures, business responded by organizing itself into large, well-funded lobbying organizations such as the Business Roundtable and the Emergency Committee for American Trade (ECAT). The National Association of Manufacturers, the country's oldest business group, founded in Cincinnati in 1895, moved its headquarters to Washington in 1973. The Chamber of Commerce morphed from a loose agglomeration of small and medium-size companies into a powerhouse voice for big business that today is routinely among the largest political donors to the Republican Party. The business lobby has won many of its biggest successes on international trade and investment issues, winning congressional support for NAFTA, China's accession to the WTO, the Central American Free Trade Agreement (CAFTA), and other trade deals that were vigorously opposed by organized labor and environmental and consumer groups and were not terribly popular with the general public. That success began with the response to the Burke-Hartke bill.

In some ways, Burke-Hartke was an easy target for business, and in retrospect labor's commitment to the bill was a huge tactical mistake. Given its still considerable influence at the time and the realistic threat to shut down production through strikes, organized labor might well have persuaded US companies to accept some modest restrictions on offshore investment and to cooperate in pressing for better international rules governing investment. Instead, labor devised a bill that one senior business executive called "the most serious legislative challenge international corporations have ever confronted."[37] Much of the bill was crude protectionism. In response to labor's fear of surging import competition, it proposed freezing the import share of the US market at the 1965–1969 average, which would have meant in some sectors slashing imports by 30 percent to fall under the quota. But it was not the quota provisions that most worried US companies; indeed, in 1971 US business remained divided between import-competing industries happy for protection and export-oriented industries worried about retaliation that might cost them sales abroad. Instead, all the companies feared the bill's proposed rules on taxation and regulation of US investment overseas. The National Association of Manufacturers, for example, took no position on the quota provisions of the bill but staunchly opposed what it called the "political control of direct foreign investment."[38]

The unions certainly understood the implications for business. By the early 1970s, they had come to view growing foreign investment by US-headquartered companies as the gravest threat the union movement had faced in more than half a century—far more significant than rising imports from Japan and Europe. The speed of the turnabout was startling. In the 1950s, most US foreign investment had been for development of petroleum and raw materials, with few jobs at stake. The unions were the first to notice the shift toward foreign investment in manufacturing in the 1960s. In consumer electronics, much of US radio and television production decamped to Mexico and Taiwan over the course of that decade. Apparel manufacturers followed. Even in a high-technology sector like aerospace, Boeing had entered into joint ventures to produce parts in Japan and Italy. US investment in Europe had surged as well. The creation of the European Economic Community in 1958 had put high tariffs around much of the European continent, giving a big advantage to producers inside the tariff wall. In an effort to skirt that tariff, US companies had increased their investments in Europe from $2 billion to $13 billion annually between 1958 and 1968. By 1968, the sales of American subsidiaries in Europe had reached $14 billion a year, which was two and half times larger than US exports to Europe.[39]

The unions had three main concerns. First, the companies investing overseas sometimes took their best technology with them and shared it with overseas joint venture partners, eroding US technological leadership. "America's newest industries are being shipped out," the AFL-CIO's legislative director Andrew Biemiller testified to the Senate. "As other nations get America's know-how in aerospace and electronics, chemicals and shipping, computers and other new industries, the job generators of the future are being lost."[40] Second, the unions feared that the growing mobility of capital would undermine the social contract at home, affecting wages, working conditions, and environmental and social legislation. "The national commitment in all these fields can be diminished by multinational action," Biemiller warned in a 1974 speech. "If a multinational corporation does not like the federal minimum wage of $1.60 an hour, or the National Labor Relations Act, it can relocate in Korea where wages run nine cents an hour, or in some country where unions are non-existent or illegal. . . . If it doesn't like a piece of environmental protective legislation which forbids pollution of the air and water, it can close down here and go to countries where such concerns are not of national priority."[41] Finally, the unions argued that the US tax system was in effect rigged against companies that remained loyal to the United States. While the United States in theory taxes corporations on their income regardless of where it is earned in the world, the system offers two big benefits for overseas investors. First, they can write off every penny of foreign tax paid as a direct credit against their US taxes; second, the taxes owed on foreign profits are "deferred" until they are returned home, either as dividends to shareholders or for reinvestment in the United States. As long as the profits remain offshore, the companies do not owe a dime to Uncle Sam. Today, with the rules largely unchanged in the last half century, US companies are holding more than $2 trillion offshore in part to avoid the US corporate tax that would be owed on repatriated profits.

The Burke-Hartke bill would have turned that system on its head. In an effort to discourage the licensing of US technology overseas and the sharing of technology through joint ventures, the president would have been authorized to block any US company from transferring technology that might have reduced employment in the United States. Proponents argued that since many of the breakthrough commercial technologies like aircraft engines and semiconductors had been developed by researchers at taxpayer-subsidized universities or with the aid of government research grants, the United States had national interests that outweighed the commercial interests of the companies themselves. Burke-Hartke further gave the president significant power to simply block offshore investments if he deemed them to be not in the interests of the United States, including in cases where they would reduce US employment. Most threatening to the large companies, as Kent Hughes wrote in his history of the legislation, the bill would have "radically altered the tax treatment of foreign source income," with the goal of "discouraging the continued outflow of U.S. capital for foreign direct investment and imposing a serious fiscal burden on existing U.S. investments abroad." It would have eliminated deferral on all overseas profits, forcing the immediate payment of taxes to the US government. And in place of the generous full credit for foreign taxes paid, it would have allowed only the deduction of those tax payments from profits. The combined effect of the two provisions would have cut the profitability of foreign investments by half or more.[42] As Representative Burke's top aide on the bill told the *National Journal,* "What we are going after is the jugular vein that makes foreign investment so attractive."[43]

Those proposals, as John Judis has written, "thoroughly alarmed business leaders." They poured money into ECAT, which had been established in 1967 by David Rockefeller of Chase Manhattan, Arthur Watson of IBM, James Linen of Time Inc., and George Moore of First National City Bank.[44] Pete Peterson too had been a member of ECAT when he ran Bell & Howell before joining the White House. The Center for Multinational Studies, a corporate-financed think tank set up in 1971 when the bill was introduced, warned in its first pamphlet, "The attack [against multinational companies], if unanswered, will at the least unnecessarily shackle international business through regulations, reporting schemes, registration and taxation, to the great detriment of the best interests of the United States."[45] The goal of the companies was not just to defeat the legislation but also to discredit the very idea that there could be a conflict between corporate interests and the well-being of the US economy. As debate over the bill grew, Donald Kendall, chairman of ECAT and chief executive of Pepsi, announced the launch of "an education campaign to inform the public and Congress of the contributions of multinational companies to American jobs, investment, exports and the balance of payments."[46] In a survey of its own member companies—at a time when the federal government was not yet collecting such data—ECAT concluded that domestic employment growth in US multinationals had been 75 percent faster than the average in all manufacturing firms. "American multinational companies do not export jobs," Kendall asserted. "They outperform other companies in making jobs. In general they make better jobs with better pay and backed by higher investment than other companies."

The business campaign was highly sophisticated and set the template for future lobbying efforts. Rather than simply trying to muscle lawmakers in Congress—as the labor unions largely did and still try to do, most recently by threatening to cut campaign funding for Democrats who voted with President Obama on trade—business mounted a massive public relations push to discredit the argument that foreign investment by US companies in any way harmed the domestic workforce. They hired out private-sector economists to crunch the numbers, largely based on selective surveys of the member companies of the lobbying organizations. The economists found, not surprisingly, that growing overseas investment by the companies did not reduce the number of jobs at home. More neutral observers were skeptical. "It is wholly unpersuasive to argue that U.S. firms have not 'exported jobs' because their domestic employment has risen faster than the average rate of domestic employment," Fred Bergsten wrote in 1973. "Since the firms involved are by definition the largest and most dynamic in the country, I would certainly hope that all aspects of their operations are growing faster than the national average—if not, something is vitally wrong!"[47] But the argument stuck and is commonly recycled today even as the number of American jobs in these multinational companies has been flat since 1999, while their overseas employment nearly doubled in the same period.

Whatever their academic merits, the corporate-funded studies were effective in raising doubts in Congress. The bill faced a chorus of media disapproval and strong opposition from the Nixon administration. By the time the AFL-CIO signaled that it was ready to bargain with business opponents of the bill, Burke-Hartke was already doomed. It died without a vote when the 92nd Congress dissolved in January 1973. When reintroduced in the next Congress, it was cleverly undermined by President Nixon, who introduced his own trade bill seeking broad negotiating authority for the next round of General Agreement on Tariffs and Trade talks and included just enough measures to co-opt Democrats who might otherwise be sympathetic to the union concerns. It was a strategy that has worked ever since.

Burke-Hartke was the wrong approach, but it asked the right question: In a world of increasingly mobile capital, what policies might best ensure that companies continued to invest in the United States even as they inevitably expanded overseas as well? That was not a question that the US government had ever really considered before. In the postwar era, the United States did not have an explicit policy on either inward or outward investment. Foreign investment has long been viewed by the US government as almost exclusively a matter for private corporations not public policy. The basic stance has been one of neutrality: the US government should neither promote nor discourage inward or outward investment but should let those decisions be made by the companies themselves in response to market forces.[48] In practice, however, there have been many exceptions to that neutrality, almost all of them in favor of offshore investments. On outward investment, the US government has actively encouraged and protected US foreign investors. Beginning with the Marshall Plan, the government has promoted overseas investment by offering insurance against political risk; the Overseas Private Investment Corporation (OPIC), set up in 1969, continues to do so today.[49] President Eisenhower similarly encouraged US businesses to invest abroad to help shore up the economies of allies in Europe and Asia. The United States has occasionally even intervened militarily in cases of outright expropriations of US private holdings by foreign governments, most famously in Guatemala in 1954 on behalf of United Fruit. Today, investor-state dispute-settlement provisions included in most investment and trade treaties at the urging of the United States allow foreign investors to seek binding arbitration if a government expropriates their holdings or takes other actions that significantly reduce the value of a company's investments.

Until very recently, the US government had done far less to encourage inward investment. President Kennedy did set up an Invest in the U.S.A. program in the Commerce Department in 1961 to encourage foreign companies to invest, but the agency had only five staff members and was later eliminated by Congress.[50] Half a century later, with no real initiatives in between, President George W. Bush in 2007 created Invest in America, a Commerce Department agency charged with attracting foreign investment to the United States. President Obama went one step further and launched what he called "the first-ever comprehensive, all hands on deck effort led by the federal government to bring jobs and investment from around the world to the U.S."[51] He renamed the program Select USA and began hosting annual investment summits aimed at selling the United States to would-be foreign investors. Despite several threats by Republicans in Congress to zero out the program, it has grown in the past several years into a significant new federal initiative. US states have been far more active—the primary function of the economic development agencies in most states is to lure investors, both domestic and foreign, and states have developed an array of tax and other incentives to attract investment. But they get too little help from Washington. While the conclusions may be a bit dated, a 2009 review by the World Bank put the United States at the bottom among Organization for Economic Cooperation and Development (OECD) countries in terms of best practices for attracting foreign investment.[52]

The oversight is glaring because there is no question that increased investment is critical for improving the competitiveness of the US economy. Competitive economies, as discussed more in chapter 7, are ones in which the productivity of workers is high and a high percentage of adults are in the labor force. Both outcomes—in effect, more technology and more jobs—require high rates of investment. And in a free market economy like the United States, the vast bulk of that investment comes from the private sector. From 1994 to 2004, when the US economy was growing strongly, unemployment was at record lows, and labor force participation was rising, private-sector investment excluding housing grew at an annual rate of 5.5 percent; over the next ten years, investment excluding housing grew by just 2.8 percent annually.[53] In the United States a great deal of that investment—more than 45 percent of all capital investment and nearly 70 percent of the private-sector research-and-development (R&D) spending that is critical for innovation—comes from US-headquartered multinational companies. Foreign-owned companies are major contributors to investment and R&D as well.[54] Persuading all these companies to invest more in the United States is vitally important for improving the competitiveness of the American economy.

Countries attract, or fail to attract, investment for all sorts of reasons, including the growth rates of their economies, the value and stability of their currencies, and the certainty of their laws and regulations. But the United States has long faced significant disadvantages for at least three reasons. First, its system of taxing corporate income favors offshore investment over investment in the United States. Second, the United States had for many years, though much less so today, a highly paid labor force, which created a big incentive for companies in some sectors to go abroad in search of lower wages. And third, the investment policies developed by the US government are mostly aimed at making it easier and safer for US companies to invest abroad rather than encouraging them to invest at home.

CORPORATE TAXES: HOW THE UNITED STATES IS LOSING INVESTMENT AND REVENUE

In May 2013, Apple's chief executive, Tim Cook, was summoned to Washington to appear before the US Senate Permanent Subcommittee on Investigations. An invitation from the committee, which for many years was chaired by the combative Michigan Democrat Carl Levin, is never good news for a company. In recent years, the committee has investigated giant banks like HSBC for allegedly facilitating money laundering and corruption, and investment banks like J.P. Morgan and Goldman Sachs for their role in triggering the financial crisis. This time the committee staff, in a detailed inquiry, had found that Apple had used clever tax strategies built around Irish subsidiaries to avoid US tax payments on nearly all of its foreign income and to reduce its US tax bill significantly as well. The committee had already interrogated executives from Microsoft and Hewlett-Packard over their tax-avoidance schemes, but the amounts were small compared to Apple's. The company's tax savings, by various counts, ran close to $10 billion annually, far more than the $6 billion the company had paid to the US Treasury in 2012. The tax-avoidance strategies were complicated, but they all boiled down to the same thing—the more of its income that Apple could earn outside the United States, or appear to be earning outside the United States, the less tax it would owe. While Apple paid more than 30 percent in federal tax on its US profits that year, the tax rate on its foreign earnings was just 2.5 percent.[55] The difference matters enormously because Apple earns the majority of its revenue outside the United States—more than two-thirds in the year Cook was testifying. While praising Apple as a "great company" and proudly waving the iPhone he carried in his pocket, Senator Levin said, "They don't have a right to decide in my book how much in taxes they are going to pay and to whom they are going to pay them." The *New York Times* reported the next day that, despite Levin's charges, the Apple CEO had most of the senators eating out of his hand. But the committee was not deferential enough for Senator Rand Paul, a libertarian Republican, who leaped to Cook's defense and accused his colleagues of conducting a "show trial." He said, "I'm offended by the spectacle of dragging in Apple executives. What we need to do is apologize to Apple and compliment them for the job creation they're doing."[56]

Taxes are the most visible of corporate costs, and there are big variations across countries. When Charlie Wilson of General Motors sought his Senate confirmation as defense secretary in 1953, corporate taxes in the United States were high—very high. The marginal federal tax rate on corporate profits for large companies was over 50 percent, and those corporate taxes totaled about 5.5 percent of US GDP. Since there were few overseas investment opportunities and the idea of using tax havens to shelter income was just emerging, companies had little choice but to pay the taxes they owed. With so little of the US economy tied up in trade, it did not much matter whether US tax rates were higher or lower than in Europe or other competing economies. Today, the marginal federal tax rate on corporate profits is 35 percent, but corporate tax revenues collected by the government total less than 2 percent of

US GDP.[57] In the past half century, American corporations have become increasingly adept at using profit shifting to low-tax or tax-haven countries to drive their tax bills lower and lower. Even as corporate profits have hit record levels, corporate taxes as a share of total federal tax payments have fallen to their lowest levels since the United States began taxing corporate income a century ago. This falling corporate share has contributed to the federal budget deficit, leaving less money for education, research, infrastructure, and other public investments that could help the United States in responding to international economic competition.

A bigger concern for the US economy is the incentive that the corporate tax system creates for US-headquartered companies to invest outside the United States rather than at home. A bedrock principle of US corporate tax policy is that it should be economically neutral. In other words, decisions on whether to invest in the United States or somewhere else should be driven by profit opportunities, not tax incentives. But the reality is that while corporate investment decisions are influenced by many things, such as transportation costs, growth rates, regulatory policies, and the quality and costs of the workforce, tax rates do matter a lot. A host of economic studies have found that when countries cut their corporate taxes, they see significant increases in foreign investment. One recent study of western Europe, where wages and other business costs are broadly similar and the creation of the euro has stabilized currency values, concluded that the corporate tax rate "is the most important factor in determining the flow of capital to core European countries."[58] For the United States, this is bad news because its corporate tax rate is high compared to nearly all its major international competitors. When the US Congress lowered the federal corporate tax rate to 35 percent as part of President Ronald Reagan's 1986 tax reform, it was the lowest rate among OECD countries; today, as other countries have slashed tax rates to attract investment, it is now the highest. And too often the easiest way for US corporations to eliminate that competitive disadvantage is by expanding outside the United States or reincorporating in another country. In recent years, several high-profile companies have undertaken what are known as "inversions," in which a US-headquartered company merges with a foreign partner and then relocates the headquarters outside the United States to take advantage of lower corporate tax rates in countries like Ireland or even Canada. The companies include drug giant Pfizer, auto parts and HVAC maker Johnson Controls, and fast-food giant Burger King. On average the tax rate on the foreign profits of US companies, which includes taxes paid both to the host countries and to the US government, is just over half the rate on their US profits.[59] Martin Sullivan of the highly respected journal *Tax Notes* says that the current US tax system "does create a significant tax incentive for U.S. corporations to move production and jobs to low-tax countries."[60]

The tax laws that created such a skewed arrangement have a long history, dating back to the creation of the first corporate income tax in 1913, and there have been only occasional and not very successful attempts to close some of the loopholes, especially in the early 1960s. No country that was seriously competing for investment would have allowed such a regime to continue with so few changes, but in the

United States it has endured for more than a century. While in theory American corporations are taxed on their income no matter where it is earned in the world (a "worldwide" system), in practice it is possible for companies to avoid US taxes on almost all their foreign income. The smaller of the two incentives is the foreign tax credit. In an effort to avoid double taxation of foreign investments, the US government permits a direct credit for taxes paid to foreign governments. In other words, if a US company had already paid the 33 percent corporate tax on profits made in France, it would owe almost no additional tax to the US government. That 33 percent tax could be directly credited against the US corporate tax rate of 35 percent. If the tax was less than 35 percent—say the 12.5 percent charged in Ireland—then the company would owe the US government the difference between the two rates. In a handful of countries, the corporate tax rates charged by the host government are high enough to fully offset the US tax that would have been owed. But in most they are not—on average, US corporations pay less than 16 percent in total taxes on their foreign profits.[61] Nonetheless, while the labor unions tried to reduce the foreign tax credit in the Burke-Hartke legislation, it is generally noncontroversial. In the absence of such a credit, US companies would face an enormous disadvantage investing abroad because they would be taxed twice on the same income.

The bigger and more controversial incentive is known as deferral. Under the theory that the corporate tax should only be levied on profits when they are distributed to shareholders, US-headquartered companies must pay US taxes on most foreign profits only if and when they are "repatriated" to the United States. In other words, if a US company earns money outside the territory of the United States and never brings it home, that company does not owe Uncle Sam a single dime, regardless of the tax rate in the foreign jurisdiction. The result is that big US companies like Apple and General Electric today mostly keep their foreign profits outside the United States to avoid having to pay US corporate tax; total US corporate profits parked offshore now total more than $2 trillion. With further clever tax planning of the sort that Apple, Starbucks, and other companies employ, the bulk of those profits can be "earned" in low-tax jurisdictions like Ireland or no-tax jurisdictions like Bermuda or the Cayman Islands. In Apple's case, according to the Senate investigation, 64 percent of the company's global pretax income (i.e., income earned outside the United States) was recorded in Ireland, even though only 4 percent of Apple's employees and 1 percent of its customers are in Ireland.[62] The losers, tax expert Dick Harvey argues, are US domestic companies with no overseas presence. He warns that in order to offset the tax disadvantage, "U.S. domestic companies may decide they need to move some of their operations offshore with the resulting loss in jobs and U.S. taxable income."[63]

The US government, recognizing the perverse incentives such a system creates, has tried at times to eliminate or reduce deferral. Douglas Dillon, President John F. Kennedy's secretary of treasury, famously said that deferral of taxes on foreign profits was "an interest-free loan from the U.S. Treasury, repayable at the option of the borrower."[64] Kennedy favored abolishing deferral entirely and proposed doing so in 1962. But he could not persuade Congress to go along and instead settled for a new and complex set of rules (known as Subpart F) designed to make it harder to shift profits to low-tax jurisdictions. The distorting effects of this system have grown year by year as opportunities for overseas investment have multiplied and more and more countries have slashed their tax rates in an effort to attract that investment. A growing number of large US corporations today report most of their profits outside the United States. The networking company Cisco, for example, booked a third of its profits offshore in the three years from 1998 to 2000; a decade later, 79 percent of its profits were reported outside the country. General Electric, which earned 39 percent of its profits abroad from 1998 to 2000, had more than doubled that to 82 percent a decade later.[65]

The US corporate tax code is a bit more generous to foreign companies investing in the United States. Foreign-headquartered companies are especially able to take advantage of the generous deduction for interest expenses allowed under US tax rules. In many cases, the US subsidiaries will borrow heavily from their foreign parent companies, and then deduct the interest payment on that debt from taxes owed to the US government. The George W. Bush administration in 2002 proposed a crackdown on this so-called earnings stripping to reduce the incentive for companies to relocate overseas, but it led to a fierce pushback from lobbyists for such blue-chip foreign companies as British Airways, Phillips, and Siemens.[66] The idea has been revived periodically during the Obama administration, causing the president of the Organization for International Investment, a lobby group for foreign-owned companies, to warn that such a move "could force companies to review their operations in the U.S."[67] Like the deferral rules, earnings stripping erodes the US tax base. But unlike the deferral rules, it at least provides an incentive for companies to invest in the United States. Nonetheless, the US share of total global direct foreign investment has dropped considerably over the past decade—from 37 percent in 2000 to 19 percent in 2013. Significantly, while much of that decline was due to the increasing attractiveness of China and other developing countries, the European share of investment actually grew slightly over the same period, to 34 percent of the global total.[68] About 6 million Americans work for foreign-owned firms in the United States, a number that has remained unchanged over the past decade.[69]

The US Congress has for many years been considering another round of tax reform, with particular attention to corporate tax. But overcoming corporate opposition has proved difficult. Dave Camp, who was Republican chairman of the tax-writing House Ways and Means committee, spent his last three years in the job producing a nearly one-thousand-page overhaul of the tax code that would, among other things, have lowered the corporate tax rate from 35 to 25 percent in an effort to improve the ability of the United States to compete for mobile investment. Bowing to long-standing demands from US multinational companies, his plan would have largely moved the United States from a worldwide corporate tax system to a "territorial" one in which US companies would be taxed on only a tiny fraction of their offshore earnings. While US companies have long lobbied for reducing the corporate tax rate and for a territorial tax system, to get there without blowing a bigger hole in the federal budget, Camp had to crack down on various tax breaks that benefit companies from manufacturers to investment banks.[70] He proposed a retroactive 8.75 percent tax on the $2 trillion of cash being held offshore by US companies and a smaller 3.75 tax on earnings that had already been reinvested abroad. The gains for companies were potentially large and penalties were small—President Obama, in contrast, has proposed lowering the corporate tax rate to 28 percent, while charging a onetime 14 percent tax on offshore earnings and a future 19 percent minimum tax on those earnings regardless of whether that are repatriated.[71] But within hours of its unveiling in February 2014, Camp's plan faced a chorus of opposition from US companies complaining that it would leave them worse off than the current system. House Republican leaders quickly reassured them that the plan had no chance of passing and becoming law.

WAGES, LABOR RIGHTS, AND INVESTMENT

In 2012, the Harvard Business School carried out a detailed survey of some ten thousand of its alumni, many of them now working in top corporate executive jobs. The survey was a first; rather than asking the executives generally about the "investment climate" in the United States and other countries, it tried to determine what factors were actually moving the money. The survey questioned business leaders about why they were, or were not, expanding their investments in the United States. In particular, it drilled down on some six hundred decisions in which companies had weighed whether to keep operations in the United States or to move abroad; in more than five hundred of those decisions, the United States had lost, primarily to China, India, Brazil, and Mexico. The reasons were varied—proximity to customers, faster-growing markets abroad, lower tax rates. But the most often cited reason—by 70 percent of the companies—was lower wages in the overseas markets where they were investing.[72] The result was not terribly surprising: according to Commerce Department statistics, the average overseas wages paid by US multinationals are less than half what they pay their employees in the United States.[73]

Rich country fears of low-wage import competition are hardly a new thing. The creation of the International Labor Organization (ILO) in 1919 at the urging of President Woodrow Wilson was intended to promote rising international labor standards and mitigate the potentially destructive effects of international economic competition. President Herbert Hoover campaigned in 1928 for higher tariffs to protect "industries which cannot now successfully compete with foreign producers because of lower foreign wages and a lower standard of living abroad."[74] Economists have long resisted the idea that low-wage competition is a problem for trade policy. They argue that trade itself will, over time, boost the wages in poorer countries. That has certainly been the case in China, for example, which attracted huge flows of foreign investment in the 1990s and 2000s to take advantage of its abundant, low-cost labor. And Chinese wages have been rising on average by 12 percent each year since 2001, eroding some of that cost advantage—though wages there are still less than a quarter of American levels.[75] Economists also point out that, historically at least, wages in any country have reflected the productivity of its workforce. As researchers for the International Monetary Fund (IMF) put it, "Important groups in the rich countries have long regarded low foreign wages and poor working conditions as a threat to their own workers' living standards and as a moral outrage. . . . From an economic point of view, these concerns are misplaced. Low foreign labor standards, like low wages, largely reflect low productivity and a low level of development rather than a form of unfair competition."[76]

The growing mobility of the multinational companies, however, has made that sanguine conclusion more problematic. The low productivity of poorly paid workers was largely a function of the low levels of investment in those economies and their low levels of technological sophistication. But the story has been a different one since the most advanced companies in the world began moving production to poorer countries. Harley Shaiken, a geographer at the University of California, Berkeley, has studied the productivity of Mexico's export sectors in the years before and after NAFTA. Mexico's overall productivity remained low even after NAFTA, he said, but in the sectors where American and other foreign companies were investing, the picture was quite different. One example: a US maker of automotive engines opened a Mexican plant in 1982 to complement its US operations; within two years the Mexican plant had achieved 85 percent of the performance of the US plant, and by 1990 its performance was nearly identical. The Mexican plant also output better quality than its US counterpart in four of the six years from 1986 to 1991.[77] The story was similar throughout the automotive sector; by the early 1990s Ford's assembly plant in Hermosillo was building some of the highest-quality cars in the world. But in the export sector overall, real wages for Mexican workers have fallen even as productivity has surged. Between the launch of NAFTA in 1994 and 2010, Mexican manufacturing productivity grew by 80 percent, but real hourly compensation including both wages and benefits fell by nearly 20 percent—in part due to the weakening of the peso.[78] US auto companies, not surprisingly, are accelerating their expansion in Mexico's auto sector, 70 percent of which is produced for the US market. The companies have announced $19 billion in new investments in just the past two years.[79] Mexico is now poised to overtake Japan and Canada as the largest exporter of cars to the United States.

Economists are far from agreed on the impacts of this sort of trade with lower-wage countries on wages and job opportunities for American workers. The consensus for a long time was that US trade with low-wage countries was too small to have any noticeable impact on US wages or jobs. But over the past two decades, that has changed. In the mid-1980s, imports from developing countries accounted for just a quarter of all US imports; today the figure is nearly 55 percent. Writing in 2008, Nobel Prize–winning economist Paul Krugman, whose own research in the 1990s had suggested that trade with developing countries had little impact on US wages and job opportunities, concluded, "It's no longer safe to assert that trade's impact on the income distribution in wealthy countries is fairly minor. There's a good case that it's big and getting bigger."[80]

In the face of such pressures, the effort to persuade or force developing countries to uphold higher labor standards emerged as a second-best option for the unions after their failure to block imports or penalize offshore investment through the Burke-Hartke bill. During the 1980s, the unions instead forged an alliance with religious and human rights activists who were concerned about the mistreatment of workers in developing countries. All agreed in principle that the United States should not trade with countries that jailed or murdered union organizers, employed children, or ignored workplace safety. And while acknowledging that lower wages were an appropriate comparative advantage for poorer countries, they believed that "lower labor costs should not result from the deliberate suppression of wages and working conditions below levels that workers' productivity should yield."[81] The new alliance found a sympathetic ear in the Democratic Congress and, after two years of negotiations, persuaded the Reagan administration to support the inclusion of labor standards in the Generalized System of Preferences (GSP). Under the GSP, created in President Nixon's 1974 Trade Act, the United States offers duty-free imports for many goods from developing countries as a way to encourage faster growth in those countries. The 1984 amendments required that in the future all GSP beneficiary countries must adhere to core ILO labor standards such as freedom of association, a prohibition on forced labor, and minimum standards for wages, working hours, and workplace health and safety.[82] Countries that violated these norms risked losing their preferential trade tariff benefits, which could drive away foreign investment.

Over the next three decades, the trade-labor linkage became the primary means by which the US labor unions tried to reduce the incentives for US companies to relocate overseas. Congress in 1985 added labor rights requirements for countries to be eligible for OPIC investment insurance and then expanded the language to other trade preference programs. The union-led coalition grew to include environmental groups, which feared that American standards on air and water pollution could be threatened if companies decamped for countries where such environmental rules were weak or left unenforced. In 1992, Democratic presidential candidate Bill Clinton, who was struggling to find a way to support NAFTA without losing his labor union backing, proposed adding binding obligations on both labor standards and environmental protection to the deal with Canada and Mexico. In a speech in Raleigh, North Carolina—a state that employed thousands of workers in two industries, textiles and furniture, that were facing unprecedented competition from low-wage countries—he offered "yes, but" support for the deal. He warned that "for a high wage country like ours, the blessings of more trade can be offset at least in part by the loss of income and jobs as more and more multinational corporations take advantage of their ability to move money, management and production away from a high wage country to a low wage country. We can also lose income because those companies who stay at home can use the threat of moving to depress wages, as many do today." He said that he would support NAFTA only if Mexico and Canada agreed to "supplemental" negotiations that would ensure that both labor and environmental laws were strictly enforced.

Since NAFTA, the US government has consistently used its trade agreements to try to strengthen labor and environmental standards in developing countries. While unable to persuade developing countries to support such a "social clause" in the WTO, the United States has insisted in every bilateral and regional deal that its trading partners accept provisions requiring better treatment of workers, with the threat of trade sanctions for countries that fail to comply. President Obama has said that the recent TPP agreement will be "the most progressive trade deal in history," one that includes strong and enforceable standards on labor and the environment—though the unions and environmental groups still remain almost unanimously opposed to the TPP. The coalition pressing for stronger labor standards has won other important victories. In response to the pressure, many multinational companies have agreed to corporate "codes of conduct," promising to boost wages and working conditions for employees in developing countries, and have invited independent monitors to keep an eye on them. Other international institutions, including the IMF and the World Bank, now consider workers' rights issues in their lending programs. And the United States has provided several hundred million dollars in foreign aid to its trading partners to help improve their compliance with labor standards.

But the track record of trade agreements in boosting labor standards has been mediocre. The effort has been most effective through the GSP, which is a unilateral trade preference program that the United States can turn off at will. But the trade agreements have so far had less impact. In order for the United States to levy sanctions for labor violations, the rules require lengthy investigations and negotiations that can drag a dispute out for many years. A 2014 study by the Government Accountability Office, the US government's internal watchdog, looked at five cases in which the United States agreed to investigate allegations of labor violations by its free trade partners. Only one of them, under the 2006 US trade agreement with Peru, has been successfully resolved—and since that case was closed, Peru has passed new laws that give a three-year grace period for companies to comply with health and safety regulations and sharply reduce the fines that could be levied against companies even if the violations continued.[83] Peru is a big exporter to the United States of clothing and agricultural products like asparagus and grapes. The country similarly has rolled back a host of environmental regulations, part of an effort "to create a more friendly environment, to reduce the impediments to investment," said Peru's minister of economy and finance.[84]

Another striking example is Guatemala. After World War II, Guatemala was a leader in Latin America in protecting labor rights; nearly a quarter of its workforce was unionized, and the country had minimum wage, social insurance, and health-coverage laws. But following the US-backed coup in 1954, the new military rulers undertook a long campaign to suppress the labor unions.[85] In 1988, US labor unions and their allies petitioned the US government to cut off GSP benefits to Guatemala, citing failures to enforce minimum wage and child-labor laws, dangerous health and safety hazards for workers, and a systematic campaign to crush union organizing. After three years of rejecting the requests, the US government finally launched an investigation in 1992. Fearing loss of their biggest export market, Guatemalan business leaders pressed the government to comply with US demands and eventually helped drive the president into exile. In 2006, however, Guatemala became part of the CAFTA with the United States, which requires countries to enforce ILO standards. Today, Guatemala has been called the "most dangerous country in the world for trade unionists" by the International Trade Union Confederation, and many of its labor laws are flouted by employers. In 2010 the Obama administration launched a labor rights enforcement case against Guatemala, threatening sanctions if the country did not address the problems, which include payment of workers well below minimum wage, firing and threatening of union organizers, and flouting of worker-safety laws. After a seven-year investigation, the United States lost the case in 2017, with the arbitration panel ruling that, while Guatemala had indeed failed to enforce its own labor laws effectively, the US had not demonstrated any adverse impacts on trade.[86]

Perhaps the most ambitious effort by the unions to seek action against weak labor standards abroad on the grounds of harm to US workers was launched by the AFL-CIO in 2004. Under Section 301 of the US Trade Act of 1988, Congress gave the president power to levy trade sanctions against any country that engages in "a persistent pattern of conduct" that violates the core ILO conventions in a manner that "burdens or restricts U.S. commerce." The provision had never before been tested, but in its lengthy submission to the US Trade Representative, the AFL-CIO argued that China's "egregious and systematic violation of workers' rights" had artificially held down Chinese labor costs at the expense of US workers. Such exploitation, the union group argued, "costs hundreds of thousands of U.S. manufacturing jobs and puts downward pressure on U.S. wages." The petition claimed that if China were to allow free collective bargaining, end the use of forced labor, and enforce its own laws on minimum wages and workplace health and safety, its manufacturing costs would rise between 10 and 77 percent, significantly reducing its competitive advantage over the United States. If accepted by the US government, the petition could have led to an epic confrontation between the United States and China over the rules for global economic competition. But a month after the petition was filed, the George W. Bush administration called a rare joint press conference, featuring not only US Trade Representative Robert Zoellick but also the secretaries of treasury, commerce, and labor, solely for the purpose of rejecting the unions' request for an investigation. "Accepting these petitions would take us down the path of economic isolationism," said Zoellick, "and that is a path we will not take."[87]

INVESTMENT: THE HOLE IN GLOBAL RULES

In 1974, as the debate over the multinational companies was still taking shape, Fred Bergsten penned a prescient article for *Foreign Affairs*. The companies, he argued, were eager to invest abroad to take advantage of more rapidly growing economies, lower labor costs, or both. Foreign countries too were growing increasingly adept at luring such investments. To attract the multinationals, many were offering not just a workforce at lower wages but also a generous array of inducements such as tax breaks, export subsidies, free land or other "location incentives," subsidized training of a local labor force, and prohibitions on strikes and other union activities. In turn, the companies were often required to transfer technology, purchase from local suppliers, and meet export requirements. While the companies chafed at the performance requirements, Bergsten wrote, "they may gain more from the incentives than they lose from the requirements." The real loser was the home country of those corporations—more often than not the United States. "Many 'U.S.-based' firms have become truly multinational and thus, quite logically and defensibly from their standpoints, pursue a set of interests which may not coincide closely with any of several concepts of U.S. national interests," he wrote. He called for the negotiation of international rules that would reduce the ability of governments to use tax subsidies and other measures that "artificially lure U.S. firms to invest abroad" and for restrictions on forced technology transfer or other performance requirements. "Traditionally," Bergsten wrote, "the United States has opposed policies which discriminated against foreign investors; now it increasingly finds its national interest threatened by policies which discriminate in favor of those firms." He feared that such policies would inevitably produce a backlash from the United States and other countries on the losing end. "For at stake is nothing less than the international division of production and the fruits thereof."[88]

Instead of fighting to attract and retain investment, however, US policy has reinforced the advantages of investing abroad through investment and trade agreements that protect the assets of US companies overseas. Those same agreements have been silent on the issue that concerned Bergsten—whether the increasing "inducements" offered by foreign governments would skew investment away from the United States. The US government (though not the states, as discussed in a later chapter) has been extremely slow to wake up to the growing international competition for investment. Indeed, the primary goal of US policy to this day continues to be opening foreign markets to US investment, with little or no concern for the ways in which those investments are solicited. The United States has long favored open investment rules that would allow US companies the same access to foreign markets that most foreign companies had to invest in the United States. From 1946 to 1968, the US government negotiated treaties of "friendship, commerce and navigation" with more than twenty countries in order to protect US investments. Since then, the United States has entered into bilateral investment treaties (BITs) with nearly fifty countries and insisted on strong investment protections in bilateral and regional trade agreements.

The rules have been broadly similar, aimed at ensuring that foreign investors are treated no less favorably than domestic ones, are protected against expropriation, and are free to move capital in and out of the host countries. The United States has also tried to eliminate, with varying degrees of success, the sort of "performance requirements" for companies that many governments began insisting on in the 1970s. The TPP chapter on investment, for example, would prohibit a long list of such measures, including export and domestic content targets and forced technology transfers.[89] The United States is currently in the midst of BIT negotiations with China, which has routinely imposed such performance requirements on foreign investors.

Most striking about these investment agreements, however, is not what is included but what has been left out. Neither the BITs nor the US trade agreements contain any restrictions on the sorts of investment subsidies or other inducements that can be offered by countries to attract and retain investments. As Kenneth Thomas has written, the agreements "are designed to protect investors rather than regulate incentives."[90] In other words, while countries are barred from using sticks against foreign investors, there are no limits on the number of carrots that may be offered. Not surprisingly, these investment inducements have run increasingly out of control. Israel offered $525 million to Intel in 2005 for a new semiconductor fabrication plant; Singapore and China later topped that to attract similar investments. Brazil's states have engaged in a growing and often self-destructive "fiscal war" to try to attract investment through tax breaks. In the Czech Republic, government investment incentives from 2010 to 2013 covered on average one-third of the capital expenditures of the projects undertaken by foreign investors—mostly auto companies such as Volkswagen, Toyota, and Hyundai.[91] The Czech incentives for investors include a tax holiday of up to ten years, training subsidies, discounted land, and even direct cash grants.[92] Even with its huge market and low-cost labor force offering a big magnet to investors, investment incentives in China have greatly sweetened the mix for foreign companies as well. Eager to attract investment to their own regions, state and local governments in China offer an array of incentives, particularly tax holidays and reductions in land prices. The central government in Beijing has at times tried to crack down on the practice, but it remains widespread.

To date, US efforts to address some of these investment distortions through international agreements have been rare and ineffective. The OECD's "Guidelines for Multinational Enterprises," which date back to the 1970s, say that companies should "refrain from seeking or accepting" exemptions from national rules regarding "environmental, health, safety, labor, taxation, financial incentives or other issues."[93] But the guidelines are "voluntary and not legally enforceable." The agreement on trade-related investment measures in the WTO has some provisions to discourage performance measures but is silent on investment inducements. More targeted efforts have been made to curb the tax-avoidance strategies of big companies. At the urging of the Clinton administration, the OECD in 1998 launched an initiative to "counter the distorting effects of harmful tax competition," which led to the creation of a blacklist of some three dozen countries deemed to be helping multinational companies avoid their tax obligations. The "name and shame" campaign was accompanied by threats from OECD countries to deny foreign tax credits and level other tax penalties against companies that used these tax havens. But the aggressive campaign did not outlive the administration. Under pressure from antitax conservatives, the George W. Bush administration withdrew its support. In a 2001 letter to his fellow G-7 finance ministers, Treasury Secretary Paul O'Neill wrote that the OECD was wrongly targeting low-tax countries that were simply trying to attract foreign investment: "Countries must be free to adopt tax policies that encourage investment and promote economic growth," he wrote. "We should not interfere in any other country's decision about how to structure its own tax system when that system does not serve as an obstacle to enforcing our own tax laws." Without US support, wrote tax analyst Martin Sullivan, the initiative "slowly dissolved into a series of toothless pronouncements, a mixture of cheerleading and scorekeeping that continues to this day."[94] More recently, the OECD, at the direction of ministers from the G-20 countries, launched the "base erosion and profit shifting" action plan. The goal is to persuade countries to voluntarily take steps that would reduce the incentives for multinational companies to shift their profits to low-tax jurisdictions. But the United States is opposed to many of the elements of that initiative, arguing that it discriminates against the overseas operations of US-headquartered companies.

Instead of fighting to curb investment inducements, the United States has become one of the world's worst offenders. Left to their own devices by the federal government and having few other tools to attract investment, US states and even cities have increasingly resorted to tax breaks and other subsidies to lure corporate investment. Many of the competitions are just among the states; Nevada, for example, recently persuaded the electric car company Tesla to locate its new $5 billion battery-manufacturing facility in the state after offering up $1.25 billion in tax breaks and other subsidies to beat out several neighboring states. The annual costs in lost tax revenues and other expenditures for US states run into the tens of billions of dollars. And the competition extends far beyond US borders. In 2006, for example, Advanced Micro Devices, which competes with companies such as IBM and NVIDIA in the global market for microchips, received a $1.2 billion subsidy from the state of New York to build a new fabrication plant north of Albany. The main competitors were the city of Dresden in Germany and several East Asian countries, led by Singapore.[95] In the 2000s Thyssen Krupp, the German steelmaker, considered offers from nearly a dozen different countries for a new steel plant, which promised twenty-seven hundred jobs, before finally settling on two US states, Alabama and Louisiana; Alabama won the competition with an $800 million incentive package.[96] It was not a good investment for the state or the company. Thyssen Krupp spent some $5 billion constructing the new plant, which provides steel to US automakers in southern states, and then sold it in 2013 to Indian Arcelor Mittal for just over $1.5 billion.[97]

THE ROAD NOT TAKEN: A MORE SENSIBLE APPROACH

A smarter US policy toward international investment in an increasingly competitive global economy would recognize at least three important goals. First, US-headquartered companies need the flexibility to invest internationally in order to maintain their profitability against overseas rivals doing the same. Significant government restrictions that harmed the ability of those companies to compete anywhere in the world would hurt both the companies and the US economy, thereby lowering living standards for Americans. If the restrictions were severe enough, it might cause those companies to leave the United States entirely and incorporate somewhere else. Second, and of equal importance, a sound policy would have aimed to encourage investment in the United States, whatever the head office location of the company doing the investing. To the greatest extent possible in line with other competing goals, policies on trade, currency, and taxes in particular would be tailored to make the United States a profitable place for companies to invest. Certainly, such an approach would try to ensure that companies paid no more in taxes for investing at home than they would if they invested outside the United States. And the government would actively solicit and promote investment in the United States, from both domestic and foreign-owned companies. Indeed, the extent to which the US government defended and promoted the interests of particular companies would be based not on the nationality of their headquarters, which is increasingly irrelevant, but on the commitment they showed by investing in the United States. By such a measure, Toyota and Siemens today are no less American companies than General Motors and Caterpillar.

Finally, to discourage what would come to be called the "race to the bottom," the United States would have led international efforts to create rules for competition over investment that reduce artificial distortions. This would have meant tackling predatory tax practices, curbing government investment subsidies, and promoting stronger labor and environmental standards in developing countries. These goals would have been tied to additional investment liberalization rather than being an afterthought. While looking back with hindsight is easy, it is possible to imagine that if the US government had consistently pursued these goals, the interests of US companies and their workers might not have diverged so sharply.

5

Helping the Losers

The Tragedy of Trade Adjustment Assistance

This issue on which the whole future of U.S. trade (and perhaps investment) policy may rest is how we decide, as a nation, to deal with the real dislocations to workers and firms caused by import competition. There are only two choices: to limit the imports themselves, or to help the dislocated workers and firms adjust to the new competition.

—C. Fred Bergsten, "The International Economy
and American Business," May 1973

On August 24, 1979, one of the most successful US makers of color television sets, Magnavox, closed a plant in Morristown, Tennessee, that made electronic components for four out of five of its US-made sets. The plant employed 575 people in a town of 20,000 in the northeast corner of the state, and its loss was a huge blow to the local economy. The employees applied to the federal government for help under a program known as trade adjustment assistance (TAA), which offered cash benefits, retraining, and relocation expense payment if needed to workers who lost their jobs as a result of import competition. The case seemed open and shut; imports of color television sets, mostly from Japan, had surged during the recession of 1973 to 1975 from 15 percent of the US color TV market to more than 35 percent. Then, in 1976 alone, Japanese color TV exports to the United States rose nearly 200 percent—a flood that even Japanese prime minister Yasuo Fukuda called a "torrential downpour"—and continued to grow in early 1977, when President Jimmy Carter negotiated an "orderly marketing arrangement" in which Japan agreed to restrain its exports a bit.[1] US TV makers could not compete with the "increasingly significant advantages from production activities in lower labor cost areas of the world," the employees argued in seeking government help. Due in part to the overvalued US dollar, production costs in Japan were about 20 percent less than in the United States.

107

Despite this surge in import competition, the Department of Labor rejected the request by the Morristown workers. For Americans making televisions, the rejection was not unusual. Between 1970 and 1973, following an earlier wave of rising Japanese imports and the relocation of US plants to Taiwan and Mexico, workers in the domestic US television industry had filed eleven petitions for assistance, more than in any sector except for shoes. All eleven were rejected. In turning down the request from the Morristown workers, the Labor Department said that Congress had only approved adjustment assistance for workers who lost their jobs directly as a result of rising imports of identical products. The Morristown plant made components, the government said, whereas the growing imports were finished, assembled TV sets. Three years later, even as Congress was considering amendments that would have extended such help to workers making parts, a US appeals court upheld the government's decision. The court wrote that, while there was little question that rising imports "accounted for an enormous displacement of American color television sales," the law was written in such a way that the Morristown workers were not eligible for assistance. "The result may appear harsh in this day of high unemployment and rising cost of living," the court wrote, "but the remedy for congressional policies that do not extend beyond lawful bonds is the legislature."[2]

The idea behind trade adjustment assistance was to help US workers harmed as a result of US government policies that opened the domestic American market to greater foreign competition. There was little question that the television industry was such a case. Japan's industry had first been built in the 1950s on borrowed US technology. The American firms RCA and General Electric (GE) had licensed their patents to Japanese producers in order to earn good profits in an otherwise closed market and were rewarded through the US tax code by the generous foreign tax credits and deferrals offered to US companies that invest offshore.[3] The strategy was highly profitable: by the late 1970s RCA was receiving $100 million in licensing fees from Japan.[4] The Kennedy Round of world trade negotiations had cut tariffs on imported picture tubes from 30 to 15 percent, and tariffs on components were lower still, with duties on receivers cut in half from 10 to 5 percent.[5] The emerging Japanese companies, such as Sanyo, Sony, and Toshiba, were in turn heavily subsidized and protected by their government, receiving direct government grants, long-term low-interest loans, and tax breaks tied to exports, all the while shielded in their home market by import quotas and restrictions on foreign direct investment. By the mid-1960s, the Japanese had developed small, lightweight black-and-white televisions that were selling well in the United States, capturing about 10 percent of the market. At the same time, US-owned companies including Zenith, RCA, GE, Sylvania, Motorola, and even Magnavox had started outsourcing production to take advantage of lower labor costs and generous government incentives. Both Mexico and Taiwan, following the advice of US consultants and academics, created low-tax, duty-free zones to attract such investment. By the early 1970s, imports of black-and-white sets made overseas in US-owned affiliates had captured more than half of the US market, and Japan controlled much of the rest. The little domestic production that remained involved assembling sets from foreign-made components. Domestic employment in the industry had fallen from a peak of more than sixty thousand in 1966 to fewer than forty thousand by the early 1970s, but none of those laid-off workers were deemed eligible for adjustment assistance, in part because much of the competition was coming from the offshore facilities of their own companies.[6]

Color television helped for a while. US companies had started making color sets in the early 1960s, and by the end of the decade those sales were far larger than those for black-and-white sets. But here too a familiar pattern played out. RCA had licensed its color technology to Japanese competitors in 1962, and by the late 1960s Japan had become a big exporter to the United States; exports of Japanese color TVs grew from 300,000 sets in 1967 to 1.5 million in 1970, more than 15 percent of the total market. Japanese companies then became the first to mass-produce solid-state TV sets, which were smaller and lighter because they were made with transistors rather than vacuum tubes. The first prototype for a solid-state TV had been developed by a US company, Motorola, in 1966, but the Japanese beat their US rivals in commercializing the technology. And the Japanese sets were generally of better quality; in the 1970s, the defect rate for Japanese-made TV sets was just 0.4 percent, ten times better than the 5 percent defect rate for US-made sets.[7] From 1973 to 1976, as imports of the new TVs surged, another twelve thousand US workers in the industry were let go. Even after President Carter's 1977 deal to stem the growth of Japanese imports, Zenith still laid off a quarter of its American workforce and moved more production to Mexico and Taiwan. The projected savings from the move was just $10 to $15 per set, but that small amount was the difference between profit and loss in an increasingly competitive market.[8]

While reeling from the surge in imports, Magnavox responded about as effectively as any US company. By the late 1970s, it had become the only one making both components and the finished sets in the United States. It consolidated operations in Greeneville, Tennessee, and expanded successfully in the 1980s by focusing on larger television sets for which shipping costs were higher and proximity to US customers was an advantage. At its peak in 1989 the company, which produced television sets under its own brand name and that of its parent company, Philips Consumer Electronics of the Netherlands, employed forty-six hundred Americans, about two thousand of them at the Greeneville plant, making it by far the town's biggest employer. By the mid-1980s, Philips was the largest color TV maker in the world, and the Dutch company, ironically, stuck longer with American production than any of its US-owned competitors. Like all the remaining US producers, Magnavox had become far more efficient in the intervening years, making more televisions with fewer workers to keep its costs competitive. In 1971, the average US production worker made about 150 TV sets in a year; by 1981 that had more than tripled to 560.[9]

But by the mid-1990s, following the passage of the North American Free Trade Agreement (NAFTA), the trickle of outsourcing to Mexico had become a flood. Most of the US companies that established "maquiladora" plants near the US border from the 1960s through the 1980s were making components for assembly in the

United States, in part to avoid import tariffs on the added value of the finished product. With the elimination of tariffs under NAFTA, much of the remaining US-based assembly also moved to Mexico. In 1997, Philips—which by then had slipped to seventh in the global rankings of color TV makers—sold the Greeneville plant, still with thirteen hundred employees, to two local Tennessee entrepreneurs, who continued to operate it under the name of Five Rivers Electronic Innovations.

By the late 1990s, the hemorrhaging seemed finally to have stopped. Five Rivers was still making TV sets under the Magnavox and Philips brands, as well as for Korean-based Samsung, and still employed about eight hundred workers. Between Five Rivers and six other domestic producers—the rest were all Japanese owned—American-based production still accounted for about 25 percent of the market for cathode-ray TVs, including both the traditional boxes and the new rear-projection models. While total US employment in the industry was now fewer than the four thousand that Philips alone had employed a decade earlier, it seemed a viable business. Five Rivers was increasingly focused on large televisions that were more expensive to ship from overseas. Mexico remained by far the biggest source of imports, supplying more than half the American market. But then the final shoe dropped. From 2001 to 2003, following China's admission to the World Trade Organization (WTO), imports of TV sets made in China grew from just 56,000 to 1.8 million, sold under new brands such as Apex as well as the established brands. It was a surge bigger than any since the Japanese competition in the 1970s. Though demand was still growing despite the US recession, big retailers like Walmart and Best Buy were slashing prices and demanding that their suppliers do the same. Despite lowering its own prices and further cutting its workforce, Five Rivers could not compete. It petitioned the Commerce Department to impose punitive duties on the Chinese producers for "dumping" televisions at less than the cost of production and won its case in 2004 when the US government slapped a 20 percent import tariff on Chinese televisions. But it was too little, too late. Later that year, Five Rivers applied for Chapter 11 bankruptcy protection, owing more than $25 million to its creditors. Revenues at the Greeneville plant had fallen from $300 million in 2002 to $65 million by 2004; Philips had cancelled one of the company's biggest contracts for HDTVs. In 2005, Five Rivers shut its doors for good, and the production equipment was sold at auction. For the next seven years, until a new start-up, Element Electronics, began making a few HDTVs in Michigan, not a single television set was made in the United States. After the shutdown, Five Rivers's remaining employees applied to the federal government for trade adjustment assistance. Unlike with the Morristown workers in 1979, their claim was approved by the government.

THE IDEA OF ADJUSTMENT ASSISTANCE

The program of "adjustment assistance" for workers who lost their jobs to import competition began with President John F. Kennedy. His signature trade legislation, the Trade Expansion Act of 1962, was a more ambitious version of authority that had been available to presidents since the mid-1930s, when Congress had renounced the protectionism of the infamous 1930 Smoot-Hawley Tariff Act and authorized President Franklin D. Roosevelt to negotiate with other nations on mutual tariff reductions. But the 1962 act contained one radical innovation. It proposed for the first time a trade adjustment assistance program aimed at helping both companies and workers harmed by import competition. Prior to the 1962 act, the federal government had only a single tool for aiding such workers or industries: temporary trade protection in the form of higher tariffs or quotas. Kennedy wanted another option, a means to continue trade liberalization while protecting American workers and companies from some of the negative consequences.

Kennedy was a committed free trader. Increasing imports would help US allies in Asia and Europe and keep them out of the Soviet orbit, he argued. At home, the tariff cuts would help the economy through lower-priced imports, which would benefit American consumers and force American companies to become more efficient, productive, and competitive. But imports would also likely hurt some sectors, driving companies out of business and forcing employees to scramble for new work. Those harmed were deserving, Kennedy argued, of government support. "When considerations of national policy make it desirable to avoid higher tariffs, those injured by that competition should not be required to bear the full brunt of the impact," Kennedy said in introducing the legislation. Under TAA, he proposed, industries lagging in the face of import competition would be eligible for government assistance, including tax breaks, technical assistance, and loans and loan guarantees for new investments that would help the company retool to meet the competition or to find other lines of business.[10] Similarly, workers who lost their jobs or faced significant reductions in working hours due to import competition would be eligible for income assistance and retraining. His proposal called for these workers to receive 65 percent of their wages for up to a year, vocational education or other retraining to develop "higher and different skills," and moving expense payment if they needed to relocate to find new employment. The goal, as suggested by the name, was not temporary income support but more lasting adjustment. The program, Kennedy insisted, "cannot be and will not be a subsidy program of government paternalism. It is instead a program to afford time for American initiative, American adaptability and American resiliency to assert themselves." The aim was "to strengthen the efficiency of our economy, not to protect inefficiencies."

The theory underlying Kennedy's trade adjustment assistance program was one long embraced by economists—that trade creates many winners but also some losers. In their classic model first published in 1933, Swedish economists Eli Heckscher and Bertil Ohlin had posited that, as a country moved from autarky to freer trade, overall national welfare would rise and consumption would increase due to falling prices as countries specialized in the production of goods in which they enjoyed an advantage. Later additions by American economists Wolfgang Stolper and Paul Samuelson, as well as others working with the same model, demonstrated that within any country, there would be winners and losers depending on the country's particular comparative advantage—its "abundant factors of production."[11] In a highly developed country like the United States, the main advantages were ample capital for investment and a highly educated and trained workforce (the United States was triply blessed because rich soil and a mild climate also gave it an advantage in agriculture). For developing countries, in contrast, or even for fairly wealthy countries that were not at the level of the United States, the primary advantage was lower-skilled, lower-wage labor. The theory suggested that as the US economy opened to the world, returns to capital were likely to increase, and higher-skilled Americans were likely to see their wages rise because markets would grow for capital-intensive and highly skilled sectors; lower-skilled Americans, however, were likely to see wages fall and work opportunities diminish because they could not compete with the many similarly skilled workers available in other countries who were paid much less. While wages for those workers in poorer countries would rise, there would be a long transition period—likely many decades—before their wages began to approach US levels. Despite these losses for some, the theory went, the total gains to the economy from freer trade far exceeded the losses to disadvantaged workers. The jobs and wages of lower-skilled Americans could be protected through higher tariffs but at a large cost to the overall economy. Therefore, rather than continuing to protect some industries through tariffs or quotas, which would reduce overall economic gains, the correct response, economists argued, was for the winners to "compensate" the losers through progressive taxation or subsidies or other forms of income transfer.

Pete Peterson, in his memo to President Richard Nixon, had embraced the same formula and recommended an acceleration of adjustment efforts. "A program to build on America's strengths by enhancing its international competitiveness cannot be indifferent to the fate of those industries, and especially those groups of workers, which are not meeting the demands of a truly competitive world economy," he wrote. "It is unreasonable to say that a liberal trade policy is in the interest of the entire country and then allow particular industries, workers, and communities to pay the whole price." He recommended that the US government set as a broad national policy the goal of "helping to facilitate the processes of economic and social change brought about by foreign competition." The adjustment program should encourage capital resources and workers to redeploy "from activities no longer economically viable to those that are." Assistance to displaced workers would have to be accelerated and in some cases even extended to whole communities. Peterson particularly stressed the need to bring organized labor on board. "Union support is critical to the program's success," he wrote. "Unions standing to lose membership through the retraining of their members for new crafts will have to be convinced that their workers will enjoy real benefits as a result."

The concept of adjustment assistance was in theory a significant advance over the economists' idea of compensation. Compensating the unemployed for not working, through welfare or disability programs or other schemes, might be a fair and reasonable way to redistribute the gains from trade but would produce no lasting benefits for the economy. In contrast, retraining workers in ways that provided them with new skills and moved them as quickly as possible back into the workforce would enhance the economy's competitiveness. In the 1960s and 1970s, as US integration into the global economy was accelerating, the idea of government assistance for workers harmed by global competition was embraced in theory by both Democratic and Republican administrations. Business went from being a skeptic in the 1960s to a supporter by the early 1970s. Fred Bergsten, Henry Kissinger's economic aide, had left the government in 1972 and headed up a Chamber of Commerce task force that in 1973 recommended a massive expansion of manpower training and other assistance in response to an increasingly competitive international economy. "Freer trade causes dislocation for a few in order to benefit all," Bergsten testified to the House Ways and Means Committee in 1973. "The personal hardships that result are often severe and must be alleviated. Those who are hurt by a policy that is thus pursued in the general interest should be compensated adequately for their losses, and the opportunity should be seized to enable them to increase their contribution to the national welfare." Donald Kendall, the chief executive of Pepsi and the chairman of the Emergency Committee for American Trade that was leading the fight against the Burke-Hartke bill, said, "It is inexcusable that instead of a national program of industrial adaptation that would allow the worker to retain pension and other rights, our economy offers only inadequate training or the dole. It is easy to understand why labor leaders call the present system of adjustment 'burial insurance.'"[12]

By 1972, when Kendall made those comments, organized labor had already moved from strong support for freer trade to deep skepticism, in part because adjustment assistance had failed to deliver on its promises. And when President Ronald Reagan came to office in 1981 on a promise to slash government spending, TAA was one of the first programs to be targeted. Payments to workers were reduced, eligibility time was cut, and the criteria tightened. While the budget for TAA has ebbed and flowed over the decades since—growing in particular as a result of the massive stimulus package approved by Congress following the 2008 financial crisis—TAA has never touched more than a fraction of the workers potentially eligible for assistance. In 2015, Democratic opponents of further trade agreements had become so frustrated that they voted to kill the TAA program in an effort to keep President Barack Obama from winning new trade-negotiating authority. While that vote was later reversed, it showed how deep the anger has become over the failure of the US government to offer more than token help for workers hurt by import competition.

The failure to help American workers adjust to the new scale and intensity of global competition is one of the bigger mistakes of US government economic policy in the last half century, one that has resulted in an enormous waste of human capacity and in eroding popular support for international trade and US engagement with the world. While many other countries have overhauled, refined, and expanded their labor market adjustment schemes, the basic structure of US federal programs remains unchanged since the creation of unemployment insurance (UI) in 1935 as part of the New Deal. That program was designed for an economy in which most unemployment was cyclical and the result of inadequate demand during temporary economic recessions; UI payments were supposed to bridge the gap for laid-off workers until the economy picked up and they were rehired by their former employers or others in the same industry. Unemployment insurance is a short-term income supplement, with no requirement that recipients retrain or upgrade their skills. Other federal job-training programs cover only a small fraction of dislocated workers, fewer than 10 percent. As both Kennedy and Nixon recognized, the challenge in an era of global competition was to redeploy workers from sectors that were uncompetitive internationally to ones that were more competitive. That required not just temporary compensation but new education and retraining to allow individuals to move into entirely new fields of work. Governments, companies, and labor unions would all need to be engaged in promoting that transition.

Other advanced countries have done far more to help their citizens adjust to competition. Denmark spends more than 2 percent of its GDP helping unemployed workers back into the workforce, about twenty times as much as the United States. France and Germany spend five times as much. Every other major economy spends at least twice what the United States does. Denmark's worker-retraining program is available throughout a career; if a factory closes, government counselors meet with each unemployed worker, drawing up individual plans for retraining and following up to make sure the goals are met. In 2006 the *Wall Street Journal* reported on the closing of a Danish meatpacking plant that had five hundred workers. Within ten months, all but sixty were back at work, one as a golf course landscaping apprentice, another as a math and science teacher.[13] Such interventions are unheard of in the United States.

The result has been pretty much what the economists would have predicted: lower-skilled American workers have seen a steady fall in both employment and wages since the early 1970s. Many of those who lost jobs in uncompetitive industries were unable to find new work at all. A 1986 task force set up by the secretary of labor looked at the plight of nearly 11 million workers who had lost their jobs as a result of plant closures in the previous five years, during the height of Japanese import competition. The findings were grim. One-third were either still unemployed in 1986 or had dropped out of the workforce entirely. Of those who found new jobs, the average loss in earnings was 10 to 15 percent, while nearly 30 percent of blue-collar workers took wage cuts of 25 percent or more.[14] Help for these workers, from either governments or companies, was "spotty and narrowly focused," the task force reported.

Two decades later, when another round of mass layoffs followed a surge in Chinese imports, the result was little different. A landmark series of studies by economists David Autor, Gordon Hanson, and David Dorn looked at the impact of Chinese competition in US communities that were competing most directly with Chinese imports, such as San Jose, California, Providence, Rhode Island, Manchester, New Hampshire, and a raft of southern cities, including Raleigh, North Carolina. They examined the effects of import competition over a fifteen-year period, from 1992 to 2007, during which Chinese imports to the United States were growing very rapidly (and prior to the 2008–2009 recession caused by the financial crisis). From 2000 to 2007, imports from all low-wage countries rose from 15 to 28 percent of total US imports, with China accounting for almost all of the growth.[15] The findings were striking: employees in the most trade-exposed industries suffered much higher unemployment and loss of earnings than those in less exposed industries. "The effects are very concentrated and very visible locally," said Autor. "People drop out of the labor force and the data strongly suggest that it takes some people a long time to get back on their feet, if they do at all." The effects are also long-lasting. "Labor market adjustment to trade shocks is stunningly slow," Autor, Hanson, and Dorn wrote in a separate paper, "with local labor-force participation rates remaining depressed and local unemployment rates remaining elevated for a full decade or more after a shock commences."[16] Trade adjustment assistance did little to help; instead, nearly 10 percent of unemployed workers applied for and received Social Security disability payments, under which injured workers can receive early retirement and Medicare benefits if they persuade a doctor that they are unable to go back to work. Few of those ever return to the workforce, instead collecting benefits until they die. In the US regions most exposed to Chinese competition, the authors found, the increase in per capita Social Security disability payments was thirty times as large as TAA payments. The total costs of these government benefits were so high as to negate much of the broader economic gains coming from lower-cost imports. But instead of using government money to help people back to work, Washington and the states are paying people to stay out of the workforce, at huge cost to the overall economy. "We do not have a good set of policies at present for helping workers adjust to trade or, for that matter, to any kind of technological change," said Autor. "We could have much better adjustment assistance—programs that are less fragmented, and less stingy." Such programs, he said, should be "directed toward helping people reintegrate into the labor market and acquire skills, rather than helping them exit the labor market."[17]

THE RISE AND FALL OF TAA: A BRIEF HISTORY

The trade adjustment assistance program could have been the innovative centerpiece of a US strategy for adapting to the competitive pressures of globalization. As a form of compensation for the losers of globalization, the idea has always made tremendous sense. A welfare system that pays people who are not working, while necessary certainly for the disabled or for single mothers with small children to raise, is expensive and wasteful; adjustment assistance, in contrast, is intended as a transitional mechanism that helps individuals return to the workforce and again contribute to the economy. Unemployment insurance that simply replaces income following the loss of a job does nothing for those who lack the skills to find new work. Broader programs offering retraining to all displaced workers regardless of cause would be even better—and presidents from Nixon to Obama have proposed them—but this has proved too ambitious for a country like the United States with its suspicion of a large federal government role. Targeted assistance to the losers in import competition, however, can easily be justified by the broader benefits, both economic and political, that come from trade liberalization. And yet it has not been possible to sustain even such a modest program. Over its life, fewer than one-tenth of the workers potentially eligible for trade adjustment assistance have received it, and most efforts to expand the program have faced significant political opposition. Throughout its history the program has enjoyed little support from either side of the debate. Businesses and free market conservatives supported TAA only reluctantly—it was the "hold your nose" price to win the congressional votes needed to allow presidents to continue pursuing trade agreements. Labor unions and most Democrats have long wanted a broader program to aid all unemployed workers and would prefer to slow or halt trade liberalization. But they have reluctantly accepted TAA as a "better than nothing" alternative. The result is that political support for trade adjustment, even half a century on, is minimal.

From its inception under President John F. Kennedy, trade adjustment assistance had one primary purpose: to encourage freer US trade with the rest of the world. Helping US workers and affected industries to rebound from import competition would, the argument went, allow the government to maintain political support for trade liberalization. The idea was first proposed by David J. McDonald, president of the United Steelworkers union and a member of the Dwight D. Eisenhower–era Randall Commission. The commission, formally known as the Commission on Foreign Economic Policy, was established by Congress and President Eisenhower as part of the 1953 agreement extending the president's trade-negotiating authority. The commission, composed equally of presidential and congressional appointees, was directed to make recommendations on US trade and international economic policy. It was chaired by Curtis Randall, chairman of Inland Steel; the vice chairman was Lamar Fleming Jr., a Texas cotton merchant, and it included several other business leaders, as well as five congressman and five senators, including Prescott Bush of Connecticut, whose son and grandson would become the forty-first and forty-third presidents, respectively. McDonald was the lone union representative. Unlike later generations of union leaders, McDonald was an enthusiastic proponent of freer trade. Over the opposition of the business executives on the commission, for example, he called for an end to the Buy American Act, which favored US over foreign companies in securing government contracts. And he urged US leadership in reducing tariff barriers even as the commission majority concluded, "Free trade is not possible under the conditions facing the United States today." McDonald believed that freer trade was indeed possible but was unlikely to be achieved without a mechanism for facilitating "adjustment" for workers and some industries that would be harmed by import competition.

As an alternative to protectionism through tariffs and quotas, he urged his fellow commissioners to support a new adjustment program. For workers displaced by cheaper imports, he wanted not just unemployment compensation but also job training and relocation expenses. Addressing objections to singling out a particular group of workers for special treatment, he argued, "Unemployment caused by government action, such as in the lowering of tariffs, should be of particular concern to the government." Affected firms should also be eligible for technical and financial assistance to help diversify or move into new lines of business, should get favorable consideration for government contracts, and should be permitted to accelerate tax write-offs on new investment. Help should be available to affected communities as well. If a plant was closed because of import competition, for example, the town or city should be eligible for funding and assistance to help it attract new job-creating investment.

The proposal was summarily rejected by every one of his fellow commissioners, most of them business executives, who argued that workers and industries would simply have to adapt with minimal government assistance.[18] Workers who lost a job due to import competition, they pointed out, were no worse off than those displaced by "technological change, alteration in consumer preferences, exhaustion of a mineral resource, new inventions, new taxes or many other causes." And since the government was not proposing to aid all those workers, singling out trade-displaced workers was unfair. The majority wrote, "No matter how great our sympathy may be for the problems of a displaced worker, or those of a business with a shrinking volume, this is but one phase of a much broader problem." Eisenhower sided with the majority.

Kennedy

While McDonald's proposal was dismissed by the commission, it was picked up by others who would ultimately prove to have more influence. John F. Kennedy, then the junior senator from Massachusetts, liked the idea and introduced it as a stand-alone bill, the Trade Adjustment Act of 1954. And with his Democratic colleague Hubert Humphrey, he tried unsuccessfully to add it to the 1958 bill extending President Eisenhower's trade-negotiating authority.[19] As an internationalist and ardent cold warrior, Kennedy believed in lowering US trade barriers to encourage imports from friendly nations in Asia and Europe. The Soviet Union and China, he warned, had signed some two hundred preferential trade arrangements in a strategy to "encircle and divide the free world," and the United States had to respond. But, at the same time, Kennedy needed the political support of the labor unions and of import-competing industries in his home state of Massachusetts that were worried about rising imports. Trade adjustment assistance was a happy marriage of the two goals; it became part of the Democratic Party platform in the 1960 election and the centerpiece of his proposal for new trade-negotiating authority.[20]

This time around, there was less opposition. The National Association of Manufacturers, which in the early 1960s was still the leading lobby for protection of American industry against imports, objected that a government-run adjustment program "seems to imply that there is something wrong with the operation of the free market."[21] Echoing the majority on the Randall Commission, the NAM argued that workers displaced by trade deserved no special consideration over other unemployed workers. House Republicans and some conservative Democrats objected strongly to a special program for trade-displaced workers and unsuccessfully demanded a separate vote on TAA.[22] But business, seeing the potential gains from opening new export markets, was mostly willing to go along. The American Bankers Association said TAA was an economically efficient way to transfer labor and capital to more competitive firms and industries, as did the US Council of the International Chamber of Commerce, though both warned against propping up "obsolete businesses." The final bill passed with nearly 300 votes in the House and by 78–8 in the Senate. In a triumphalist editorial on the eve of the Senate vote headlined "Protectionism Has Had Its Day," the *New York Times* wrote, "The provision of adjustment assistance, however, will cushion the shock. But it is not to be a permanent subsidy, nor will it protect the inefficient. On the contrary, it is aimed at increasing the competitiveness of industry and enhancing the technical skills of labor. In the long run, this will contribute to trade expansion."

The unions were not entirely happy with Kennedy's proposal: the retraining period was too short, they argued, and the benefits too low; government loan guarantees for affected business should be larger and interest rates lower. But in the end the American Federation of Labor and Congress of Industrial Organizations (AFL-CIO) endorsed the trade bill, arguing that the marriage of trade liberalization and adjustment assistance would expand exports, safeguard companies and workers hurt by import competition, and strengthen the economy by boosting the efficiency and productivity of business. It was the last time the AFL-CIO would ever support a major piece of trade legislation.

From Johnson to Nixon

The unions, while supporting TAA, had been wary throughout the process. But even the most pessimistic union leader could not have predicted what actually happened. As written, the bill specified that adjustment assistance would only be available to workers who suffered "serious injury," generally meaning job loss, caused primarily by a rise in imports that was a direct result of tariff cuts made by the US government. And the decisions on those narrow criteria were made by a Tariff Commission whose appointees were generally less than sympathetic to workers. The result was that from 1962 to 1968, not a single US worker or firm received benefits under TAA; twenty-five petitions were denied in all by the commission.[23] Even after the program was expanded under President Lyndon B. Johnson in 1965 to cover the US-Canada Auto Pact and tweaked in 1968 to ease eligibility requirements, just forty-six thousand workers received benefits over the next five years, and almost none of those actually entered retraining programs. From 1969 to 1975, just thirty-five hundred workers received any retraining at all.[24] The unions were apoplectic—the director of research for the AFL-CIO wrote as early as 1963 that growing protectionism "is a real and serious threat that is aggravated by the Tariff Commission's rigidly technical interpretation of the Trade Expansion Act."[25] By 1965, support for TAA was eroding among lawmakers and labor unions alike, with AFL-CIO leaders warning that the Tariff Commission's stringency in rejecting applications for adjustment assistance threatened to "[fan] latent protectionist sentiment in local unions."[26]

While less sympathetic to the labor unions than Democrat Johnson, Richard Nixon had, if anything, an even broader vision of how adjustment assistance should operate. In keeping with Republican critics like Prescott Bush, he opposed the idea of special aid to trade-displaced workers. It was too hard to determine, he believed, whether the job losses had been caused by imports, technology, consumer changes, or simply incompetent management. But unlike the earlier Republicans, Nixon favored a far broader government role. In 1969, he proposed to Congress the most ambitious overhaul of the unemployment insurance program ever contemplated, which would have created for the first time a comprehensive national standard. The original UI program enacted under President Roosevelt in 1935 had recommended that unemployed workers receive at least 50 percent of their wage in government benefits. But since individual states determined the actual eligibility, level, and duration of benefits, few were that generous. Nixon wanted a single national standard that would be imposed by Washington on states that refused to comply. Many states also actively discouraged any sort of retraining, instead preferring to save money by forcing the unemployed to return to work as quickly as possible at whatever meager wages they could find. In 1960, all but three states denied unemployment benefits to workers who chose to seek retraining, and even by the end of the decade, half the states still did so. These states, Nixon said, "continue to discourage retraining by denying benefits to workers in such programs on the theory that they are not 'available for work.' On the contrary, the workers are trying to keep themselves available by learning new techniques and technologies, and government should certainly stop penalizing them for doing something that government, business and labor all want to encourage."[27] Finally, in periods of high unemployment—then defined as anything above 4.5 percent for three consecutive months—he wanted automatic extensions of benefits, ending the practice of extending benefits only through special congressional legislation that sometimes came long after benefits had expired or not at all. To pay for the new benefits, he proposed doubling the wage cap beyond which employees were exempt from the Social Security tax, in effect calling for a new tax on higher-income earners.

The Democratic Congress, however, rejected the broader approach. Nixon's UI proposal faced heavy opposition from state insurance commissioners who feared a federal takeover of the program, as well as from business, which opposed the higher taxes needed to pay for more generous benefits.[28] Unions were also opposed because of a provision that would deny UI benefits to striking workers. All lobbied Congress heavily to reject Nixon's program. In the wake of that failure, Nixon continued to push for his more comprehensive approach, and in the trade bill he presented to Congress in 1973, he urged a substantial reduction in TAA. Instead, Congress expanded the program significantly, with quiet but enthusiastic support from Nixon's

State Department and the economic agencies that favored trade liberalization and saw TAA as a necessary price for passage of the trade act.[29] The unions were divided. The AFL-CIO, wedded to the Burke-Hartke approach, insisted that no improvements to TAA would win their support for further trade liberalization. But the United Auto Workers supported the trade bill, and autoworkers would prove to be the major beneficiaries of the expanded program.

The Trade Act of 1974 ushered in changes that, for a brief period, came as close as they would ever come to the sort of program that David McDonald of the steelworkers' union had originally envisioned—though still with gaping loopholes of the sort that denied benefits to the five hundred Magnavox workers in Morristown, Tennessee. It eased the qualification requirements and raised benefits—employees no longer had to prove that they had been harmed by specific tariff cuts; they needed to show only that growing imports had "contributed importantly" to job losses. The benefits were increased to 70 percent of the worker's previous wage, or up to 80 percent including UI benefits. With the crisis in the US auto industry in the late 1970s, including the bankruptcy and bailout of Chrysler, TAA claims surged. The Department of Labor replaced the Tariff Commission as the certifying body, and it was far more generous in accepting petitions.[30] From 1975 to 1981, more than 1.3 million workers received TAA benefits, nearly 700,000 in the recession year of 1980 alone, including 500,000 auto workers.[31]

The cost was significant—nearly $4 billion between 1975 and 1981 compared with just $85 million between 1962 and 1975.[32] But while the cash benefits were far more generous, the promise of retraining still remained empty. Among all those TAA-eligible workers, only forty-three thousand, or just 4 percent, actually entered training programs. Fewer still, about fifty-two hundred, received job-search assistance, and only forty-four hundred got relocation payments to help move to another job. While workers were by law required to undergo retraining in order to receive the payments, successive administrations refused to enforce the provision and often failed to provide the promised retraining funds. A 1978 survey found that 78 percent of laid-off Chrysler workers wanted to be trained for different jobs, but almost none received that training.[33] The program was poorly administered as well. The federal government did little to alert workers to the benefits available, relying on state employment agencies to inform employees of their eligibility. As a result, many employees took months before applying for assistance. And the Labor Department was slow in processing petitions, unable to keep up with the crush of demand. Assessments at the time suggested that on average workers did not receive any government support until fourteen months after they had lost their jobs; more than half had returned to work before they even received their first payment.

Reagan

The growing costs and poor administration of TAA made it a fat target for critics of government spending. President Jimmy Carter had to amend his 1981 budget proposal to Congress just a month after he submitted it because growing TAA claims had added nearly $1 billion in unanticipated costs, swelling a government budget deficit that had approached $40 billion the previous year. The uproar over that disclosure killed a congressional amendment that would have extended TAA to cover parts suppliers like the Morristown workers.[34] Republicans called the program expensive, inefficient, and inequitable. President Ronald Reagan, in his first budget submission to Congress, targeted TAA as part of a broader crackdown on government spending. In his first major economic address to Congress in February 1981, he said, "We wind up paying greater benefits to those who lose their jobs because of foreign competition than we do to their friends and neighbors who are laid off due to domestic competition. Anyone must agree that this is unfair."[35] Reverting to UI-level payments for these workers would save about $1.5 billion per year. Reagan's opposition to TAA was bolstered by a January 1980 report by the General Accounting Office, the congressional watchdog that was supposed to sniff out waste and fraud in federal programs. The report found that nearly three-quarters of those eligible had used none of the retraining, job search, or relocation services, either because they were unaware they were available, didn't need them, or were unwilling to move to find a job.[36] Among recipients, nearly two-thirds had returned to their old jobs, suggesting that TAA had become simply a more generous UI program rather than a true adjustment program. A separate survey by Mathematica Policy Research in 1979 had found that TAA did little to encourage workers to move into new sectors; just 15 percent of recipients in its sample had switched to a new industry, and only 25 percent had switched to a new occupation.[37] The result was not entirely surprising since so few workers had entered training programs that might actually prepare them for another career, but it still became more ammunition against the program.

It was easy to conclude from the first big test of TAA that it had failed. Few workers received the promised retraining, and evidence of benefits for those who did was sparse. But instead of tweaking the program, the Reagan administration took an axe to it. Overall spending on the program was cut by nearly $3 billion from 1982 to 1984, in part by making TAA available only after employees had exhausted their UI benefits. And Congress tightened the eligibility criteria as well, so that the approval rate for TAA petitions, which had risen to a high of 81 percent in 1980, fell to just 14 percent in 1981.[38] By 1984, the program had shrunk dramatically, with only sixteen thousand workers receiving about $50 million in aid that year.[39] Reagan tried several more times to eliminate the program entirely, while Congress just barely kept it alive.

Clinton to Obama

By the 1990s, TAA had become inextricably linked with the president's trade-negotiating authority; with President Bill Clinton unable to persuade members of his own party to restore that authority following the ratification of NAFTA in 1993 and the creation of the WTO in 1994, there was no opportunity to revisit TAA. It was not until 2002, when President George W. Bush requested new fast-track

trade-negotiating authority, that Congress again expanded both eligibility and benefits. For the first time, addressing the issue that had deprived the Morristown workers
of any benefits, Congress said that workers who produced components for finished
goods would be covered if import competition was increasing for the finished products. The bill experimented for the first time with wage insurance, an idea that had
first been proposed in the mid-1980s to top up the wages of those who were forced
to move from highly paid manufacturing work to lower-wage jobs.[40] And it again
extended the term of benefits for up to two years for workers enrolled in retraining.
The 2002 trade bill also established a health coverage tax credit covering 65 percent
of a displaced worker's monthly health insurance premiums.[41] The expansion of the
program and growing import competition from China in the 2000s produced a
significant increase in eligibility. In 2002, more than 235,000 workers were covered,
compared with fewer than 100,000 in 2000.[42] A higher percentage of the workers
eligible for TAA, nearly half, were actually using the program, and the majority of
those were enrolling in job retraining.

Finally, President Obama's stimulus package, formally known as the American
Recovery and Reinvestment Act of 2009, restored TAA to a scale and level of generosity not seen since the late 1970s. In the face of a crippling recession, it expanded
the health coverage tax credit, provided an additional twenty-six weeks of trade-
readjustment allowance payments (up to 2.5 years) for those enrolled in full-time
training, and increased payments for job-search costs and relocation allowances.
Between March 2009 and May 2011, when unemployment rates rose to levels not
seen since the recession of the early 1980s, more than 500,000 workers applied for
benefits, and 80 percent of the petitions, covering 450,000 workers, were approved.
And in a strong sign of how global competition had changed, twice as many workers
were covered because they lost their jobs due to outsourcing rather than to import
competition.[43] Funding for training also doubled for 2009 and 2010, and about half
of those eligible enrolled in retraining.[44]

Like Nixon before him, Obama also pushed for a larger overhaul of unemployment insurance. In place of TAA, he aimed to create a comprehensive displaced-
worker program that would offer TAA-type benefits to all workers. Included would
be seventy-eight additional weeks of income support for all workers enrolled in a
training program, which, added to the traditional twenty-six weeks of UI, would
mean a full two years of support. Individuals would also be eligible for a $1,250
job-search allowance and a $1,250 relocation expense allowance. Those choosing to
retrain in certain high-growth, high-demand occupations like computers or health
care would receive an additional $8,000 voucher. And for workers over fifty, wage
insurance would top up payments if they were forced to accept a lower-paying job.
The administration estimated the program would help about 1 million workers
each year, at a cost of about $4 billion annually. Congress has never taken up that
proposal. Instead, House Republicans have called for workforce-training programs
to be cut across the board by about 30 percent.

COULD ADJUSTMENT ASSISTANCE HAVE WORKED?

On May 20, 1983, Ford closed an auto assembly plant just northeast of San Jose, California, that employed more than twenty-four hundred workers making the smaller Ford Escorts. The Escort had been Ford's desperate response to imports of smaller, fuel-efficient Japanese cars following the oil price shocks of the 1970s. In just three years, from 1978 to 1980, US auto production had plummeted from 9 million vehicles to just 6.5 million; Ford's market share in the United States fell from 24 to 16.6 percent. While the San Jose plant was among the company's most productive, Ford's sales in California especially had taken a beating; Japanese imports had captured half of the California auto market and 70 percent of the small car market. In early 1982, the plant was targeted for closure.

What followed was an experiment that experts in labor market programs said could have become a model for the country. Under its agreement with the United Auto Workers, Ford had agreed to give six months advance notice of any plant closing. The announcement was made on November 18, 1982. Nearly all the workers were eligible for TAA benefits that would allow for up to two years of income support, and the company had agreed to pay for health insurance throughout that period. Before the plant had even closed, the company and union had paid for educational assessments for all of the workers to see whether they would need basic remedial education in English or reading or could move directly to vocational retraining. Thirty-seven percent of the workforce had less than eleven years of schooling, 41 percent had completed high school, and 27 percent had done some post–high school education or training. More than 500 employees took the basic adult education courses that were offered at the plant during the first five months of 1983, and about 160 completed their high school equivalence. Vocational courses in personal computers, welding, auto mechanics, upholstery, forklift operation, and other skills were also launched at the plant and continued after its closure; more than 2,100 workers participated, with 750 taking intensive, full-time vocational training.

When assessed two years later, the results did not suggest that retraining had been transformative, but it had clearly made a significant difference. Nearly 17 percent of the workers were still unemployed, and on average those with new jobs had taken about a 20 percent pay cut. The new careers were many and varied: salesman, microwave technician, plumber, welder, machine operator, truck driver. Notably, some 25 percent of former Ford workers had managed to find jobs in the emerging high-technology industries in Silicon Valley, exactly the sort of transition from lower- to higher-growth industries that labor market adjustment programs are supposed to facilitate. Older workers, those in their fifties and above, faced a harder time finding new jobs. There was no question, however, that the retraining programs had helped considerably. The most striking statistic was that, of the workers who had enrolled in retraining, only 14 percent were unemployed as of 1985, and the number was just 10 percent for those who had received vocational training; among those who had not participated in any of the programs, 33 percent were still without a job nearly three years later.[45]

The Ford experience in California was a big influence on a task force convened by President Reagan's secretary of labor in 1986 to look into the experiences of some 10.8 million workers who had lost jobs due to plant closings or other events "suggesting that the job losses would be permanent." During the 1981–1982 recession, it found, more than half of layoffs were permanent, significantly more than during previous recessions in the early 1960s and early 1970s. And even though the economy was growing strongly again by 1986 and creating jobs in record numbers, those workers faced huge hurdles in finding their way back into the labor market. The task force called for a new national public effort, at a cost of about $900 million per year, "to provide an early and rapid response to the needs of workers permanently displaced from employment." Reagan rejected the scheme.

Other efforts to create a more ambitious trade adjustment program have largely been stymied as well. More than fifty years after the program was first created by President Kennedy, there is neither political consensus nor substantive agreement on how to help American workers adjust to the profound impacts of the country's growing integration into the global economy. Worker training continues to be an ideological target for conservative critics. The Heritage Foundation says that TAA "provides overly generous benefits for a small fraction of laid-off workers" and does little to help them find better jobs.[46] The Cato Institute, which also advocates abolishing the program, argues, "The very existence of trade adjustment assistance perpetuates the myth that freeing trade creates special 'victims' who deserve special programs simply because of the reason for their unemployment."[47] Most congressional Republicans remain opposed to the program to this day and would kill it if they could.

Adjustment assistance is not an easy sell. Even under the best of economic circumstances, observed labor leader Sol Chaikin as American industrial jobs were disappearing in the early 1980s, "occupational adaptability is far from perfect." Given the enormous variation of education and skills, he wrote, "fitting people into job slots is a complex and frequently disheartening exercise, especially when an industry or substantial fraction of it is phased out of existence."[48] In other words, if the steel plant closes and the only other jobs in town are for nurses at the hospital, then the prospects for unemployed steelworkers are pretty grim whether retraining is available or not. Proponents of TAA are also hampered by the lack of data on the program's effectiveness. Astonishingly, when the program was created, Congress did not require any ongoing assessments of the labor market outcomes of those enrolled. In other words, did TAA participants fare any better than other workers who lost their jobs for nontrade reasons? It is only in recent years that the government has begun doing ongoing evaluations of the outcomes of those enrolled in the program. Under a Department of Labor contract, Mathematica Policy Research took detailed samples of TAA recipients from 2004 to 2008, comparing their outcomes to a comparable group of laid-off workers who did not receive the same assistance (though they may have been eligible for unemployment insurance and other government retraining programs). The results were not definitive; those in TAA retraining lost significant earnings in the first two years, most likely because they were in retraining programs. Even at the end of the four-year evaluation period, TAA participants were earning slightly less than those in the control group. But given the four-year window for the research, it is impossible to know whether the retraining will pay off in higher earnings in the medium or long term.

Other studies have suggested that retraining does help, but the obstacles are formidable. TAA recipients on average tend to be older and more difficult to reemploy. Many had been working in unionized sectors, so their odds of finding work at comparable wages are much smaller, particularly as the unionized share of the workforce continues to shrink. And much of the job loss in manufacturing, in particular, has been concentrated in smaller towns and cities where there are few other opportunities for work. Retraining for new jobs often requires moving to where those new jobs are, and Americans for a variety of reasons are becoming less rather than more mobile.

Federal government retraining programs are hardly a model. There has never been a national scheme for workforce development; instead there is a fragmented mix of national and state-level training schemes operating with a range of mandates. Most other advanced countries do better. The United States spends just 0.1 percent of GDP on "active labor market policies"—those designed to move the unemployed back into better jobs—which is seven times less than the average Organization for Economic Cooperation and Development (OECD) country. The OECD has found that most European countries, as well as Canada and Australia, have training systems that are "more comprehensive and stable" than those in the United States.[49]

A better model would involve both companies and labor unions, as was the case at the Ford plant. But business has been not much help. One of the consistent findings from the research is that on-the-job training is far more cost-effective than any form of outside training; this is no great surprise because instead of being trained for jobs that labor economists predict will be in demand, individuals train for real jobs at real companies. Yet in the past decade, according to the Labor Department, programs that combine on-the-job training with classroom education have fallen by 40 percent. Many companies don't want to pay the financial costs for training, hoping the government will do it for them or fearing that the employees they train will be lured away by competitors.[50] Yet US companies today complain bitterly that they are unable to find the skilled workers they need and then blame the educational system. While large business organizations like the Chamber of Commerce and the Business Roundtable continue to support TAA, it is only as a side payment to win congressional support for further trade liberalization.

Still, there seems little question that retraining could make a significant difference to at least some displaced workers. Jobs in the so-called middle-skill segment—requiring some sort of community college or vocational degree—are forecast to grow over the next decade faster than low-skilled jobs and nearly as fast as those requiring a full college education.[51] With a little bit of help, many of those losing their jobs to trade competition could attain those credentials.

THE BROKEN PROMISE

Trade adjustment held out the promise of being an American solution to the challenge of helping workers face up to growing global competition. The more generous European unemployment programs, which are available to all workers, coupled with work rules that make it difficult for employers to fire workers, have their own unintended consequences. France has struggled with high unemployment, especially high youth unemployment, for decades. Germany overhauled its unemployment insurance programs during the 2000s to make them less generous in an effort to push the unemployed back to work. The European example that is perhaps most relevant to the United States is Denmark. There, job protections are weak, much like in the United States, but significant financial support and retraining are quickly available for all workers who lose their jobs. Unemployment benefits cover up to 60 percent of lost income for as long as four years, but the unemployed are not left to idle and collect benefits. Instead, the government works closely with companies and labor unions to train individuals for jobs that are in demand; unemployed workers are required to enroll in retraining and job-search programs to retain their benefits. Despite such generous aid for the unemployed, the jobless rate in Denmark over the past decade has been consistently lower than in the United States. Even in the midst of the deep recession of 2010, some 70 percent of unemployed Danes said they were confident of finding new jobs. But Denmark is not the United States, of course. It is a much smaller country with a much higher tolerance for taxation; labor unions represent almost 70 percent of Danish workers, compared with just 11 percent in the United States. It is hard to imagine such a scheme taking hold here.

Adjustment assistance for workers facing rising import competition was conceived as a more modest, achievable aim for a country making the difficult transition from relative autarky to deeper integration in a highly competitive global economy. A successful program might have at least forestalled, if perhaps not entirely prevented, the labor unions from turning against free trade. And it could have helped millions of American workers manage the wrenching transition from the old economy to the new. Its failure to do any of these is one of the great tragedies in America's efforts to build a more competitive economy with widely shared benefits. Fred Bergsten had written in 1973 that the nation had only two choices in confronting the disruptions caused by rising import competition: limit imports or help dislocated firms and workers adjust to the new competition. Unfortunately the United States made a third choice: it remained open to imports and did little or nothing to aid those harmed by the new competition.

6

Tiger Moms and Failing Schools

Competitive Challenges at Home

Amy Chua was a student of international economic competition before she became the infamous tiger mother. In her 2007 book *Day of Empire*, the Yale law professor wrote a rich historical study of how the most successful nations, from ancient Rome to the modern United States, had prospered by opening their doors to immigration and successfully assimilating the best and brightest from many countries. But she was little known until she made the issue personal. The *Battle Hymn of the Tiger Mother*, her story about raising her two half-Chinese daughters, is a witty account, filled with considerable self-parody, chronicling her not always triumphant battles to cultivate uber-successful children. Following an excerpt in the *Wall Street Journal* under the provocative headline "Why Chinese Mothers Are Superior," the book touched off a national debate—with some excoriating Chua as an abusive parent, while others worried that perhaps she was actually onto something. Published in 2011, after a decade in which China's trade advantages over the United States had continued to grow while the US economy stagnated, her arguments about the superiority of Chinese over Western parents, said Britain's *Guardian*, fed into growing "insecurity about a rising China and the slide of the west."[1] *Slate* magazine wrote that Chua "has clearly tapped into deep-seated anxieties among American parents and educators about the country's children increasingly slipping behind their counterparts in the rising economic giants of the East."[2] In the *Washington Post*, columnist Alexandra Petri wrote, "The Tiger Mother Debate has exploded nationwide not simply because it's about parenting . . . but because it's about competitive, cross-cultural parenting. We want our kids to compete—so long as they win."[3] She quoted former Pennsylvania governor Ed Rendell, who was furious that a scheduled December 2010 football game between the Philadelphia Eagles and Minnesota Vikings had been called off due to snow: "We've become a nation of wusses," Rendell said. "The Chinese are kicking our butt in everything. If this was in China, do you think the Chinese would have called off the game? People would have been marching down to the stadium. They would have walked, and they would have been doing calculus on the way down." In his campaign for the presidency in 2016, real estate mogul Donald Trump lamented, "We don't win anymore. We lose to China. We lose to Mexico, both in trade and at the border. We lose to everybody."[4]

"Excellence demands competition," President Ronald Reagan said. "Without a race there can be no champion, no records broken, no excellence—in education or any other walk of life."[5] The virtue of competition has long been a staple for presidents trying to sell the country on deeper economic ties with the rest of the world. Bill Clinton, challenging his party during the debate over the North American Free Trade Agreement (NAFTA), had insisted that the United States must "compete, not retreat" from the trade challenges it faced. Two decades later, President Barack Obama used virtually the same language to drum up congressional support for the Trans-Pacific Partnership trade deal. "We're not going to be able to isolate ourselves from world markets," he said in a speech at the Oregon headquarters of Nike. "We've got to be in there and compete."

But how prepared are Americans to succeed in that competition? In 1983, when concerns over Japan's growing export success were at their peak, a blue-ribbon panel convened by the National Academy of Sciences (NAS) issued a report titled *A Nation at Risk* that shocked the country by warning that American students were falling behind their peers in the rest of the world. Mass education, more than any other single government policy, had helped propel the United States to world leadership by providing the human capital to build and man the most sophisticated industries in the world. By the mid-nineteenth century, the United States had a higher percentage of its children in school than any country; in 1960, nearly 70 percent of its young people graduated from high school, far more than any other nation. But the NAS panel said those distinctions were all in the past: "Our once unchallenged preeminence in commerce, industry, science, and technological innovation is being overtaken by competitors throughout the world," it warned. "The educational foundations of our society are presently being eroded by a rising tide of mediocrity that threatens our very future as a nation and a people. What was unimaginable a generation ago has begun to occur—others are matching and surpassing our educational attainments." While critics later charged, with some merit, that the report was overly alarmist, it sold more than half a million copies and led the *New York Times* to declare that it had put the education issue "to the forefront of political debate with an urgency not felt since the Soviet satellite shook American confidence in public schools in 1957."[6]

Two decades later, this time under the shadow of a rising China, the NAS convened a similar group to examine US performance in science and technology. In that 2005 report, *Rising above the Gathering Storm*, the committee of scientists, engineers, and business leaders chaired by former Lockheed-Martin chief executive Norman Augustine said it was "deeply concerned that the scientific and technical building blocks of our economic leadership are eroding at a time when many other nations are gathering strength." The report continued, "A substantial portion of our workforce finds itself in direct competition for jobs with lower-wage workers around the globe, and leading-edge scientific and engineering work is being accomplished in many parts of the world." In order to maintain its prosperity in such a world, "the United States must compete by optimizing its knowledge-based resources, particularly in science and technology, and by sustaining the most fertile environment for new and revitalized industries and the well-paying jobs they bring. We have already seen that capital, factories, and laboratories readily move wherever they are thought to have the greatest promise of return."[7]

While it is sometimes hard to separate legitimate concerns from self-interested hype, there has been a growing chorus of critics arguing that the United States has fallen far short in preparing itself for international economic competition. The American Society of Civil Engineers (ASCE) gives the United States a D+ for the condition of its basic infrastructure, including roads, dams, bridges, and ports.[8] The Business Roundtable, which represents large multinational companies, says that US policies do more to discourage highly skilled immigration than those of any other wealthy country except for Japan.[9] While the United States continues to be the most fertile country in the world for innovation, the federal government's chronic budget deficit—fueled by a combination of low taxes and the high costs of the military and health and safety net programs for senior citizens—has left less money for investments in research and technology that could boost future economic growth.

Pete Peterson, in his memo to Richard Nixon in 1971, had told the president that the ability of the United States to succeed in a more competitive global economy would depend above all else on its actions at home. Better trade rules would open new markets, and a more reasonably priced dollar would help US exports. Without changes to international rules and more responsible behavior by other countries, it was going to be difficult for the United States to compete internationally regardless of what it did at home. But a fairer, more balanced international system was only part of the answer. Unless the United States took steps to improve the competitiveness of its own economy by boosting productivity, educating its workforce, and leading in research and innovation, then it would continue to lose ground. "It is important to emphasize that development of those competitive strengths depends mainly *on our own efforts* rather than the actions of other countries," he wrote, highlighting the phrase. "A strong foreign economic policy for the United States begins in a strong domestic economy." Raising living standards for Americans, he argued, "depends on more new investment in plant and equipment, more growth in research and development and more progress in training appropriate talent and manpower, particularly in the new skills U.S. workers will require as our society moves increasingly to more industrial sophistication and services."[10] The goal should be "to *increase* our competitiveness, our productivity and, in general, enlarge the areas of comparative advantage vis-à-vis the rest of the world." Achieving that goal would require, he said, "conscious and deliberate steps to make our economy more competitive with those abroad." Peterson did not suggest the United States should slavishly follow the example of other countries. For all his admiration of Japan's success, for example, he argued that a US strategy for improving its competitiveness "[did] not mean adopting the system of Japan or any other particular country." But it did require, he argued, some sort of coherent national strategy. The United States would need to pursue its own "long-range economic and technological objectives" designed to strengthen its competitiveness.

A NATIONAL COMPETITIVENESS STRATEGY

The idea of a national "competitiveness strategy" is a controversial one in the United States. As a recent National Research Council report put it, "The United States is one of the few industrialized countries whose policymakers have traditionally not thought strategically about the composition of the nation's economy."[11] To many critics, any such effort smacks of government direction of the economy, "picking winners and losers" instead of letting the market decide outcomes. While the US government played a big role in the nineteenth and much of the twentieth centuries in supporting American industries by building or subsidizing critical infrastructure such as roads and rail, promoting technological innovation, and expanding access to education, many today question whether government can perform even those basic functions effectively. The debate over picking winners and losers has always been something of a phony one. The US government has long favored some industries over others, though generally for reasons other than economic competition. US agriculture has been heavily subsidized in the name of a safe and reliable food supply and the well-being of rural communities, the aircraft and computer industries were nurtured to strengthen national defense, the auto companies have been rescued several times to prevent massive job losses, and big banks and smaller savings and loan companies have been bailed out by taxpayer dollars to avoid panic in financial markets. But much of the government's intervention has been ad hoc, without a clear vision of the sort that Peterson advocated. And there has been strong resistance to changing that pattern.

The idea that the United States needed a national strategy to bolster its global economic competitiveness began to gain serious attention in the early 1980s, as imports from Japan surged and US manufacturing stalled, and it has continued to shape public policy debates since then. The competitiveness agenda was given its biggest push, ironically, by President Reagan, who was staunchly opposed to the idea that the United States needed such a strategy. By the mid-1980s, a broad group of business and political leaders had begun to coalesce into what Kent Hughes has called "a competitiveness movement." And by the end of that decade, the goal of bolstering US economic competitiveness had become a staple of American political rhetoric. In 1987, incoming Democratic House Speaker Jim Wright of Texas declared that competitiveness was "the dominant economic issue of the remaining years of the 20th century. Failure to deal with this crisis . . . could doom future generations of Americans to a steadily declining standard of living and eventual status as poor inhabitants of a once-rich land."[12] Robert Reich, a future secretary of labor under President Clinton, wrote that the idea of competitiveness "has become America's great national Rorschach test. It's an ink blot on which we discern our highest hopes and worst fears. . . . The idea that we are no longer competitive in world markets has caused a collective slow burn, and everyone seems ready to do something about it."[13] And Richard Gephardt, the House Democratic leader, warned, "The sharp increase in global competition is the single greatest economic challenge to face the country since the Great Depression. If we do not meet and master that challenge, we will not be able to meet our obligations at home or our commitments abroad."[14]

At times, support for "competitiveness" has shaded over into trade protectionism, but even the advocates of protection have mostly agreed that restraining imports is at best a temporary measure to allow companies and workers to retool to better meet the foreign competition. "Instead of turning away from global competition," Hughes wrote, "the competitiveness strategy focused on the need for public policies and private practices that would make American institutions, companies and workers competitive on the world stage."[15] They sought a virtuous circle—greater government support for research, for example, would lead to innovations and breakthroughs that would boost US exports and generate the profits to finance the next wave of innovations. A world-class infrastructure of roads, rail lines, and airports would ensure that US products moved quickly to global markets. Improved education, worker training, and liberal high-skilled immigration would build the scientific and engineering workforce to man these sophisticated companies. While some industries, such as semiconductors or renewable energy, might need special attention because they were the building blocks for future innovations, the idea was not to create a national industrial policy in which the government tried to identify and support certain sectors. Instead, the role of government should be to help build what Harvard Business School professors Michael Porter and Jan Rivkin have called the "business commons" that would allow companies and their employees to flourish in the United States—educating and training a skilled workforce, financing public infrastructure, and supporting basic scientific research.[16]

The idea of competitiveness has proved to be a compelling one. There are few political leaders today who do not at least give lip service to the notion that the United States needs to become a more competitive economy. Presidents from both parties have embraced the idea, though with varying degrees of enthusiasm. In 1992, then Arkansas governor Bill Clinton campaigned in support of a comprehensive national competitiveness strategy.[17] President George W. Bush became a champion of education reform and backed what he called an American Competitiveness Initiative (ACI), a ten-year plan to double federal spending on basic scientific research and train tens of thousands of new science and math teachers. Under his watch, Congress passed the America Competes Act, which aimed at boosting investment in basic research, encouraging students to pursue science and engineering careers, and promoting commercially relevant innovation. In his 2011 State of the Union address, President Obama urged Congress to unite around a plan to "win the future" by investing in new technologies that would help the United States keep its economic lead over China, India, and other rising powers. "We need to out-innovate, out-educate and out-build the rest of the world," he said. "We have to make America the best place on earth to do business."[18] He created a Council on Jobs and Competitiveness, stacked with A-list chief executives and experts to advise the White House on how to "ensure the competitiveness of the United States," and launched a slew of new efforts to promote advanced manufacturing in the United States.

The result of these efforts is, at best, incomplete. The good news is that, after falling as low as seventh in the annual ranking by the World Economic Forum (WEF) of the world's most competitive economies, the United States has climbed back up into a tie for third with Germany and Japan, primarily as a result of its growing lead in innovation. Only the small countries of Switzerland and Singapore came out higher in the overall rankings.[19] The WEF rankings, which are based on surveys of business executives, look almost exclusively at how well a nation's companies are competing, and many US companies are doing very well. Yet, on the measures that look at whether Americans as individuals are developing the capabilities to prosper in the global economy, the results are more troubling. In the year that Amy Chua's book extolling the virtues of Chinese parenting was published, international student test results showed that students from Shanghai, the only city tested in China, were besting their peers in every other country in all three of the core areas: math, reading, and science. American students tested thirty-sixth in math (between Lithuania and the Slovak Republic), twenty-eighth in science (between Denmark and Lithuania), and twenty-fourth in reading (between Denmark and the United Kingdom).[20] US high school graduation rates were the highest in the world a generation ago but have since fallen behind many other countries, including not only leaders such as Japan, Canada, and South Korea but nearly every western European country as well. While other countries were moving forward, "we simply flat-lined," Education Secretary Arne Duncan told the Council on Foreign Relations in 2010. "We stagnated, we lost our way, and others literally passed us by."[21] Education reform has made some significant strides in improving standards and accountability, and high school graduation rates are rising. But US students remain far behind their peers in the best-performing countries, and reform efforts continue to face state and local opposition. US investment in basic infrastructure such as roads, bridges, rail lines, and ports has declined precipitously, with the United States slipping from fifth in the world in overall infrastructure quality in 2002 to sixteenth a decade later.[22] Efforts to boost spending have floundered in the face of Republican opposition to new taxes or borrowing. US spending on basic research is also falling, and while corporate research and development (R&D) has filled some of the gap, companies tend to focus on projects that offer near-term returns for shareholders rather than on future breakthrough technologies with broader societal benefits. Partisan battles over federal priorities have made it impossible to overhaul badly outdated and dysfunctional policies on corporate taxes, entitlement spending, and immigration.

While both Republicans and Democrats talk about the importance of making the US economy more competitive, they have had very different notions of what is required, and those differences have not narrowed over the past three decades. Most Republicans since Reagan have embraced a version of free market conservatism that focuses primarily on reducing costs to business by cutting regulations, shrinking government, lowering taxes, and weakening labor unions. The concerns of small businesses, most of which are not competing internationally, have outsized influence in the GOP. Most Democrats want a more active government role in raising American living standards, including mandates for employers to provide health care and raise minimum wages, and they want higher taxes to boost federal spending for job training and infrastructure. More often than not, the differences between the parties have produced a stalemate. There have even been steps backward. The US Export-Import Bank, which was created by President Franklin D. Roosevelt in 1934 to support US exports to developing countries, was forced by Congress to stop making new loans for several months in 2015 in the face of criticisms from House Republicans that it amounted to "corporate welfare" for a handful of large companies like Boeing and Caterpillar. Every other major exporting country has similar export credit agencies to help their companies sell to developing world customers; China does five times as much business as the Export-Import Bank.[23]

And unfortunately, even the big companies that should be the strongest advocates for such competition-driven reforms no longer care as much as they once did about improving the business environment inside the United States. Thomas Friedman and Michael Mandelbaum argue that American business has increasingly "dropped out of the national debate" over how to strengthen competitiveness. Historically, they wrote, big companies could be counted on to lobby in Washington "not just on behalf of their own businesses but more broadly for better education, infrastructure, immigration, free trade and rules to promote constructive risk-taking." But increasingly "business leaders are less and less interested in the whole pie and more and more interested in their own slice."[24] The reality is that most of the big companies have other options. If the United States is failing to graduate enough scientists and engineers to fill corporate research labs, so be it; they can move R&D to Singapore or India instead.

Finally, many of the challenges facing the United States, while far from insurmountable, are genuinely difficult. Education reform, for example, involves not just the fifty states that control most of the funding but also thousands of semiautonomous local school districts and hundreds of teacher-education programs, not to mention the students and their parents. And nearly a quarter of the nation's K–12 schools are privately run, enrolling more than 10 percent of all students. Even with the most determined efforts, changes in such a system are likely to come slowly and in fits and starts. To take another example, investments in basic research make long-term sense, but the payoffs are unclear and the time horizons uncertain, making such spending harder to protect against competing priorities at a time when budget deficits remain high and politicians are opposed to tax increases. Infrastructure spending seems easy to defend, especially when borrowing is so cheap, but competing local priorities and pork barrel politics mean that the money often goes to the wrong places. The shadow of the infamous "Bridge to Nowhere" in Alaska—a proposed $400 million project to connect fifty residents of a tiny island to the mainland—remains.

More than three decades since the idea of bolstering "competitiveness" became part of the national agenda, the federal government's response has been sporadic, inconsistent, and mostly ineffective. The fear that the United States might be losing its competitive edge launched a national debate that continues to this day over the quality and effectiveness of key American institutions, from education to science to government. But there has been at best modest progress in addressing these challenges. The failure of the competitiveness movement to produce better results may just be part of the broader dysfunction of current American politics, which has left many hard issues unaddressed. But it also reflects the particular challenges that the United States has faced in moving from a largely self-sufficient economy to one that is much more deeply integrated into the global economy. For most other advanced countries, the need to compete internationally has long been ingrained. For the United States, it is a much more recent challenge. While the United States is far more trade exposed than it used to be, it is still much less trade dependent than all of its major competitors except for Japan, which imports so little. The competitiveness movement's core claim—that sweeping policy changes must be made to improve American success in global markets—therefore carries less weight than in most other countries in which overall prosperity depends more heavily on trade.

The result is that, while there has certainly been progress, Pete Peterson's vision of a "competitiveness strategy" that would help the United States stay on top in a new era of global competition remains unrealized. Competitiveness seems entrenched as a staple of national political rhetoric, but the accomplishments have fallen far short of the promises.

THE COMPETITIVENESS MOVEMENT—TWO STEPS FORWARD AND ONE BACK

It began with a tennis match in the spring of 1983. Edwin Harper, President Reagan's top advisor for domestic policy, had been invited to speak to the Business Council, a group of about a hundred of the nation's leading chief executives. Before joining the Reagan White House, Harper had been a vice president at Emerson Electric, which was founded in St. Louis in 1890 and nearly a century later had grown into the largest US maker of fans, power tools, and other electrical appliances. By the time Harper went to Washington, however, the company was reeling. Competitors from Japan and Taiwan were undercutting its prices by as much as 30 percent and quickly eroding its market share. Emerson had reacted aggressively to stop the slide, moving more than three thousand jobs to Mexico and other low-wage countries and closing a fifth of its 250 US factories.[25] Harper's doubles opponent that day was John Young, chief executive of Hewlett-Packard, the oldest of the Silicon Valley companies that was becoming a major force in the emerging business of personal computers. While Hewlett-Packard was doing far better than Emerson at the time, Young feared the trends he was seeing, in particular the growing dominance of Japan and other countries in the consumer electronics business. Even in high-technology sectors like semiconductors, airplanes, and telecommunications equipment, the United States had been losing market share to Japan and Europe. On the sidelines of the Business Council meeting, the two—both lifelong Republicans—began talking.[26]

Edwin Harper's boss was not especially sympathetic to the idea that the United States had a competitiveness problem. In February 1983, even as the US trade deficit was hitting record levels and US unemployment had topped out at a post–World War II high of nearly 11 percent, President Reagan's Council of Economic Advisers had concluded that there was little to worry about. "Much of the concern about long-run competitiveness is based on misperceptions," they wrote in the annual Economic Report to the President. While the rising dollar had created a temporary challenge, "the overall performance of the United States . . . does not suggest a problem of competitiveness."[27] The president's advisors opposed any sort of targeted interventions to address the challenges facing specific sectors. But if Reagan's impulse was to do nothing, the politics dictated otherwise. Republicans had lost twenty-four seats in the November 1982 congressional election, and the president's own popularity had fallen to a low of 35 percent. Democrats in Congress were increasingly calling for some kind of national industrial policy, modeled loosely after best practices in Japan and Germany. Reagan's advisors suggested a delaying tactic—appoint a commission to study the problem. Harper picked up the phone and called John Young, and in June 1983 Reagan appointed Young to chair the President's Commission on Industrial Competitiveness.

Its report, delivered eighteen months later, was a watershed in Washington's thinking about the problem of competitiveness. The commission was composed primarily of business leaders and academics and, at Young's insistence, included two union representatives as well. Directed by Harvard Business School's Michael Porter, regarded as the nation's leading thinker on competitiveness, it framed the issue as one not just of corporate competition but of American living standards. It was not enough, the report argued, for US-based companies to do better in facing growing overseas competition; they had to do so in a way that also left most Americans better off. The commission defined competitiveness as "the degree to which a nation can, under free and fair market conditions, produce goods and services that meet the test of international markets while at the same time maintaining or expanding the real incomes of its citizens." The last clause was crucial; the challenge, the commission wrote, "is to maintain a high standard of living in an increasingly competitive world environment."[28] By those standards, the report made clear, it was certainly no "misperception" that the US economy faced a long-term competitive challenge. It identified five trends that added up to a "declining ability to compete": productivity growth that had lagged behind major competitors, stagnation in real hourly wages, falling profits in the manufacturing sectors, record trade deficits, and declining global market share in the very high-technology industries where the United States ought to have a competitive advantage.

The commission's recommendations honed in on four issues: technology and innovation, the availability of capital for investment, education and human resources, and international trade. The four were tightly linked. Technology, Young argued, was the strongest US advantage in global economic competition and should be nurtured through government support for R&D to help universities and companies both develop and commercialize the latest innovations. Following new breakthroughs, the availability of capital at low cost would allow entrepreneurs to launch new companies and expand existing ones. Improvements in education and training would produce the scientific and engineering leaders and the skilled workers to man those new industries. And finally, a fair trading environment would help US companies sell those new products and services on world markets. Young rejected the criticism that his prescriptions would somehow increase the government's role in the economy. Instead, he said, "The commission did not identify any new roles for government. Rather what it tried to make clear is the fact that government has not effectively performed the legitimate roles it already has. Government is responsible for creating an environment within which American business can effectively compete. That basic goal has not been achieved."[29] The commission proposed a series of reforms, including the creation of new cabinet-level departments of trade, science, and technology.

Young's nod to the antigovernment sentiments of the Reagan White House was not enough, however, to win the president's support for his recommendations. When he and Porter briefed the president and his cabinet in early February 1985, the reception was desultory. Reagan had won reelection in a landslide, and the economy was roaring back to life, growing by more than 7 percent in 1984, the strongest showing since the late 1950s. Secretary of State George Shultz, the former treasury secretary and Office of Management and Budget director who had recruited Pete Peterson into Nixon's White House, asked a couple of questions, but the president and the rest of the cabinet were quiet. Reagan passed a note to Shultz: if the United States really has such problems, it said, why did every other country still want to be like America?[30] Reagan's chief of staff, Donald Regan, told Young there was no money in the budget for any of the programs proposed by the commission. And when the report was made public, it was released by the Commerce Department, not by the White House.[31] Young was frustrated but not discouraged by the poor reception. Instead of quietly accepting that his work would languish on some dusty shelf, he decided to press forward on his own. With seed money from the National Association of Manufacturers, he launched a new think tank, the Council on Competitiveness, to push the competitiveness agenda. The council's first president, Alan Magazine, said later that he originally had to preface his public speeches by pointing out that the Council on Competitiveness had nothing at all to do with the Olympics. Within a year, however, he had stopped doing that. "I'd test the audience and say, 'Tell me what issues we should be concerned about in terms of our competitiveness.' And the audience would throw out productivity, quality of products, and keep going and going."[32]

The Democratic Congress proved more fertile ground for Young's agenda than the Reagan White House. The Congressional Caucus on Competitiveness, which topped out at nearly two hundred members, was established in 1987 and called for "comprehensive solutions in such areas as research and development, worker retraining and intellectual property rights."[33] "We have met the enemy and it is us," said Max Baucus, then a new senator from Montana who helped found the caucus. "Even if we get the level playing field, we need to outhustle and outcompete other nations. . . . People are beginning to realize America has to make basic changes to compete in the world."[34] In 1988, Congress passed the Omnibus Trade and Competitiveness Act, and the name was no coincidence. The last major trade bill passed by Congress had been called simply the Trade Act of 1974; Kennedy's signature trade bill in 1962 had been called the Trade Expansion Act. But the 1988 act was aimed at linking US trade performance to reforms at home that would improve the ability of the United States to compete for investment and export shares. Alongside a host of trade-related measures and the effort discussed in chapter 3 to crack down on currency manipulation by US trading partners, the 1988 bill directed the Commerce Department to create a new Advanced Technology Program that would provide research grants to small businesses and seed money for joint research ventures. It launched the new National Institute of Standards and Technology to provide federal support for civilian technology research.[35] And it created—despite a veto threat from Reagan—a new advisory council, known as the Competitiveness Policy Council, charged with developing "a coherent, comprehensive, long-run competitiveness strategy." The new council included representatives of business, government, labor, and public interest groups, appointed equally by the president and the leadership of both parties in Congress, with the hope that a robust consensus could be built on how to respond to the challenge. The chairmanship of the new council went to an old hand: Pete Peterson's friend and former colleague Fred Bergsten. In his first report to Congress in 1992, Bergsten told the lawmakers, "There is plenty of blame to go around, over an extended period of time, for the decline in America's competitive position. The issue now is whether the country as a whole can come to understand the fundamental seriousness of the problem, devise remedies that will effectively meet the challenge, and create and sustain a domestic political consensus to do so."

But the council's efforts to lead the country toward a competitiveness strategy never really got off the ground. Even in Congress, where there was at least strong rhetorical support from some members, the political backing was extremely limited. While the labor unions stood to benefit, for example, from a big investment in infrastructure, the primary goal of the unions was to restrict imports from Japan. Big business was mildly supportive, but its larger priorities were cutting taxes and expanding trade through NAFTA and the Uruguay Round. The council's first big recommendation—that Congress require a "competitiveness impact statement" to assess the effects of major new legislation on US competitiveness—was never taken up in Congress. Republicans in particular were wary, seeing almost every proposal as an unnecessary federal government intrusion into the economy that ran counter to the Reagan narrative of government as the problem, not the solution. In 1991, for example, President George H. W. Bush dipped a toe in the water when he launched a new federal initiative to help beat the Japanese in developing the world's fastest supercomputer and announced a "national technology initiative" to promote commercial applications for new technologies developed in the national laboratories run by the Department of Energy. But Bush was worried about any program that could be tagged by conservative critics within his party as government meddling in the economy. Following the launch of the new technology schemes, one of his officials had pleaded with a *Time* magazine reporter not to call it "industrial policy." Just call it "George Bush's incredibly forward-looking applied research and development initiatives," he said.[36] In an effort to head off the Democrats, Bush had also created a new White House Council on Competitiveness shortly after taking office in 1989, chaired by his vice president, Dan Quayle. But the commission's mandate was narrow: "to review regulations issued by Federal agencies, with the aim of insuring that they do not unduly harm the competitiveness of American business." Critics charged that Quayle's council was a secret back door for industries seeking to undermine environmental and consumer protection laws. The link between overregulation and declining competitiveness was not without merit—paperwork burdens on US companies have roughly doubled over the past fifteen years, and the United States has not overhauled its regulatory system since the early 1980s.[37] But Quayle's group resisted any broader look at the competitiveness problem. Bush never successfully overcame the divisions in his own administration over how to approach the competitiveness issue. The president had signed legislation, for instance, that required the White House Office of Science and Technology Policy to develop a list of "critical technologies" that had "broad potential applicability across civilian and military sectors." But on the eve of its release, staff from Vice President Quayle's office strongly objected to any suggestion of a government role in identifying "winning" technologies, and the White House backed away from the report.[38]

Bill Clinton, as a southern governor working hard to attract investment to a poor state, probably understood better than any president before him the challenges of adjusting to a more competitive global economy. Clinton had asked John Young for a briefing in the summer of 1991 before he had even announced his run for the White House, and Young would later break with the Republicans and endorse Clinton over Bush in the 1992 election.[39] In a campaign speech he gave to textile workers in Raleigh, North Carolina, on the eve of the election, Clinton captured the challenges succinctly. A little more than a generation ago, the world was a far simpler place, he said. "American workers, consumers, and companies lived almost entirely within the American economy. . . . We could support free trade and open markets and still maintain a high wage economy because we were the only economic superpower, and our capacity to control our destiny was largely within our own hands." But that world had changed forever, he said. A Carolina textile worker was now competing with textile workers in Asia; "an 'American' car may have more foreign parts in it than a foreign car that happens to be made in an American assembly plant." The only way for the United States to prosper in such a world was to create advantages that could not easily be replicated by other countries: a highly skilled workforce, including not just university graduates but skilled technicians; more investments in research and development and in "moving ideas from the laboratory to the marketplace"; and controlling business costs, especially health care and energy. "The issue here," he said, "is not whether we should support free trade or open markets. Of course we should. The real issue is whether or not we will have a national economic strategy to make sure we will reap the benefits."[40]

But instead of advancing a comprehensive competitiveness strategy, much of Clinton's presidency was spent fighting off demands from the conservative wing of the Republican Party to dismantle the few federal programs that had been put in place in the late 1980s. Many of his signature initiatives faced crippling opposition. In the 1992 campaign, for example, Clinton had proposed a new 1.5 percent tax on the payrolls of all but the smallest companies to fund worker-training programs. Companies could have avoided the tax by setting up their own in-house training; government would set standards, and companies themselves would do the actual training.[41] But corporate opposition to the new tax was so fierce that Clinton dropped the idea right after taking office.[42] Clinton wanted a big increase in infrastructure spending—his campaign platform had called for creating a Rebuild America Fund seeded with a modest $20 billion in annual federal funding to encourage private and public pension funds to invest in toll roads and other infrastructure. But the proposal was denounced by some Republicans as a "raid on pension funds" and never got off the ground. Then following the Republicans' sweeping takeover of Congress in the 1994 midterm elections, the new Speaker of the House, Newt Gingrich, tried to dismantle several of the government agencies that Clinton and his supporters had counted on to lead the new push for greater competitiveness. Freshman representative Sam Brownback of Kansas, who would later become governor of his home state and lead a similar effort to slash government spending, called for the elimination of the US Departments of Education, Commerce, and Energy. Many of the new freshman class had business experience, but it was almost exclusively with small businesses that did not compete internationally.[43] Tom DeLay of Texas, who would go on to become House Republican leader, got his start as an exterminator in Houston and was so angered by a city ordinance that required him to obtain a business license that he won a seat in the Texas legislature and passed a law abolishing the licensing requirement.[44] Their concerns were primarily with reducing the costs of doing business at home, including taxes, regulations, and paperwork, not with supporting industries that could compete globally.[45] While the Gingrich Republicans did not succeed in eliminating any federal departments, they got one scalp—Bergsten's Competitiveness Policy Council. In 1996, the House cut off funding, and the council closed its doors.

Those same divisions have limited the ambitions of presidents since. President Obama came to office with a competitiveness agenda similar to Clinton's. He favored a massive overhaul of federal job-retraining programs, a new wage insurance scheme, and the creation of a national infrastructure bank that would use federal dollars to leverage private-sector investment in roads, rails, and sewer systems. But like Clinton, he mostly ran into a solid wall of Republican opposition. The Tea Party Republicans elected in 2010 were heirs to the Gingrich class of 1994 and included many small businessmen and libertarians who were strongly opposed to any policies that smacked of an expanded government role in the economy. Instead Obama moved forward with smaller initiatives of his own using executive authority, but with limited congressional support. In particular, the administration focused on promoting "advanced manufacturing" aimed at boosting information technology, biotechnology, robotics, and other cutting-edge sectors and subsidized new initiatives in clean energy. The president faced some opposition even among his own supporters. For example, in his 2011 State of the Union address, he called for tax breaks to encourage manufacturing companies to invest and expand in the United States, but his own recently departed chair of the Council of Economic Advisers, Christina Romer, penned a *New York Times* article denouncing the proposal for favoring one sector over another.[46]

EDUCATION, INFRASTRUCTURE, AND INNOVATION: THE FOUNDATIONS OF COMPETITIVENESS

Three of the core issues for the competitiveness movement—education, infrastructure, and innovation—demonstrate the challenges the United States has faced in trying to reorient its domestic institutions to better meet international competition. Proposals for reform in each have had largely the same goal: improving the ability of US-based businesses to thrive in international markets while also raising the living standards of Americans. All three are aimed at boosting the productivity of American companies, ensuring that the United States will be in the forefront of new technological breakthroughs, and creating the higher-paying jobs that should accompany that success. Yet despite a strong political consensus on those goals, the progress has remained modest.

Education

Over the past four decades, the link between education and success in the job market has grown ever tighter. Good jobs have all but vanished for those without advanced educations. Since 1970, real earnings for the median male worker with no more than a high school education have fallen by nearly half. Men who fail to complete high school are doing even worse, making less than half as much as they did in 1970, in part because nearly one-quarter are no longer working at all.[47] Even college-educated men have seen few pay increases in the last generation, but at least they have held their ground. Women have done better, with college-educated women seeing big salary increases in the 1990s, though for women too wages have been flat for the past decade.[48] Over the course of his or her lifetime, an American with a bachelor's degree will earn about $1 million more than those with just a high school diploma, while an associate's degree is worth an extra $325,000.[49] Yet educational attainment has stalled in the United States, while other countries have continued to move forward. Led by smaller countries like Finland, Poland, and Korea, many nations have overhauled curricula and the delivery of educational services in an effort to educate citizens to higher levels so they have the ability to thrive in a more competitive global economy.[50] The United States has taken notice. As Michael Greenstone of the Massachusetts Institute of Technology has written, "Strengthening our K–12 education system and increasing college-completion rates are . . . imperative to improving living standards for future generations."[51]

The performance of American students has not improved much in decades, even as many other countries have found ways to move ahead faster. For the generation of Americans aged fifty-five to sixty-four, the United States ranks first in high school completion among Organization for Economic Cooperation and Development (OECD) countries and third in college and university completion. The generation aged twenty-five to thirty-four is roughly as educated as its parents' generation, but in that cohort the United States has fallen to tenth in the world in high school completion and thirteenth in postsecondary completion. Such rankings are far from disastrous, but they have eroded what used to be a big American competitive advantage: the ready availability of highly educated and skilled labor to man the most sophisticated companies in the world. Today, companies in the United States, especially in the competitive manufacturing sectors, say they face enormous challenges in finding the employees they need. In a recent survey of Harvard Business School alumni working in senior management jobs, the availability of skilled labor was cited as a growing problem for locating or expanding business in the United States. Astonishingly, among senior managers at companies considering moving operations overseas, 31 percent of executives cited "better access to skilled labor" as a rationale for moving out of the United States versus just 29 percent who cited it as a reason for staying.[52] The issues are varied. Not all companies are looking for top research scientists or the best computer programmers, though such individuals are in high demand. Many complain instead about the lack of "soft skills," such as communication, teamwork, and adaptability. Others are looking for technicians of the sort best trained in community colleges rather than universities. Companies themselves have all but abandoned training their own workforces; the number of apprenticeships has declined more than 40 percent over the past decade, putting even more pressure on schools and community colleges to fill the gaps.[53] The one common area of agreement has been that improving the performance of K–12 education is vital to meeting any of these demands.

Every president since Reagan has pledged to restore the United States to leadership in educational attainment. In 1989 after taking office, President George H. W.

Bush convened a landmark education summit in Charlottesville, Virginia, that was attended by forty-nine of the nation's fifty governors. It was only the third time in American history that a president had come together with nearly all the governors on an issue of national concern—the others being in 1908 when Theodore Roosevelt had summoned the governors to back his land conservation initiatives and in 1933 when the newly inaugurated Franklin Roosevelt sought their support for emergency measures to lift the country out of the Great Depression.[54] The motivation for most of the governors was the economic competitiveness of their states. The early leaders of the modern educational reform effort were southern governors—among them liberals like Bill Clinton of Arkansas and conservatives like Lamar Alexander of Tennessee—who were eager to persuade manufacturers to move their operations to the South. While the low-wage, nonunion environment of the southern states was attractive to many big companies, those states also had the worst educational record in the country. Unless the companies could be assured of a skilled workforce, these governors feared, business would look elsewhere.[55]

The problems that had produced America's slipping education performance were many, and not all of them could be laid at the feet of the schools themselves. Even the best schools struggle to deal with the growing number of children from poorer households who start school with big learning deficits, while the worst schools are overwhelmed. To President Bush and the governors, the challenges that seemed most amenable to solution were fragmentation and accountability. The United States has a long tradition of local control of education, so both content and standards vary widely from state to state. In some states, like Massachusetts and Minnesota, elementary students test better in math and science than those in all but a handful of countries, but few states are at that level.[56] At the Charlottesville summit, the president and the governors pledged for the first time to develop and implement a set of national standards, with the goal of boosting achievement across the country. "The President and the nation's Governors agreed that a better educated citizenry is the key to the continued growth and prosperity of the United States," their final statement said. While reaffirming that education was and should remain a state responsibility and a local function, they agreed that "as a Nation we must have an educated workforce, second to none, in order to succeed in an increasingly competitive world economy." Therefore, "we believe that the time has come, for the first time in U.S. history, to establish clear, national performance goals, goals that will make us internationally competitive."

That objective has been pursued quite consistently over the past three decades. President Clinton signed into law in 1994 a bill that required states to develop content and performance requirements for their schools and to make "continuous and substantial" progress toward academic proficiency for all students.[57] He also backed school choice to create competition that it was hoped would spur improvements in public schools, and he encouraged the creation of new charter schools. President George W. Bush worked closely with congressional Democrats to pass the 2001 No Child Left Behind (NCLB) Act, which set the goal of making all students "proficient" in the core subjects of math and reading in just over a decade. Unlike during the Clinton era, the Bush law also tried to use federal funding as a club to force improvements in student performance; schools that failed to meet performance targets, as measured by annual testing of students, would face increasingly harsh penalties up to and including dismissal of staff and even closure. In reaction to NCLB, which was criticized for setting unachievable standards and imposing draconian penalties, President Obama tried to replace sticks with carrots. Under the Race to the Top program, the federal government offered generous cash incentives to state and local districts that improved teacher evaluation and effectiveness, adopted "college-ready" standards such as the so-called Common Core, closely tracked student performance, and encouraged competition through high-quality charter schools. Despite some difference in emphasis, all three presidents were committed to benchmarking the United States against international standards, to rigorous testing, and to accountability as a tool for raising educational performance. Building consensus on educational reform has been easier than in some other areas because the issue is not primarily money. The United States spends a great deal on education. Per-pupil spending is nearly $12,000 annually in K–12, 35 percent higher than the average in OECD countries, while per-student spending for postsecondary education is nearly twice the OECD average.[58] Most of the debate has focused on spending education dollars more effectively rather than spending more.

The results of more than two decades of reform efforts remain mixed, however. While American students continue to lag in international tests, there have been some positive developments. Enrollment in pre-K programs has nearly doubled in the past decade, though it is still well behind peer countries. Nearly all four-year-olds in France, Germany, the United Kingdom, and Japan attend preschool, but in the United States it is still just seven out of ten.[59] High school graduation rates have been inching up and in 2014 reached more than 80 percent, the highest on record. And more of those graduates are continuing their education. In 1980, just half of US high school graduates went on to enroll at a college or university in the next two years. Today that figure is 70 percent, though nearly half of those who enroll in postsecondary education still have not graduated six years later, and the United States has the highest dropout rate in the developed world. These figures conceal huge variations. In particular, American students from poorer households enter kindergarten already behind and tend to fall further behind once they are in school. While all students are making gains, children of wealthier families are pulling away from their lower-income compatriots—the achievement gap between high- and low-income students is far larger than a generation ago. As a 2013 Council on Foreign Relations report on federal education policy noted, "The influence of parental wealth on student achievement is stronger in the United States than anywhere else in the developed world."[60] The way US schools are funded reinforces the divisions: because most revenue for public schools comes from local property taxes, public schools in wealthy neighborhoods are better resourced than schools in poor neighborhoods. In most other developed countries, the opposite is true, with governments spending more per pupil in lower-income districts. National education reform efforts have not made much difference in tackling these problems. A recent assessment of NCLB concluded that at best it produced only small achievement gains.[61] The most recent renewal of the federal education law, in December 2015, rolled back much of NCLB and returned more power to the states to make their own assessments of educational progress.

Finally, little progress has been made on what most education experts agree is the key to better performance: developing and retaining the best teachers possible. The best school systems in the world have highly selective entry requirements for teacher training, recruit teachers from the top students in their universities, and retain them through generous salaries and workplace autonomy—the opposite of the American approach in which teachers are generally not the top college students, salaries are relatively low and based on seniority rather than merit, and teachers face an ever-changing array of top-down mandates on how they are supposed to teach. Many states are now experimenting with more rigorous teacher training, and some school districts have instituted merit pay to boost salaries for the best teachers. But change has come very slowly, and there is strong resistance even to some of the reforms that have already been implemented. The Common Core standards, which were developed by the state governors in an effort to emulate the curriculum and performance requirements of the world's best education systems, have faced a strong local backlash from many states and from teachers worn out by decades of top-down mandates. Further improvements in education performance are likely to be slow in coming. As author Steven Brill, who has chronicled the effects of education reforms, has put it, "Anything we do today to fix our failing public schools will take fifteen to twenty years to show significant results."[62]

Infrastructure

Roads, bridges, rail lines, and airports are the arteries of an economy. For an economy to be productive, individuals need to move efficiently within their communities and around the country, and companies need to move goods rapidly to market. Fast and secure data sharing is increasingly vital for modern business. Good roads, speedy freight and passenger rail service, efficient airports and seaports, and secure broadband networks all help countries stand out as good places to do business. But much as with education, the United States has failed to take the steps to maintain the competitive advantages it once had. At the beginning of the 2000s, the World Economic Forum still rated the overall quality of US infrastructure fifth in the world. Since then it has fallen to sixteenth, passed not only by Canada, Japan, and Korea but even by Portugal and Spain.[63] US public spending on infrastructure has dropped sharply since the mid-1970s. From 1950 to 1974, US public investment grew by an average rate of 4.3 percent annually; since then it has dropped to just over 2 percent annually.[64] On transportation infrastructure such as roads, rails, and bridges, the United States currently spends just 1.6 percent of its GDP annually, putting it last among OECD countries.[65]

Some of the slowdown in spending is understandable. Since the construction of the national highway system in the 1950s, there has been no need for a project of comparable scale. Developing countries like China and India have massive infrastructure requirements of the sort the United States faced half a century or more ago and should rightly be spending more. But even with those caveats, the US effort has fallen far short. The ASCE estimates that it would cost nearly $2 trillion by 2020 just to rebuild roads, bridges, and sewer systems that are desperately in need of refurbishing. In Washington, DC, cars were washed down a major road in 2008, and nine people had to be freed by rescue workers from a wall of water, after the fifty-year-old water pipe from the Potomac River to the city burst. In many parts of the country, aging pipes are leaching lead into the drinking water of households, potentially causing brain damage in children that can last a lifetime. The ASCE says that drinking-water pipes in most cities are "nearing the end of their useful life."[66] Freight rail traffic has been booming, but congestion is so bad in cities like Chicago that it can takes hours for trains to get through. US passenger rail systems are among the slowest in the world, even as China and Europe have been investing billions of dollars in high-speed rail. US airports move far more people than any other in world, more than twice as many as the runner-up, China; yet investment in airport infrastructure—runways, control towers, passenger terminals—has been falling for a decade. Not a single US airport ranks in the top twenty-five in the world, and no US airline ranks in the top ten globally for on-time performance.[67] As a 2011 report led by then New York mayor Michael Bloomberg and former governors Ed Rendell of Pennsylvania and Arnold Schwarzenegger of California put it, "We have let more than a half-century go by without devising a strategic plan on a national scale to update our freight and passenger transport systems."[68]

The failure of the United States to maintain and upgrade its infrastructure is both an economic and a political puzzle. Economically, there has scarcely been a time in US history when the payoffs would be larger. With long-term interest rates near historic lows for close to a decade, the costs of borrowing to invest in long-term projects are minimal. And with unemployment still moderately high and labor force participation at its lowest level since the 1970s, new construction spending would create well-paying jobs and boost the economy. Critics have argued that public infrastructure spending might crowd out private-sector investment, but there is little evidence of such an effect.[69] Corporate investment levels have been weak for years, and the cost of capital has rarely been lower. Politically, infrastructure is one of the few issues on which US companies and labor unions are in complete agreement, with the Chamber of Commerce and the American Federation of Labor and Congress of Industrial Organizations both favoring a big boost in infrastructure spending. And the proponents of greater infrastructure spending have been willing to entertain virtually any financing option acceptable to Republican critics—including one-offs like a temporary tax reduction to encourage companies to repatriate foreign profits. Yet it has still been impossible to move forward. For more than a decade, for example, Congress has failed to find new ways to pay for highway infrastructure. Most federal spending on highways is financed by an 18.4-cents-per-gallon tax on gasoline. The tax has not been increased in more than twenty years, even though revenues have fallen because modern cars are far more fuel efficient.

Infrastructure spending is a conspicuous victim of the declining confidence in government. For too long, federal allocations were set by political rather than economic priorities. Federal transportation dollars were spread thinly around the country to ensure political support, while powerful members of the congressional appropriations committees were able to earmark even more dollars to their pet projects. Perhaps the most egregious offender was Democratic senator Robert Byrd of West Virginia, who for a decade chaired the Senate appropriations committee and funneled federal transportation dollars to his state. Even today, the state is putting the finishing touches on a mountain-top, four-lane highway named after Senator Byrd that will connect Wardensville (population 272) with Elkins (population 7,214) and very little in between. At roughly $20 million per mile, it is one of the most expensive highways ever built in the country. And unlike most highway projects, in which the state picks up most of the cost, the new highway has been paid for almost entirely by Washington. In theory the new road might funnel travelers from Washington and other East Coast cities into the state, but Virginia has refused to expand the winding two-lane highway that links the state's freeway to its neighbor. One consequence of such folly has been a backlash against federal project spending; House Republicans succeeded in banning earmarks in 2010, but rather than leading to more rational infrastructure spending, it has just resulted in less of it.

As with education, most of the responsibility for infrastructure lies not in Washington but at the state and local levels. More than 90 percent of public infrastructure funding comes from state and local governments, and heavily indebted state governments do not have as much flexibility to borrow for big capital projects as they once did.[70] But unlike in education, the federal government has made little effort to increase funding or to use that funding to influence local and state priorities. Ironically, the opposition to a greater federal role is explained as a way to avoid trampling on state and local priorities. Yet, especially in transportation, where the federal government does account for about a third of all spending, state and local governments cannot move ahead without Washington's help. Republicans in Congress have been staunchly opposed to the simplest response, an increase in the gas tax. But efforts to find other creative ways to pay even to maintain current spending levels have fallen short. President Obama's idea for a national infrastructure bank, which would have used just $10 billion in federal seed money to encourage hundreds of billions of private-sector investments in infrastructure projects, could not override Republican opposition. Some members of Congress simply objected to a new federal role, arguing that many states already have their own infrastructure banks. Other countries have managed to find a way around similar ideological gridlock. When the Conservative government in the United Kingdom launched its 2010 austerity program aimed at cutting a fifth from the budgets of government agencies, it nonetheless committed to a five-year, $320 billion plan to invest in transportation, energy, broadband, and water infrastructure.[71]

States, municipalities, and the private sector have partly filled the gap. On broadband, for example, where most of the build-out has been done by the private sector, a recent survey put the United States tenth in overall broadband speed, well behind the leaders, Japan and South Korea.[72] The ideal combination seems to be a mixture of public and private initiatives. Chattanooga, Tennessee, has one of the fastest Internet connections in the world, thanks to a local government initiative.[73] Google has done the same through Google Fiber, its own high-speed network. Kansas City was the first to open the door for Google, with Atlanta, Nashville, Charlotte, Raleigh-Durham, and Salt Lake City next in line.[74] Indiana's Republican governor Mitch Daniels in 2005 launched his Major Moves initiatives for building and fixing roads across the state, which has invested nearly $3 billion over ten years. The state raised the money by selling the sixty-year-old Indiana Toll Road to a private Spanish and Australian investment consortium; when the new investors declared bankruptcy on the project in 2014 following the deep recession and drop in tolls, it was resold to another Australian toll operator for $5.7 billion. And with the Panama Canal expansion project nearing completion, a new generation of giant transport ships will be able to travel from East Coast ports to Asian markets. As a consequence, many of the East Coast port cities such as Charleston and New York have plans to spend billions of dollars to deepen harbors, though many of the projects are moving slowly due to regulatory delays and lack of financial support from Washington.[75]

Innovation

In the summer of 2015, the National Museum of American History in Washington opened its new forty-five-thousand-square-foot Innovation Wing, paid for in good part by donations from innovative American companies such as Intel, Motorola, and Monsanto. The exhibition is a remarkable chronicle of American ingenuity—from the cotton gin to the Internet. By many different measures, the United States has long been, and continues to be, the most innovative economy in the world. The United States spends more on research and development than any other country, with roughly two-thirds coming from private companies and one-third from government. It produces more cutting-edge scientific research than any other country and attracts more of the top scientists from around the world. US companies have been among the most successful in sectors such as pharmaceuticals, information technology, and complex manufacturing, where innovation plays a big role. Knowledge-intensive industries accounted for 39 percent of the US economy in 2014, well ahead of the 30 percent in the European Union and Japan and the 20 percent shares in developing countries like China and India.[76] The United States also has a vibrant start-up culture of young companies hoping to hit it big with new ideas. There is no single reason for US success in innovation. As the 2013 Council on Foreign Relations report on US innovation policy put it, "A successful innovation system is a complex web that requires substantial investment and brings together business, universities and human capital. Few countries are seriously challenging the United States in any of those areas in quality or scale. U.S. government policy, though not without flaws, deserves credit for creating a nurturing innovation environment, and for directly promoting innovation where the private market cannot."[77] On innovation, Washington seems to have found the sweet spot in which the government has reinforced the innovative capacity of the private sector rather than detracted from it.

The federal government historically played a significant role in encouraging technological innovation, though it was long dominated by the needs of the military. Boeing's first commercial jetliners were closely modeled after planes designed for the US Air Force. The first electronic digital computer was designed under a contract for the US Army and first used for a simulated hydrogen bomb detonation, while IBM's first foray into commercial computers was supported by the air force. The early development of both the semiconductor industries and the Internet were underwritten by defense contracts.[78] In many cases, it took years or even decades for the technologies to move from military to commercial applications. Vernon Ruttan has pointed out that while the Pentagon commissioned the first Internet-related research in the early 1960s and the Internet was first demonstrated at an international conference in 1972, it wasn't until 1994 that Netscape launched the first widely available commercial Internet browser.[79] For most of those three decades, the only real customer for the new technology was the Pentagon. Yet such "government interference" was widely accepted by both parties in Washington. As economist Ann Markusen has written, "What made defense such a powerful underwriter of innovation and a reliable market for incipient high-tech industries was the consensus that national defense was in the public interest, providing a public good not achievable through purely market mechanisms."[80]

As the competitiveness movement began to gain momentum in the 1980s, one of its chief policy goals was to build the same sort of government support for commercially relevant R&D that had long existed for military R&D. When President Clinton took office, he pledged to spend much of the "peace dividend" from the end of the Cold War on commercially relevant research, some $30 billion over four years on such projects as robotics, smart roads, biotechnology, machine tools, and fiber-optic communications.[81] Clinton's technology plan, which was written for the candidate by John Young with help from two of the top tech industry CEOs, Larry Ellison of Oracle and John Sculley of Apple, called for a shift away from military-driven R&D.[82] "America cannot continue to rely on trickle-down technology from the military," the Clinton plan said. "Civilian industry, not the military, is the driving force behind advanced technology today. Only by strengthening our civilian technology base can we solve the twin problems of national security and economic competitiveness."[83]

But the early battles were frustrating for the proponents, and Clinton lost more often than he won. His plans for a big increase in civilian R&D spending were sharply scaled back in his first budget proposal in an effort to reduce the budget deficit he inherited, and Congress gave him even less than he asked for. He backed ambitious umbrella legislation, the National Competitiveness Act, which would have increased government support for developing commercial technologies. The act would have provided huge boosts in funding for two of the new programs created by the 1988 Trade Act—the Advanced Technology Program and the Manufacturing Extension Partnerships—to provide business and technical advice to small manufacturing companies, modeled after the US agricultural extension program that had long provided similar services for small farmers. But the proposal triggered a backlash from Republicans. The conservative Heritage Foundation charged that such new initiatives would only "spawn new political pork projects siphoning funds from other, more productive ventures." While some of the individual programs survived in smaller form, the National Competitiveness Act died in Congress. Specific initiatives were rarely any more successful. At the beginning of the Clinton's first term, for example, the administration pulled together an interagency task force to come up with strategies for developing a globally competitive flat-panel industry for the new generation of television sets and computer screens, targeting a 15 percent global market share. Flat-panel digital displays had been invented and first produced in the United States in the 1950s and 1960s, but as with so many other technologies, the Japanese had seized the commercial lead. Even here there was a defense link; flat panels were increasingly being used in airplane cockpits and tanks, and because the Japanese constitution prohibited arms exports, the Pentagon could not rely on Japanese suppliers.[84] But even with the Defense Department leading the effort, congressional opposition was fierce. The administration developed a plan to subsidize new commercial research into flat-panel technology, with the hope that it would lure new US companies back into the business. But the idea was fiercely rejected by many Republicans and their supporters as a thinly veiled government effort to "pick winners and losers."[85] Today, flat-panel production is dominated by companies in Taiwan and Korea.

Republican opposition has been inconsistent, however. Following the release of the NAS's *Gathering Storm* report in 2005, a bipartisan group of lawmakers came together to pass the 2007 America Competes Act. George W. Bush, sounding an awful lot like Bill Clinton, said on signing the law, "ACI is one of my most important domestic priorities because it provides a comprehensive strategy to help keep America the most innovative nation in the world by strengthening our scientific education and research, improving our technological enterprise, and providing 21st-century job training." But he criticized congressional Democrats for creating several new programs, among them one "to fund late-stage technology development more appropriately left to the private sector."[86] It has also been possible to find loopholes in the conservative opposition to a greater federal role in encouraging commercialization of research. In 1982, for example, President Reagan signed the

Small Business Innovation Research Act, which for the first time offered early-stage financial support for R&D in small companies; the goal was to help bridge what is sometimes called "the valley of death" between good research ideas that may not be sufficiently ripe to attract private venture capital and commercial success.[87] The idea had broad appeal in both parties. On signing, Reagan said, "As we meet here today, there's some fellow or gal in a research park or a garage inventing something that will make our future healthy or more productive or more comfortable. I believe the bill recognizes the contributions of small high-technology firms to the Nation's growth, productivity, and competitiveness."[88] The bill originally required all federal agencies to set aside 1.5 percent of their R&D spending for small businesses; over successive reauthorizations by Congress, that has grown to 2.8 percent, or about $2.5 billion per year, which is awarded on a competitive basis to some six thousand small businesses annually. Among the once small companies that received funding from the program in the 1980s were Apple, Intel, and Compaq; in a recent survey, only 3 percent of the companies that received funds said they would have been able to move ahead without government support.[89]

The Obama administration has managed to nudge the government still further down the road of encouraging the development of technologies that are likely to be important for future competitive advantage. It has launched new initiatives to support advanced manufacturing in the United States—such as 3-D printing or nano technologies—and to bolster commercialization of renewable energy technologies. The administration has created a network of institutes, known as the National Network for Manufacturing Innovation, which is modeled after Germany's famed Fraunhofer Institutes and is intended to facilitate the commercialization of new manufacturing research. These are also closely modeled after Sematech, the public-private research consortium launched during the Reagan administration to help US semiconductor companies compete with Japan. The first manufacturing institute, focused on 3-D printing, was set up in Youngstown, Ohio, in 2012 and in its first year attracted seventy-six member companies and cofunded seven projects with the private sector. Others are focusing on next-generation semiconductors (North Carolina) and lightweight metals and composites to build stronger, fuel-efficient vehicles for civilian and military uses (Detroit). President Obama has set a goal of building forty-five similar institutes over the next decade to "guarantee that the next revolution in manufacturing is made right here in America." In renewable energy—despite the collapse of Solyndra—the administration has managed to win a big boost in funding. The government has developed new Energy Frontier Research Centers, which are similar in design to the manufacturing institutes, and has created a new Advanced Research Projects Center for energy modeled after the Pentagon's Defense Advanced Research Projects Agency.[90]

The United States will need similar efforts and more to sustain its lead in innovation. Sometime in the next decade, China is likely to surpass the United States in total R&D spending. US corporations have been increasing their overseas R&D investments much faster than they have been growing in the United States. US companies over time have been spending less on basic research and focusing more on marketable products. The federal government had filled that gap until about the mid-2000s, but since then federal spending on basic research has been flat. And the huge US trade deficit in advanced technologies will create further incentives for companies to move R&D offshore. Until 2002, the United States ran a global trade surplus in these products, which include computers, semiconductors, robotics, and biotechnology. Since then the trade deficit in these goods has grown almost every year, reaching $92 billion in 2015.[91] With increasingly fragmented global supply chains, many US companies such as Apple and Intel continue to do most of their innovative research and development in the United States even though their manufacturing is conducted mostly overseas and contributes to the US technology deficit. But Willy Shih and Gary Pisano of the Harvard Business School have argued that in many industries, R&D naturally follows manufacturing. New technological innovations often come from what is learned in the manufacturing and development of earlier technologies, so that countries that lose their manufacturing capability will be hard-pressed to maintain the lead in innovation. Kodak, where Shih once worked, is a classic example. The conventional story is that Kodak failed to see the coming transformation from film to digital photography. In fact, the company had long been working on digital technologies and made one of the first consumer digital cameras in 1994. But Kodak had largely exited the camera business in the 1960s, deciding (quite logically at the time) that the real profits were in film. The camera business moved offshore to Japan. As a result, when Kodak decided to begin making digital cameras in the United States, there was no supplier network; all the critical components were being made in Japan. In 1998, Kodak shut down its digital assembly line in Rochester and moved it to Japan to be closer to suppliers.[92]

AN ELUSIVE CONSENSUS

Pete Peterson had hoped that the United States would develop a national strategy for bolstering its competitiveness through reforms at home; instead, it has proved politically impossible to build and sustain a consensus in Washington around that goal. For powerful interest groups, other priorities have dominated. US multinational companies, with their global footprint, have at times been a strong voice for pro-competitive initiatives. But generally they have been more concerned with holding down taxes and opening up trade opportunities that allow them to prosper on a global scale rather than with supporting public initiatives that would make the United States more competitive as a business location. Labor unions, while favoring more infrastructure spending, have put most of their remaining political muscle into fighting off additional trade deals. Small companies that still make up most of American business are more concerned with competition down the street than across the world. As a consequence, while progress has been made in some areas, Washington has been mired for decades in foundational debates over the appropriate role of government in supporting a more competitive economy.

In its final report to President Obama at the end of 2011 before it was disbanded, the president's Jobs and Competitiveness Council once again urged the federal government to adopt a broader competitiveness strategy. "With other nations raising their game, an agenda for American renewal won't happen by accident. We need a strategy. We need to reach a new, pragmatic consensus on the role of the public and private sectors in fueling the next generation of growth. And we need a sense of urgency; in this global era, if you're standing still, you're falling behind."[93] But in his introduction to the report, Jeff Immelt, the council's chairman and the chief executive of General Electric, was openly skeptical about the prospects for such a consensus: "It is hard to say that jobs and competitiveness are supported by a national sense of urgency," he wrote. "If they were, we would be further along."[94]

7

How to Think about Economic Competitiveness

Today, the language of competitiveness is everywhere. The World Economic Forum (WEF), which every year hosts the tony summit in Davos, Switzerland, of global business and political elites, publishes an annual report with country-by-country competitiveness rankings. State governments are getting into the game: Georgia has its Competitiveness Initiative, Arizona offers a Competitiveness Package, California touts its Competitiveness Agenda, and Minnesota has a Global Competitiveness Initiative. These efforts all arise from a premise that is obvious to political leaders trying to attract investment and jobs—that in an increasingly integrated global economy, national prosperity depends in no small part on exporting goods and services, encouraging investment, and competing successfully with imports. That was not the case for the United States half a century ago, but it is certainly so today. Such concerns are hardly confined to the United States. The European Commission issues an annual *Global Competitiveness Report* on Europe that runs to more than two hundred pages.

But what does it actually mean to say that a country is "competitive" or that it is not? For the United States to develop and implement a genuine competitiveness strategy, it is important to have a clear idea of what "competitiveness" means. But it is a difficult idea to define with any precision. First, many economists have challenged the notion that the United States is, to any important degree, actually competing with other countries.[1] Most economists are firmly committed to the idea, based on the theory of comparative advantage, that increased trade and investment make all countries better off. So there is no competition to speak of in the sense of some countries winning and others losing. Trade is about mutual benefits, the argument goes, not about competition. Second, even those who accept that countries are to some degree in economic competition with each other differ markedly in how to assess the winners and the losers. Should we look at trade deficits? At relative productivity? At overall living standards? At the policy environment? The World Economic Forum's *Global Competitiveness Report*, the most ambitious undertaking of its kind, uses an index with 123 different variables in an effort to rank the relative competitiveness of 148 nations. This is impressively comprehensive but does not help solve the definitional problem. Finally, even if a greater consensus could be reached on what national competitiveness is and how to measure and evaluate it, there are deep intellectual and political divisions over what policies countries should enact to improve their competitiveness. There is more than one way for countries to become more competitive against their rivals, and the core economic policy debates of our time are largely about those choices.

DO COUNTRIES COMPETE?

There is no mystery about what competition means in a sporting event—the better team wins, and the weaker team loses. It is also reasonably clear among companies in a free economic marketplace—those that provide goods and services that meet customer demand at a price customers are willing to pay will prosper, while those that don't will decline and perhaps go bankrupt. Similarly, it is fairly easy to understand how individuals compete with one another economically—those who possess knowledge or skills or work habits that are valued by society will be rewarded more than those who don't. Failure in that competition means a life of low pay and precarious work. There are certainly gray areas—in sports we consider it unfair, for example, if the better team loses because of poor or biased officiating. In markets, we put rules in place to prevent companies from colluding or manipulating prices in order to drive otherwise sound competitors out of business. Need-based college scholarships, student loans, and affirmative action schemes are efforts (though not terribly successful) to ensure that children from better-off families do not get an unfair head start on their peers in the competition for education and skills. But generally, competition is seen to be a good thing; teams, companies, and individuals possessing greater talents and a stronger work ethic will succeed, while those that don't will fail. Indeed, the idea that competition is what drives societies to advance is the animating principle of modern capitalism, and nowhere has that idea been embraced more fully than in the United States.

Do countries, though, compete in the same way that sporting teams, companies, or individuals compete? When Americans were fretting over Japanese competition in the 1980s, the intuitive answer was yes. Best-selling books like Lester Thurow's *Head to Head: The Coming Battle among America, Japan, and Europe* painted the world as a giant arena of economic competition in which power and riches would flow to the winners, and the losers would be left behind. Certainly many governments behave as if they are engaged in such a competition. Several times a year, the chancellor of Germany will lead delegations of business leaders overseas to promote exports of German-made goods. China's government heavily subsidizes its state-owned industries to give them an edge against Western competitors. The US government has sometimes intervened with foreign governments to try to persuade their national airlines to buy American-made Boeing aircraft rather than the European-made Airbus. The Canadian province of Ontario buys full-page ads in the *Economist* urging companies to invest there.

If many governments are persuaded, however, economists remain skeptical. Writing in the 1990s, Nobel Prize–winning economist Paul Krugman rejected the whole idea that countries compete as "a dangerous obsession," chalking it up to simplistic thinking that failed to recognize that trade is mutually beneficial, not zero-sum. "It is simply not the case," Krugman wrote in a famous 1994 essay in *Foreign Affairs*, "that the world's leading nations are to any important degree in economic competition with each other, or that any of their major economic problems can be attributed to failures to compete on world markets." Krugman has become more concerned recently with some of the negative impacts of trade competition, but he has continued to argue that a country's success or failure in international economic competition is not particularly important in determining its well-being.[2] Trade and international investment are not at all like a sporting competition with clear winners and losers, he argued. Even countries that are inefficient and unproductive will do better trading with others than going it alone; they can specialize in whatever they do best while importing goods at lower costs than could be produced domestically. So unlike in sports, it is quite possible in a global economy to have many winners and few losers and even for the losers to be relatively better off than they would have been if they never played the game in the first place. This is unquestionably true.

Krugman also argued that countries are not at all like companies. Coke and Pepsi, for example, "are almost purely rivals," with the success of one coming largely at the expense of the other; such is not the case for nations. Here he probably overstated his case. Boeing and Airbus, for example, are the only two companies in the world producing large passenger aircraft, and they compete head-to-head for almost every sale. Yet as long as the overall market is growing, both companies can prosper even as they lose out on individual sales. Boeing earned more than $7 billion in 2015, while Airbus earned more than $4 billion; clearly the market is big enough for both. Similarly, while Pepsi and Coke compete for market share, the market is a growing one. Over the past decade, even with declining US consumption, the global market for soft drinks has nearly doubled, allowing both companies to do well, even though Coke's lead over Pepsi grew substantially. The companies are certainly direct competitors, but the competition is not entirely zero-sum. For both companies and countries, a rising tide can lift all boats, though some companies and countries will do better than others.

Krugman was certainly right, however, that there are differences between competition among companies and competition among countries. Companies that are uncompetitive can go out of business and cease to exist, and many do so every year. Countries that are unsuccessful economically may limp along and see the living standards of their citizens eroded. Sometimes, like Argentina in 2001 or Iceland following the 2008 financial crisis, countries can even go bankrupt. But unlike companies, even the most uncompetitive country is unlikely to disappear. A more realistic threat, as Richard Haass and others have highlighted, is that countries that do not succeed economically will matter less in global affairs, become more vulnerable militarily, and depend on other nations for their security.[3] Even if a country is growing economically, it can become relatively weaker in international affairs if its rivals are growing more rapidly.

A second big difference between companies and countries is that pretty much anything sold by a company faces some sort of competition. This is the case whether its competitors are down the street or across the world. True monopolies are exceedingly rare. That is not true for countries. Most sectors of the economy in any country—particularly in a large one like the United States—are not directly exposed to international competition. The best estimates suggest that about one-quarter of US jobs are in sectors that face direct international competition; indeed, the huge job losses in US manufacturing in the first decade of the twenty-first century have actually left a slightly smaller percentage of American employees working in traded sectors than was the case two decades ago.[4] Housing and office construction and most government services are not in any appreciable way affected by foreign competition. International competition is growing in both education, especially higher education, and health care, with the rise in medical tourism. For the most part, however, US schools and hospitals do not compete directly with foreign providers either—though the price of education and health care affects the overall costs of doing business in the United States for all companies. Modern computer and communications technologies are making it possible to outsource a greater number of what were once purely domestic activities, such as back-office accounting or the reading of patient X-rays. The effects still remains fairly small, though the impact could become much bigger. Economist Brad Jensen suggests that as much as 70 percent of business services—which are in generally high-paying industries like computer programming, publishing, Internet services, finance and insurance, and legal and consulting services—could be done across borders. These business services already account for about 25 percent of US jobs, more than twice the share of manufacturing, and the share is growing.[5] Economist Alan Blinder has predicted that the number of service jobs facing international competition—largely as a result of data moving freely across borders—could eventually be two to three times as large as the number in manufacturing.[6] So the competitive challenges that have faced US manufacturing are likely to face an even greater portion of the economy in the future. The challenge of adjusting successfully to that competition is not one that will disappear.

Where countries must behave most like companies is with respect to these internationally competitive sectors. If a fast-food chain raises the price of its hamburgers, it may lose sales to local rivals who hold their prices down. But consumers are not going to order their burgers shipped from Mexico. However, if aerospace workers for Boeing are overpaid or production inefficiencies prevent the delivery of aircraft in a timely fashion, some sales could be lost to Airbus, resulting in less economic activity in the United States (though Airbus is increasing its US investments). Boeing may even choose to assemble its aircraft in another country instead; it has already outsourced much of its component production. Similarly, if US-made cars are too expensive or perform poorly, Americans will buy imported cars instead, reducing jobs for US workers and cutting profits for US-based companies. If financial regulations on Wall Street are seen as too onerous, business may move to London or Hong Kong rather than New York.

Competitiveness is an issue, therefore, primarily for those large sectors of the economy where businesses located all or in part in the United States face direct competition with similar enterprises in other countries. In these sectors, the United States as a country is competing with other countries for investment, for exports, for jobs, and for commercially valuable innovations. Companies that are exporting goods or services or facing import competition must constantly be concerned with how they are performing against international competitors. And countries, including the United States, end up competing with one another to develop, retain, and attract companies that can succeed in international markets. As Rob Atkinson of the Information Technology and Industry Foundation has written, "Competitiveness relates only to the economic health of a nation's traded sectors," those that are competing every day with similar entities outside the United States.[7] Success in that competition, Atkinson argues, means developing, attracting, and retaining more production that is competitive in international markets.

It is important to emphasize that the competition is not just about retaining or attracting existing companies. As research by the Kauffman Foundation has shown, nearly all net job growth in the United States since 1980 has come from new companies, those that are less than five years old.[8] The most important attribute of a competitive economy may well be its ability to nurture the development of new companies; the US lead in innovation helps in this regard, though there has been a puzzling and disturbing slowdown in the rate of new company formation in recent decades.[9] But it also matters greatly what happens to those companies after they succeed. It makes a big difference to Americans whether they continue to expand in the United States and use this country as a platform for serving world markets or whether much of the economic activity moves elsewhere. General Motors (GM), perhaps the most successful US company of the pre-1971 world, directly employed more than six hundred thousand Americans at its peak and supported hundreds of thousands of others working in auto parts and related industries; Apple, perhaps the most successful modern US company, directly employs about fifty thousand and indirectly supports roughly another three hundred thousand.[10] Most of its actual production, however, takes place in Asia, and most of the jobs have been created there. That is not to diminish Apple's huge economic impact—its products have created vast spin-off industries in developing applications and likely boosted the productivity of companies and their employees across the economy, much as GM cars and trucks made Americans more mobile and more efficient. But Apple's footprint in the United States is considerably smaller than GM's was half a century ago.

Retaining and attracting big, successful companies is not enough to ensure strong economic growth, but it matters enormously. US-headquartered multinational companies such as Boeing, IBM, Caterpillar, Amazon, and hundreds of others account for nearly one-quarter of all private-sector jobs and output in the country, more than 40 percent of all private-sector investments, and more than 80 percent of private-sector research-and-development spending. They dominate both exporting and importing. Large companies (those with more than five hundred workers) account for two-thirds of all US exports and more than 80 percent of manufacturing exports.[11] These companies in turn support a huge base of domestic suppliers. And these companies pay their workforces much better than companies that are competing purely in the domestic market.

The expansion or contraction of these companies in the United States has a big impact on the overall health of the economy, particularly on the most innovative parts of the economy. The impact of companies that succeed in the internationally competitive parts of the economy usually outweighs that of those that succeed in purely domestic sectors like retailing. Gene Sperling, who chaired the White House National Economic Council during Barack Obama's first term, described it this way: "If an auto plant opens up, a Wal-Mart can be expected to follow. But the converse does not necessarily hold—that a Wal-Mart opening does not definitely bring an auto plant with it."[12] As the Council on Foreign Relations 2011 Independent Task Force on US Trade and Investment Policy put it, these globally engaged companies "are larger, more capital intensive, more skill intensive, and more productive" than purely domestic firms.

THE CATERPILLAR WAY

To understand better how countries compete for economic gains, let's take a closer look at Caterpillar, the Peoria, Illinois–based company that is the world's largest maker of construction and mining equipment and one of the biggest US exporters to the developing world. Caterpillar is, by any definition, a company that competes successfully in international markets. Its US exports in 2014 totaled more than $15 billion to nearly every region in the world.[13] It is also a remarkable turnaround story, having lifted itself from the verge of bankruptcy to become one of the fastest-growing large US companies over the past decade. Travel to almost any country and you will see Caterpillar earth movers working alongside those made by Japan's Komatsu and Hitachi or Sweden's Volvo. Construction equipment is a highly competitive market, and Caterpillar could quite easily have gone the way, for example, of Zenith, RCA, and other US television makers who were driven out of business in the 1980s by Asian and European rivals. In 1978, RCA and Zenith ranked third and fourth in the world, respectively, in production of color television sets; by 1997 not a single US company remained in the top ten, with Japanese and Korean firms dominating the market. Caterpillar's Japanese rival, Komatsu, first emerged as a serious challenger in the early 1980s. Komatsu was an innovator in lower-cost "lean manufacturing" techniques, while the weak yen helped it push Caterpillar out of some overseas markets and even allowed Komatsu to gain market share in the United States.[14] Caterpillar, unable to adjust quickly, began to rack up rising losses, including a record $428 million loss in 1984, before engineering an impressive turnaround. There is little question that, as a company, Caterpillar has long been directly competing with foreign companies that are making largely similar products and targeting many of the same customers. Today, Caterpillar's global market share for construction and mining equipment is nearly twice that of Komatsu and four times that of Volvo.[15]

But the competition is not just business versus business. The United States is also competing directly with many other countries as a location for making earthmoving equipment. In the early 1980s, when Caterpillar was struggling, it needed the US government's help to return to profitability. The 1985 Plaza Accord, the international agreement engineered by the Ronald Reagan administration to reverse the long run-up in the value of the dollar, began the turnaround in the company's fortunes. Within a year, the dollar had fallen 40 percent versus the yen, giving the company what its chroniclers Craig Bouchard and James Koch called "a pause that enabled it to reinvent itself." Part of that reinvention meant becoming an even more global company. Caterpillar has long been among the United States' most internationally oriented companies—even in the early 1960s foreign customers accounted for more than 40 percent of its revenue. Today the company earns more than 60 percent of its revenues outside the United States, responding to the huge demand in developing countries for equipment to build roads, sewers, water, and other large construction projects.

To simplify greatly, Caterpillar has three choices for serving those fast-growing overseas markets. It can make its machines in the United States and export them. It can make them closer to their final markets, diversifying production around the world. Or it can manufacture only overseas and serve the US market as well by exporting back to the United States. In reality, it does all three. Today Caterpillar has fifty production facilities in the United States but more than sixty abroad, including Japan, China, Brazil, and India. Most of this has been driven by faster growth in overseas markets and the economic logic of producing large machinery closer to its final delivery destination. As Bouchard and Koch write, "Caterpillar is no longer a conventional American company that sells to foreign customers. It has mutated and now is a global company that happens to be headquartered in the United States."

Much as Caterpillar is competing with Komatsu or Volvo for market share overseas, the United States is competing with Japan, China, Korea, Sweden, and other nations for the jobs and economic spin-offs created when earthmoving equipment is made here instead of somewhere else. Caterpillar's decision in recent years to bring back some production from Japan has been hailed as a "reshoring" success, and the company was praised by President Obama for the decision.[16] But while the United States has certainly benefited greatly from being the company's headquarters, the American share of the pie has been shrinking. From 2005 to 2014 Caterpillar's workforce grew in North America from about forty-four thousand to more than fifty-one thousand jobs, though the company announced a round of layoffs in 2015 in the face of slowing global demand. But the growth in the company's overseas employment over the same period was enormous, particularly in Asia, where its workforce quadrupled from just over six thousand to more than twenty-five thousand employees.[17] In 2005, just over half of Caterpillar's workforce was in North America, including plants in Canada; today that number is down to about 45 percent. In many ways these numbers are a "win-win"—the company's success internationally has allowed it to create more jobs in the United States and more jobs abroad. The US economy is better off as a result, and so are other countries. But there is also a competition among countries to win a bigger share of those gains, and here the United States has been slowly losing ground, even if it has gained in absolute terms.

The international competition for jobs also gives companies like Caterpillar tremendous leverage over governments, which are frequently pressed by the companies to make concessions either to retain existing jobs or to attract future investments. In 2011, for example, Caterpillar announced plans to open a new heavy-equipment plant and distribution center in the United States, relocating from Japan to be closer to core markets in the United States and Europe. The announcement touched off a frenzied bidding war among several US states, which was won by Georgia after it offered $45 million in tax credits and grants plus a new state job-training scheme, while the local counties chipped in another $30 million in free land and new road construction.[18] The new heavy-equipment plant and distribution center near Athens, Georgia, is set to employ as many as fourteen hundred workers by 2018.

Caterpillar is a particularly successful example for the United States; if one looks at US-headquartered multinational companies over the last decade, all of the job growth has been overseas. The number of Americans working for these companies is roughly the same as a decade ago, between 22 million and 23 million. But employment in their overseas affiliates grew from about 9 million jobs to more than 12 million; over the past two decades, these US-based multinational companies have gone from employing 80 percent of their workforce in the United States to employing about 65 percent.[19] It is reasonable to argue that this changing share simply reflects growing prosperity in developing countries and that US companies are responding appropriately to meet those new market opportunities. But it also poses a serious challenge for the United States. These jobs are some of the best paying and the companies are among the most research intensive. If the United States continues to lose ground in competing for these investments, the costs will be substantial.

ASSESSING NATIONAL COMPETITIVENESS

In the competition for investment and jobs, how do we know which countries are winning? How should we keep score? While US political leaders frequently describe their favored policies as means for boosting economic competitiveness, it's hard to make any assessment unless there's at least some general agreement on how to measure progress.

One possibility is simply to add up which country sells more of its goods on international markets than any other. By that measure, the most competitive country in the world is China, which exported nearly $2.3 trillion worth of goods in 2015; the United States was second.[20] If competitiveness means that a country exports more than it imports—that it runs a large trade surplus, in other words—then the most competitive country in the world is Germany, followed by China and the Netherlands; the United States would be the least competitive country by this definition.[21] Or perhaps we should measure competitiveness by which country has the biggest trade surplus relative to the size of its economy. If so, then Kuwait was the most competitive economy in the world, followed by Brunei and Qatar, all three as a result of large oil exports; the United States is in the bottom half here, between Canada and Guatemala.[22]

But are any of these good measures of competitiveness? Surely there are very few Americans who would trade their economy for any of the countries on this list, with the possible exception of Germany. China is a manufacturing powerhouse, which is increasingly making more sophisticated goods and paying higher wages to workers. But its chief competitive advantages are a huge, relatively low-cost labor force, government subsidies, and a weak currency. Chinese living standards remain far below the United States; GDP per capita in 2014 was just over $7,500, compared to nearly $55,000 in the United States.[23]

Trade Balances

Trade balances clearly matter, though there is huge debate among economists on exactly how. The debate became far more urgent as US concerns over competitiveness first arose, in part because the US trade deficit began to grow sharply precisely at the time that US integration into the global economy accelerated. From 1900 to 1970, the United States ran a trade deficit just once—in the Depression year of 1935. Since 1970, it has run a trade surplus only twice—in 1973 and 1975. As a percentage of GDP, the deficit rose to more than 3 percent in the late 1980s, fell back to less than 1 percent in the early 1990s, and rose to a record 6 percent in 2006 before falling back under 3 percent after the deep 2008–2009 recession. It has remained below 3 percent since, though it has begun to creep up again with the stronger dollar.

The chronic US trade deficit, as economist Robert Blecker has argued, is the result of at least three factors: the low savings rate in the United States compared to domestic investment, which necessitates foreign borrowing from surplus countries, where savings rates are generally higher; the large purchases of US dollars, mostly in the form of Treasury securities, by foreign central banks, especially in China and Japan, which is often a deliberate strategy by surplus countries to hold down the value of their currencies; and, finally, US competitive weakness in manufacturing and other tradable sectors as more and more production takes place offshore.[24]

Economists disagree considerably on which of these three factors is most responsible and on whether the trade deficit represents a serious problem. But there would be wider agreement that the trade balance on its own is not an especially good indicator of US competitive performance. It fluctuates in part with the relative health of different economies. A stronger US economy sucks in imported goods, while weaker growth overseas reduces exports. In turn, when the US economy is in a slump and other countries are growing more strongly, the deficit closes.[25] That's why the deep recession of 2009 cut the trade deficit down to less than 3 percent of GDP, the lowest it had been since the mid-1990s. The only thing that has consistently reduced the trade deficit is a US recession that lowers demand for imported consumer goods. It would be an odd statement to claim that the US economy was somehow more competitive in 2009 than it had been a decade earlier when the deficit was comparatively higher. Repeated recessions are not a recipe for economic competitiveness. A rising or falling trade deficit is not, on its own, an adequate measure of competitiveness. It is certainly influenced by the competitiveness of US-based industries. As Blecker has argued, all other things being equal, innovations that improved the competitive advantage for US-based sectors would increase exports, reduce imports, and increase both wages and corporate profits, thereby increasing US savings and reducing the trade deficit.[26] But simply comparing trade deficits across countries tells us only a partial story about their underlying competitiveness.

For policymakers, the question is whether a concerted effort to reduce the trade deficit makes sense as a policy goal. The answer must be no, because the policies that would do most to reduce the trade deficit—import protection, aggressive efforts to devalue the US dollar, or a deliberate slowing of economic growth to reduce imports—would all harm the US economy and leave Americans worse off. But the chronic trade deficit is symptomatic of problems that do need to be addressed—from the mercantilist, export-led growth strategies of some US trading partners to the weak US export performance.

Foreign Investment Flows

If trade balances are not by themselves a good measure of competitiveness, a second alternative might be to follow the flow of investment dollars. Direct investment by companies may be a better measure of competitiveness than trade balances. In a world of increasingly mobile capital, the decisions that companies make about where to build plants, locate facilities, or acquire other companies reflect the judgments of corporate executives about the potential returns offered by different locations. On that measure, the United States looks better. The United States has been the largest single recipient of foreign direct investment (FDI) over the past decade.[27]

That success, however, is in good part simply a result of the size of the American economy. Adjusted for size, the United States is roughly in the middle among advanced economies for inward foreign investment flows as a percentage of GDP, and it has lost ground compared to some other rich economies over the past decade. The

United States' share of the total stock of FDI around the world fell from 37 percent in 2000 to 19 percent by 2013.[28] Most FDI takes place through acquisitions of existing companies, which can bring value in greater efficiencies, improved management, and new markets but not necessarily much increased economic activity. The biggest benefits come from so-called greenfield investment, such as Volkswagen's 2011 assembly operation in Chattanooga, Tennessee, which employs some two thousand Americans making the company's Passat model, or the steady expansion of Siemens in North Carolina, where the German conglomerate has built facilities for everything from gas turbines to medical imaging equipment. Such greenfield investment has been declining sharply over the last decade, however, falling 6 percent year over year during the 2000s, again suggesting a less-than-stellar US performance.[29] In an effort to compare performance across countries, the Conference Board of Canada has measured the success of advanced economies in attracting foreign direct investment relative to the size of their economies. In 2011, the United States ranked tenth out of sixteen peer countries, behind the United Kingdom, Canada, Sweden, Australia, and Ireland, but slightly ahead of France and Germany and well ahead of Japan.[30]

Yet investment too can be misleading as a measure of competitiveness, since investment normally follows growth opportunities. Older, slower-growing economies like the United States and Europe can therefore be expected to see their shares slip relative to faster-growing emerging economies. Over the past decade, not surprisingly, the strongest growth in foreign investment has been in developing economies; in 2012, for the first time total FDI flows to developing countries, led by China and Brazil, exceeded those to the advanced economies.[31] And in the past several years, no region of the world has seen faster growth in foreign investment than Africa. It would be odd, however, to use that statistic to claim that Africa is somehow the most competitive business location in the world today.

As with exports, policymakers should be focused on policies that encourage expanded business investment, whether from foreign or domestic sources. These can include reforms to corporate taxes, streamlining of duplicative regulations, and training and immigration policies that provide a strong, educated workforce. The level of foreign investment is a good indicator of success or failure in that effort. But on its own it is not enough to guide a competitiveness strategy.

The Global Rankings

Perhaps in reaction to the difficulty of finding a single measure of national competitiveness, the most ambitious efforts to assess the relative competitiveness of countries have gone to the other extreme of relying on multiple measures. The two main competitiveness rankings—the *Global Competitiveness Report* of the Davos-based WEF and the annual *World Competitiveness Yearbook* of the Institute for Management Development (IMD)—both rely on elaborate indices that blend objective economic data with surveys of business leaders' perceptions. The WEF report is by far the better known and has emerged as a kind of *Michelin Guide* for national competitiveness ranking. The WEF has built an entire industry around the rankings, highlighted by hosting the annual Davos summit in January of business and government leaders to share thoughts on prospects for the global economy.

The WEF index uses a weighted average of 123 variables spread out among twelve "pillar" categories to come up with one composite ranking for 148 countries. The pillars include the quality of a country's institutions (e.g., government regulations, corruption), macroeconomic environment, infrastructure, education, financial services, and technological sophistication, among others. The IMD uses 333 variables spread among nine "factors" to rank fifty-nine countries. Both also rely heavily on surveys of business leaders, who are asked structured questions about the relative attractiveness of different countries for business investment.

The theoretical basis for these indices is pretty weak. In the absence of any clear conception of what makes nations more or less competitive, the WEF and IMD have tried to make their indicators as comprehensive as possible. But there appears to be little relationship between these competitiveness rankings and a country's economic growth prospects, suggesting that the rankings have little predictive value. And they are not terribly helpful as a guide to policymakers trying to boost a nation's competitiveness, other than to point out the obvious fact that there are many policies that can boost a country's competitiveness and many that can weaken it.

Productivity

The most widely accepted approaches to assessing national competitiveness all look in one way or another at productivity. As Krugman has put it, "Productivity isn't everything, but in the long run it's almost everything. A country's ability to improve its standard of living over time depends almost entirely on its ability to raise output per worker." In his classic *The Competitive Advantage of Nations*, Michael Porter of Harvard Business School writes, "The only meaningful concept of competitiveness at the national level is national productivity. A rising standard of living depends on the capacity of a nation's firms to achieve high levels of productivity and to increase productivity over time."[32] Productivity—generating more output per worker, largely due to investments in technology or improvements in the production or delivery process—is in turn the main determinant of living standards. Assuming that the distribution of returns to management, investors, and employees remains relatively constant, wages rise or the price of goods falls only if productivity rises.

International trade and investment should contribute to faster productivity growth. The increasing specialization permitted by an interconnected global economy is likely to increase productivity. This is true both for companies competing in export markets and for companies facing new import competition. The bigger the market, the greater the competitive pressures that companies will face and the greater the rewards for success. And in such an environment, less productive companies will fail while their stronger competitors remain standing. The high rewards for success and the big costs of failure should in turn induce companies to invest in increasing output and lowering costs—raising productivity, in other words. Studies of Canadian manufacturing after the 1989 United States–Canada Free Trade Agreement, for example, showed significant increases in productivity in the industries that were most affected by the tariff reductions.[33]

For the United States, the productivity statistics tell a mixed story. Growth in US labor productivity compared with that in other advanced economies over the past three decades has been reasonably good. There have been periods of strong growth—especially from 1995 to 2004, likely as a result of heavy investment in new information technologies—and periods of stagnation, especially in the 1970s and 1980s. Japan enjoyed very strong productivity growth, nearly 6 percent annually, through the late 1980s, before it fell sharply throughout the 1990s. Labor productivity in the core European Union states grew more rapidly than in the United States throughout the postwar period up to 1995 but since then has stalled even as it was improving in the United States.[34] From 2007 to 2013—from the onset of the Great Recession through the slow recovery that followed—US productivity averaged just over 1 percent annually, and more recently the performance has been still weaker. But even those minimal gains were slightly better than those for Europe and Japan.[35] When adjusted for purchasing power, the United States tends to rank above all but a handful of European economies in output per worker.[36]

Compared to itself over time, the US productivity story is less impressive. According to the Bureau of Labor Statistics, average nonfarm productivity growth in the 1947–1973 period, when the US economy was relatively self-sufficient, was 2.8 percent, considerably stronger than it has been since, with the exception of the surge of the late 1990s and early 2000s.[37] Productivity growth in the 1970s and 1980s was roughly half of what it had been in the previous period. Economic historian Robert Gordon suggests that future productivity growth will remain weaker than it was in the pre-1973 period, though likely better than that of the 1970s and 1980s.[38]

Government policies that helped to boost US productivity would pay benefits across the board, both in the traded and nontraded sectors of the economy. But as Gordon argues, it is difficult to know which sorts of policies are likely to be most effective in raising productivity, and in practice the big productivity gains in the past have been the result of breakthrough, one-off innovations like railroads, electricity, and the automobile. As discussed in the final chapter, governments can and should do things to encourage productivity growth—including expanding educational opportunity, investing in infrastructure, and supporting research initiatives that may foster future innovations. But targeting productivity alone is not enough, on its own, to boost a country's competitive position.

WHAT MAKES A COUNTRY COMPETITIVE?

Competitiveness is a means, not an end. Making the United States a more competitive business location is beneficial because it helps encourage more investment by companies that are competing globally. These are companies that create more than their share of high-paying jobs and that play a leading role in developing and commercializing new and valuable goods and services. A productive economy—one in which the workforce is skilled and efficient, new innovations can be brought to market easily, and sound infrastructure makes it easy to move goods and people—is important for attracting and retaining these kinds of investments. Indeed, there can be a virtuous circle in which rising productivity attracts new investments that in turn generate higher future productivity. The end goal is higher living standards for more Americans.

But even a highly productive country may still not be able to gain the necessary edge in the competition for these traded industries. A country could be highly productive but also a very costly place to do business. High taxes, burdensome regulations, uncompetitive wages, and excessive costs for health care could all drive companies not to invest or expand even in high-productivity countries. In a recent paper for the National Bureau of Economic Research, Michael Porter and his colleagues tried to tackle this problem by arguing that a competitive country is "one which provides low factor costs compared to potential productivity," with potential productivity defined as both high output per worker and a high labor force participation rate.[39] The paper looked at a host of factors that shape the underlying attractiveness of a country for investors—from the stability of its political institutions to its macroeconomic policies to more targeted policies to support the country's business environment. It then plotted those alongside the costs of doing business in that country. In a first cut at applying this methodology, Porter and his colleagues came up with results that seem intuitively correct. The three countries that come out highest in terms of their underlying competitive strengths (high productivity and high workforce participation) are Sweden, Switzerland, and Finland. The United States is ranked twentieth, just behind France and just ahead of Japan. When this index is adjusted for business costs (using hourly labor costs as a measure), highly productive countries with relatively high labor costs such as Denmark and Norway still come out on top. The United States also ranks highly, about the same as Germany and ahead of France and the United Kingdom, largely because its labor costs are lower than those of the big European economies. But lower-productivity countries like India, Malaysia, and China also rank quite highly because their costs are low compared to the output of the workforce.

This approach is a good one because it captures the core challenge for policymakers in trying to build a more competitive economy. A country could see its competitiveness slip if it tries to maintain high wages and generous social programs but fails to boost the overall productivity of its workforce to keep pace with those costs. France, for example, is a great place to be an employee; it has a thirty-five-hour workweek, six weeks of mandatory vacation, and legal protections that make it extremely difficult to get fired. But it is a difficult place to be an employer; the employer's share of payroll taxes is nearly half of the typical employee's gross salary, the overall tax burden is the highest in the European Union, and regulatory barriers pose a web of restrictions on competition. The *Global Competitiveness Report* ranks France 144th out of 148 countries in "hiring and firing practices," 137th in "effect of taxation on incentives to invest," and 130th in "burden of government regulation." In such a country, improving competitiveness requires cutting costs, greatly boosting productivity, or some combination of the two. A 2013 report to the French president by industrialist Louis Gallois concluded that France needed a "competitiveness shock," including a deep cut in payroll taxes. Similarly, an already low-cost country, such as China, could see its competitiveness falter if it fails to make productivity improvements and loses factories and future investment to still lower-cost countries like Vietnam and Indonesia.[40] As the huge migration from the country to the cities has slowed and the overall number of workers has stopped growing, Chinese wages have more than doubled since 2007. Yet China's productivity growth has slowed significantly.[41] The sweet spot for a competitive economy is the juncture at which both output per worker and workforce participation are high and business costs are moderate.

The other value of this measure is that it captures the political struggle at the heart of the debate over competitiveness. When politicians and business leaders talk about improving US competitiveness, they are almost always talking about one of two things: increasing productivity or cutting costs. Both are relative to other countries of course; if China's costs go up due to higher wages or curbing of government subsidies to business, for example, that amounts to a de facto cost cut for the United States in competing with China. But those are the only two options for improving competitiveness—produce more and better goods and services for the same cost or cut costs. The right balance between the two and the best ways for achieving it have largely defined the US debate over competitiveness.

HOW TO COMPETE: TWO ROADS

The argument here is that countries do indeed compete with one another, though the majority of US output does not come from sectors that are in direct competition with foreign economies. This competition is different from a sporting competition in that trade and foreign investment offer mutual benefits such that there can be many more winners than losers. It is also different from competition among companies, both because countries do not compete across the board the way most companies do and because they do not face the same prospect of bankruptcy and dissolution. But much like companies, countries are competing for relative shares of investment, exports, jobs, innovation, and other economic goods in those sectors that are internationally traded. The best measure of the relative competitiveness of economies is to look at cost-adjusted productivity—in other words, output per worker and the number of working-age people who are in the labor market compared to the costs of doing business in that country.

How does this competition take place in practice? Broadly speaking, companies can compete in two ways. They can compete on quality by developing better products or services than their competitors or by creating new products and services that find new markets. Or they can compete on price by lowering their costs so that they can undercut the prices of competitors selling largely similar products. The two classic modern examples are Apple and Amazon. Both are rightly hailed as examples of American ingenuity, and both are extremely competitive companies by any measure. Apple perfected entirely new categories of products, such as the digital music player and the computer tablet, and did it so well that it has been able to charge high prices and earn large profits from each sale. Even as competitors like Samsung, Google, and Microsoft have developed competing products, Apple's high quality has allowed it to earn outsized returns. Amazon, in contrast, was barely profitable for many years; yet it has enjoyed explosive growth that has shoved aside many other retailers and led to rising returns, with online sales increasing from 10 to 25 percent annually thanks to deep discounting and a fast and efficient distribution network.[42]

Countries can compete in much the same way, by lowering the costs of doing business in their territories or by offering other advantages that justify higher costs.[43] Much of the debate over competitiveness is about precisely that choice—should the United States compete for business on quality and innovation, on price, or on some combination of both? In other words, the United States could certainly make itself more attractive as an investment location by making it cheaper to do business here—reducing wages for employees, cutting taxes on corporations and perhaps on personal income as well, reducing the burden of social programs on employers, and limiting other regulations that impose higher costs on business. Government subsidies to corporations have roughly the same effect—reducing the costs to business but at the same time diverting taxpayer money that could be spent on something else like education or roads or police and fire protection. All of these actions lower costs for companies and make it more profitable for them to do business in this country.

There are others who argue that the United States should not try to compete on cost and should instead work to make itself a highly productive location so that companies can pay higher wages and higher taxes, absorb the costs of regulations and social programs, and still find this country a desirable place to do business. But if the United States—or any country—wants to attract business in this way, it will have to offer something that offsets the higher costs. These could include a particularly well-educated, skilled workforce, an intellectual and policy environment that encourages innovation, excellent roads and other infrastructure to get products to markets efficiently, a stable and predictable legal environment, a network of trade agreements to reduce costs on imports and exports, a highly developed financial system to help companies raise capital, and developed intellectual property rules that protect innovators against theft.

Discussions over national competitiveness have rarely confronted the "costs versus productivity" choice directly because it's an uncomfortable one. John Young, the Hewlett-Packard chief executive named by President Reagan to lead the 1983 US Commission on Industrial Competitiveness, put it succinctly: "As a nation, we are not going to lower our wages in order to compete. At least no one I have met has ever offered to cut his or her paycheck in honor of this worthy cause." Young's commission tried to make rising living standards central to its definition of competitiveness. But it is quite possible for companies to be highly competitive while paying their workers less. Caterpillar, for example, is under no illusions that higher wages will somehow help its competitive edge. The company pursued a series of labor disputes throughout the early 1990s, locking out its workers and bringing in replacements in an effort to bring down wage and benefit costs. The battles continue to this day. In January 2012 the company locked out 450 employees at its London, Ontario, diesel locomotive plant and then closed the facility a month later when the union refused to accept wage cuts of as much as 50 percent, elimination of the company's defined benefit pension plans, and additional benefits cuts. Later that year, Caterpillar's management forced nearly eight hundred union workers at its Joliet, Illinois, plant—which makes the hydraulic parts, like hoses, cylinders, and pumps, for much of the company's heavy equipment—to accept a six-year wage freeze, a pension freeze, and higher employee contributions to health insurance, even though company profits at the time were hitting record levels. The company is unapologetic. Chief executive Doug Oberhelman has said that if Caterpillar had not faced down its unions, it would have gone the way of the "Big Three" car companies in Detroit.

Consulting firms are similarly under no illusions that wage gains are necessary for improved competitiveness. A widely cited 2011 Boston Consulting Group study on US manufacturing competitiveness, for instance, predicted a renaissance in US manufacturing in part because "certain U.S. states, such as South Carolina, Alabama and Tennessee, will turn out to be among the least expensive production sites in the industrialized world."[44] The three states rank, respectively, forty-eighth, forty-second, and thirty-fourth out of the fifty states in per capita income.[45] They are indeed highly competitive as business locations, but they are not, as John Young would have wished, leaders in "expanding the real income" of their citizens.

Given the choice, it seems obvious that any country would prefer the high-productivity/high-wage road to competitiveness rather than the alternative. But getting there is far from straightforward. Higher productivity comes from a more educated populace, a modern infrastructure to support business, and basic and applied scientific research that leads to commercially successful innovations. But each of these takes time, and the returns on investment are uncertain. In the meantime, countries—and even more state and local governments—are competing every day for investments by global companies whose location decisions are extremely sensitive to small price advantages, whether in terms of labor costs, taxes, or regulatory burdens. Countries that resist competing on costs could find themselves with a shrinking share of investment, which would slow economic growth and erode the tax receipts needed to finance productivity-enhancing investments. If the costs of doing business in a country become too high, then this approach becomes self-defeating.

The two paths—one focused on improving productivity and encouraging innovation, the other on controlling costs—have sometimes been called the "high road" and the "low road" to international competitiveness. But that is unnecessarily simplistic and not particularly conducive to creating a more competitive US economy.

Democrats who argue in favor of more spending on education and infrastructure and government support for research and development have a point; if the United States does not invest in the foundations of a high-productivity economy, it will be unable to improve living standards for its people. At the same time, Republicans who fret over taxes, budget deficits, government regulations, and labor unions also have a point; if costs are too high, the United States will not be able to attract and sustain the business investment needed to produce jobs and higher living standards.

A successful competitiveness strategy would be one that tries to find the sweet spot between the two. It would requires the United States to pursue economic policies internationally that do more to create fair terms for competition, especially reducing the distortive effects of subsidies and currency manipulation that make it difficult to attract and retain investment in the United States in the traded sectors of the economy. The United States should compete more aggressively for investment and for exports and do more to sell itself and its products to the world. Governments should invest in the things that are most likely to pay off in higher future productivity and greater participation in the labor force, especially education, retraining of workers, modern infrastructure, and support for innovation. And governments should focus on controlling the costs of doing business, especially those costs—like corporate taxes—that are directly within the government's control and have big effects on investment location decisions.

None of this is possible without an active federal government role. But devising and implementing such a strategy directly out of Washington is probably a bridge too far in the current political environment. There is simply too much skepticism in the country today—primarily, though far from exclusively, among Republicans—about the ability of Washington to lead on these issues in ways that won't waste taxpayer dollars or descend into cronyism. But there is another way. State and local governments in the country, under the leadership of both Democratic and Republican governors and legislatures, are increasingly embracing economic development strategies built around competing for investment and nurturing companies that can win in global markets. What they need from Washington is a federal government that stands behind them.

8

A Strategy for Competing in a Globalized World

Buffalo, like so many industrial American cities, has fallen on hard times over the last half century. The city was built by cheap energy and good transportation. The completion of the Erie Canal in 1825, connecting Lake Erie to the Hudson River, made Buffalo the critical link in bringing midwestern grain to New York and other eastern seaboard cities and to European markets as well. The city became the center of the country's milling industry, with General Mills, Pillsbury, and other companies setting up milling operations that by the 1960s were providing flour to one-third of all Americans.[1] Its proximity to Niagara Falls also meant that electricity costs were among the lowest in the nation, attracting such energy-intensive industries as steel, aluminum, autos, and auto parts. In the 1950s, General Motors had seven plants in the city, and Ford had one, employing more than twenty thousand people in total. The city boomed, with its population hitting some 580,000 in 1950. But by the end of that decade, Buffalo's best days were already behind it. The opening of the St. Lawrence Seaway in Canada in 1957 offered a cheaper route from the Great Lakes to Europe, and the city's population began to decline. Then in the 1970s the local economy was pummeled by new competition from Asia and Europe in industries like steel, autos, and auto parts and from southern US states that offered lower business costs and a warmer climate and were urging companies to move. More than one hundred thousand residents left the city in a single decade. By the end of the 2000s, Buffalo's population had shrunk to just 270,000, less than half of its peak in the 1950s. Government policies did not help either. In 1975, the first ranking of the "business climate" in the lower forty-eight states, carried out by the site-location consultant Fantus, put New York at the bottom of the list due largely to the state's high corporate taxes and high labor costs. Buffalo's municipal property taxes were also among the steepest in the country.[2] While such rankings were at least in part a self-interested effort by consultants to encourage companies to move to the southern states, Buffalo had little capacity to lure new industries to replace the ones it was losing.[3]

Today, Buffalo is hoping that its future can be built on a new kind of energy. In November 2013, the US solar panel maker Silevo announced that it would open the largest solar panel facility in the Western Hemisphere on the site of a former steel mill, Republic Steel, which shrank throughout the 1970s and shut its doors for good in 1984. Six months later, Silevo was acquired by distributor SolarCity, a California company chaired by Elon Musk, the entrepreneur behind electric car maker Tesla and SpaceX, the commercial space company. SolarCity is pushing to begin operations in 2017 and plans to employ some fifteen hundred new workers, with another two thousand spin-off jobs being created in the local economy. The jobs are expected to pay about $45,000 a year for manufacturing to more than $100,000 for engineering positions—good wages in a city that was recently named by *Forbes* as the most affordable in the nation.[4] Local community colleges are offering new certificate programs in semiconductor manufacturing to help fill the anticipated need for skilled workers.[5]

The decision by SolarCity to pick a cold, derelict city like Buffalo for its most ambitious project is the coming together of a series of trends that could finally be working in the competitive favor of the United States. China continues to dominate the world's solar panel production, and like so many industries in which China is a big player, the solar panel market is plagued with oversupply created in no small part by Chinese industrial subsidies. The United States currently imports more than 90 percent of its solar panels, most of them from China. But the solar market in the United States has also seen explosive growth, with photovoltaic installations growing sevenfold between 2010 and 2014. And the decision by the Commerce Department in 2014 to slap new import duties on Chinese and Taiwanese producers to offset the subsidies has at least temporarily raised the cost of solar panel imports. SolarCity is primarily an installation company and currently supplies more than one-third of the US residential market, relying on imported panels. The Buffalo factory is a gamble that Silevo's technology, which relies on conventional silicon but uses innovative production methods, can produce more efficient panels at a cost and quality that can compete with China. And SolarCity is promising that within the next decade, all its installations will include battery backup systems, with the batteries primarily supplied by Tesla's new gigafactory in Nevada.[6]

The new plant would never have got off the drawing board, however, without the active involvement of state and local governments. Silevo, before it was acquired by SolarCity, looked seriously at simply expanding its existing facility in Huangzhao, China, where it operates in partnership with the municipal government. But the company's executives wanted to diversify their locations, and the rapid growth of solar use in North America made it the logical choice. The company hired site-location consultants to explore options and narrowed them down to three states: New Mexico, Arizona, and New York. New York was ready. As part of a program championed by Governor Andrew Cuomo known as the Buffalo Billion, the state had chosen the city of Buffalo as a test project for whether targeted government incentives could help rebuild the city's economy. The state's goal was to identify and encourage industries that either bolstered the city's strong medical cluster, built around the University of Buffalo's medical school, or leveraged its still cheap hydroelectric power. The Silevo executives met with officials from New York's Empire State Development Corporation, the state's economic development agency, who tried to sell the company's executives on the city. Buffalo met three key criteria for SolarCity: ready availability of skilled labor at lower cost than in states like California and Arizona, good research and engineering universities, and cheap hydropower.[7] And the state went further, agreeing to pay the full costs of acquiring the former Republic Steel plant and purchasing the production machinery as a hedge against the company's relocating in the future. The total investment from New York taxpayers will be close to $750 million, while the company says it will invest $5 billion.

The risks of such deals are high, but so are the potential rewards. Buffalo has a sorry history with government development initiatives, including billions of dollars spent on building public housing, redeveloping the city's waterfront, and building a metro rail system.[8] None of those did anything to build the city's employment base except to provide temporary construction jobs. And government support for solar companies has failed spectacularly before—the Barack Obama administration infamously made a failed $535 million bet on Solyndra, a company with unproven technologies whose executives, according to an inspector general's report, misled the Energy Department in winning federal loan guarantees.[9] The state of Massachusetts also lost the nearly $60 million it invested in Evergreen Solar, which was driven out of business by cheaper Chinese competition. SolarCity, with its huge and growing customer base, looks to be a better gamble, but it is far from a sure thing. And Governor Cuomo is facing charges of political favoritism in doling out contracts for Buffalo—including renovation of a downtown building to house IBM and other technology companies—to companies that contributed to his political campaigns.[10] Even as construction is proceeding, SolarCity's share price has bounced more down than up, with investors wary of the costs of the project. For the moment, however, city and state officials are excited about the prospects. "When people think of Buffalo now, they're not just going to think of chicken wings, the Bills and snow," said an Erie County executive. "They're going to think of the largest production site for solar panels in the Western Hemisphere."[11]

Buffalo is a latecomer to the economic planning fervor that has taken hold in many American cities. It is following a well-worn path in which targeted government investments are reinforcing US competitive advantages in research and high-skilled labor to help states and cities build and attract companies in globally competitive industries. Austin, Texas, built itself as a high-technology center after it was chosen in the late 1980s as the headquarters for Sematach, the Defense Department/industry research consortium designed to seize leadership in microchip design back from the Japanese. The city went further by sweetening its natural advantages—a mild climate and the University of Texas—with development incentives such as property tax rebates to attract tech companies. Until the tech industry slowed following the dot-com crash of 2001, its growth even outstripped such success stories as Silicon Valley, Raleigh-Durham, and Phoenix.[12] Portland, Oregon, has long been a leader in computer and electronics exports because of the presence of Intel in nearby Hillsboro, and it also had a strong athletic and outdoor industry built around Nike. But decades of careful urban planning have also made it one of the greenest cities in the country, with the highest percentage of bicycle commuters and a downtown filled with energy-efficient buildings. So in 2012 the city launched its We Build Green Cities marketing and business platform in an effort to persuade cities in other countries to hire its architecture, engineering, and clean-tech firms to carry out similar plans. Portland targeted four countries with which it already had strong trade links— Japan, Colombia, China, and Brazil—and in 2014 the Japanese city of Kashiwanoha, north of Tokyo, hired three Portland engineering firms to design and build a new "eco-district" in the city.[13]

Over the past several decades, the United States has seen a surge of efforts by governments to boost the country's economic competitiveness. They have offered tax incentives to attract investment by big manufacturing companies. They have built roads and bridges and deepened ports to speed products to national and global markets. They have set up training programs to ensure that their citizens have the skills for the new jobs that are available. They have launched incubators and created venture capital funds to encourage small start-up businesses. They have even set up offices overseas to solicit foreign investment and promote exports. But little of this has come from Washington. Instead, while the nation's capital has remain gridlocked over the proper role of government in the economy, US state and local governments have taken the lead in trying to attract foreign investment, boost exports, promote entrepreneurship, and train workers for the jobs that are created. The efforts have crossed party lines, with Democratic and Republican governors and legislatures and urban mayors of all political stripes eagerly embracing an activist role. Today, most state governments and many large municipalities spend enormous time and resources identifying and promoting their comparative economic advantages, not just against other parts of the country but against the world. They have worked closely with companies, hired economists and consultants to identify economic strengths and weaknesses, and partnered with universities to develop and disseminate new technologies. They have, in other words, developed competitiveness strategies.

This was not a role that state and local governments went looking for. "Most of the history of economic development is notable for the absence of planning," wrote Peter Eisinger in his comprehensive history of the rise of state-level economic development in the United States.[14] State governments historically did not pursue conscious development strategies. But with the rise of global economic competition in the 1970s, many state governments made a very different choice than the one made in Washington. Rather than assuming that the global market would sort itself out to the benefit of the United States, they worried about which pieces would land in their states. The disappearance of manufacturing jobs in steel, autos, textiles, consumer electronics, and other once high-paying industries forced many state and local governments to begin thinking in detail about where the jobs of the future would come from and how to win a share for themselves. Far too often the strategy has been to lure companies from other states by promising lower labor or regulatory costs and offering tax breaks or other subsidies. Over time, however, many states and cities have become more sophisticated in identifying and promoting sectors in which they have the potential for competitive advantage. The new strategies rely more on helping entrepreneurs and young companies, training skilled workers, and seizing new market opportunities.[15] Today, states and cities are trying to position themselves as strongly as possible within a global market by encouraging sectors in which they can develop the scale to compete internationally. This new local activism was born in the early 1980s as a response to rising foreign economic competition that pummeled the manufacturing industry in many parts of the country. In an increasingly competitive economy in which states were not only competing with each other but with other countries as well, states felt impelled to focus their limited resources on encouraging those sectors most likely to produce job growth. Today, nearly every state has such a plan.[16]

States see themselves as in direct competition with other states, regions, and the world for investment, exports, and jobs that, while in no way finite, are far from limitless. While the particulars differ, most have adopted conscious strategies to gain advantage in attracting or developing the industries that will best promote the prosperity of their states and cities. The commitment to local and state economic development is not unique to either political party. Sometimes the tools for encouraging growth are different—with Republicans leaning toward lower taxes, for example, and Democrats favoring investments in infrastructure or education—but the goals are the same. And surprisingly often, the initiatives rise above any ideology. While Republicans in Washington have slammed the Obama administration over its subsidy programs for renewable energy, for example, reliably Republican Texas has become the country's largest producer of wind power due in no small part to state government subsidies and new investments in transmission lines.[17]

State and local governments are trying to step into the vacuum created by Washington's failure to respond to global economic competition. Pete Peterson, in his memo to President Richard Nixon some forty-five years ago, saw with remarkable foresight the competitive challenges that would face the United States in adapting to a global economy. An effective response, he argued, required two things—first, negotiating better rules so that the terms of global economic competition would be as fair as possible, and second, taking steps to ensure that Americans were prepared to thrive in a more competitive world. Peterson had little doubt that smart public policy would make a big difference in whether the United States prospered or withered in the face of the new competition. Over the past half century, however, the United States—and the federal government in particular—has too often fallen short in rising to the challenges he identified. The international trading system negotiated under US leadership has been unable to come to grips with the clever mix of subsidies and discriminatory regulations that too many countries use to gain artificial advantages in trade. International monetary rules have done too little to restrain countries from manipulating the value of their currencies to gain competitive advantage, and the US government has too rarely pushed back. Investment treaties negotiated with other countries have encouraged American companies to expand globally but have done nothing to crack down on subsidies and other inducements that distort investment decisions. At home, the US government has done too little to help Americans adjust to the growing pressures of economic competition. Education and worker retraining have not kept pace with demands for a highly skilled labor force, and immigration rules written half a century ago discourage too many skilled migrants. The United States has invested too little in infrastructure, and its corporate tax policies were designed for another era in which there was little competition for investment. The federal government has until very recently done little to encourage foreign investment in the United States.

But the flowering of locally led economic competitiveness strategies could offer a way forward for the country. States and cities have embraced with a mixture of pragmatism and zeal the task of trying to attract or nurture companies that pay higher wages and can compete successfully in global markets. This local revolution in economic planning should be the foundation for a larger national economic competitiveness strategy, one that builds on local and regional efforts rather than supplanting them. There are sensible reasons, quite apart from the ideological arguments over the role of government, to prefer a more limited federal role in promoting economic competitiveness. State and local governments are much closer to the companies that operate in their communities and are better able to understand the competitive challenges they face. Local governments can shape the physical environment—roads, transit, parks, bike paths—that make their states and cities attractive places to live and work. State governments are the largest funders of community colleges and research universities and pay for most infrastructure investments. Many of the pieces of a competitiveness strategy are in state and local hands.

There are severe limitations, however, to what these governments can do on their own to promote the competitiveness of their own regions, much less to strengthen the competitiveness of the United States as a whole. They have little or no capacity to shape the terms of international economic competition. State governments, for example, can offer tax breaks and train a local workforce to entice companies, the way New York has done in persuading semiconductor companies such as IBM and AMD to choose the state as a location for chip design and manufacturing. But New York State has no influence at all on the international rules governing trade in semiconductors. It was not part of the latest round of global negotiations on a new Information Technology Agreement to free up trade in high-technology goods. It cannot influence China's indigenous innovation policy, which is aimed at discouraging imports of semiconductors and instead developing its own national industry, potentially influencing the location decisions of big chip manufacturers. It has no ability to protect those companies' technologies against intellectual property theft.

The state has no power to discourage other governments from offering even more in the way of subsidies or tax breaks to attract the same investments. It has no influence on the value of currencies; if the dollar rises too much and undercuts the profitability of New York as a location, the state and its people will be the losers, but there is no way for state governments to become involved in managing currencies. State and local governments, in short, lack many of the tools they need to promote their ambitious economic development goals. Only the federal government has the capacity to address these larger competitive challenges.

Further, without support from the national government, it is hard for states to avoid a race to the bottom in competition with other states and with overseas competitors. Too often, the easiest way that states can encourage companies to remain or relocate is through cutting taxes, easing government regulations, and passing right-to-work laws that discourage union organizing and help keep a lid on wages. As discussed in the last chapter, such strategies can certainly enhance the competitiveness of a country or region by lowering the costs of doing business there. But it is a costly strategy for state governments, reducing significantly the tax revenues available for education, infrastructure, or research that could help boost a state's economy in the longer term. States now forgo some $80 billion in tax revenues annually as part of deals made to attract or retain investment.[18] And as a strategy for increasing living standards, it is likely to fail. Purely cost-driven companies are more likely to pick up and move again if costs start to rise. The US film-production industry is a notorious example, having jumped from California to New York to Canada and almost everywhere in between, chasing local tax incentives and then picking up and leaving when the incentives dried up or a better offer came around. Amazon was persuaded to open a new national distribution facility in Irving, Texas, in 2005 after local government officials offered the company a big reduction on local taxes. The jobs were not great ones—paying between $11 and $15 an hour. Nonetheless, in 2011 Amazon abruptly closed the facility rather than pay Texas a $269 million bill for sales tax that the company had never collected on its sales to customers in Texas.[19] The low-cost road to competitiveness has not been a terribly successful one for states so far. While Texas has an impressive job-creation record, the benefits are less obvious for many of the other states that have competed most aggressively through tax incentives and other promises to reduce business costs. Ranked by median income, the southern states that have been most successful in recruiting companies to relocate by promising lower costs—such as South Carolina, Tennessee, Alabama, and Mississippi—all remain in the bottom ten nationally.[20]

For US states and cities to reap the maximum benefits from their competitiveness strategies, they need support from Washington. Such a "bottoms-up" competitiveness plan should be built around two components. First, the US government's international trade and investment negotiating strategy should be aimed at ensuring that state and local authorities face as few barriers as possible in trying to promote investment in their regions by internationally competitive companies and their suppliers. The federal government should give state and local development officials a much bigger voice in setting Washington's international negotiating priorities. Currently, too much of the advice that US policymakers solicit on trade comes from large, US-headquartered companies. Yet such companies now have global strategies that may or may not fit with the larger interests of the United States in attracting and retaining job-creating investments. State and local officials are committed to that mission—and are in a position to understand how the US negotiating posture can support or detract from it—far more than the representatives of global companies.

Second, Washington needs to encourage states and cities to pursue a race to the top rather than a race to the bottom. At their worst, the strategies of some states amount to little more than poaching companies and jobs from neighboring states. Former Texas governor Rick Perry went so far as to take out television ads in California urging companies to "get their business moving to Texas."[21] From a national perspective, poaching is simply wasteful—it creates no net benefits for the country and costs tax dollars both for the states that lose investments and for the states that attract them, depending on the size of the incentives package. The federal government has a strong interest in promoting state and local competitiveness strategies that provide a boost for the whole country rather than just for individual states. A growing number of states are trimming their incentive programs and instead investing in worker retraining, export promotion, commercially relevant research, and helping start-up companies. The federal government should support such efforts and encourage strategies that build new businesses and create new jobs rather than just move the pieces.

HOW WASHINGTON CAN
HELP STATE AND LOCAL COMPETITIVENESS

The emergence of state and local competitiveness strategies was a direct response to the growing mobility of capital and, as the competition became a global one, to the absence of a national response. As it became easier for companies to move all or parts of their operations around the country, and then later across the world, it also became possible for state and local governments to influence those location choices. No state wanted to be on the wrong end of that deal. As economic consultant David Robinson has written, "The creation of economic winners and losers across the United States and a lack of national coordination on economic development strategy turned economic development into a competitive business at the state and local level."[22] It started in the southern states: Mississippi created its Balance Agriculture with Industry program in the 1930s, a fancy name for an industrial subsidy scheme that first succeeded in luring Reliance, a Chicago-based maker of men's dress shirts and pajamas, by offering to pay the $85,000 cost of a new factory and to train a local workforce. A dozen other companies soon followed, most of them lower-wage textile and apparel companies.[23] The Mississippi Industrial Act of 1936 created a huge new corporate subsidy known as industrial revenue bonds. These low-interest bonds were used to build or purchase factories, but because they were issued by the government for the public purpose of developing the economy, they were exempt from federal taxes in the same way municipal bonds for building transit or schools are tax exempt. The state would then lease the facilities back to private companies, which were then also exempted from property taxes because the buildings were government owned.[24]

While Mississippi's program produced some grumbling in the northern industrial states, it wasn't until the emergence of global competition that more states began to follow its lead. Before the 1980s, only a handful of US states, mostly in the South, had developed plans to promote industries that were deemed important to the state's economy; between 1983 and 1985, seventeen states for the first time created such plans, led by northern industrial states such as Michigan, Wisconsin, New York, and Pennsylvania.[25] The Mississippi bond scheme was quickly adopted by its neighbors, such as Tennessee and Alabama, and then copied by most of the northern states in the late 1970s and 1980s.[26] The economic development mission has increasingly become an international one for states as well. In 1980, just four state governments had offices anywhere outside the United States. New York State opened the first one in Europe in 1954; today, the states operate more than 175 overseas trade offices in twenty-eight different countries. South Carolina, for example, has permanent foreign offices in Shanghai, Tokyo, and Munich working to recruit investments; Florida has international offices in thirteen countries.[27] China is the biggest target for US states, with twenty-eight state trade offices, followed by Japan and Mexico with nineteen each.[28]

The most elaborate economic planning effort of the 1980s was, ironically, rejected by voters in one of the rare cases where a state put its development plans to a referendum. In the early 1980s, the state of Rhode Island commissioned Ira Magaziner, a private economic development consultant, to develop a new state economic strategy. Magaziner, a Brown university graduate who volunteered his time to the project, would go on to play a major role in the Bill Clinton administration as the architect of Clinton's equally ill-fated health-care plan. Magaziner's team produced a 976-page document known as the Greenhouse Compact that has been called "the most comprehensive study of a single state's economy ever conducted."[29] It was supported by the state's business leaders, as well as by the leadership of the American Federation of Labor and Congress of Industrial Organizations, and was endorsed by both houses of the Rhode Island legislature. The Greenhouse Compact ("greenhouse" referred at that time to the incubation of new companies, not to contemporary concerns with global warming) proposed that the state spend some $250 million over seven years to create new local venture capital programs, build research centers, launch new small-business accelerators, and fund job-training programs. The goal was to create sixty thousand new high-wage jobs, which would have brought Rhode Island close to full employment. But the state's voters torpedoed the proposal in a referendum, seeing it as an expensive plan foisted on them by the state's establishment.

The Greenhouse Compact was a spectacular failure, but it was also ahead of its time. Many states have gone on to embrace strategies that look quite like those that

Magaziner recommended. The Mississippi model of luring companies through tax breaks and low-cost labor remains a popular one today. Indeed, a huge "site location" industry has emerged in which lawyers and consultants negotiate on behalf of big companies to extract the maximum in tax concessions and other subsidies from state and local governments. But over time states have focused increasingly on building new companies and targeting incentives only at those companies seen as offering an edge in international markets. Export-oriented industries have advantages over industries that do not compete in international markets. Firms that compete in international markets on average are more productive and pay significantly higher wages than companies that do not, and they carry out most of the corporate research and development that results in new products and processes that drive economic growth. They have strong multiplier effects, supporting networks of local parts suppliers and service industries. And more states are trying to lure or build "advanced industries" that are especially research intensive, such as pharmaceuticals, autos, aerospace, software design, and telecommunications; the list includes both manufacturing and internationally competitive service industries such as architecture and engineering, computer systems design, and medical diagnostics.[30] If we look at which companies are receiving state and local incentives, it is clear how much governments prize these big, internationally competitive companies. Of the top twenty-five most expensive subsidy packages ever offered by states, eighteen were to lure or retain big, global manufacturing companies in such sectors as autos, aerospace, semiconductors, and steel.[31]

Economists who focus on regional development have long drawn a distinction between local-serving and export-serving businesses. Companies that sell goods or services outside the region or state or that export overseas bring money back in the form of wages and benefits to workers, the creation of local supplier businesses, and perhaps reinvestment by the company in the community. Rob Atkinson and Stephen Ezell of the Information Technology and Industry Foundation use the example of the Maytag plant and corporate headquarters in Newton, Iowa, which closed its doors in 2007 after the company was acquired by Michigan-based Whirlpool. The washing machine company employed one in four of the town's working residents. Local-serving businesses—dry cleaners, barbers, restaurants, hardware stores, bowling alleys—all benefited from the wages paid to the Maytag workers. If one or more of those small businesses had closed, it would have had little effect on the community; as long as the demand was there, another business would spring up to take its place. But the disappearance of Maytag immediately hurt all the local businesses as paychecks for the factory's employees disappeared.[32] Since the plant's closure, Newton's recovery plan has explicitly focused on luring new export-serving businesses through tax breaks and other incentives and encouraging new start-ups through state and federal loans. The town has become a center of wind-turbine production encouraged by federal tax credits.[33] Unemployment in the town, after spiking to nearly 10 percent in 2011, well above the Iowa state average, is now less than 5 percent, and strong job growth is predicted for the future.

Tax incentives and other subsidies for corporate relocation do, unfortunately, affect the location decisions of many companies. Andrew Liveris, the chief executive of Dow Chemical, says that his biggest concern in deciding where to locate a new facility is how to minimize risk for the company's shareholders. If a government comes forward and offers financial help—say a tax break or low-interest loan for construction or subsidies that lower the price of raw material inputs—"they just eliminated a very big risk for me compared to an alternative investment in the United States. They are removing my uncertainty."[34] Indeed, the petrochemical industry has increasingly migrated to countries where government support is the strongest. The United States and Europe accounted for more than 60 percent of global production in 1980, but Singapore, China, and India have each used a mixture of direct subsidies, investments in research and development (R&D) and education, and protectionist measures to capture a growing share of production. The US share of the global market has fallen by half, from 32 to 16 percent, since 1980.[35] Ronald Pollina, a US site-location consultant, argues that without incentives, US states will find themselves at a serious disadvantage in competing not just with each other but with Mexico, China, Vietnam, Brazil, and other countries.[36]

For some states, their economic development plans begin and end with tax incentives designed to poach business from their neighbors. New Jersey, for example, spent some $4 billion in 2010 alone to entice Manhattan-based companies to jump across the river. In one case, the New Jersey Economic Development Corporation even offered some $34 million in incentives to encourage New York Life Insurance to move 325 employees from Parsippany, New Jersey, to Jersey City, fearing that otherwise the firm would be lured to New York.[37] For some states, such incentives are extraordinarily expensive. A *New York Times* analysis in 2012 concluded that Oklahoma and West Virginia forgo taxes amounting to nearly one-third of their state budgets.[38]

But many states are adopting more positive-sum strategies. More local governments today are pursuing strategies that instead focus on encouraging new start-up companies, training the workforce, supporting business in finding new markets, and building research connections with universities to encourage innovation.[39] Virginia, for example, was among the first southern states to largely reject the poaching strategy in favor of efforts to diversify its economy. It launched the Commonwealth Center for Advanced Manufacturing in 2013, a research-based collaboration between state universities and manufacturers to carry out applied research in several areas of advanced manufacturing. The state has also produced a regional industries priority list that provides a comprehensive analysis of the competitive advantages of the state's ten regions and then works with university, public, and private partners to try to build on those advantages. Virginia also has a workforce retraining fund to subsidize companies that are retraining their employees. The state's direct incentives to businesses have fallen. New York State has a similarly ambitious strategy. In particular, the state has created a series of incubators to encourage new start-up companies under the name Startup-NY. The incubators are located on most of the state university campuses and provide office space, technical assistance, and financing for new firms.

Tennessee has been among the most aggressive states in targeting big manufacturers like Volkswagen and Nissan through tax incentive and job-training programs, but it too has increasingly focused on nurturing new companies. And Tennessee has been among the most ambitious in promoting exports and foreign investment, with export offices in Mexico, the United Kingdom, Germany, and China and investment recruitment offices in Canada and Japan. The National Governors Association has created a list of best practices from the most successful state-development efforts. The prescriptions are easier to articulate than to carry out in practice, but they all involve creating a friendly business climate through competitive taxation and transparent regulations and putting entrepreneurial activity at the top of the economic agenda. The goal is to nurture small companies to become high-growth ones and then help them to find new customers in the state, the nation, and overseas.[40]

Such state initiatives are far from being sure things. All states face political pressure, for example, to spread the benefits across their states rather than focusing on regions and sectors with the best possibilities for success. New York's start-up project, for example, has been spread across seventy-one educational institutions, yet has so far attracted just over 120 companies.[41] More successful start-up incubators have been concentrated in a smaller number of locations to encourage the development of new clusters of talent. There will certainly be high-profile bets that fail, potentially causing much closer scrutiny of state economic development efforts than most have seen to date. Too many states may end up chasing the same sort of "advanced manufacturing" projects, which means there will almost certainly be overinvestment in regions that have no obvious competitive advantages in those sectors. Mississippi, for example, has spent a decade and hundreds of millions of dollars luring new "clean tech" firms, but with few success stories.[42] But while many states are changing direction, they show no sign of backing away from developing and implementing ambitious competitiveness strategies.

A BOTTOMS-UP COMPETITIVENESS STRATEGY

Even the best development strategies can only do so much to influence private-sector investment decisions, which are driven primarily by economic costs and opportunities that are mostly beyond the control of any governments. The good news for the United States today is that many of these larger trends are working in its favor. Over the decade from 2004 to 2014, manufacturing costs in the United States fell against every single one of the other nine largest goods-exporting nations, including China, Germany, and Japan, according to research by the Boston Consulting Group. Among those ten, the United States is now the second-lowest-cost location after China, and the gap with China has narrowed significantly in a decade. Even among a broader group of the top twenty-five exporting nations, the United States is less costly than all but China, Mexico, Taiwan, India, Thailand, and Indonesia.

While stagnant wages have not been good for the American workforce, they have brought down costs even as wages have been rising rapidly in China. Adjusted for productivity gains, wages in China have tripled over the past decade while rising just 25 percent in the United States.[43] Shale gas and oil have brought US energy costs down below most of the world; European energy costs in particular are far higher than in the United States. And the productivity of the US manufacturing workforce is higher than any of the other top exporting nations.

While such trends are encouraging, cost advantages can also shift against the United States quickly, as the history of the past four decades has sometimes painfully demonstrated. Exchange rates in particular can move quickly in ways that hurt the US competitive position. To capitalize on the opportunities, the United States needs a competitiveness strategy that helps it to adapt and adjust to these trends and to do everything possible to build on its competitive advantages. Yet, as we have seen throughout this book, the US government has never adopted a coherent competitiveness strategy that would shape both its international negotiating positions and its domestic economic development strategies. Where economic competitiveness concerns have clashed with diplomatic or security priorities, they have often taken a back seat. Successive administrations have rarely insisted on trade, currency, and investment rules that strengthen the ability of the United States to build, attract, and retain internationally competitive businesses. And even when the federal government has embraced elements of a competitiveness strategy, there has been deep skepticism—often reflected in congressional opposition—that Washington can set sensible national priorities or spend taxpayer dollars wisely. As long as the focus remains on what Washington will or will not do, it is unlikely that these practices will change.

But the growing role of states and cities in shaping their own economic futures in the global economy offers another path—a "bottoms-up" competitiveness strategy in which the federal government more actively supports the efforts by US states and cities to attract and develop competitive industries. It should also be one in which Washington tries to influence those state and local strategies—and those of its international trading partners as well—to avoid "race to the bottom" competitions. The federal government should encourage states and cities to pursue a high road to improved competitiveness, one that raises living standards while also allowing US goods and services to be competitive in international markets. What follows is a series of recommendations for federal action under such a bottoms-up strategy. The list is neither inclusive nor exhaustive. The great virtue of competition is that it sharpens and improves performance; you learn from what you are doing wrong and get better. Over the past three decades, even as they have made mistakes, US states have learned a great deal about how to use the tools of government more effectively to develop competitive industries. The best way to improve the performance of the federal government is for Washington also to finally get serious about making America more competitive in the global economy.

Compete on Costs

States and cities know that in order to build or attract the sorts of companies that can pay good wages and compete in international markets, they have to capitalize on every advantage they can offer. But they are too often competing with one hand tied behind their backs. Instead of receiving the support they need from Washington, they find themselves having to offer ever more generous local incentive packages just to offset the drag from Washington policies.

Perhaps the biggest drag comes from the corporate income tax. As discussed in chapter 4, corporate taxes have become increasingly important in corporate location decisions, and the US system for taxing corporate income too often rewards US-headquartered companies for investing outside the United States. Those basic rules have remained largely unchanged for more than half a century, and while the federal corporate rate was cut in the late 1980s to 35 percent, it is now the highest among the advanced countries as a result of even more aggressive tax reductions by America's competitors. While the overall tax burden on US companies is not out of line with companies headquartered in other Organization for Economic Cooperation and Development (OECD) nations, that is mostly because US companies are investing more overseas, deferring their tax obligations, and shifting profits to low-tax jurisdictions to reduce their US tax bill.[44] The result is the worst of both worlds—a high statutory tax rate that discourages investment in the United States and tax rules that reward US-domiciled companies for overseas investing and aggressive tax planning. Many states and cities find themselves in the position of having to offer up tax breaks to companies in order to offset the high federal tax rate. Despite bipartisan agreement in Washington on the need to lower the corporate tax rate to bring it more in line with other advanced economies, there is still much disagreement on the particulars. Republicans have favored cutting the rate to 25 percent, which would bring the United States to roughly the midpoint among OECD countries; President Obama proposed a reduction to 28 percent, which would still leave the United States with the third-highest rate after Japan and France. Both parties would offset the reduced tax revenue by eliminating some deductions and effectively raising taxes on some foreign profits.[45]

The debate over corporate taxes has been caught between two competing priorities. The first is to ensure that US-headquartered companies can compete on a global basis and are not disadvantaged against rivals from Europe, Japan, and increasingly China and other emerging markets. The second is to rebalance tax rules so that investing in the United States is no less favorable for companies than investing offshore. The challenge is that revenue-neutral corporate tax reform tends to fail one or the other test; the reduction in rates is offset either by reducing domestic tax breaks such as accelerated depreciation or by raising rates on overseas income by reducing deferral or levying some new minimum tax on foreign earnings. A better and simpler solution would be simply to lower rates to somewhere near the OECD average and make up the lost revenue from reduced corporate taxes through other taxes. This should be accompanied by US support for efforts by the OECD and many European nations to curb the tax-avoidance strategies of the large companies. Certainly, any effort to cut corporate taxes will raise objections that companies are not shouldering their fair share of the tax burden. But the reality for many years now has been that corporate taxes have been a shrinking part of the nation's tax base; the corporate share of total taxes collected fell sharply in the 1970s and 1980s and has not risen since, despite record corporate profits. In the United States, corporate taxes account for just 11 percent of total tax revenues.[46] The highest tax rates are paid by relatively immobile companies—retailers like Target and Walmart or mining and construction firms. The mobility of capital in the competitive, traded sectors makes it extremely hard to tax corporations effectively, however upsetting that may be to advocates of a fairer tax system.

There is an obvious way to make up the lost revenue, however, in a fashion that would enhance US competitiveness in global markets rather than eroding it. The United States remains the only country in the OECD that does not use a value-added tax (VAT). VATs are consumption taxes charged to companies at each stage of the production process and then to consumers at final sale. In most OECD countries, consumption taxes are the largest single source of tax revenues, accounting for one-third or more of total revenues. The rates vary widely—from lows of just 5 percent in Canada and Japan to upward of 20 percent in many European countries. VATs have three advantages over both corporate and individual income taxes. First, they are easy to collect and administer. In the 2011 Harvard Business School survey of its alumni working in senior corporate positions at US companies, simplifying the tax code was the most cited recommendation for improving US competitiveness (reducing corporate taxes was third).[47] Second, under World Trade Organization (WTO) rules, the VAT collected by a company is automatically rebated when it exports a good or service, and the VAT is conversely charged on imported goods and services. The logic is that companies in VAT-collecting countries would be at a competitive disadvantage if imports could escape the tax or if their exports were competing in foreign markets with products that did not face a VAT. But for a non-VAT country like the United States, the tax is a big disadvantage: US exports to France, for example, face a 20 percent tax, while French companies get a rebate of that same tax when they export to this country. By lowering its corporate taxes and substituting a small VAT to make up the lost revenue, the United States would immediately become more attractive as an investment and export location. The final advantage for the United States is that consumption taxes quite naturally tend to lower consumption by raising the final cost of goods and services to consumers. The United States is already the world's most consumption-dependent economy, with consumer spending accounting for more than three-quarters of GDP. Much as China needs to reduce the investment and export shares of its economy and increase its consumption share, the United States needs to do the opposite. By tamping down consumption and offering new tax reductions that would encourage investment for export and discourage consumption, a VAT would help with that rebalancing.

Federal regulations are another area where Washington should look for cost savings. US companies in general do not face greater regulatory burdens than their

European or Japanese competitors, though that benchmark has become somewhat
less meaningful with the rise of big competitors from emerging markets. But where
the United States has fallen behind is in reviewing—and eliminating, where necessary—old regulations that no longer serve their purpose. Australia, Canada, and
the United Kingdom have all developed automatic reviews of old regulations and
systems to better screen the cost-effectiveness of new regulations. Britain has even
adopted a "one-in, two-out" policy, in which two regulations must be eliminated
when a new one is added.[48] Rob Atkinson and Stephen Ezell have similarly proposed
that the White House carry out a "competitiveness screen" on proposed new regulations that would examine the effect of those regulations on US companies facing
international competition and consider ways to mitigate any negative impacts.[49]
More broadly, Congress should revisit Fred Bergsten's idea from the early 1990s that
Congress establish a "competitiveness impact statement" to assess the effects of major
new legislation on US competitiveness.

Compete for Investment

Even the largest and wealthiest of the US states face significant disadvantages
in competing on their own for investments and trying to build export-oriented
companies. Too often they are competing not with other states but with national
governments. Consider Intel, the California-based firm that is the world's largest
semiconductor manufacturer. Intel still makes about three-quarters of its chips in
the United States—with facilities in Arizona, Oregon, New Mexico, and Massachusetts—even as the industry generally has been moving more and more of its manufacturing to Asia. But the competition is fierce. The range of incentives offered by
foreign governments—including lower taxes, specific tax incentives, free land, and
worker training—can shave as much as $1 billion off the roughly $5 billion cost of
building a new fabrication facility, the company has said.[50] Intel's former CEO Paul
Ottelini has said that the cost advantages of building a new facility in China, for
example, have little to do with lower labor costs. Instead, 90 percent of the savings
come from the Chinese government providing Intel with capital and equipment
grants, tax holidays, and other incentives.[51] Similarly, Intel has invested more than
$7 billion in Israel but received $1.2 billion in subsidies from the Israeli government;
in Vietnam, Intel received a four-year corporate tax holiday, a 50 percent tax break
for the following nine years, and a permanent rate of just 10 percent after that.[52] No
American state on its own can compete with those sorts of incentives from national
governments.

The federal government should not be emulating Israel or Taiwan, but it should
be doing far more to help US states that are directly involved in such investment
competitions. With corporate profits likely to be squeezed in the future, companies
are going to become even more determined to drive hard bargains with governments
trying to lure investments.[53] The only way for state and local governments to ensure
they are not wasting tax dollars is to be far better armed for such negotiations than

they are today, and the only way that will happen is if the federal government is fully engaged. The good news is that federal policy on investment promotion has undergone a quiet but potentially enormous transformation over the past decade. Led by a small Commerce Department agency called Select USA, the US government has for the first time in its modern history started to play an active role in encouraging foreign investors to come to the United States. Select USA, which started during the George W. Bush administration with a skeleton staff, has grown to more than sixty employees in Washington and abroad. The agency works closely with state governors and economic development organizations to solicit foreign investment and compete aggressively with other countries to win those investments. Select USA has three missions: marketing and promotion of the United States as an investment location, facilitation of deals, and playing an "ombudsman" role to sort through problems that are blocking particular deals. It has assembled a database of all state and federal incentives that are available to foreign investors, making it easier for site-selection consultants and the companies themselves to compare the United States with foreign locations. And the US government now hosts an annual Select USA summit to promote the United States for foreign investors, bringing companies from more than seventy countries together with top US government officials and state and local economic development officials from across the United States.

Select USA has chalked up some significant victories already. Lufthansa Technik, a division of the German airline, in 2014 chose Puerto Rico as the headquarters for a new aviation maintenance and repair facility after a tough competition with Mexico.[54] The new facility will employ about four hundred workers on the island, which has been hit hard by a debt crisis and the shrinking of the island's pharmaceutical industry after a federal tax credit for the companies expired in 2006. The University of Puerto Rico has already set up a new technical institute near the facility to train workers, which the company said was critical to closing the deal.[55]

The ramped-up federal effort has also had knock-on effects when it comes to attracting or retaining investment by US-headquartered companies as well. While Select USA will steer clear if, say, Arizona and New York are competing for an IBM plant, if the competition involves a foreign location, Washington will weigh in on behalf of the states involved. Such efforts can include gathering open-source intelligence on what foreign governments are doing to lure that investment and sharing it with state and local economic development officials. And in some cases, senior members of the administration, including the secretary of commerce and even the vice president, have lobbied companies to encourage them to choose US locations.

Encouraging as these are, the federal efforts to date are only a small first step. US states and regions today increasingly find themselves competing not just with other US states but with foreign governments that have far more resources and experience in the competition for investment. Washington needs whenever possible to weigh in on the side of the states. That includes much bigger efforts to brand the United States internationally as an attractive place to invest and do business. When it comes to specific deals, the federal government should be assembling and sharing with the states information on what the other side is putting on the table—corporate tax rates, special incentives, land deals, local subsidies, and anything else that might influence a corporate location decision. Without hard numbers on the costs of doing business in, say, Taiwan or Korea and intelligence on specific deals, it is extremely difficult for US states and cities to compete effectively. On certain occasions, top federal officials can and should reach out directly to company executives to encourage them to choose the United States. For many states and regions, a growing share of business deals are international ones. In the Greater Phoenix region, for example, nearly 25 percent of the new companies being attracted to the region today are foreign owned, compared with less than 1 percent a decade ago.[56] Without federal help, it is hard to compete in that arena.

There are other things Washington could do to support state efforts. As in the Lufthansa–Puerto Rico deal, employee training is often critical to attracting investment by large companies. Federal workforce-training dollars could be mobilized to aid states that are trying to close big deals. Infrastructure upgrades such as new highway connections are often critical as well, and the federal Economic Development Administration has significant discretionary funds to support such projects under the umbrella of community development. The federal government could also play a greater role in helping states and cities to identify their advantages in the competition for investment. Basic data is lacking for many states and cities on the strengths and weaknesses of their economies in international markets. Much of that work is currently being done for cities either by private paid consultants or by think tank efforts such as the Brookings/J.P. Morgan Global Cities Initiative.[57] The federal government could help to plug that hole.

Compete on Exports

In 2010, the Obama administration launched the National Export Initiative (NEI), setting a goal of doubling US exports over the next five years and supporting 2 million new jobs. The target proved far too ambitious: while exports grew strongly coming out of the recession, they have slowed in the past several years in the face of a rising dollar and weaker growth in big export markets like Europe and China. But the NEI did have the positive effect of focusing the US government in a sustained way on the goal of boosting exports and on providing greater help to companies, especially small and medium-size ones, that are trying to break into export markets. The Obama administration has pursued the initiative at the highest levels, building on the model established by Commerce Secretary Ron Brown during the Bill Clinton administration. Obama's first secretary of state, Hillary Clinton, launched a new initiative she called "economic statecraft," mobilizing the United States' diplomatic resources, including its network of more than three hundred embassies and consulates overseas, to help boost American exports and attract foreign investment to the United States. In a 2011 speech to the New York Economic Club, Clinton said, "America's economic strength and our global leadership are a package deal. A strong economy has been a pillar of American power in the world." Therefore, she argued, it should be a central goal of US foreign policy to "help drive domestic economic renewal."[58] Much as Ron Brown had done in the 1990s, Clinton used her extensive travels to help secure several deals for US companies, persuading Australia to buy US-made communications satellites and Japan to purchase Lockheed-Martin fighter jets.[59]

The NEI is a federal initiative that aligns very closely with the priorities of a growing number of US states and regions. California, for example, has long been a US leader in both exports and foreign investment, but competition from other states led it in 2014 to develop its first statewide international trade and investment strategy. The Brookings Institution has worked to develop export plans for many US cities designed to identify and promote each region's most competitive industries. Many states are targeting their help to small and medium-size businesses, which face especially big challenges in breaking into export markets. The federal government, because of its network of embassies and consulates positioned to open doors to foreign markets, is crucial for reaching those goals.

But the commitment to export promotion by Washington remains too weak and poorly institutionalized. Such commercial diplomacy has long been practiced by America's competitors—Germany, for instance, maintains four government-funded German Industry and Commerce offices in China whose sole mission is to help German companies export to China.[60] The Shanghai office alone has more than one hundred staff. German chancellor Angela Merkel makes an annual trade mission visit to China to help German companies secure deals there. But in President Obama's first six years in office, in contrast, he visited China just once, in 2009, and not on a trade mission. While the German economy is just a quarter the size of the US economy, Germany exports two-thirds as much to China as does the United States.

A Competitive Dollar

The United States should replace the "strong dollar" policy with a "competitive dollar" policy, signaling its determination to make sure the dollar is valued at a reasonable level that allows US-based goods and services to compete internationally. The goal, as Martin Feldstein, the former chair of President Ronald Reagan's Council of Economic Advisers, has put it, should be "a competitive exchange rate relative to the other major currencies of the world—an exchange rate that will make American goods more attractive to foreign buyers and that will cause American consumers and firms to choose American made goods and services."[61] Like the strong dollar policy, a competitive dollar policy would be as much rhetorical as substantive—it would signal to the markets and to US trading partners that the US government is prepared to act if and when the dollar rises to a level that significantly disadvantages the United States as a business location. While critics have focused on currency manipulation by other countries, which is a real and persistent problem, the US government itself has too often been indifferent to the consequences of an overvalued dollar. When the Reagan administration got serious about bringing down the dollar in the mid-1980s, largely because of mounting pressure from Congress, the adjustments happened very quickly. Similarly, when the George W. Bush administration started putting pressure on China in its second term—again in the face of retaliation threats from Congress—China began to move, albeit far more slowly, to revalue.

When the United States gets serious about an overvalued dollar, other countries tend to adjust. As Bergsten has argued, "There is no example of successful global monetary cooperation without a lead from the United States."[62] But it gets serious too rarely. The best approach would be ongoing, cooperative international efforts to address currency misalignments. Former secretary of treasury, James Baker, the architect of the 1985 Plaza Accord agreement that brought down the value of the dollar and helped briefly eliminate the US trade deficit in the early 1990s, wrote in his 2006 memoirs, "The need for aggressive economic policy coordination today is, if anything, more acute now than in 1985."[63] Such coordination, he rightly noted, "is very difficult politically for all countries involved." No country wants to limit its flexibility on monetary, domestic fiscal or exchange rate policy. And indeed there have been, and will be, many times in which domestic economic officials will simply decide that other economic goals, such as raising interest rates to tamp down inflation or permitting higher budget deficits to stimulate the economy, take priority over managing the value of the dollar. But the United States cannot afford to ignore the impact of exchange rate fluctuations on its competitiveness. What Baker wrote in 2006 remains equally true today: "The United States has a policy, not quite 'benign neglect,' of hoping the dollar will fall, but not saying or doing much about it. Our trading partners appear to be less interested in currency stability than in maintaining their trading advantages against the United States."[64] Ending that benign neglect is the first step.

What might be possible today is a more targeted effort—backed by US enforcement action where appropriate—to discourage foreign governments from intervening to artificially hold down the value of their currencies. There have been long and largely inconclusive debates about whether such coordination should be led by the International Monetary Fund (IMF) or by high-level coordinating bodies like the G-7 or G-20 or should be brought into trade agreements like the Trans-Pacific Partnership (TPP). The best answer is "all of the above." The United States should increase pressure on the IMF to play a more assertive surveillance role in policing currency manipulation. It should insist that the issue remain high on the agenda for the meetings of G-7 and G-20 finance ministers and leaders. And it should bring the currency issue into trade agreements. Encouragingly, while the Obama administration slapped down efforts by Congress to require binding provisions in trade agreements, it has pushed its partners in the TPP talks to set up a separate committee of TPP member countries to discuss allegations of currency manipulation.[65] That will at least produce some greater transparency. Finally, the currency issue is only part of the larger international discussion about rebalancing and should be approached in that context. Steps by other countries—China most notably, but also Germany, Japan, and others as well—to increase the consumption shares of their GDP and thereby reduce their trade surpluses and increase global demand would do a great deal to ease tensions over currency values.[66]

In order to maintain a competitive dollar, the United States needs to have a credible threat of unilateral action when foreign governments intervene repeatedly in exchange markets in order to hold down the value of their currencies. An accurate and complete accounting of the problem is the first step. Congress understood this in the 1988 Trade Act when it required the administration to report twice a year on the currency practices of US trading partners and identify those that were manipulating their exchange rates. But successive administrations have let this tool atrophy. Throughout the 2000s, when there was a strong consensus among economists that China's renminbi was undervalued, China was never cited for manipulation in the Treasury report. The administration needs to start living up to the letter of the 1988 Trade Act and naming countries that meet the criteria for currency manipulation. The "intensified evaluation" provisions that were ordered by Congress as part of the 2015 Trade Enforcement Act are a positive step in that direction.[67] But naming and shaming alone is likely to have limited impact on its own. While negotiated resolutions to currency disputes are almost always preferable, Fred Bergsten and Joe Gagnon of the Peterson Institute for International Economics have developed a menu of enforcement tools for the US government that they argue would be consistent with both IMF guidelines and WTO rules.[68] The most powerful of the options they recommend is countervailing currency intervention by the Treasury and the Federal Reserve against countries that are purchasing dollar assets in order to hold down the value of their currencies. The goal would be to offset the impact of such currency interventions by buying up the currencies of the countries doing the manipulating. In the case of China, which does not have a fully convertible currency, they argue for either restrictions or taxes on Chinese purchases of US Treasury securities that would limit China's ability to drive up the value of the dollar. Such actions, they argue, "would be only a logical and systematic extension of actions the United States has taken for many decades when it concluded that dollar overvaluation had become too costly for its economy."

Deciding on the timing of such actions, of course, is no easy matter. In the case of China, such an aggressive US response would almost certainly have helped the US economy in the mid-2000s, when Chinese exports were booming due in part to the undervalued renminbi and the global economy was reasonably stable. With the renminbi more fairly valued today and the global economy weaker, such intervention would not likely be warranted, though there are certain countries, including Korea and several other smaller Asian countries, that continue to intervene to hold down their currencies. Administration officials will also have to resist political pressure to act in circumstances other than clear currency manipulation. Some US auto companies, for example, had pushed for action against Japan over the policy of monetary easing, which had weakened the yen, though Japan's policies are essentially indistinguishable from policies pursued by the United States coming out of the Great Recession. Interest rate cuts to stimulate economic growth are a different animal from intervention in exchange markets to hold down currency values; the former tend to increase economic growth, which encourages imports and benefits trading partners, while the latter is a classic beggar-thy-neighbor policy of shifting spending from foreign competitors to domestic producers.[69]

Such countervailing interventions by the United States should be rare, because they would be disruptive to markets. As Bergsten and Gagnon write, large-scale intervention by the United States to counter currency manipulation by others "would shatter the longstanding conventional view of the dollar as the unique and passive 'nth' currency in the global system," its value determined by the combined actions of the markets and intervention by other countries. A more active US stance would make bets for currency traders less predictable than in the past by introducing the new variable of US government intervention—a positive side effect.

A New Trade and Investment Agenda: Reducing Market Distortions

Even as it is ramping up its efforts to compete more aggressively for investment and to support exporting industries, the United States needs to take the lead in trying to mitigate the market distortions caused by government subsidies, discriminatory regulations, intellectual property theft, and location incentives. Washington should embrace a new international trade and investment negotiating agenda that is aimed at reducing such distortions and allowing US states and cities to compete on a genuinely level playing field. The US trade and investment negotiating agenda for the past half century has been highly successful in removing barriers to international commerce and investment, spurring international competition that has lifted up many poorer countries, and lowering the cost of consumer goods around the world. But that traditional trade agenda has largely run its course. Trade negotiations have been extremely effective in removing visible barriers to international trade such as tariffs and quotas. With most tariffs in advanced countries already in the single digits and many in developing countries not much higher than that, the gains from further traditional trade liberalization are small. Most of the traditional investment barriers such as ownership restrictions have also been eliminated or eased, and most countries today are eager to attract international investment rather than discourage it. But the consequence is that less visible distortions such as government regulations, tax incentives, and subsidies now play a far larger role in determining the winners and losers in international economic competition.[70]

The future priority for US trade policy should be finding ways to minimize such competitive distortions and level the playing field in a way that permits all countries to compete on a more equal footing. There are encouraging signs of such an approach emerging in some recent trade negotiations. The Trans-Pacific Partnership, for example, has a chapter that would take small steps aimed at ensuring that state-owned enterprises, which control a large share of the economy in emerging market economies such as Vietnam and China, compete on a fair commercial basis with other companies and do not enjoy special government subsidies or regulatory preferences. There has also been a much greater focus in the TPP than in previous trade negotiations on regulatory distortions and on improving enforcement of intellectual property rights. The bilateral US "strategic and economic dialogue" with China has increasingly focused on regulations that hurt US companies competing with China.

The best opportunity to chart a new course, however, is the current Transatlantic Trade and Investment Partnership (TTIP) talks with Europe. For decades, the United States and the European Union were the big players in setting the rules for global trade. The first nine rounds of the General Agreement on Tariffs and Trade negotiations and the creation of the WTO were largely US-EU initiatives. But with the rise of powerful new economies, including China, India, and Brazil, the influence of the United States and the European Union in setting global trade priorities has waned. The fifteen-year failure to conclude the Doha Round of the WTO talks reflects a long stalemate between the traditional trading powers and their new competitors. The TTIP, however, could put the United States and the European Union back at the center of the global trading system, reasserting some of the influence they relinquished two decades ago.[71] By establishing new rules for the two biggest consumer markets in the world, the United States and the European Union would put enormous pressure on other countries to adopt the same or similar rules.

The TTIP negotiations are already focused primarily on ensuring that government regulations are as nondiscriminatory as possible while respecting the rights of governments to regulate in the interests of consumer health and safety and environmental protection. Such an agreement on regulations could help drive higher standards globally. As former US trade official (and Council on Foreign Relations [CFR] colleague) Thomas Bollyky has argued, the unbundling of production and the creation of global supply chains for most goods and services mean that unclear, excessive, or duplicative regulations can have high economic costs and particularly discourage smaller companies from entering export markets. And consumer health and safety are increasingly dependent on regulatory standards in other countries that are difficult to monitor. The TTIP and other big regional agreements, including the TPP, are important vehicles for encouraging countries to adopt international standards that meet regulatory goals while reducing discrimination and duplication. As Bollyky argues, such initiatives would "avoid a race to the bottom on regulation" while helping to achieve US trade goals.[72]

The TTIP should also tackle the issue of investment distortions—again as much to establish a benchmark for the rest of the world as to influence US-EU trade and investment. The European Union has gone further than any other region in trying to curb both investment and tax distortions. Its state aid code, agreed to as part of the 1957 Treaty of Rome that established the European Economic Community, sets tight restrictions on the ability of governments to use investment incentives. Member states can only give individual businesses a subsidy under certain conditions—for example, if the subsidy benefits a region that is economically depressed or serves an environmental purpose. Most subsidies must be preapproved by the European Commission, which carries out a cost-benefit analysis on a case-by-case basis. The commission also regularly tallies and reviews existing subsidies and requires national governments and localities to list subsidies online, along with the companies that are significant beneficiaries. Member states found in violation of the state aid law can face fines and other penalties, and the companies can be required to pay back the financial benefits.[73] The European Commission has gone aggressively after several countries—Ireland, Luxembourg, and the Netherlands—over tax breaks used to benefit such companies as Apple, Fiat, and Starbucks.[74] A US-EU deal could aim at extending these restrictions to the United States as well, so that both the United States and the European Union would have similar rules for when investment subsidies would be permitted and when they would be discouraged. The purpose would not be primarily to restrict US-EU competitions for investment—which are relatively rare—but to establish a standard for the rest of the world. That standard could then be pursued through the myriad of bilateral investment treaties and regional agreements in which both the United States and the European Union participate. The United States is currently negotiating a bilateral investment treaty (BIT) with China, for example. If the TTIP were to establish a set of agreed rules on investment incentives, the United States could demand similar rules in its BIT with China, where the distortions caused by such incentives are far greater.[75]

Such an effort would be difficult, to be sure. From the US side, it would require building some consensus among the US states on which sorts of investment subsidies to companies should be permitted and which should be restricted. The US government has faced challenges over several decades in trying to get states to cooperate in other areas of trade, such as opening state government procurement to international competition. And even a US-EU deal would only be a first step—the United States would still be competing with the rest of the world, which would not be bound by any new restrictions. The new rules would have to recognize that US states would remain unrestricted in competing with countries that were not abiding by the same rules. But a common front on the subsidies issue between the United States and the European Union could allow both to finally put the issue on the table in the WTO and in other regional trade negotiations. As the most advanced economies in the world—and the ones that have generally shown the most commitment to playing by the spirit as well as the letter of international trade rules—the United States and the European Union share common ground in minimizing such distortions.

To encourage this new direction on trade and investment policy, the US government needs to pay far more attention to state and local economic development officials who are busy every day trying to compete for jobs and investment. Congress should create a Federal-State International Trade and Investment Policy Commission that would become the new vehicle for coordination between Washington and the states on trade issues. The idea was first put forward a decade ago by members of Intergovernmental Policy Advisory Committee on Trade (IGPAC) of the US Trade Representative (USTR), the sole advisory group that allows state and local governments any input into the trade and investment negotiating process (almost all the other committees represent only business interests, with a smattering of labor and NGO representatives). As the members of the IGPAC argued in calling for a new commission, "State and local governments are at the front lines of the international marketplace." They are largely responsible for assisting businesses trying to engage in global competition, for operating worker-training and -assistance programs, and for mitigating the impacts of trade competition. Those voices should be much louder ones in the formulation of federal trade policy. The new advisory commission would have bipartisan leadership from both the states and Washington and would include top trade and economic development officials from the administration, Congress, and state and local governments. It would be supported by a nonpartisan staff with expertise in trade and investment issues.[76] Other countries have long had similar models in place. Canada has a developed federal-provincial model for trade consultations, and the European Union has an elaborate system for ensuring that both member states and regional governments have significant input into EU trade priorities.

New Enforcement Strategies

None of these new trade and investment initiatives will have a significant impact in the absence of greater will by the United States (and ideally Europe and others as well) to enforce the rules. Trade enforcement is difficult. The dispute-settlement procedures in the WTO and other trade agreements require intensive research by the government and industry to build a case and then can take years to resolve. Unilateral tools such as antidumping and countervailing duty laws are blunt instruments to block imports, which can have unintended and damaging consequences on other parts of the economy. Nonetheless, every new US administration promises to be more vigorous than its predecessors in trade enforcement.

There are two crucial issues with enforcement: resources and priorities. The first is the easier to fix. Enforcement has long been the poor cousin to negotiation in US trade policy. The US Trade Representative, the agency charged with negotiating and enforcing international trade rules, is tiny by US government standards, with just over two hundred staff in total. Most of that manpower is focused on negotiating new agreements rather than enforcing existing ones. As Rob Atkinson and Stephen Ezell have rightly argued, "Political leadership in the USTR more often than not focuses on promoting trade openness rather than on enforcing existing trade agreements. Because success for USTR is often defined as signing new trade agreements, it has less incentive to be a tough negotiator." The easiest response is for Congress to insist that enforcement be a greater priority for the USTR and to back it up with more resources and manpower. Congress, for example, could authorize in statute the new Interagency Trade Enforcement Center (ITEC), which was established by the Obama administration to coordinate the actions of more than half a dozen government agencies on trade enforcement. The ITEC should take charge of leading a comprehensive review—building on the USTR's annual *National Trade Estimates* report—of potential violations of the WTO and other trade agreement rules by America's trading partners.

An equally important issue is the question of priorities. Current US enforcement strategies are essentially scattershot and driven largely by the global interests of particular industries. Instead, US trade enforcement should be realigned to support the efforts of state and local economic planners to develop internationally competitive industries. For example, the electric car maker Tesla is facing big competitive challenges from China. In an effort to develop its own domestic electric car industry, China imposes high tariffs compared to the United States and requires foreign companies to have joint venture partners to assemble vehicles in China. While China has encouraged consumers to purchase electric vehicles, Tesla has still had little success breaking into the market. Meanwhile, Chinese firms that are investing in Tesla's competitors face no similar obstacles in the United States.[77] Nevada has gambled more than $1 billion on the success of Tesla's new battery factory, but the state has no ability to address these competitive challenges without help from Washington. Helping ensure that Tesla does not face unfair competition from China should be a top enforcement priority. The solar industry is another good example. The first round of US efforts to develop a competitive solar industry were undermined in no small part by huge subsidies from the Chinese government to that country's solar panel industry. But the US government did nothing until a German-owned company with a small solar plant in Oregon, SolarWorld, filed antidumping and countervailing duty complaints against the Chinese producers. With many state governments, as well as the federal Energy Department, working to encourage solar production in the United States, the enforcement of laws covering trade in the sector should not be left to the discretion of individual companies.

Two options exist for the more effective use of domestic trade laws to discourage foreign government subsidies and other practices that distort competition. The first is for the US government itself to play a more active role in "self-initiating" cases rather than waiting for companies or, as is often the case today, labor unions to come forward. Traditionally such cases have been triggered by US companies that were facing import competition. But fewer companies are availing themselves of those remedies. The rules were built for a trading system in which most companies here had American owners and produced all or most of their products inside the United States. There was thus a common interest among those companies in protecting themselves against unfair import competition. But few US sectors are structured that way anymore. In most cases, US-owned companies now maintain global supply chains and have interests that could be harmed if the United States slaps tariffs on imports. And many US industries now have significant foreign ownership, which again makes those companies less likely to bring cases. When Congress beefed up the unfair trade rules in the 1970s, leaving initiation primarily in the hands of industry made some sense. It no longer does. In many cases, the United States can be harmed in particular by foreign subsidies that displace US production or encourage US companies to invest abroad, even if the companies themselves are not harmed to the point where they wish to initiate trade action. WTO rules, however, permit governments to "self-initiate" either antidumping or countervailing duty cases on their own, regardless of whether the domestic industry is willing to launch such an action. The administration has long had the authority to self-initiate, but the practice has been allowed to atrophy and has not been used since the early 1990s.[78]

Self-initiation would also allow the US government to use its trade tools more strategically to open markets to US exports. In the late 1980s, for example, the Reagan administration self-initiated a dumping case on semiconductors against Japan with the purpose not of closing the US market but of opening Japan's market. A more proactive government role in trade cases would enable such strategic calculations to be made by Washington rather than allowing the US government's priorities to be set entirely by the wishes and interests of particular industries.[79] And again, the choice of when and where to self-initiate a case should be determined in close consultation with state and local governments. When particular state and local economic development efforts are being impeded by subsidies or other trade-distorting measures by other countries, those cases should be a high priority for federal action. A second and not mutually exclusive option is to give state and local governments themselves the standing to bring unfair trade cases to the Commerce Department—an authority currently restricted to companies, unions, and the federal government. Unlike with federal self-initiation, giving standing to state and local governments would require congressional legislation. But with so many states and regions working to develop and attract internationally competitive industries, these governments need new tools to assist those industries that are facing market-distorting competition.

Ultimately, the goal of such unilateral enforcement actions by governments should not be primarily to protect US companies against unfair import competition but instead to encourage other countries to eliminate their trade distortions and open their markets. Enforcement is most effective when it is linked to a larger trade strategy. A willingness by the United States to use the current enforcement system to its fullest would help identify the shortcomings in the current rules and put pressure on other countries to help fix them.

Help Americans Compete, Not Just American Companies

While international competition revolves around companies, what matters most for Americans working in the economy is their jobs and their incomes. And many are competing for those jobs and wages not just with other Americans but increasingly with others across the world. Yet, as we saw in chapter 5, the United States has never had a comprehensive workforce-training plan, and the most generous of the initiatives—trade adjustment assistance (TAA)—has expanded and contracted dramatically depending on the political mood in Washington and the importance of TAA as collateral to win votes for further trade liberalization. The United States is far behind almost every other country in workforce training, especially in the so-called middle skills, such as computer-assisted design or basic computer coding skills, that are needed by many manufacturing and technology companies. US spending on "active labor market" programs to help workers build the skills to find new employment has shrunk by half as a percentage of GDP over the past two decades. While the United States is second only to the Netherlands in the share of its population with university degrees, it ranks sixteenth in the share with middle-skills degrees, which can include both four-year degrees and community college certificates. Not surprisingly, despite the large number of job seekers, many US companies continue to say they have a hard time finding employees qualified for the jobs available.

The skills shortage is not, for the most part, a problem created by the US educational system. As Ricardo Hausmann of Harvard has written, "Most of the skills that a labor force possesses were acquired on the job. What a society knows how to do is mainly in its firms, not its schools."[80] The jobs thrown up by new technologies—especially in competitive sectors like manufacturing or financial services—often require skills that are not taught in schools. Consider graphic design. Traditionally, design schools taught students to work in print. But demand today is mostly for web and mobile designers, and certificate programs for those specialties are only being developed slowly. Even then, the standards and requirements for such work are changing rapidly. Employers too often don't know whether prospective hires have the skills they need, and prospective employees don't know what skills to acquire.[81]

Historically, American companies understood this and trained much of their own workforces through apprenticeships or mid-career training. But companies are increasingly reluctant to shoulder those expenses, partly just to cut costs but partly out of fear that they will train employees only to lose them to competitors. Over the past decade, for example, the number of apprenticeships offered by companies has fallen by 40 percent; just 0.2 percent of American workers are in some kind of apprenticeship program. In comparison, more than 60 percent of German high school students—nearly 2 million each year—go through some kind of apprenticeship training to help launch their careers.[82] Companies are increasingly asking governments to help in providing them with the skilled workers they need. Some state and local governments have stepped up. South Carolina launched a statewide apprenticeship program in 2007 in cooperation with local businesses and the state's Technical College System. The state offers tax incentives for companies to train apprentices and offers tuition assistance for apprentices to build on their skills through college courses.[83] Some of the best examples involve close collaborations between companies and local governments. Volkswagen, for example, has partnered with Chattanooga State Community College to develop an advanced auto mechanics program—modeled after similar programs in Germany—that combines five semesters of academic and practical training with four semesters of paid, on-the-job training at the Volkswagen plant in the city.[84] Other initiatives have similarly focused on a specific industry in a regional labor market. Per Scholas, a nonprofit in New York City that offers free training for the unemployed and young adults in the skills needed to work as computer technicians in local information technology companies, has been highly successful in leading its graduates to good jobs.[85]

The federal government needs to follow that lead. Current federal workforce-training programs, under the umbrella of the Workforce Investment Act, have generally been too small, too fragmented, and too bureaucratic. In comparison to other advanced countries, the United States spends a pittance on worker training. In the whole of the OECD, only Mexico and Chile spend less on workforce training.[86] The money is fragmented—with nearly fifty different programs across nine federal agencies—and outside TAA most unemployed workers only qualify for job-search support rather than training. And the eligibility requirements are often strict, excluding many who need assistance.

Instead Washington should be supporting state and local training initiatives that are designed to build the workforces those regions need to attract competitive companies. The Obama administration has taken some encouraging steps in that direction. The White House in 2014 created a $100 million American Apprenticeship Fund that has offered competitive grants to state and local governments and nonprofit groups that are partnering with companies or labor unions to implement new apprenticeship training programs. The president has called for Congress to create a $2 billion fund to double the number of apprenticeships over the next five years. The administration has also launched projects to help states and regions collaborate and share the results of the most successful local programs. And the Commerce Department has launched a formal collaboration with the government of Germany to promote cooperation in career and technical education and training—a rare example of the United States learning from the best practices adopted by other countries.[87] A range of other innovations could fall under the same umbrella—including expanded tax incentives to encourage employers to invest in retraining and to let employees deduct the costs of upgrading their own skills, whether for a current job or a future one.[88] Wage insurance—in which the salaries of workers who are forced by technology or global competition to move to a lower-paid job are temporarily topped up by the government while the worker gains experience in a new sector—was first proposed in the mid-1980s when Japanese competition was growing.[89] It is an idea that has enjoyed bipartisan support, and in his 2016 State of the Union address President Obama again called for Congress to pass a broad program of wage insurance.[90]

A Race to the Top

In an effort to help states and cities help themselves, Washington should adopt a race-to-the-top strategy for supporting local economic development priorities. The race-to-the-top idea was popularized by the Obama administration's education policy; in place of the top-down mandates of the George W. Bush–era No Child Left Behind law, Race to the Top has instead used federal financial incentives to try to encourage states to adopt national education priorities, such as implementation of the Common Core curriculum. Similarly, under this approach, rather than trying to create a national competitiveness strategy, the federal government should offer financial and other incentives for states and cities that adopt positive-sum strategies for competing.

There is a growing consensus among the states that such positive-sum strategies should be encouraged. A recent report from the National Governors Association, for example, called for "a different breed of policy than the usual formula of enticing public companies to build plants in this country. It will be built on a combination of worker education, business innovation, and public and private sector entrepreneurship." The benefits would accrue not just to the states themselves, and not even just to the United States as a whole, but potentially to the world by finding innovative solutions to challenges in energy, water, food, health, security, and public infrastructure.[91] The Obama administration pursued a series of initiatives that closely follow this model. The White House plan for a national network of public-private manufacturing institutes was designed to create new research centers in regions of the country that have strong clusters of companies working to commercialize new technologies. The model is competitive proposals, in which state and local economic development officials, private companies, and universities come together to design new programs for pushing forward research on promising technologies and developing commercial applications. Cost sharing is designed to limit the up-front risks for both companies and taxpayers. And the new institutes, which work in close partnership with universities, are also aimed at educating a new generation in the skills that advanced manufacturing requires.

The administration developed a similar model around federal support for local economic development. In 2013 it launched the Investing in Manufacturing Communities Partnership with the stated goal of encouraging states and cities to stop "smokestack chasing" and start building their own industries. "Smart companies decide where to locate facilities and hire workers based on the quality of a community's infrastructure, institutions, and human capital—its industrial ecosystem," the Commerce Department said in 2013 when it launched the program. "However, communities all too often rely on . . . subsidies and tax breaks to attract a single firm. Evidence shows this approach results in a low return on taxpayer investment."[92] The initiative is aimed at encouraging and assisting communities to "launch strategic plans to strengthen their industrial ecosystems." The administration started by helping some forty communities design such plans and then awarded more than $1 billion in federal economic development assistance in each of 2014 and 2015 to a dozen communities that developed the most competitive proposals.[93] These approaches should be studied to see what works best, refined as needed, and expanded.

Similar initiatives are needed on infrastructure. Ideally, Congress will finally get serious about the need to address America's infrastructure deficit and sharply increase spending, either through a long-overdue increase in the gas tax and/or the creation of a national infrastructure bank to leverage private-sector investments in infrastructure. Certainly the current low price of oil should make such a tax increase far more politically palatable than it has been in the recent past. But in the meantime, there are easy things that Washington can do to encourage states and cities to launch their own initiatives. As my CFR colleague Heidi Crebo-Rediker has argued, other governments around the world have set up small project finance divisions that work with their local governments to facilitate private-sector investments, mostly from large pension funds seeking modest, long-term returns.[94] Canada has seen a surge of such investment in part as the result of federal support. The Obama administration launched a similar effort in 2014 with its Build America Investment Initiative, which offers federal help for state and local governments trying to use public-private partnerships to build roads, bridges, or local rail networks.[95] Congress could also make a series of small changes to help state and local governments fund their own projects—including removing current restrictions on tolls for interstate highways, offering new tax advantages for municipal bonds and other state and local funding vehicles, and speeding up federal review of new projects.[96]

Finally, both state and federal governments need to help nurture the biggest competitive advantage that the United States still enjoys: its leadership in innovation. The United States is home to sixteen of the twenty universities in the world that produce the highest-impact scientific research. The share of US output from knowledge-intensive industries like pharmaceuticals, financial services, and high-technology manufacturing is now nearly 40 percent; no other large economy has even reached 30 percent. And total public and private US spending on research and development is higher than at any time since the early 1960s. Only Japan invests as much in R&D as a percentage of its economy, and the US lead in total R&D spending is enormous.[97] Sensible public policy has made a big difference, from the R&D tax credit for companies to more direct government support. For example, the Small Business Innovation Research (SBIR) program, which was launched by President Reagan in 1982, is one of the most effective competitiveness initiatives ever launched by the federal government. Through the SBIR, Washington allows small companies the opportunity to compete for loans and grants to help them bridge the so-called valley of death that so many new start-ups face between coming up with new ideas and developing the commercial products that will make their companies attractive to investors. Intel, Apple, and Compaq all received SBIR funds in the 1980s, and 97 percent of SBIR companies said those grants had been essential to their later successes.[98] Other countries have followed the US lead, with Germany, the United Kingdom, Israel, and China all launching similar schemes. Building on its existing advantages in innovation is the lowest-hanging fruit for the United States as it works to build a more competitive economy. Government funding for basic research, as opposed to commercially oriented development research, should be increased; it received a big bump in the 2000s but has since declined sharply. The US patent system is poorly designed for the modern innovation economy, especially in information technology; the Apple iPhone, for example, has 250,000 patented components. And while the United States, thanks to its top-flight universities, continues to attract the lion's share of the brightest immigrants, US quotas on high-skilled immigration are outdated and overly restrictive and drive away too many who might otherwise stay.[99]

A SECOND CHANCE

Some forty-five years ago, the first White House official tasked with understanding the challenges that would face the United States in a more competitive global economy warned President Nixon, "The rising pace of change poses adjustment policy problems which simply cannot be ignored." In the long run, Pete Peterson wrote, market forces would reach some new equilibrium—exchange rates and trading practices would adjust and "take care of the employment and dislocation effects" caused in the United States by rising economic competition. But the long run, he feared, was too long to wait. "In practice, these adjustments come slowly and the disruptive effects come quickly, leaving long periods when the transition is painful beyond endurance." It would be hard to come up with a more apt description of what far too many Americans have faced in the transition over the past half century. The integration of the United States into a more competitive global economy, while enormously beneficial to the world and to most Americans as well, also created serious adjustment challenges that produced harmful consequences for far too many. The failure to adjust has been paid for by millions of Americans—both older ones already in the workforce and those entering today—who have seen their prospects for a good job at good wages diminish. Peterson's solution was for the United States to develop policies that would cushion that adjustment, make the transition smoother, and help more Americans prosper from the new order. At the same time, he argued, the United States would need to work carefully to "carry out these changes without unduly disrupting the interests of other countries or the international economic system as a whole."

In the early 1970s, when Peterson wrote his memo, the United States had the luxury of adapting from a position of strength. That it did not do so more effectively was a massive failure of public policy. But after the economic disruptions of the last decade, the United States again finds itself in a position of somewhat greater strength to pursue the adaptations that Peterson had encouraged. The United States remains at the center of the world's trade and monetary systems, with more power than any other country to persuade other countries to adopt better and fairer rules for competition. And after a decade in which the economies of Asia seemed on an unstoppable rise, the United States has become a far more attractive place for businesses to invest. With the right support from governments—federal, state, and local—the ingredients are there to build an American economy that not only competes with the best in the world but does so in a way that once again raises the living standards of more of its citizens.

In policy, as in life, sometimes there are second chances.

Notes

FOREWORD

1. John F. Kennedy, "Remarks at a Rally in Monessen, Pennsylvania, 13 October 1962," John F. Kennedy Presidential Library, https://www.jfklibrary.org/Asset-Viewer/Archives/JFK WHA-138-001.aspx.

2. "Complete History Part 4 Pittsburgh Steel Company Monessen Works, Monessen Pennsylvania," Historic Structures, http://www.historic-structures.com/pa/monessen/monessen _steel4.php.

3. Cassandra Vivian, *Monessen: A Typical Steel Country Town* (Pennsylvania: Arcadia Publishing, 2002), 145.

4. "Full transcript: Donald Trump's jobs plan speech," *Politico*, June 28, 2016, http://www .politico.com/story/2016/06/full-transcript-trump-job-plan-speech-224891.

5. Michael Oreskes, "Trump Gives a Vague Hint of Candidacy," *New York Times*, September 2, 1987, http://www.nytimes.com/1987/09/02/nyregion/trump-gives-a-vague-hint-of -candidacy.html.

6. Edward Alden, "The Biggest Issue that Carried Trump to Victory," *Fortune*, November 10, 2016, http://fortune.com/2016/11/10/trump-voters-free-trade-globalization/.

7. Mark Muro and Sifan Liu, "Another Clinton-Trump divide: High-output America vs low-output America," The Brookings Institution, November 29, 2016, https://www.brookings .edu/blog/the-avenue/2016/11/29/another-clinton-trump-divide-high-output-america-vs-low -output-america/.

8. David Autor, David Dorn, Gordon Hanson, Kaveh Majlesi, "Importing Political Polarization? The Electoral Consequences of Rising Trade Exposure," The National Bureau of Economic Research (NBER working paper no. 22637), September 2016, http://www.nber .org/papers/w22637.

9. Edward Alden and Robert E. Litan, "A Winning Trade Policy for the United States," Council on Foreign Relations, September 2016, and "A New Deal for the Twenty-First Century," Council on Foreign Relations, May, 2017.

10. Edward Alden, "Trumponomics: The way forward: Don't belittle his jawboning, wheeling and dealing—build on it," *New York Daily News*, December 10, 2016, http://www.nydailynews.com/opinion/trumponomics-article-1.2905352.

11. Jan W. Rivkin and Michael E. Porter, The Strategic Context: "We should have been worried before the Great Recession," *Harvard Magazine*, September-October 2012, http://harvardmagazine.com/2012/09/the-strategic-context.

12. Edward Alden, "Jeff Immelt of GE Gives The Most Important Foreign Policy Speech of the Year," The Council on Foreign Relations, May 24, 2016, http://blogs.cfr.org/renewing-america/2016/05/24/jeff-immelt-of-ge-gives-the-most-important-foreign-policy-speech-of-the-year/.

13. Aaron Pressman, "Can AT&T Retrain 100,000 People?" *Fortune*, http://fortune.com/att-hr-retrain-employees-jobs-best-companies/.

14. Angela Hanks, "President Trump's Budget Breaks His Promise to Workers—Again," Center for American Progress, March 17, 2017, https://www.americanprogress.org/issues/economy/news/2017/03/17/428535/president-trumps-budget-breaks-promises-workers/

15. David Riker, "Export-Intensive Industries Pay More on Average: An Update," U.S. International Trade Commission, April 2015, https://www.usitc.gov/publications/332/ec201504a.pdf.

16. Joseph Parilla and Mark Muro, "US metros most exposed to a Trump trade shock," The Brookings Institution, January 30, 2017, https://www.brookings.edu/blog/the-avenue/2017/01/27/u-s-metros-most-dependent-on-trade/.

17. "Map: The Most Common* Job in Every State," National Public Radio, February 5, 2015, http://www.npr.org/sections/money/2015/02/05/382664837/map-the-most-common-job-in-every-state.

CHAPTER 1

1. Anthanasios Vamvakidis, "How Robust Is the Growth-Openness Connection? Historical Evidence," *Journal of Economic Growth* 7 (2002): 57–80, http://www.cer.ethz.ch/resec/teaching/seminar_aussenwirtschaft_wt_04_05/vamvakidis_JEG.pdf.

2. "On the Move," *Economist*, January 13, 2014, http://www.economist.com/blogs/free exchange/2014/01/european-labour-mobility.

3. Anne O. Krueger, "Protectionist Pressures, Imports, and Employment in the United States," National Bureau of Economic Research, March 1980, http://www.nber.org/papers/w0461.pdf.

4. "Employment, Wage, and Benefits," US Department of Labor, http://www.dol.gov/oasam/programs/history/herman/reports/futurework/report/chapter2/#chart2–1.

5. C. Fred Bergsten, "The United States and the World Economy," *Annals of the American Academy of Political and Social Science* 460 (March 1982): 11–20, http://www.jstor.org/stable/1044592?seq=2.

6. Bureau of Economics, Staff Report, "The United States Steel Industry and Its International Rivals," Federal Trade Commission, November 1977, https://www.ftc.gov/sites/default/files/documents/reports/u.s.steel-industry-and-its-international-rivals-trends-and-factors-determining-international/197711steelindustry.pdf.

7. "International Competition: Trade Flows and Industry Structure," in Automobile Panel, Committee on Technology and International and Trade Issues of the Office of the Foreign Secretary, National Academy of Engineering, and the Commission on Engineering and Technical Systems, National Research Council, *The Competitive Status of the U.S. Auto Industry: A Study of the Influences of Technology in Determining International Industrial Competitive Advantage* (Washington, DC: National Academies Press, 1982), http://www.nap.edu/openbook .php?record_id=291&page=52.

8. "Jerry Brown on the 'Reindustrialization of America,'" *Washington Post*, January 14, 1980, http://search.proquest.com/news/docview/147148532/1375113D4C761DEE5DD/6 ?accountid=37722.

9. David H. Autor, David Dorn, and Gordon H. Hanson, "Untangling Trade and Technology: Evidence from Local Labor Markets," National Bureau of Economic Research, Working Paper No. 19838, April 2013, http://www.nber.org/papers/w18938.

10. "International Trade/Global Economy," PollingReport.com, http://www.pollingreport .com/trade.htm.

11. Jan W. Rivkin, Karen G. Mills, and Michael E. Porter, with contributions from Michael I. Norton and Mitchell B. Weiss, "The Challenge of Shared Prosperity: Findings of Harvard Business School's 2015 Survey on U.S. Competitiveness," Harvard Business School, September 2015, http://www.hbs.edu/competitiveness/Documents/challenge-of-shared-pros perity.pdf.

12. "Historical Income Tables: Households," US Census Bureau, http://www.census.gov /hhes/www/income/data/historical/household. See also Carmen DeNavas-Walt and Bernadette D. Proctor, "Income and Poverty in the United States: 2014," *Current Population Reports*, US Census, September 2015. http://www.census.gov/content/dam/Census/library/publications /2015/demo/p60-252.pdf.

13. Molly Selvin, "Study: Men's Earnings Shrink," *Los Angeles Times*, May 26, 2007, http:// articles.latimes.com/2007/may/26/business/fi-men26.

14. David Leonhardt and Kevin Quealy, "The American Middle Class Is No Longer the World's Richest," *New York Times*, April 22, 2014.

15. "United States: Tackling High Inequalities, Creating Opportunities for All," OECD, June 2014, http://www.oecd.org/unitedstates/Tackling-high-inequalities.pdf.

16. Brian Keeley, "Income Inequality: The Gap between Rich and Poor," December 15, 2015, OECD Insights, http://www.oecd-ilibrary.org/docserver/download/0115391e .pdf?expires=1453488804&id=id&accname=guest&checksum=2EF4A6746AEC6278258 60E7300708125.

17. Stanford Center on Poverty and Inequality, *State of the Union: The Poverty and Inequality Report 2016*, special issues of *Pathways* (2016), http://inequality.stanford.edu/sites/default /files/Pathways-SOTU-2016.pdf.

18. Edward Gresser, "American Families Have Cut Their Bills for Food and Home Goods by 40 Percent since the 1970s," *Progressive Economy*, http://www.progressive-economy.org /trade_facts/american-families-have-cut-their-bills-for-food-home-goods-by-40-percent-since -the-1970s.

19. Gary P. Pisano and Willy Shih, *Producing Prosperity: Why America Needs a Manufacturing Renaissance* (Boston: Harvard Business Review Press, 2012).

20. Robert D. Putnam, *Our Kids: The American Dream in Crisis* (New York: Simon & Schuster, 2015).

21. See Daniel J. Sargent, *A Superpower Transformed: The Remaking of American Foreign Policy in the 1970s* (Oxford: Oxford University Press, 2014).

22. Peter G. Peterson, *The Education of an American Dreamer: How a Son of Greek Immigrants Learned His Way from a Nebraska Diner to Washington, Wall Street, and Beyond* (New York: Twelve, 2009).

23. Peterson, *The Education of an American Dreamer*.

24. C. Fred Bergsten, *Towards a New International Economic Order: Selected Papers of C. Fred Bergsten, 1971–1974* (Lexington, MA: Lexington Books, 1975), 499.

25. Robert A. Pastor, *Congress and the Politics of U.S. Foreign Economic Policy, 1929–1976* (Berkeley: University of California Press, 1980).

26. AFL-CIO, "An American Trade Union View on International Trade and Investment," February 21, 1971, in *Multinational Corporations: A Compendium of Papers Submitted to the Subcommittee on International Trade of the Committee on Finance in the United States Senate*, ed. US Senate, Committee on Finance, Subcommittee on International Trade (Washington, DC: US Government Printing Office, 1973), 71.

27. Howard Rosen, "Trade Adjustment Assistance: The More We Change, the More It Stays the Same," in *C. Fred Bergsten and the World Economy*, ed. Michael Mussa (Washington, DC: Peterson Institute for International Economics, 2006), 81.

28. Peterson, *The Education of an American Dreamer*.

29. Dom Bonafede, "Peterson Unit Helps Shape Tough International Economic Policy," *National Journal* 3, no. 46 (November 13, 1971): 2238–48.

30. "Memorandum from C. Fred Bergsten of the National Security Council Staff to the President's Special Assistant for National Security Affairs (Kissinger)," Washington, DC, April 21, 1971, in *Foreign Relations of the United States, 1969–1976, Vol. 3: Foreign Economic Policy; International Monetary Policy, 1969–1972*, ed. Bruce F. Duncombe (Washington, DC: United States Government Printing Office, 2001), document 64.

31. See Edward Alden and Rebecca Strauss, *How America Stacks Up: Economic Competitiveness and U.S. Policy* (New York: Council on Foreign Relations, February 2016).

32. Alden and Strauss, *How America Stacks Up*.

33. Bob Davis and Valerie Bauerlein, "South Carolina GOP Voters Feel the Benefits of Free Trade—but Also the Scars," *Wall Street Journal*, February 17, 2016.

CHAPTER 2

1. "Mickey Kantor's Riverboat Gamble," *Chicago Tribune*, May 19, 1995; "Lexis and Hubris: Car Tariffs Are Infinitely Dumb," *San Jose Mercury News*, May 19, 1995.

2. Martin Kenney, "The Shifting Value Chain: The Television Industry in North America"; see also "The Decline of the US TV Industry: Manufacturing," Princeton University, http://www.princeton.edu/~ota/disk2/1990/9007/900709.PDF.

3. Douglas A. Irwin, "Trade Policies and the Semiconductor Industry," in *The Political Economy of American Trade Policy*, ed. Anne O. Krueger (Chicago: University of Chicago Press, 1994).

4. Quoted in Jeffrey A. Frankel and Peter R. Orszag, *American Economic Policy in the 1990s* (Cambridge, MA: MIT Press, 2002), 284.

5. William J. Clinton, "Remarks on the Signing of NAFTA," Miller Center, December 8, 1993, http://millercenter.org/president/speeches/speech-3927.

6. "Kantor Letter to Ruggiero on Autos," *Inside U.S. Trade*, May 12, 1995.

7. Recorded by author at press conference following meeting of trade ministers from the "Quad" countries (United States, Japan, Canada, and the European Union) at Whistler, British Columbia, May 3–5, 1995; see also David Holley, "Trade Minister Emerges as Japan's New-Style Politico: Asia: The Nation's Point Man in the U.S. Auto Talks, Ryutaro Hashimoto, Stands Out like a Samurai Warrior," *Los Angeles Times*, June 9, 1995.

8. "Japan to Charge U.S. in WTO with Violation of MFN, Bound Tariffs," *Inside U.S. Trade*, May 17, 1995, http://insidetrade.com/inside-us-trade/japan-charge-us-wto-violation -mfn-bound-tariffs.

9. Paul A. Volcker and Toyoo Gyohten, *Changing Fortunes: The World's Money and the Threat to American Leadership* (New York: Times Books, 1992), 11.

10. Robert A. Pastor, *Congress and the Politics of U.S. Foreign Economic Policy, 1929–1976* (Berkely: University of California Press, 1980), 125.

11. Robert O. Keohane, "American Policy and the Trade-Growth Struggle," *International Security* 3, no. 2 (fall 1978).

12. Jeffrey E. Garten, "Japan and Germany: American Concerns," *Foreign Affairs* (winter 1989–1990).

13. Robert O. Keohane and Joseph S. Nye Jr., "Power and Interdependence Revisited," *International Organization* 41, no. 4 (autumn 1987), http://www.jstor.org/stable/2706764.

14. Martin Wolf, *Why Globalization Works* (New Haven, CT: Yale University Press, 2005).

15. Branko Milanovic, "Global Income Inequality by the Numbers: In History and Now," World Bank, http://elibrary.worldbank.org/doi/pdf/10.1596/1813-9450-6259.

16. Floyd Norris, "Era of Cheap Apparel May Be Ending for US," *New York Times*, January 17, 2014, http://www.nytimes.com/2014/01/18/business/era-of-cheap-apparel-may-be -ending-for-us.html.

17. Gary P. Pisano and Willy C. Shih, *Producing Prosperity: Why America Needs a Manufacturing Renaissance* (Boston: Harvard Business Review Press, 2012).

18. National Science Board, "Chapter 6: Industry, Technology, and the Global Marketplace: Trade and Other Globalization Indicators," in *Science and Engineering Indicators 2014*, National Science Foundation, http://www.nsf.gov/statistics/seind14/index.cfm/chapter-6#s3.

19. "U.S. Exports Support a Record 11.7 Million Jobs in 2014," US Department of Commerce, March 4, 2015, https://www.commerce.gov/news/press-releases/2015/03/us-exports -support-record-117-million-jobs-2014.

20. Robert E. Scott, "Heading South: U.S.-Mexico Trade and Job Displacement after NAFTA," Economic Policy Institute, May 3, 2011, http://epi.3cdn.net /fdade52b876e04793b_7fm6ivz2y.pdf.

21. David H. Autor, David Dorn, and Gordon H. Hanson, "The China Syndrome: Local Labor Market Effects of Import Competition in the United States," *American Economic Review* 103, no. 6 (2013): 2121–68.

22. Edward Alden, "Behind the New View of Globalization," *Economix* (blog), *New York Times*, August 29, 2012, http://economix.blogs.nytimes.com/2012/08/29/changing-views-of -globalizations-impact.

23. Robert Z. Lawrence, "Adjustment Challenges for US Workers," in *Bridging the Pacific: Toward Free Trade and Investment between China and the United States*, ed. C. Fred Bergsten et al. (Washington, DC: Peterson Institute for International Economics, 2014).

24. A. Michael Spence and Sandile Hlatshwayo, "The Evolving Structure of the American Economy and the Employment Challenge," Council on Foreign Relations, working pa-

per, March 2011, http://www.cfr.org/industrial-policy/evolving-structure-american-economy-employment-challenge/p24366.

25. "The Low-Wage Recovery: Industry, Employment and Wages Four Years into the Recovery," National Employment Law Project, data brief, April 2014, http://www.nelp.org/content/uploads/2015/03/Low-Wage-Recovery-Industry-Employment-Wages-2014-Report.pdf.

26. Elise Gould and Alyssa Davis, "Sluggish Wage Growth over the Last Year Is Not Due to the Mix of Jobs Being Created," Economic Policy Institute, April 24, 2015, http://www.epi.org/blog/sluggish-wage-growth-over-the-last-year-is-not-due-to-the-mix-of-jobs-being-created.

27. See Lawrence Edwards and Robert Z. Lawrence, *Rising Tide: Is Growth in Emerging Economies Good for the United States?* (Washington, DC: Peterson Institute for International Economics, February 2013).

28. See Susan M. Collins, ed., *Imports, Exports and the American Worker* (Washington, DC: Brookings Institution, 1998).

29. "WSJ Interview Transcript: President Obama on TPP, China, Japan, Pope Francis, Cuba," *Wall Street Journal*, April 27, 2015, http://blogs.wsj.com/washwire/2015/04/27/wsj-interview-transcript-president-obama-on-tpp-china-japan-pope-francis-cuba.

30. Shanker A. Singham, "Freeing the Global Market: How to Boost the Economy by Curbing Regulatory Distortions," Council on Foreign Relations, http://www.cfr.org/world/freeing-global-market-boost-economy-curbing-regulatory-distortions/p29123.

31. "Meeting Japan's Challenge: The Need for Leadership," A Study Conducted for Motorola by Yankelovich, Shelly, and White Inc., 1982.

32. Edson W. Spencer, "Japan: Stimulus or Scapegoat," *Foreign Affairs* 62, no. 1 (fall 1983), https://www.foreignaffairs.com/articles/asia/1983-09-01/japan-stimulus-or-scapegoat.

33. John Zysman and Stephen S. Cohen, "Double or Nothing: Open Trade and Competitive Industry," *Foreign Affairs* 61, no. 5 (summer 1983), https://www.foreignaffairs.com/articles/1983-06-01/double-or-nothing-open-trade-and-competitive-industry.

34. Michael L. Dertouzos, Richard K. Lester, and Robert M. Solow, *Made in America: Regaining the Productive Edge* (New York: Harper Perennial, 1989).

35. Donald W. Katzner and Mikhail J. Nikomarvo, "Exercises in Futility: Post-War Automobile Trade Negotiations between Japan and the United States," University of Massachusetts Economic Working Paper Series, 2005, https://www.umass.edu/economics/publications/2005-16.pdf.

36. Lisa Brown, "Rawlings Accelerates Foreign Sales Push," *St. Louis Post-Dispatch*, April 10, 2014, http://www.stltoday.com/business/local/rawlings-accelerates-foreign-sales-push/article_9967aabf-b597-5154-b646-3df8d45420cf.html.

37. Ernst-Ulrich Petersmann, *The GATT/WTO Dispute Settlement System: International Law, International Organizations and Dispute Settlement*. Nijhoff Law Specials (Boston: Kluwer Law International, 1997), 164.

38. See "2015 National Trade Estimate Report on Foreign Trade Barriers," Office of the United States Trade Representative, https://ustr.gov/sites/default/files/2015%20NTE%20Combined.pdf; National Trade and US Foreign and Commercial Service, "Doing Business in Japan: 2014 Country Commercial Guide for U.S. Companies," iberglobal, http://www.iberglobal.com/files/2015/japan_ccg.pdf.

39. See Edward Alden, "Anatomy of a Compromise," *Newsweek Japan*, June 6, 1994.

40. David E. Sanger, "A Deal on Auto Trade: The Agreement; U.S. Settles Trade Dispute, Averting Billions in Tariffs on Japanese Luxury Autos," *New York Times*, June 29, 1995, http://www.nytimes.com/1995/06/29/us/deal-auto-trade-agreement-us-settles-trade-dispute-averting-billions-tariffs.html.

41. "Free Trade Is Good for Everyone: Making the Trans-Pacific Partnership a Win-Win-Win for All Member Countries," Japan Automobile Manufacturers Association, March 2013, http://www.jama-english.jp/publications/tpp_pr_feb2012.pdf.

42. "Ford to End Japan Operations by End of 2016, Citing Lack of Profitability," *Inside U.S. Trade*, January 25, 2106.

43. Samuel Benka and Bill Krist, "The Auto Industry Has a Lot at Stake in TPP and TTIP," Washington International Trade Association, March 28, 2014, http://americastrade policy.com/the-auto-industry-has-a-lot-at-stake-in-tpp-and-ttip/#.U_-NHbHQp8E.

44. Rep. Sander Levin, "An Open Letter to Progressives: TPP Is Not Yet 'The Most Progressive Trade Agreement in History,'" *Huffington Post*, May 11, 2015, http://www.huffingtonpost.com/rep-sander-/an-open-letter-to-progres_b_7257776.html.

45. Alan Wm Wolff, "China's Rise: Dealing with State Capitalism—Again."

46. Edward J. Lincoln, *Troubled Times: U.S.-Japan Trade Relations in the 1990s* (Washington, DC: Brookings Institution Press, 1999), 207.

47. Testimony of Treasury Secretary Lawrence Summers, US House of Representatives, Committee on Banking and Financial Services, Hearing on Permanent Normal Trade Relations for China (PNTR), May 11, 2000.

48. Robert B. Zoellick, "Whither China: From Membership to Responsibility?," remarks to National Committee on US-China Relations, New York City, September 21, 2005.

49. Testimony of US Trade Representative Charlene Barshefsky, US Senate, Committee on Banking, Hearing on the China WTO Agreement and Financial Services, May 9, 2000.

50. "U.S.-China Business Council Welcomes Administration Move on Permanent Normal Trade Relations with China," PR Newswire, January 10, 2000, http://www.prnewswire.com/news-releases/us-china-business-council-welcomes-administration-moves-on-permanent-normal-trade-relations-with-china-72012377.html.

51. Ernest H. Preeg, "The U.S. Trade Deficit in Manufactures and the Chinese Surplus Continued to Surge in 2012," MAPI Policy Analysis, February 13, 2013, https://www.mapi.net/research/publications/chinese-surplus-continued-surge.

52. Wayne M. Morrison, "China's Economic Rise: History, Trends, Challenges, and Implications for the United States," Congressional Research Service, June 14, 2015, http://fas.org/sgp/crs/row/RL33534.pdf.

53. "2014 Report to Congress on China's WTO Compliance," US Trade Representative, December 2014, https://ustr.gov/sites/default/files/2014-Report-to-Congress-Final.pdf, 2–3.

54. "The Impact of International Technology Transfer on American Research and Development," testimony of Robert D. Atkinson, president of Information Technology and Innovation Foundation, US House of Representatives, Science Committee, Subcommittee on Investigations and Oversight, December 5, 2012.

55. "The Impact of International Technology Transfer on American Research and Development."

56. Usha C. V. Haley and George T. Haley, *Subsidies to Chinese Industry: State Capitalism, Business Strategy, and Trade Policy* (Oxford: Oxford University Press, 2013).

57. "Chinese State Owned Enterprises and US Policy on China," testimony of Derek Scissors, US-China Economic and Security Review Commission, February 15, 2012.

58. Robert D. Atkinson, "The Explosive Rise of Subsidies to Chinese Industry," Breakthrough Institute, November 24, 2013, http://thebreakthrough.org/index.php/programs/economic-growth/the-explosive-rise-of-subsidies-to-chinese-industry.

59. Keith Bradsher, "Solar Panel Maker Moves Work to China," *New York Times*, January 14, 2011, http://www.nytimes.com/2011/01/15/business/energy-environment/15solar.html.

60. Keith Bradsher, "Despite Trade Rulings, Beijing Gains from Delay Tactics," *New York Times*, August 30, 2009, http://www.nytimes.com/2009/08/31/business/global/31iht-trade.html.

61. Bill Canis and Wayne M. Morrison, "U.S.-Chinese Motor Vehicle Trade: Overview and Issues," Congressional Research Service, August 16, 2013, 12.

62. Usha C. V. Haley, "Putting the Pedal to the Metal: Subsidies to China's Auto-Parts Industry from 2001 to 2011," Economic Policy Institute, January 31, 2012, http://www.epi.org/publication/bp316-china-auto-parts-industry.

63. Canis and Morrison, "U.S.-Chinese Motor Vehicle Trade," 8.

64. "Trends in U.S. Vehicle Exports," US Department of Commerce, International Trade Administration, August 2015, http://www.trade.gov/td/otm/assets/auto/ExportPaper2015.pdf.

65. "Trends in U.S. Vehicle Exports."

66. Haley, "Putting the Pedal to the Metal," 15.

67. Fabrice Defever and Alejandro Riano, "China's Pure Exporter Subsidies: Protectionism by Exporting," *Vox*, January 4, 2013, http://www.voxeu.org/article/china-s-pure-exporter-subsidies-protectionism-exporting article.

68. "2015 National Trade Estimate Report on Foreign Trade Barriers," 79.

69. Haley and Haley, *Subsidies to Chinese Industry*, 36–39.

70. Derek Scissors, "Statement before the Senate Committee on Banking, Housing, and Urban Affairs Subcommittee on Economic Policy on 'Rebuilding American Manufacturing': The Importance of Chinese Subsidies," December 11, 2013, http://www.banking.senate.gov/public/_cache/files/87eaf06c-3510-4222-ae9b-f9bc243f3d2a/23C6AE00CC53D93492511CC744028B5E.scissorstestimony121113.pdf.

71. Louise Keely and Brian Anderson, "Sold in China: Transitioning to a Consumer-Led Economy," Demand Institute, 2015.

72. "A Decade of Unprecedented Growth: China's Impact on the Semiconductor Industry, 2014 Update," PriceWaterhouseCoopers, August 2014, http://www.pwc.com/gx/en/technology/chinas-impact-on-semiconductor-industry/assets/2014-update.pdf.

73. Gordon Orr and Christopher Thomas, "Semiconductors in China: Brave New World or Same Old Story?," McKinsey and Co., August 2014, http://www.mckinsey.com/insights/high_tech_telecoms_internet/semiconductors_in_china_brave_new_world_or_same_old_story.

74. John Zysman and Laura Tyson, eds., *American Industry in International Competition: Government Policies and Corporate Strategies* (Ithaca, NY: Cornell University Press, 1983), 143.

75. Zysman and Tyson, *American Industry in International Competition*, 155.

76. Kenneth Flamm, *Mismanaged Trade: Strategic Policy and the Semiconductor Industry* (Washington, DC: Brookings Institution, 1996).

77. Clair Brown and Craig Linden, *Chips and Change: How Crisis Reshapes the Semiconductor Industry* (Cambridge, MA: MIT Press, 2009).

78. Zysman and Tyson, *American Industry in International Competition*, 145.

79. John Kunkel, *America's Trade Policy towards Japan: Demanding Results* (London: Routledge, 2003), 83.

80. Kunkel, *America's Trade Policy towards Japan*, 91.

81. Irwin, "Trade Policies and the Semiconductor Industry," in *The Political Economy of American Trade Policy*, ed. Anne O. Krueger (Chicago: University of Chicago Press, 1996).

82. Irwin, "Trade Policies and the Semiconductor Industry," 54.

83. Flamm, *Mismanaged Trade*, chapter 5.

84. Brown and Linden, *Chips and Change*.

85. Flamm, *Mismanaged Trade*, 436.

86. "Request for Comments on Negotiating Objectives with Respect to Japan's Participation in the Proposed Trans-Pacific Partnership Trade Agreement," Docket Number USTR-2013-0022, Semiconductor Industry Association, June 9, 2013, http://www.semiconductors .org/clientuploads/Trade%20and%20IP/SIA_Comments_on_Japan%27s_Participation_in _TPP-_FINAL.pdf.

87. U.S. Commerce Department, International Trade Administration, "2015 Top Markets Report: Semiconductors and Semiconductor Manufacturing Equipment," July 2105.

88. Falun Yinug, "U.S. Semiconductor Industry Employment," Semiconductor Industry Association, January 2015.

89. John Newhouse, *Boeing versus Airbus: The Inside Story of the Greatest International Competition in Business* (New York: Vintage Books, 2007).

90. Matthew Lynn, *Birds of Prey: Boeing versus Airbus, a Battle for the Skies* (New York: Four Walls Eight Windows, 1998), 224.

91. Jeffrey D. Kienstra, "Cleared for Landing: Airbus, Boeing and the WTO Dispute over Subsidies to Large Civil Aircraft," *Northwestern Journal of International Law and Business* (summer 2012).

92. See Douglas A. Irwin and Nina Pavenik, "Airbus versus Boeing Revisited: International Competition in the Aircraft Market," National Bureau of Economic Research, Working Paper 8648, December 2001.

93. Daniel Michaels, Jon Ostrower, and David Pearson, "Airbus's New Push: Made in the USA," *Wall Street Journal*, July 2, 2012, http://www.wsj.com/articles/SB100014240527023 04211804577502000504183004; Robin Wright, "Airbus Seeks to Unlock Commercial Jet Market with New Factory," *Financial Times*, September 22, 2014, http://www.ft.com/intl /cms/s/0/f2bfe83e-3f47-11e4-a5f500144feabdc0.html#axzz3loxk1T7l.

CHAPTER 3

1. "Debate Transcript," *New York Times*, December 7, 2008, http://www.nytimes .com/2008/02/27/world/americas/27iht-26textdebate.10457266.html.

2. White House, "Here's the Deal: The Trans-Pacific Partnership," November 6, 2015, https://www.whitehouse.gov/blog/2015/11/06/heres-deal-trans-pacific-partnership.

3. Senator Rob Portman, "Portman Urges Passage of Amendment on Currency Manipulation," YouTube, May 20, 2015, https://www.youtube.com/watch?v=vM2PUeL4AA4.

4. C. Fred Bergsten, "Currency Wars, the Economy of the United States and the Reform of the International Monetary System," Stavros Niarchos Foundation Lecture, May 16, 2013.

5. "IMF Involvement in International Trade Policy Issues," International Monetary Fund, 2009, http://www.ieo-imf.org/ieo/files/completedevaluations/Trade_Main_Report.pdf, 78.

6. See the discussion in C. Randall Henning, "Congress, Treasury, and the Accountability of Exchange Rate Policy: How the 1988 Trade Act Should Be Reformed," Peterson Institute for International Economics, working paper, September 2007, http://www.piie.com/publications/interstitial.cfm?ResearchID=801.

7. Bergsten, "Currency Wars." See also Michael Pettis, *The Great Rebalancing: Trade, Conflict, and the Perilous Road Ahead for the World Economy* (Princeton, NJ: Princeton University Press, 2013).

8. Robert Z. Lawrence, *Can America Compete?* (Washington, DC: Brookings Institution, 1984), 3.

9. About 63 percent of official foreign exchange reserves are in dollars, compared with 27 percent in euros, while 86 percent of all foreign exchange transactions are carried out in dollars. See Richard Dobbs et al., "An Exorbitant Privilege? Implications of Reserve Currencies for Competitiveness," McKinsey Global Institute, 2009, http://www.mckinsey.com/global-themes/employment-and-growth/an-exorbitant-privilege.

10. C. Randall Henning, *Currencies and Politics in the United States, Germany and Japan* (Washington, DC: Institute for International Economics, 1994), 1.

11. Alan Greenspan, *The Age of Turbulence: Adventures in a New World* (New York: Penguin Press, 2007), 347.

12. C. Fred. Bergsten, "Addressing Currency Manipulation through Trade Agreements," Peterson Institute for International Economics, January 2014, http://www.iie.com/publications/interstitial.cfm?ResearchID=2549.

13. Kenneth Austin, "Systemic Equilibrium in a Bretton Woods II–Type International Monetary System: The Special Role of Reserve Issuers and Reserve Accumulators," *Journal of Post Keynsian Economics* 36, no. 4 (summer 2014): 607–34, http://econpapers.repec.org/article/mespostke/v_3a36_3ay_3a2014_3ai_3a4_3ap_3a607-634.htm.

14. See Barry Eichengreen, "Global Imbalances and the Lessons of Bretton Woods," National Bureau of Economic Research, Working Paper 10497, May 2004, http://www.nber.org/papers/w10497.

15. Paul A. Volcker and Toyoo Gyohten, *Changing Fortunes: The World's Money and the Threat to American Leadership* (New York: Times Books, 1992), 40.

16. See Joanne Gowa, *Closing the Gold Window: Domestic Politics and the End of Bretton Woods* (Ithaca, NY: Cornell University Press, 1983).

17. See John S. Odell, *U.S. International Monetary Policy: Markets, Power and Ideas as Sources of Change* (Princeton, NJ: Princeton University Press, 1982).

18. Volcker and Gyohten, *Changing Fortunes*, 73.

19. Eichengreen, "Global Imbalances and the Lessons of Bretton Woods."

20. Douglas A. Irwin, "The Nixon Shock after Forty Years: The Import Surcharge Revisited," *World Trade Review* 12, no. 1 (January 2013): 29–56, http://www.nber.org/papers/w17749.

21. Thomas W. Zeiler, "Nixon Shocks the Trade System," Western University History Department, July 17, 2010, http://history.uwo.ca/Conferences/trade-and-conflict/files/zeiler.pdf.

22. Volcker and Gyohten, *Changing Fortunes*, 104.

23. Otto Eckstein et al., *The DRI Report on U.S. Manufacturing Industries* (New York: McGraw-Hill, 1984).

24. "The U.S. Economic Contraction and Trade Deficit: Quantifying Exchange Rate Fluctuations' Impact on International Trade Flows," Penn Wharton Public Policy Initiative,

June 10, 2015, http://publicpolicy.wharton.upenn.edu/live/news/727-the-us-economic-con
traction-and-trade-deficit.

25. Thomas Klitgaard and James Orr, "Evaluating the Price Competitiveness of U.S. Exports," *Current Issues in Economics and Finance* 4, no. 2 (February 1998), http://www.new yorkfed.org/research/current_issues/ci4-2.pdf. The effect holds even when comparing exports to a particular market, which helps to correct for faster or slower growth in certain regions. Germany's exports were slowed overall in the first half of the 1990s by weak growth in its major European export markets. Yet while German exports to Europe grew by just 9 percent from 1991 to 1997, US exports to Europe rose 24 percent over the same period.

26. "U.S. International Trade in Goods and Services," Bureau of Economic Analysis, April 2016, http://www.bea.gov/newsreleases/international/trade/tradnewsrelease.htm.

27. Martin S. Feldstein, *American Economic Policy in the 1980s* (Chicago: University of Chicago Press, 1994).

28. Arthur Burns, "The American Trade Deficit in Perspective," *Foreign Affairs* 62, no. 5 (summer 1984), https://www.foreignaffairs.com/articles/united-states/1984-06-01/american -trade-deficit-perspective.

29. Quoted in Robert Schaeffer, *Understanding Globalization: The Social Consequences of Political, Economic, and Environmental Change* (Lanham, MD: Rowman & Littlefield, 1997), 41.

30. Feldstein, *American Economic Policy in the 1980s*.

31. C. Randall Henning and I. M. Destler, "From Neglect to Activism: American Politics and the 1985 Plaza Accord," *Journal of Public Policy* 8, nos. 3/4 (July–December 1988), http:// www.jstor.org/stable/4007187.

32. See Michael D. Bordo, Owen F. Humpage, and Anna J. Schwartz, *Strained Relations: U.S. Foreign-Exchange Operations and Monetary Policy in the Twentieth Century* (Chicago: University of Chicago Press, 2015).

33. Henning, *Currencies and Politics*, 136–38.

34. I. M. Destler and C. Randall Henning, *Dollar Politics: Exchange Rate Policymaking in the United States* (Washington, DC: Institute for International Economics, 1989), 23.

35. Clyde H. Farnsworth, "Talking Business with Treasury Secretary Donald T. Regan; Seeking Stable Money Rates," *New York Times*, March 29, 1983, http://www.nytimes .com/1983/03/29/business/talking-business-with-treasury-secretary-donald-t-regan-seeking -stable-money.html.

36. Jeffrey A. Frankel, "Exchange Rate Policy," in *American Economic Policy in the 1980s*, ed. Martin Feldstein (Chicago: University of Chicago Press, 1994).

37. Clyde H. Fansworth, "Dollar Rise Is Defended by Regan," *New York Times*, February 23, 1984, http://www.nytimes.com/1984/02/23/business/dollar-rise-is-defended-by-regan .html.

38. Quoted in William Greider, *Secrets of the Temple: How the Federal Reserve Runs the Country* (New York: Simon & Schuster, 1987), 597–98.

39. Henning, *Currencies and Politics*, 273–74.

40. Henning and Destler, "From Neglect to Activism," 321.

41. I. M. Destler, "The Dollar and U.S. Trade Politics," Peterson Institute for International Economics, 2003, http://www.piie.com/publications/chapters_preview/360/4iie3519.pdf.

42. Feldstein, *American Economic Policy in the 1980s*.

43. Burns, "The American Trade Deficit in Perspective."

44. Henning and Destler, "From Neglect to Activism," 322.

45. James Risen, "Caterpillar Tries to Dig Itself Out," *Los Angeles Times*, January 13, 1985, http://articles.latimes.com/1985-01-13/business/fi-8949_1_caterpillar-products.

46. "Still Losing, Caterpillar Struggles On," *Milwaukee Journal*, January 22, 1985, http://news.google.com/newspapers?nid=1499&dat=19850122&id=Rm4aAAAAIBAJ&sjid=JCoE AAAAIBAJ&pg=6339,1046130.

47. See Destler and Henning, *Dollar Politics*, 124–29.

48. Greider, *Secrets of the Temple*, 593.

49. Robert E. Scott, "Currency Manipulation: History Shows That Sanctions Are Needed," Economic Policy Institute, April 29, 2010, http://www.epi.org/publication/pm164.

50. Destler and Henning, *Dollar Politics*, 38–40.

51. James Baker, *Work Hard, Study . . . and Keep Out of Politics!* (New York: G. P. Putnam's Sons, 2006), 451.

52. Baker, *Work Hard*, 429.

53. Baker, *Work Hard*, 431.

54. William R. Cline, "The Case for a New Plaza Agreement," Institute for International Economics, December 2005, http://www.iie.com/publications/pb/pb05-4.pdf.

55. Baker, *Work Hard*, 432.

56. Feldstein, for example, insisted for many years that the correction was entirely market driven and that, while the Plaza intervention produced a small downward movement in the dollar, the fall had begun six months before the announcement and continued at roughly the same pace afterward, suggesting "the inappropriateness of interpreting the dollar's decline after September 1985 as evidence that coordinated intervention was effective." See "New Evidence on the Effects of Exchange Rate Intervention," National Bureau of Economic Research, Working Paper 2052, October 1986, http://www.nber.org/papers/w2052. However, in a 2006 speech to the Stanford Institute for Economic Policy Research titled "The Case for a Competitive Dollar," Feldstein suggested that the coordinated government action at Plaza had indeed played a decisive role. In making the case that a new round of devaluation was needed to correct the record trade imbalance, Feldstein called for a new Plaza Accord. His version this time was that, following the G-5 statement in September 1985 that the dollar needed to decline, "the markets did the rest, confident that the U.S. government did not have a sudden plan to punish those who sold dollars by engineering a sudden reversal of the dollar." That claim is odd in the extreme, since—as Feldstein well knows—prior to the surprising Plaza announcement, the Reagan administration had made a blanket, repeatedly stated refusal to intervene in currency markets. Whatever was preventing a fall in the dollar prior to 1985, it was surely not investor fears that the US government would "engineer a sudden reversal of the dollar."

57. "H.R. 4848—100th Congress: Omnibus Trade and Competitiveness Act of 1988," US Department of the Treasury, http://www.treasury.gov/resource-center/international/exchange-rate-policies/Documents/authorizing-statute.pdf.

58. Phillip Bowring, "The Plaza Accord Worked . . . ," *Asia Sentinel*, November 15, 2010, http://www.asiasentinel.com/econ-business/the-plaza-accord-worked.

59. Christina D. Romer, "Needed: Plain Talk about the Dollar," *New York Times*, May 21, 2011.

60. Robert E. Rubin, *In an Uncertain World: Tough Choices from Wall Street to Washington* (New York: Random House, 2003), 182–83.

61. Keith Bradsher, "Treasury Chief Says Strong Dollar Isn't a Threat to Trade," *New York Times*, August 17, 1995, http://www.nytimes.com/1995/08/17/business/international-business-treasury-chief-says-strong-dollar-isn-t-a-threat-to-trade.html.

62. Rubin, *In an Uncertain World*, 182–83.

63. Michael D. Bordo et. al, *Strained Relations*, pp. 320–21.

64. Thomas I. Palley, "The Overvalued Dollar and the US slump," in *Dollar Overvaluation and the World Economy*, ed. C. Fred Bergsten and John Williamson (Washington, DC: Institute for International Economics, February 2003), http://www.piie.com/publications/chapters_preview/360/7iie3519.pdf.

65. Robert A. Blecker, "The Benefits of a Lower Dollar," Economic Policy Institute Briefing Paper, May 2003.

66. C. Randall Henning, *Accountability and Oversight of U.S. Exchange Rate Policy* (Washington, DC: Peterson Institute for International Economics, June 2008), http://bookstore.piie.com/book-store/4198.html, 4.

67. Eswar S. Prasad, *The Dollar Trap: How the U.S. Dollar Tightened Its Grip on Global Finance* (Princeton, NJ: Princeton University Press, 2014), 144.

68. C. Fred Bergsten, "The Dollar and the Renminbi," statement before the Hearing on "U.S. Economic Relations with China: Strategies and Options on Exchange Rates and Market Access," Subcommittee on Security and International Trade and Finance, Committee on Banking, Housing and Urban Affairs, US Senate, May 23, 2007.

69. Henning, *Accountability*, 21.

70. Henning, *Accountability*, 35.

71. Henning, *Accountability*, 32–33.

72. Henning, *Accountability*, 3.

73. Henning, *Accountability*, 45.

74. "IMF Staff Completes the 2015 Article IV Consultation Mission to China," International Monetary Fund, http://www.imf.org/external/np/sec/pr/2015/pr15237.htm.

75. Louise Keely and Brian Anderson, "Sold in China: Transitioning to a Consumer-Led Economy," Demand Institute, July 22, 2015, http://demandinstitute.org/sold-in-china.

76. "The Path to Sustainable Growth in China," testimony of Esward Prasad, US-China Economic and Security Review Commission, April 22, 2015.

77. Christopher Alessi, "Raw Nerve: Germany Seethes at US Economic Criticism," *Spiegel Online*, October 31, 2013, http://www.spiegel.de/international/germany/germany-defends-trade-surplus-after-critical-us-treasury-report-a-931126.html.

78. Martin Feldstein, "The Case for a Competitive Dollar," remarks to the Economic Summit of the Stanford Institute for Economic Policy Research, March 3, 2006.

79. Bergsten, "Currency Wars."

CHAPTER 4

1. George Meany, "Trade, Progress, and Prosperity," quoted in Aly Bower, ed., *American Trade Policy* (Columbia, MO: Artcraft Press, 1962.)

2. "Foreign Trade and Tariff Proposals: Hearings before the Committee on Ways and Means," House of Representatives, 90th Congress (1968), Stewart and Stewart, http://www.stewartlaw.com/Content/Documents/HR%20-%20Foreign%20Trade%20and%20Tariff%20Proposals%20part%203.pdf.

3. Thomas W. Zeiler, *American Trade and Power in the 1960s* (New York: Columbia University Press, 1992), 144–45.

4. John B. Judis, *The Paradox of American Democracy* (New York: Routledge, 2001), 110–11.

5. Carolyn C. Perrucci et al., *Plant Closings: International Context and Social Costs* (New York: Aldine de Guyter, 1988).

6. National Association of Manufacturers, *U.S. Stake in World Trade and Investment: The Role of the Multinational Corporation* (New York: National Association of Manufacturers, 1972), 2.

7. Jefferson Cowie, *Capital Moves: RCA's Seventy-Year Quest for Cheap Labor* (New York: New Press, 1999).

8. C. Fred Bergsten, Thomas Horst, and Theodore H. Moran, *American Multinationals and American Interests* (Washington, DC: Brookings Institution, 1978), 10.

9. Judis, *The Paradox of American Democracy*, 114.

10. Judis, *The Paradox of American Democracy*, 112.

11. "Foreign Trade and Tariff Proposals."

12. "Foreign Trade and Tariff Proposals."

13. Quoted in Kent H. Hughes, *Trade, Taxes, and Transnationals: International Economic Decision Making in Congress* (New York: Praeger, 1979), 122.

14. See Edward Alden, "American Workers Need a Powerful Voice, not Mere Bluster," *Washington Post*, May 6, 2015, https://www.washingtonpost.com/opinions/american-workers-need -a-powerful-voice-not-mere-bluster/2015/05/06/af642bf4-f3e7-11e4-bcc4-e8141e5eb0c9 _story.html.

15. "World Trade in the 1970s," report of the Economic Policy Committee to AFL-CIO Executive Council, February 20, 1973.

16. See Scott article in Bruce R. Scott and George C. Lodge, eds., *U.S. Competitiveness in the World Economy* (Boston: Harvard Business School Press, 1985). See also Charles W. L. Hill, Michael A. Hitt, and Robert E. Hoskisson, "Declining U.S. Competitiveness: Reflections on a Crisis," *Academy of Management Executive* 2, no. 1 (February 1988): 51–60, http://www.jstor .org/stable/pdf/4164795.pdf.

17. Michael L. Dertousoz, *Made in America: Regaining the Productive Edge* (Cambridge, MA: MIT Commission on Industrial Productivity, MIT Press, 1989), 43.

18. Dertousoz, *Made in America*, 47.

19. Suzanne Berger, *How We Compete: What Companies Around the World Are Doing to Make It in Today's Global Economy* (New York: Doubleday, 2005).

20. Edward Alden and Rebecca Strauss, *How America Stacks Up: Economic Competitiveness and U.S. Policy* (New York: Council on Foreign Relations, February 2016).

21. Floyd Norris, "Corporate Profits Grow and Wages Slide," *New York Times*, April 4, 2014, http://www.nytimes.com/2014/04/05/business/economy/corporate-profits-grow-ever -larger-as-slice-of-economy-as-wages-slide.html.

22. Sam Ro, "CHART: A Breakdown of Where S&P 500 Companies Get Overseas Business," *Business Insider*, June 27, 2012, http://www.businessinsider.com/chart-sp-500-revenue -geography-2012-6.

23. Martin Neil Baily and Robert M. Solow, "International Productivity Comparisons Built from the Firm Level," *Journal of Economic Perspectives* 15, no. 3 (summer 2001): 151–72.

24. "Making the United States Competitive," *Harvard Magazine*, May 16, 2013, http:// harvardmagazine.com/2013/05/competitiveness-conference.

25. Thomas Anderson, "Summary Estimates for Multinational Companies: Employment, Sales, and Capital Expenditures for 2011," Bureau of Economic Analysis, April 18, 2013, http://www.bea.gov/newsreleases/international/mnc/2013/_pdf/mnc2011.pdf.

26. Laura Tyson, "Are US Multinationals Abandoning America?," *Project Syndicate*, April 3, 2012, http://www.project-syndicate.org/commentary/are-us-multinationals-abandoning -america.

27. James K. Jackson, "Outsourcing and Insourcing Jobs in the U.S. Economy: Evidence Based on Foreign Investment Data," Congressional Research Service, June 21, 2013.

28. Yingying Xu, "The Employment Effects of US Multinationals' Overseas Expansion," Manufacturers Alliance for Productivity and Innovation, August 2012.

29. Robert Lipsey, "Home and Host Country Effects of FDI," National Bureau of Economic Research, Working Paper 9293, October 2002.

30. Gary Clyde Hufbauer, Theodore H. Moran, and Lindsay Oldenski, *Outward Foreign Direct Investment and US Exports, Jobs, and R&D: Implications for US Policy*, Policy Analyses in International Economics, Peterson Institute, August 2013.

31. Charles Duhigg and Keith Bradsher, "How the U.S. Lost Out on iPhone Work," *New York Times*, January 21, 2012, http://www.nytimes.com/2012/01/22/business/apple-america -and-a-squeezed-middle-class.html.

32. Juann H. Hung and Priscila Hammett, "Globalization and the Labor Share of Income in the United States," Graduate Institute of International Economics, February 25, 2013, http://econ.ccu.edu.tw/graduate/20130304.pdf.

33. Matthew J. Slaughter, "How America Is Made for Trade," HSBC, 2014, https:// globalconnections.hsbc.com/us/en/articles/comprehensive-trade-agenda-could-create-10-mil lion-us-jobs-new-report-finds.

34. Michael W. L. Elsby, Bart Hobijn, and Aysegul Sahin, "The Decline of the U.S. Labor Share," *Brookings Papers on Economic Activity*, fall 2013, http://www.brookings.edu/~/media /Projects/BPEA/Fall%202013/2013b_elsby_labor_share.pdf.

35. Kate Bronfenbrenner, "Uneasy Terrian: The Impact of Capital Mobility on Workers, Wages, and Union Organizing," Cornell University Research Studies and Reports, September 6, 2000.

36. Peter G. Peterson, *The United States in a Changing World Economy* (Washington, DC: US Government Printing Office, 1971), iii.

37. Charles Culhane, "Economic Report: Labor and Industry Gear for Major Battle over Bill to Curb Imports, Multinationals," *National Journal*, January 15, 1972, 108–19.

38. Hughes, *Trade, Taxes, and Transnationals*, 131.

39. Robert A. Pastor, *Congress and the Politics of U.S. Foreign Economic Policy, 1929–1976* (Berkeley: University of California Press, 1980), 207.

40. Statement of Andrew J. Biemiller, director, Department of Legislation, AFL-CIO, before the Subcommittee on Multinational Corporations of the Senate Committee on Foreign Relations, December 10, 1975.

41. Andrew J. Biemiller, speech to the John Bassett Moore Society, School of Law, University of Virginia, March 15, 1974, AFL-CIO Collection, University of Maryland Special Collections, Volume 7, Box 7.

42. Hughes, *Trade, Taxes, and Transnationals*, 24.

43. Culhane, "Economic Report," 112.

44. Hughes, *Trade, Taxes, and Transnationals*, 114.

45. Pastor, *Congress and the Politics of U.S. Foreign Economic Policy*, 133.

46 News Release, "ECAT Will Lead Campaign for Multinational Companies," February 24, 1972, in *Multinational Corporations: A Compendium of Papers Submitted to the Subcom-*

mittee on International Trade of the Committee on Finance in the United States Senate, ed. US Senate, Committee on Finance, Subcommittee on International Trade (Washington, DC: US Government Printing Office, 1973), 734.

47. C. Fred Bergsten, *Towards a New International Economic Order: Selected Papers of C. Fred Bergsten, 1971–1974* (Lexington, MA: Lexington Books, 1975), 466.

48. Elliott L. Richardson, "United States Policy toward Foreign Investment: We Can't Have It Both Ways," *American University International Law Review* 4, no. 2 (1989), http:// digitalcommons.wcl.american.edu/cgi/viewcontent.cgi?article=1675&context=auilr.

49. Pastor, *Congress and the Politics of U.S. Foreign Economic Policy*, 213.

50. Pastor, *Congress and the Politics of U.S. Foreign Economic Policy*, 221.

51. "President Obama to Announce First-Ever Federal Effort to Attract Job-Creating Foreign Investment to the United States," White House Office of the Press Secretary, October 31, 2013, http://www.whitehouse.gov/the-press-office/2013/10/31/president-obama-announce -first-ever-federal-effort-attract-job-creating-.

52. "Global Investment Promotion Benchmarking 2009, Summary Report," World Bank Group, May 2009, https://www.wbginvestmentclimate.org/uploads/GIPB2009.Summary Report.pdf.

53. "Gross Private Domestic Investment," Bureau of Labor Statistics, last modified December 8, 2015, http://www.bls.gov/emp/ep_table_405.htm.

54. Slaughter, "How America Is Made for Trade," 12.

55. Timothy D. Cook, testimony of Apple Inc. before the Permanent Subcommittee on Investigations, US Senate, May 21, 2013; testimony of J. Richard (Dick) Harvey Jr. before the Permanent Subcommittee on Investigations, US Senate, May 21, 2013.

56. Nelson D. Schwartz and Brian X. Chen, "Disarming Senators, Apple Chief Eases Tax Tensions," *New York Times*, May 21, 2013, http://www.nytimes.com/2013/05/22/technology /ceo-denies-that-apple-is-avoiding-taxes.html.

57. "Historical Source of Revenue as Share of GDP," Tax Policy Center, February 4, 2015, http://www.taxpolicycenter.org/taxfacts/displayafact.cfm?Docid=205.

58. Nahid Kalbasi Anaraki, "Does Corporate Tax Rate Affect FDI? Case Study of Core European Countries," *Journal of Global Economy* 11, no. 2 (June 2015).

59. Edward Alden and Rebecca Strauss, "Standard Deductions: US Corporate Tax Policy," Council on Foreign Relations, http://www.cfr.org/tax-policy/standard-deductions-us-corporate -tax-policy/p32655, January 2016.

60. Martin A. Sullivan, *Corporate Tax Reform: Taxing Profits in the 21st Century* (New York: Apress, 2011).

61. Melissa Costa and Jennifer Gravelle, "Taxing Multinational Corporations: Average Tax Rates," American Tax Policy Institute, http://www.americantaxpolicyinstitute.org/pdf /Costa-Gravelle%20paper.pdf.

62. Harvey testimony, May 21, 2013.

63. Harvey testimony, May 21, 2013.

64. Quoted from Office of Tax Policy, Department of the Treasury, "The Deferral of Income Earned through U.S. Controlled Foreign Corporations: A Policy Study," December 2000.

65. Sullivan, *Corporate Tax Reform*, 80.

66. Michael R. Sesit, "Firms with US Units Face a Taxing Problem," *Wall Street Journal*, August 9, 2002, http://www.wsj.com/articles/SB10288186069620280.

67. Ama Sarfo, "'Earning Stripping' Fix Could Blunt Foreign Investment," Law360, August 22, 2014, http://www.law360.com/articles/569682/earnings-stripping-fix-could-blunt -foreign-investment.

68. "Foreign Direct Investment in the United States: 2014 Report," Organization for International Investment, http://www.ofii.org/sites/default/files/FDIUS2014.pdf.

69. Jackson, "Outsourcing and Insourcing Jobs in the U.S. Economy," 9.

70. Eric Lipton and Jonathan Weisman, "Corporate Lobbyists Assail Tax Overhaul They Once Cheered," *New York Times*, April 2, 2014, http://www.nytimes.com/2014/04/02/busi ness/tax-lobby-works-to-defeat-overhaul-it-once-cheered.html.

71. Kelsey Snell and Kim Dixon, "Obama Budget Pitch: Tax Offshore Profits to Fix US Roads," *Politico*, February 2, 2015, http://www.politico.com/story/2015/02/barack-obama -2015-budget-proposal-taxes-offshore-114799.html.

72. Michael E. Porter and Jan W. Rivkin, "Prosperity at Risk: Findings of the Harvard Business School's Survey on U.S. Competitiveness," Harvard Business School, January 2012, http://www.hbs.edu/competitiveness/Documents/hbscompsurvey.pdf.

73. Jackson, "Outsourcing and Insourcing Jobs in the U.S. Economy," 6.

74. Edward Gresser, "78 Percent of US Imports from Developing Countries Are Duty-Free," Progressive Policy Institute, January 14, 2015, http://www.progressive-economy.org /trade_facts/78-percent-of-u-s-imports-from-developing-countries-are-duty-free.

75. "A Tightening Grip: Rising Chinese Wages Will Only Strengthen Asia's Hold on Manufacturing," *Economist*, May 14, 2015, http://www.economist.com/news/briefing/21646180 -rising-chinese-wages-will-only-strengthen-asias-hold-manufacturing-tightening-grip.

76. Stephen S. Golub, "International Labor Standards and International Trade," IMF Research Department, working paper, April 1997, http://www.imf.org/external/pubs/ft/wp /wp9737.pdf.

77. Harley Shaiken, "Going South," *American Prospect*, December 19, 2001, http://pros pect.org/article/going-south.

78. Harley Shaiken, "The Nafta Paradox," *Berkeley Review of Latin American Studies* (spring 2014), http://clas.berkeley.edu/research/trade-nafta-paradox.

79. Bill Vlasic, "Wariness as Detroit's Big 3 Look to Mexico for Growth," *New York Times*, July 23, 2015, http://www.nytimes.com/2015/07/23/business/wariness-as-auto-industry -eyes-mexico-for-growth.html.

80. Paul R. Krugman, "Trade and Wages, Reconsidered," Brookings Panel on Economic Activity, spring 2008, http://www.brookings.edu/~/media/projects/bpea/spring-2008/2008a _bpea_krugman.pdf.

81. Lance A. Compa and Jeffrey S. Vogt, "Labor Rights in the Generalized System of Preferences: A 20-Year Review," *Comparative Labor Law & Policy Journal* 22, no. 2/3 (2000–2001): 201.

82. Robert Rogowsky and Eric Chyn, "In Global Trade, Labor Standards Have a Long History," American Enterprise Institute, July 18, 2007, http://www.aei.org/publication/in -global-trade-labor-standards-have-a-long-history.

83. "Peru: Legal Reforms Encourage More Local and Foreign Investment," Oxford Business Group, http://www.oxfordbusinessgroup.com/overview/legal-reforms-encourage-more -local-and-foreign-investment.

84. Brian Finnegan, "Peru Supersizes Its Backslider Regulation," *AFL-CIO Now* (blog), July 22, 2014, http://www.aflcio.org/Blog/Global-Action/Peru-Supersizes-Its-Backslider-Legislation.

85. Compa and Vogt, "Labor Rights."

86. Alex Lawson, "US Loses First Trade Cases as Guatemala Prevails," Law 360, New York, June 26, 2017, at https://www.law360.com/internationalarbitration/articles/938456/us-loses -first-labor-trade-case-as-guatemala-prevails.

87. Elizabeth Becker, "Bush Reject's Labor's Call to Punish China," *New York Times*, April 29, 2004, http://www.nytimes.com/2004/04/29/business/29trade.html.

88. C. Fred Bergsten, "Coming Investment Wars," *Foreign Affairs* 53, no. 1 (October 1974).

89. "TPP Full Text," Office of the United States Trade Representative, https://ustr.gov /trade-agreements/free-trade-agreements/trans-pacific-partnership/tpp-full-text.

90. Kenneth P. Thomas, *Investment Incentives and the Global Competition for Capital* (New York: Palgrave McMillan, 2010), 17.

91. Vale Columbia Center, "Investment Incentives: The Good, the Bad, and the Ugly: As-sessing the Costs, Benefits, and Options for Policy Reform" (background paper for the Eighth Columbia International Investment Conference, Columbia University, New York, November 13–14, 2013).

92. "Investment in the Czech Republic," KPMG, 2014, https://www.kpmg.com/CZ /cs/IssuesAndInsights/ArticlesPublications/Factsheets/Documents/KPMG-Investment-in-the -Czech-Republic-2014.pdf.

93. Vale Columbia Center, "Investment Incentives," 91–92.

94. Martin A. Sullivan, "Lessons for the Last War on Tax Havens," Tax Analysts, July 30, 2007, http://www.taxanalysts.com/www/features.nsf/Articles/F3AA18739F0EFF008525744 B0066459B?OpenDocument.

95. Jack Lyne, "New York's Big Subsidies Bolster Upstate's Winning Bid for AMD's $3.2-Billion 300-MM. Fab," *Site Selection*, July 10, 2006, http://siteselection.com/ssinsider /bbdeal/bd060710.htm.

96. Thomas, *Investment Incentives*, 50.

97. John W. Miller and Alex MacDonald, "Steel Giants to Buy Alabama Plant," *Wall Street Journal*, December 1, 2013, http://www.wsj.com/articles/SB100014240527023045794045 79232181239548744.

CHAPTER 5

1. Alan Wolff, "The Role of U.S. Trade Policy," in *U.S. Competitiveness in the World Econ-omy*, ed. Bruce R. Scott and George C. Lodge (Boston: Harvard Business School Press, 1985).

2. *Morristown Magnavox Former Employees v. Marshall*, 671 F.2d 194 (6th Cir. 1982).

3. Clyde V. Prestowitz, *Trading Places: How We Allowed Japan to Take the Lead* (New York: Basic Books, 1988), 200.

4. Martin Kenney, "Shifting Value Chain: The Television Industry in North America," in *Locating Global Advantage*, ed. Martin Kenney and Richard L Florida (Stanford, CA: Stanford University Press, 2004).

5. Alfred E. Eckes, *Opening America's Market: U.S. Foreign Trade Policy since 1776* (Chapel Hill: University of North Carolina Press, 1995), 206.

6. Most of this section draws on James E. Millstein, "Decline in an Expanding Industry: Japanese Competition in Color Television," in *American Industry in International Competition*, ed. John Zysman and Laura Tyson (Ithaca, NY: Cornell University Press, 1983).

7. Kenney, "Shifting Value Chain."

8. Kenney, "Shifting Value Chain."

9. John A. Alic and Martha Caldwell Harris, "Employment Lessons from the Electronic Industry," *Monthly Labor Review*, February 1986, http://stats.bls.gov/opub/mlr/1986/02 /art4full.pdf.

10. Eleanor Roberts Lewis and Harry J. Connolly Jr., "Trade Adjustment Assistance for Firms and Industries," *Journal of International Law* 10, no. 4 (1988), http://scholarship.law .upenn.edu/cgi/viewcontent.cgi?article=1629&context=jil.

11. Wolfgang Stolper and Paul Samuelson, "Protection and Real Wages," *Review of Economic Studies*, 1941.

12. "ECAT Will Lead Campaign for Multinational Companies," February 24, 1972, in *Multinational Corporations: A Compendium of Papers Submitted to the Subcommittee on International Trade of the Committee on Finance in the United States Senate*, ed. US Senate, Committee on Finance, Subcommittee on International Trade (Washington, DC: US Government Printing Office, 1973).

13. Jonathan Cohn, "Great Danes," *New Republic*, January 1, 2007, http://www.new republic.com/article/politics/great-danes.

14. *Economic Adjustment and Worker Dislocation in a Competitive Society: Report of the Secretary of Labor's Task Force on Economic Adjustment and Worker Dislocation*, Washington, DC, December 1986, http://hdl.handle.net/2027/mdp.39015014879665.

15. David H. Autor, David Dorn, and Gordon H. Hanson, "The China Syndrome: Local Labor Market Effects of Import Competition in the United States," *American Economic Review* 103, no. 6 (October 2013), http://economics.mit.edu/files/6613.

16. David H. Autor, David Dorn, and Gordon H. Hanson, "The China Shock: Learning from Labor Market Adjustment to Large Changes in Trade," National Bureau of Economic Research, Working Paper 21906, January 2016, http://www.nber.org/papers/w21906.

17. Peter Dizikes, "When (and Where) Work Disappears," MIT News Office, February 24, 2012, http://newsoffice.mit.edu/2012/manufacturing-overseas-competition-0224.

18. Richard A. Givens, "The Search for an Alternative to Protection," *Fordham Law Review* 30, no. 1 (1961), http://ir.lawnet.fordham.edu/cgi/viewcontent.cgi?article=1698&context=flr.

19. J. F. Hornbeck and Laine Elise Rover, "Trade Adjustment Assistance (TAA) and Its Role in U.S. Trade Policy," Congressional Research Service, July 19, 2011, http://fpc.state .gov/documents/organization/169173.pdf.

20. Givens, "The Search for an Alternative to Protection."

21. Howard Rosen, "Trade Adjustment Assistance: The More We Change, the More It Stays the Same," in *C. Fred Bergsten and the World Economy*, ed. Michael Mussa (Washington, DC: Peterson Institute for International Economics, 2006), 80.

22. Hornbeck and Rover, "Trade Adjustment Assistance (TAA) and Its Role in U.S. Trade Policy."

23. James A. Dorn, "Trade Adjustment Assistance: A Case of Government Failure," *Cato Journal* 2, no. 3 (winter 1982), http://citeseerx.ist.psu.edu/viewdoc/download?doi=10.1.1.198 .4326&rep=rep1&type=pdf.

24. Steven T. O'Hara, "Worker Adjustment Assistance: The Failure and the Future," *Northwestern Journal of International Law and Business* 5, no. 2 (summer 1983), http://schol arlycommons.law.northwestern.edu/cgi/viewcontent.cgi?article=1145&context=njilb.

25. Nat Goldfinger, "Adjustment Assistance," letter, *Washington Post, Times Herald*, September 23, 1963.

26. Arlen J. Large, "Firms, Workers Hurt by Imports May Win Aid from Washington," *Wall Street Journal*, May 21, 1965.

27. Richard Nixon, "Special Message to the Congress on Unemployment Insurance," American Presidency Project, July 8, 1969, http://www.presidency.ucsb.edu/ws/?pid=2117.

28. George P. Shultz and Kenneth W. Dam, *Economic Policy behind the Headlines*, 2nd ed. (Chicago: University of Chicago Press, 1988), 145.

29. Charles R. Frank Jr., *Foreign Trade and Domestic Aid* (Washington, DC: Brookings Institution, 1977).

30. Steve Charnovitz, "Worker Adjustment: The Missing Ingredient in Trade Policy," *California Management Review* 28. no. 2 (winter 1986).

31. J. F. Hornbeck, "Trade Adjustment Assistance (TAA) and Its Role in U.S. Trade Policy," Congressional Research Service, August 5, 2013, https://www.fas.org/sgp/crs/misc/R41922.pdf.

32. Dorn, "Trade Adjustment Assistance."

33. Charnovitz, "Worker Adjustment."

34. See Thomas G. Donlan, "Hands across the Sea: Trade Adjustment Benefits Will Cost Uncle Sam Plenty," *Barron's*, May 5, 1980; Art Pine, "Billion-Dollar Mistake Snags New Budget," *Washington Post*, April 9, 1980, http://www.washingtonpost.com/archive/politics/1980/04/09/billion-dollar-mistake-snags-new-budget/7d0e8f0d-3ab9-4949-8202-7cbc42d0d1a8.

35. Ronald Reagan, "Address before a Joint Session of the Congress on the Program for Economic Recovery," American Presidency Project, February 18, 1981, http://www.presidency.ucsb.edu/ws/?pid=43425.

36. O'Hara, "Worker Adjustment Assistance."

37. Dorn, "Trade Adjustment Assistance."

38. "Trade Adjustment Assistance: New Ideas for an Old Program," US Office of Technology Assessment, June 1987, http://ota.fas.org/reports/8730.pdf.

39. Kenneth B. Noble, "Reagan Move for Job Funds," *New York Times*, November 9, 1985, http://www.nytimes.com/1985/11/09/business/reagan-move-for-job-funds.html.

40. Stephen A. Wandner, "Wage Insurance as a Policy Option in the United States," Upjohn Institute, Working Paper 16-250, 2016, http://research.upjohn.org/cgi/viewcontent.cgi?article=1268&context=up_workingpapers.

41. Hornbeck, "Trade Adjustment Assistance (TAA) and Its Role in U.S. Trade Policy."

42. Lori G. Kletzer and Howard Rosen, "Easing the Adjustment Burden on U.S. Workers," in *The United States and the World Economy: Foreign Economic Policy for the Next Decade*, ed. C. Fred Bergsten (Washington, DC: Peterson Institute for International Economics, 2005), https://www.piie.com/publications/chapters_preview/3802/10iie3802.pdf.

43. Howard Rosen, "Trade Adjustment Assistance: Facts versus Fiction," June 14, 2011.

44. "Trade Adjustment Assistance: Changes to the Workers Program Benefited Participants, but Little Is Known about Outcomes," Government Accountability Office, September 2012, http://www.gao.gov/assets/650/648980.pdf.

45. Gary B. Hansen, "A Follow-Up Survey of Workers Displaced by the Ford San Jose Assembly Plant Closure," Gary B. Hansen Collection, Utah State University, http://garybhansen.com/pdfs/worker/fllwup.pdf.

46. David B. Muhlhausen, "Trade Adjustment Assistance: Let the Ineffective and Wasteful Job Training Program Expire," Heritage Foundation, January 8, 2014, http://www.heritage.org/research/reports/2014/01/trade-adjustment-assistance-and-ineffective-job-training-program.

47. Sallie James, "Maladjusted: The Misguided Policy of Trade Adjustment Assistance," Cato Institute, November 8, 2007, http://www.cato.org/sites/cato.org/files/pubs/pdf/tbp -026.pdf.

48. Sol Chaikin, "Trade, Investment and Deindustralization: Myth and Reality," *Foreign Affairs* 60, no. 4 (spring 1982), https://www.foreignaffairs.com/articles/united -states/1982-03-01/trade-investment-and-deindustrialization-myth-and-reality.

49. Thomas J. Hilliard, "Building the American Workforce," Council on Foreign Relations, working paper, July 2013, http://www.cfr.org/united-states/building-american-work force/p31120.

50. Lauren Weber, "Apprenticeships Help Close the Skills Gap. So Why Are They in Decline?," *Wall Street Journal*, April 27, 2014, http://online.wsj.com/news/articles/SB10001424 052702303978304579473501943642612.

51. Hilliard, "Building the American Workforce."

CHAPTER 6

1. Kira Cochrane, "The Truth about the Tiger Mother's Family," *Guardian*, February 7, 2014, http://www.theguardian.com/lifeandstyle/2014/feb/07/truth-about-tiger-mothers -family-amy-chua.

2. Ray Fisman, "Mary Gates and Karen Zuckerberg Weren't Tiger Moms," *Slate*, February 9, 2011, http://www.slate.com/articles/business/the_dismal_science/2011/02/mary_gates _and_karen_zuckerberg_werent_tiger_moms.html.

3. Alexandra Petri, "State of the Union: Competitiveness, the Super Bowl, and Amy Chua," *Washington Post*, January 25, 2011, http://voices.washingtonpost.com/compost /2011/01/state_of_the_union_competitive.html.

4. Edward Alden and Rebecca Strauss, "Is America Great? How the United States Stacks Up," *Foreign Affairs*, February 1, 2016, https://www.foreignaffairs.com/articles/united -states/2016-02-01/america-great.

5. Ronald Reagan, "Remarks to the National Catholic Education Association, Chicago, Illinois," American Presidency Project, April 15, 1982, http://www.presidency.ucsb.edu /ws/?pid=42399.

6. Quoted in Maris A. Vinovskis, "The Road to Charlottesville: The 1989 Education Summit," Department of History, Institute for Social Research, and School of Public Policy, University of Michigan, September 1999, http://govinfo.library.unt.edu/negp/reports /negp30.pdf, 10–11.

7. *Rising above the Gathering Storm: Energizing and Employing America for a Brighter Economic Future* (Washington, DC: National Academies Press, 2005), http://engineering .columbia.edu/files/engineering/rising.pdf.

8. "2013 Report Card for America's Infrastructure," American Society of Civil Engineers, 2013, http://www.infrastructurereportcard.org.

9. "The State of Immigration," Business Roundtable, http://businessroundtable.org /state-of-immigration.

10. Peter G. Peterson, *The United States in a Changing World Economy* (Washington, DC: US Government Printing Office, 1971), 33–34.

11. National Research Council, *Rising to the Challenge: U.S. Innovation Policy for the Global Economy* (Washington, DC: National Academies Press, 2012), xiv.

12. Stuart Auerbach, "Parties Vie to Embrace American Competitiveness: U.S. Competitiveness Trumpeted," *Washington Post*, December 21, 1986, http://search.proquest.com/docview /138755485/1376A914169575EF5E4/32?accountid=37722.

13. Robert B. Reich, "The New 'Competitiveness' Fad," *New York Times*, January 14, 1987, http://search.proquest.com/docview/110610458/1376A914169575EF5E4/14?account id=37722.

14. Stuart Auerbach, "Competitiveness Moves to Forefront: Politicians Vie to Seize Initiative," *Washington Post*, December 7, 1986, http://search.proquest.com/news/docview/138856 312/13751CAF6927D14EFD/2?accountid=37722.

15. Kent H. Hughes, *Building the Next American Century: The Past and Future of American Economic Competitiveness* (Washington, DC: Woodrow Wilson Center Press, 2005), 5.

16. "The Strategic Context," *Harvard Magazine*, September–October 2012, http://harvard magazine.com/2012/09/the-strategic-context.

17. Michael Kantor, *Building the American Dream: Jobs, Innovation, and Growth in America's Next Century* (Washington, DC: US Department of Commerce, 1996).

18. Sheryl Gay Stoltberg, "Obama Calls for Bipartisan Effort to Fight for U.S. Jobs," *New York Times*, January 25, 2011, http://www.nytimes.com/2011/01/26/us/politics/26speech.html.

19. "Competitiveness Rankings," World Economic Forum, 2015, http://reports.weforum .org/global-competitiveness-report-2014-2015/rankings.

20. "Snapshot of Performance in Mathematics, Reading and Science," Organization for Economic Cooperation and Development, 2013, http://www.oecd.org/pisa/keyfindings /PISA-2012-results-snapshot-Volume-I-ENG.pdf.

21. Thomas L. Friedman and Michael Mandelbaum, *That Used to Be Us: How America Fell Behind in the World It Invented and How We Can Come Back* (New York: Farrar, Straus and Giroux, 2011), 235.

22. Rebecca Strauss, "Road to Nowhere: Federal Transportation Infrastructure Policy," Council on Foreign Relations, January 2016, http://www.cfr.org/infrastructure/road-nowhere -federal-transportation-infrastructure-policy/p28419.

23. "The Global Export Credit Dimension," National Association of Manufacturers, http://www.nam.org/Issues/Global-Export-Credit-Dimension-Web.

24. Friedman and Mandelbaum, *That Used to Be Us*, 139.

25. Bill Saporito and Cynthia Hutton, "Companies That Compete Best," *Fortune*, May 22, 1989, http://archive.fortune.com/magazines/fortune/fortune_archive/1989/05/22/72010 /index.htm.

26. This account is based on Hughes, *Building the Next American Century*, and Max Holland, "Mr. Young Goes to Washington," *Washington Decoded*, December 5, 1999, http://www .washingtondecoded.com/site/1999/12/mr-young-goes-t.html.

27. "Economic Report of the President Transmitted to the Congress February 1983 Together with the Annual Report of the Council of Economic Advisers," American Presidency Project, http://www.presidency.ucsb.edu/economic_reports/1983.pdf, 52–53.

28. John A. Young, "Global Competition—the New Reality: Results of the President's Commission on Industrial Competitiveness," Channeling Reality, http://www.channelingreality .com/Competitiveness/Global_Competition_New_Reality_typed.pdf.

29. Young, "Global Competition."

30. Holland, "Mr. Young Goes to Washington."

31. Max Holland, *The CEO Goes to Washington* (Knoxville, TN: Whittle Direct Books, 1994), 12.

32. Holland, *The CEO Goes to Washington.*

33. Hughes, *Building the Next American Century*, 187.

34. Auerbach, "Competitiveness Moves to Forefront."

35. Hughes, *Building the Next American Century*, 190.

36. Kevin P. Phillips, "U.S. Industrial Policy: Inevitable and Ineffective," *Harvard Business Review*, July–August 1992, https://hbr.org/1992/07/us-industrial-policy-inevitable-and -ineffective.

37. Philip J. Hilts, "At Heart of Debate on Quayle Council: Who Controls Federal Regulations?," *New York Times*, December 16, 1991, http://www.nytimes.com/1991/12/16/us /at-heart-of-debate-on-quayle-council-who-controls-federal-regulations.html; Rebecca Strauss, "Quality Control: Federal Regulation Policy," Council on Foreign Relations, March 2015, http://www.cfr.org/corporate-regulation/quality-control-federal-regulation-policy/p36110.

38. Hughes, *Building the Next American Century*, 256.

39. Holland, *The CEO Goes to Washington*, 21.

40. Bill Clinton, "Expanding Trade and Creating American Jobs," ibiblio, October 4, 1992, http://www.ibiblio.org/pub/academic/political-science/speeches/clinton.dir/c151.txt.

41. Phillips, "US Industrial Policy."

42. John Judis, *The Paradox of American Democracy*, 209; James Risen, "Clinton Drops Plans to Impose Job Training Tax, Officials Say," *Los Angeles Times*, June 4, 1993, http:// articles.latimes.com/1993–06–04/news/mn-43333_1_job-training.

43. Hughes, *Building the Next American Century*, 331.

44. Linda Killian, *The Freshmen: What Happened to the Republican Revolution?* (Boulder, CO: Westview Press, 1998), 124.

45. Richard S. Dunham and Amy Barrett, "The House Freshmen," *Bloomberg Businessweek*, January 28, 1996, http://www.bloomberg.com/bw/stories/1996-01-28/the-house-freshmen.

46. Christina D. Romer, "Do Manufacturers Need Special Treatment?," *New York Times*, February 4, 2012, http://www.nytimes.com/2012/02/05/business/do-manufacturers-need -special-treatment-economic-view.html.

47. Michael Greenstone and Adam Looney, "Trends: Reduced Earnings for Men in America," Milken Institute Review, 2011, http://www.brookings.edu/~/media/research/files /papers/2011/7/men%20earnings%20greenstone%20looney/07_milken_greenstone_looney .pdf.

48. "Income," US Census Bureau, https://www.census.gov/hhes/www/income/data/his torical/people.

49. Jaison R. Abel and Richard Deitz, "Do the Benefits of College Still Outweigh the Costs?," *Current Issues in Economics and Finance* 20, no. 3 (2014), http://www.newyorkfed .org/research/current_issues/ci20-3.html.

50. See Amanda Ripley, *The Smartest Kids in the World: And How They Got That Way* (New York: Simon & Schuster, 2013).

51. Michael Greenstone and Adam Looney, "The Uncomfortable Truth about American Wages," *New York Times*, October 22, 2012, http://economix.blogs.nytimes.com/2012/10/22 /the-uncomfortable-truth-about-american-wages.

52. Edward Alden, "Why Companies Are Leaving the United States, and How to Get Them Back," *Renewing America* (blog), Council on Foreign Relations, March 6, 2012, http:// blogs.cfr.org/renewing-america/2012/03/06/why-companies-are-leaving-the-united-states -and-how-to-get-them-back.

53. Robert Maxim, "No Helping Hand: Federal Worker-Retraining Policy," Council on Foreign Relation, January 2016, http://www.cfr.org/labor/no-helping-hand-federal-worker -retraining-policy/p35885.

54. Stanley Meisler, "Governors Bring Years of Concern to Education Summit: Bush Calls a Meeting of All State Leaders for Only 3rd Time in History," *Los Angeles Times*, September 27, 1989, http://articles.latimes.com/1989-09-27/news/mn-160_1_american-education.

55. Vinovskis, "The Road to Charlottesville," 6.

56. Rebecca Strauss, "Remedial Education: Federal Education Policy," Council on Foreign Relations, January 2016, http://www.cfr.org/united-states/remedial-education-federal-education -policy/p30141.

57. Andrew Rudalevige, "The Politics of No Child Left Behind," *Education Next* 3, no. 4 (fall 2003), http://educationnext.org/the-politics-of-no-child-left-behind.

58. "Education Expenditures by Country," National Center for Education Statistics, May 2015, http://nces.ed.gov/programs/coe/indicator_cmd.asp.

59. Strauss, "Remedial Education."

60. Strauss, "Remedial Education."

61. Michael Hout and Stuart W. Elliott, *Incentives and Test-Based Accountability in Education* (Washington, DC: National Academies Press, 2011), http://www.nap.edu/catalog /12521/incentives-and-test-based-accountability-in-education.

62. Steven Brill in "Education Reform and U.S. Competitiveness," Council on Foreign Relations, September 12, 2011, http://www.cfr.org/competitiveness/education-reform-us -competitiveness/p25816.

63. Strauss, "Road to Nowhere."

64. Robert Pollin and Dean Baker, "Public Investment, Industrial Policy and U.S. Economic Renewal," Political Economy Research Institute and Center for Economic Policy Research, December 2009, http://www.peri.umass.edu/fileadmin/pdf/working_papers /working_papers_201-250/WP211.pdf.

65. Strauss, "Road to Nowhere."

66. Alana Semuels, "Aging Pipes Are Poisoning America's Tapwater," *Atlantic*, July 29, 2015, http://www.theatlantic.com/business/archive/2015/07/dont-drink-the-water/399803.

67. Steve Markovich, "U.S. Aviation Infrastructure," Council on Foreign Relations, June 2, 2015, http://www.cfr.org/infrastructure/us-aviation-infrastructure/p36579.

68. "Falling Apart and Falling Behind: Transportation Infrastructure Report 2012," Building America's Future, 2012, http://www.bafuture.org/pdf/Building-Americas-Future -2012-Report-32013.pdf.

69. Pollin and Baker, "Public Investment, Industrial Policy and U.S. Economic Renewal."

70. Andrew Flowers, "Why We Still Can't Afford to Fix America's Broken Infrastructure," FiveThirtyEight, June 3, 2014, http://fivethirtyeight.com/features/why-we-still-cant-afford -to-fix-americas-broken-infrastructure.

71. Robert Puentes, "Slashing Spending and Boosting Infrastructure in the U.K.," Brookings Institution, October 26, 2010, http://www.brookings.edu/blogs/the-avenue /posts/2010/10/26-transportation-puentes.

72. Curt Woodward, "US 10th in Average Internet Speed Rankings, S. Korea Still No. 1," *Xconomy*, April 23, 2014, http://www.xconomy.com/boston/2014/04/23/u-s-10th-in -average-internet-speed-rankings-s-korea-still-no-1.

73. James O'Toole, "Chattanooga's Super-Fast Publicly Owned Internet," *CNN Money*, May 20, 2014, http://money.cnn.com/2014/05/20/technology/innovation/chattanooga-internet.

74. Jamal Carnette, "Can You Guess Which City Is Getting Google Fiber Next? (Hint: It's Not Washington, D.C.)," *Motley Fool*, March 29, 2015, http://www.fool.com/investing general/2015/03/29/can-you-guess-which-city-is-getting-google-fiber-n.aspx.

75. Ryan Holeywell, "Panama Canal Expansion Has U.S. Ports Rushing," *Governing*, July 2012, http://www.governing.com/panama-canal-expansion-has-us-ports-rushing.html.

76. National Science Board, Science and Engineering Indicators 2016.

77. Rebecca Strauss, "Keeping the Edge: U.S. Innovation," Council on Foreign Relations, January 2016, http://www.cfr.org/innovation/keeping-edge-us-innovation/p37127.

78. Vernon W. Ruttan, *Is War Necessary for Economic Growth? Military Procurement and Technology Development* (New York: Oxford University Press, 2006).

79. Quoted in Pollin and Baker, "Public Investment, Industrial Policy and U.S. Economic Renewal," 19.

80. Pollin and Baker, "Public Investment, Industrial Policy and U.S. Economic Renewal," 20.

81. William J. Broad, "Clinton to Promote High Technology, with Gore in Charge," *New York Times*, November 10, 1992, http://www.nytimes.com/1992/11/10/science/clinton-to -promote-high-technology-with-gore-in-charge.html.

82. Holland, *The CEO Goes to Washington*, 21.

83. Broad, "Clinton to Promote High Technology, with Gore in Charge."

84. Hughes, *Building the Next American Century*, 307–8.

85. Hughes, *Building the Next American Century*, 307–8; Kenneth S. Flamm, "In Defense of the Flat-Panel Display Initiative," *Issues in Science and Technology* 11, no. 3 (spring 1995), http://www.freepatentsonline.com/article/Issues-in-Science-Technology/16864733.html.

86. George W. Bush, "Statement on Signing the America COMPETES Act," American Presidency Project, August 9, 2007, http://www.presidency.ucsb.edu/ws/?pid=75650.

87. Strauss, "Keeping the Edge."

88. Ronald Reagan, "Remarks on Signing the Small Business Innovation Development Act of 1982," Ronald Reagan Presidential Library and Museum, July 22, 1982, http://www .reagan.utexas.edu/archives/speeches/1982/72282c.htm.

89. Strauss, "Keeping the Edge."

90. Strauss, "Keeping the Edge."

91. "Trade in Goods with Advanced Technology Products," US Census, https://www .census.gov/foreign-trade/balance/c0007.html.

92. Edward Alden, "Why Manufacturing Really Matters: Gary Pisano and Willy Shih on Innovation," *Renewing America* (blog), Council on Foreign Relations, February 4, 2013, http://blogs.cfr.org/renewing-america/2013/02/04/why-manufacturing-really-matters-gary -pisano-and-willy-shih-on-innovation.

93. "Road Map to Renewal," 2011 year-end report, President's Council on Jobs and Competitiveness, http://files.jobs-council.com/files/2012/01/JobsCouncil_2011YearEndReport1 .pdf, 9.

94. "Road Map to Renewal," 5.

CHAPTER 7

1. Paul Krugman, "Competitiveness: A Dangerous Obsession," *Foreign Affairs*, March– April 1994, https://www.foreignaffairs.com/articles/1994-03-01/competitiveness-dangerous -obsession.

2. Paul Krugman, "Competitiveness and Class Warfare," *New York Times*, August 11, 2015, http://krugman.blogs.nytimes.com/2015/08/11/competitiveness-and-class-warfare.

3. Richard Haass, *Foreign Policy Begins at Home* (New York: Basic Books, 2013).

4. Lawrence Edwards and Robert Z. Lawrence, *Rising Tide: Is Growth in Emerging Economies Good for the United States?* (Washington, DC: Peterson Institute for International Economics, February 2013), 62.

5. J. Bradford Jensen, "Globalization and Business Services: A Growth Opportunity?," Georgetown University McDonough School of Business, November 2009, http://www.gcbpp .org/files/EPV/EPV_Jensen-ServiceExports_1109.pdf.

6. Alan S. Blinder, "Offshoring: The Next Industrial Revolution?," *Foreign Affairs*, March/ April 2006, http://www.foreignaffairs.com/articles/61514/alan-s-blinder/offshoring-the-next -industrial-revolution.

7. Robert D. Atkinson, "What Really Is Competitiveness?," *Globalist*, September 20, 2013, http://www.theglobalist.com/really-competitiveness.

8. Dane Stangler, "Where Will the Jobs Come From?," Ewing Marion Kauffman Foundation, April 30, 2011, http://www.kauffman.org/what-we-do/research/firm-formation-and -growth-series/where-will-the-jobs-come-from.

9. Robert Litan, "Start-Up Slowdown," *Foreign Affairs*, January–February 2015, https:// www.foreignaffairs.com/articles/americas/2014-12-15/start-slowdown.

10. "Creating Jobs through Innovation," Apple, http://www.apple.com/about/job-creation.

11. "A Profile of U.S. Importing and Exporting Companies, 2009–2010," US Census Bureau, April 12, 2012, http://www.census.gov/foreign-trade/Press-Release/edb/2010/edbrel .pdf.

12. Gene Sperling, remarks at the Conference on the Renaissance of American Manufacturing, March 27, 2012, Whitehouse.gov, https://www.whitehouse.gov/sites/default/files /administration-official/sperling_-_renaissance_of_american_manufacturing_-_03_27_12 .pdf.

13. Caterpillar annual report, December 31, 2014, http://s7d2.scene7.com/is/content /Caterpillar/C10428589.

14. Eric N. Berg, "Thinking Long Term Is Costly to Caterpillar," *New York Times*, November 24, 1989, http://www.nytimes.com/1989/11/24/business/thinking-long-term-is-costly -to-caterpillar.html.

15. Craig Bouchard and James Koch, *The Caterpillar Way: Lessons in Leadership, Growth and Shareholder Value* (New York: McGraw-Hill, 2013).

16. Mina Kimes, "Caterpillar's Doug Oberhelman: Manufacturing's Mouthpiece," *Bloomberg Businessweek*, May 16, 2013, http://www.businessweek.com/articles/2013-05-16/cater pillars-doug-oberhelman-manufacturings-mouthpiece.

17. For the 2007 employee data, see Caterpillar's 2007 annual report at http://www .slideshare.net/finance5/caterpillar-2007-annual-report. For the 2014 employee data, see "Number of Caterpillar Employees in FY2014, by Region," Statista, http://www.statista.com /statistics/267818/number-of-caterpillar-employees-by-region.

18. Laura Diamond, Misty Williams, and J. Scott Trubey, "Landing Caterpillar Plant a Major Economic Victory for Georgia," *Atlanta Journal-Constitution*, February 17, 2012, http:// www.ajc.com/news/business/landing-caterpillar-plant-a-major-economic-victory/nQRQ3.

19. Thomas Anderson, "Summary Estimates for Multinational Companies: Employment, Sales, and Capital Expenditures for 2011," Bureau of Economic Analysis, April 18, 2013,

http://www.bea.gov/newsreleases/international/mnc/2013/_pdf/mnc2011.pdf; "Activities of U.S. Multinational Enterprises, 2009–2013," Bureau of Economic Analysis, http://www.bea .gov/international/di1usdop.htm.

20. "Country Comparison: Exports," CIA World Factbook, https://www.cia.gov/library /publications/the-world-factbook/rankorder/2078rank.html.

21. "List of Sovereign States by Current Account Balance," Wikipedia, http://en.wikipedia .org/wiki/List_of_sovereign_states_by_current_account_balance.

22. "List of Countries by Current Account Balance as a Percentage of GDP," Wikipedia, http://en.wikipedia.org/wiki/List_of_countries_by_current_account_balance_as_a_percent age_of_GDP.

23. "GDP per Capita (Current US$)," World Bank, http://data.worldbank.org/indicator /NY.GDP.PCAP.CD.

24. "The Trade Deficit: Is It a Problem or Not?," Council on Foreign Relations, March 9, 2015, http://www.cfr.org/budget-debt-and-deficits/trade-deficit-problem-not/p36375.

25. Daniel Griswold, "Are Trade Deficits a Drag on U.S. Economic Growth?," Cato Institute, March 12, 2007, http://www.cato.org/publications/free-trade-bulletin/are-trade-deficits -drag-us-economic-growth.

26. Robert A. Blecker, "The Trade Deficit and U.S. Competitiveness," in *Competitiveness Matters: Industry and Economic Performance in the U.S.*, ed. Candace Howes and Ajit Singh (Ann Arbor: University of Michigan Press, 2000).

27. "Foreign Direct Investment in the United States," Department of Commerce and the President's Council of Economic Advisers, October 2013, http://www.whitehouse.gov/sites /default/files/2013fdi_report_-_final_for_web.pdf.

28. Edward Alden et al., "Trading Up: U.S. Trade and Investment Policy," Council on Foreign Relations, January 2016, http://www.cfr.org/trade/trading-up-us-trade-investment -policy/p31813.

29. Luke A. Stewart and Robert D. Atkinson, "Restoring America's Lagging Investment in Capital Goods," Information Technology and Industry Foundation, October 2013, http:// www2.itif.org/2013-restoring-americas-lagging-investment.pdf, 24.

30. "Inward Foreign Direct Investment (FDI) Performance Index," Conference Board of Canada, 2011, http://www.conferenceboard.ca/hcp/details/economy/inward-fdi-perfor mance.aspx.

31. *World Investment Report 2013: Global Value Chains: Investment and Trade for Development*, United Nations Conference on Trade and Development, 2013, http://unctad.org/en /PublicationsLibrary/wir2013_en.pdf.

32. Michael Porter, *The Competitive Advantage of Nations* (New York: Free Press, 1990), 6.

33. Douglas A. Irwin, *Free Trade under Fire* (Princeton, NJ: Princeton University Press, 2002), 50–55.

34. Robert J. Gordon, "Revisiting U.S. Productivity Growth over the Past Century with a View of the Future," National Bureau of Economic Research, March 2010, http://www.nber .org/papers/w15834.

35. "2014 Productivity Brief—Key Findings," Conference Board, 2014, https://www .conference-board.org/pdf_free/economics/TED3.pdf.

36. "List of Countries by GDP (PPP) per Hour Worked," Wikipedia, http://en.wikipedia .org/wiki/List_of_countries_by_GDP_(PPP)_per_hour_worked.

37. "Labor Productivity and Costs," Bureau of Labor Statistics, August 11, 2015, http:// www.bls.gov/lpc/prodybar.htm.

38. Robert J. Gordon, "Is U.S. Economic Growth Over? Faltering Innovation Confronts the Six Headwinds," National Bureau of Economic Research, August 2012, http://www.nber.org/papers/w18315.

39. Mercedes Delgado et al., "The Determinants of National Competitiveness," National Bureau of Economic Research, Working Paper 18249, July 2012, http://www.nber.org/papers/w18249.

40. Kiyoaki Aburaki, "China's Competitiveness: Myth, Reality, and the Lessons for the United States and Japan," Center for Strategic and International Studies, January 2013, http://csis.org/files/publication/130129_competitiveness_Aburaki_Web.pdf.

41. "Total Economy Database—Key Findings," Conference Board, May 2015, http://www.conference-board.org/data/economydatabase.

42. David Streitfeld, "Amazon's Revenue Soars, but No Profit Is in Sight," *New York Times*, October 24, 2013, http://www.nytimes.com/2013/10/25/technology/amazons-revenue-soars-but-no-profit-in-sight.html.

43. Laura D'Andrea Tyson, "Economic Competitiveness in the U.S.," in *Proceedings: Technology and Governance in the 1990s*, ed. US Congress, Office of Technology Assessment. OTA-A-564 (Washington, DC: US Government Printing Office, April 1993).

44. Harold L. Sirkin, Michael Zinser, and Douglas Hohner, "Made in America, Again: Why Manufacturing Will Return to the U.S.," Boston Consulting Group, August 2011, http://www.bcg.com/documents/file84471.pdf.

45. "A Chart and Map Book of Population and Selected Economic Indicators for the U.S. and States," vol. 1, no. 3. University of New Mexico Bureau of Business and Economic Research, December 2012.

CHAPTER 8

1. Mark Goldman, *City on the Lake: The Challenge of Change in Buffalo, New York* (Buffalo, NY: Prometheus Books, 1990), 171.

2. Edward L. Glaeser, "Can Buffalo Ever Come Back?," *New York Sun,* October 19, 2007, http://www.nysun.com/opinion/can-buffalo-ever-come-back/64879.

3. Greg Leroy, *The Great American Jobs Scam: Corporate Tax Dodging and the Myth of Job Creation* (San Francisco: Berrett-Koehler, 2005), chap. 3.

4. Erin Carlyle, "America's Most Affordable Cities," *Forbes,* March 11, 2014, http://www.forbes.com/sites/erincarlyle/2014/03/11/americas-most-affordable-cities.

5. David Robinson, "SolarCity Aims to Create 1,460 jobs," *Buffalo News,* July 13, 2015, http://www.buffalonews.com/business/solarcity-aims-to-create-1460-jobs-20150713.

6. Zachary Shahan, "Every SolarCity Customer Will Get Battery Backup within 5–10 Years," *CleanTechnica,* September 22, 2014, http://cleantechnica.com/2014/09/22/every-solarcity-customer-will-get-battery-backup-within-5-10-years.

7. Adam Bruns, "Multiple Visions," *Site Selection*, October 2014, http://siteselection.com/onlineInsider/solar.cfm.

8. Glaeser, "Can Buffalo Ever Come Back?"

9. "Solyndra Misrepresented Facts to Get Loan Guarantee, Report Says," *Wall Street Journal,* August 26, 2015, http://www.wsj.com/articles/solyndra-misrepresented-facts-to-get-loan-guarantee-report-says-1440632222.

10. Jim Heaney, "Watchdog Report: Buffalo Billion's Lack of Transparency," *Democrat and Chronicle*, June 21, 2015, http://www.democratandchronicle.com/story/news/2015/06/21 /buffalo-billion-andrew-cuomo-solarcity-transparency/29054685.

11. "SolarCity Investing $5B in Buffalo, Creating 3,000 jobs," WIVB News 4, September 23, 2014, http://wivb.com/2014/09/23/solarcity-investing-5b-in-buffalo-creating-3000-jobs.

12. Michael Oden, "Building a More Sustainable Economy: Economic Development Strategy and Public Incentives in Austin," Livable City, May 2008, http://www.soa.utexas .edu/files/csd/FinalIncentiveStudy.pdf.

13. Brad McDearman and Ryan Donahue, "The 10 Lessons from Global Trade and Investment Planning in U.S. Metro Areas," Brookings Institution, May 27, 2015, http://www .brookings.edu/research/reports/2015/04/21-global-trade-investment-planning-us-metro -areas-mcdearman-donahue; Aimee Rawlins, "Is Your City the Next Portlandia?," *CNN Money*, October 7, 2014, http://money.cnn.com/2014/10/07/smallbusiness/portland-export -kashiwanoha.

14. Peter K. Eisinger, *The Rise of the Entrepreneurial State: State and Local Economic Development Policy in the United States.* (Madison: University of Wisconsin Press, 1988).

15. Mark Drabenstott, "Rethinking Federal Policy for Regional Economic Development," *Economic Review*, Federal Reserve Bank of Kansas City, First Quarter 2006, https://www .kansascityfed.org/publicat/econrev/PDF/1q06drab.pdf.

16. Drabenstott, "Rethinking Federal Policy for Regional Economic Development," 21.

17. Roger Real Drouin, "How Conservative Texas Took the Lead in U.S. Wind Power," *Yale Environment 360*, April 9, 2015, http://e360.yale.edu/feature/how_conservative_texas _took_the_lead_in_us_wind_power/2863.

18. Louise Story, "As Companies Seek Tax Deals, Governments Pay High Price," *New York Times*, December 1, 2012.

19. Louise Story, "Lines Blur as Texas Gives Industries a Bonanza," *New York Times*, December 2, 2012.

20. "List of U.S. States by Income," Wikipedia, https://en.wikipedia.org/wiki/List _of_U.S._states_by_income.

21. Arlette Saenz, "Rick Perry in California to Lure Businesses to Texas," ABC News, February 11, 2013, http://abcnews.go.com/blogs/politics/2013/02/rick-perry-in-california -to-lure-businesses-to-texas.

22. David Robinson, *Economic Development from the State and Local Perspective: Case Studies and Public Policy Debates* (New York: Palgrave Macmillan, September 2014), 38.

23. Connie Lester, "Economic Development in the 1930s: Balance Agriculture with Industry," *Mississippi History Now*, May 2014, http://mshistorynow.mdah.state.ms.us/articles/224 /economic-development-in-the-1930s-balance-agriculture-with-industry.

24. Leroy, *The Great American Jobs Scam*, 71.

25. Eisinger, *The Rise of the Entrepreneurial State*, 28.

26. Leroy, *The Great American Jobs Scam*, 84.

27. Thomas Stringer, "How U.S. States Are Targeting Foreign Direct Investment," *Area Development*, 2015, http://www.areadevelopment.com/LocationUSA/2015-US-inward -investment-guide/how-us-states-target-fdi-strategies-2727261.shtml.

28. Jennifer Burnett, "State Overseas Trade and Investment Offices, 2013," Council of State Governments, June 18, 2013, http://knowledgecenter.csg.org/kc/content/state-overseas -trade-and-investment-offices-2013.

29. Dan Weisman, "Greenhouse: Why a Good Plan Failed," *Labor Research Review* 1, no. 9 (1986), http://digitalcommons.ilr.cornell.edu/cgi/viewcontent.cgi?article=1086&context=lrr.

30. Mark Muro et al., "America's Advanced Industries," Brookings Institution, February 2015, http://www.brookings.edu/research/reports2/2015/02/03-advanced-industries#/M10420.

31. "Subsidy Tracker," Good Jobs First, http://www.goodjobsfirst.org/subsidy-tracker.

32. Robert D. Atkinson and Stephen J. Ezell, *Innovation Economics: The Race for Global Advantage* (New Haven, CT: Yale University Press, 2012), 273.

33. Charles Riley, "Iowa's Turnaround Town," *CNN Money*, January 3, 2012, http://money.cnn.com/2012/01/03/news/economy/Iowa_Newton.

34. Andrew N. Liveris, *Make It In America: The Case for Re-inventing the Economy* (Hoboken, NJ: John Wiley & Sons, 2011), 62.

35. Jaap Kalkman and Alexander Keller, "Global Petrochemicals—Who Is Really Benefitting from the Growth in the New World?," Roland Berger, November 2012, https://www.rolandberger.com/media/pdf/Roland_Berger_Global_Petrochemicals_20121113.pdf.

36. Ronald R. Pollina, "In Defense of Business Subsidies," *Renewing America* (blog), Council on Foreign Relations, May 19, 2014, http://blogs.cfr.org/renewing-america/2014/05/19/in-defense-of-business-subsidies.

37. "New York Life Weighs Move to Goldman's Jersey City Tower," *Bloomberg Businessweek*, April 15, 2015, http://www.bloomberg.com/news/articles/2015-04-14/new-york-life-weighs-move-to-goldman-s-jersey-city-tower.

38. Story, "As Companies Seek Tax Deals, Governments Pay High Price."

39. Erin Sparks, "Top Trends in State Economic Development," National Governor's Association, August 2013, http://www.nga.org/files/live/sites/NGA/files/pdf/2013/1308TopTrendsinStateEconDevPaper.pdf.

40. Erin Sparks and Mary Jo Waits, "Making Our Future: What States Are Doing to Encourage Growth through Innovation, Entrepreneurship and Investment," National Governors' Association, January 2013.

41. Andrew M. Cuomo, "Opportunity Agenda: End of Session Report 2015," Office of the Governor of New York State, June 2015, https://www.governor.ny.gov/sites/governor.ny.gov/files/atoms/files/2015_End_of_Session_Report_FINAL.pdf.

42. Becky Gillette, "Mississippi Gambles on Technology Developments Some Deem to Be Too Risky," *Mississippi Business Journal*, January 18, 2013, http://msbusiness.com/2013/01/mississippi-gambles-on-technology-developments-some-deem-to-be-too-risky.

43. Harold L. Sirkin, Michael Zinzer, and Justin R. Rose, "The Shifting Economics of Global Manufacturing," Boston Consulting Group, August 2014, https://www.bcgperspectives.com/Images/The_Shifting_Economics_of_Global_Manufacturing_Aug_2014.pdf.

44. Edward Alden and Rebecca Strauss, "Standard Deductions: U.S. Corporate Tax Policy," Council on Foreign Relations, January 2016, http://www.cfr.org/tax-policy/standard-deductions-us-corporate-tax-policy/p32655?co=C044801.

45. Alden and Strauss, "Standard Deductions."

46. Alden and Strauss, "Standard Deductions."

47. Michael E. Porter and Jan W. Rivkin, *Prosperity at Risk: Findings of the Harvard Business School's Survey on U.S. Competitiveness*, Harvard Business School, January 2012, http://www.hbs.edu/competitiveness/Documents/hbscompsurvey.pdf.

48. Rebecca Strauss, "Quality Control: Federal Regulation Policy," Council on Foreign Relations, January 2016, http://www.cfr.org/corporate-regulation/quality-control-federal-regulation-policy/p36110.

49. Stephen J. Ezell and Robert D. Atkinson, "Fifty Ways to Leave Your Competitiveness Woes Behind: A National Traded Sector Strategy," Information Technology and Innovation Foundation, September 2012, http://www2.itif.org/2012-fifty-ways-competitiveness-woes-behind.pdf.

50. Noel Randewich, "Insight: As Chip Plants Get Pricey, U.S. Risks Losing Edge," *Reuters*, May 1, 2012, http://www.reuters.com/article/2012/05/01/us-semiconductors-manufact uring-idUSBRE8400N920120501.

51. Richard McCormack, "Intel CEO Says U.S. Would Lose No Tax Revenue by Providing Companies with Tax Holidays to Open Plants and Hire Workers," *Manufacturing and Technology News* 17, no. 17 (October 29, 2010), http://www.manufacturingnews.com/news /newss/intel102.html.

52. Atkinson and Ezell, *Innovation Economics*, 174–75.

53. Richard Dobbs et al., "Playing to Win: The New Global Competition for Corporate Profits," McKinsey Global Institute, September 2015, http://www.mckinsey.com/insights /corporate_finance/the_new_global_competition_for_corporate_profits.

54. Danica Coto, "Lufthansa Plans Puerto Rico Aviation Facility," *USA Today*, April 14, 2014, http://www.usatoday.com/story/todayinthesky/2014/04/14/lufthansa-unit-plans -puerto-rico-aircraft-maintenance-facility/7692305.

55. Bill Carey, "Lufthansa Technik Set to Open New MRO Base in Puerto Rico," *Aviation International News Online*, July 14, 2015, http://www.ainonline.com/aviation-news/air -transport/2015-07-14/lufthansa-technik-set-open-new-mro-base-puerto-rico.

56. Telephone interview with Chris Camacho, executive vice president, business development, Greater Phoenix Economic Council, September 2015.

57. See the Global Cities Initiative at http://www.brookings.edu/about/projects/global -cities.

58. Hillary Clinton, "Secretary Clinton's Speech at Economic Club of New York," Bureau of International Information Programs, US Department of State, October 14, 2011, http://iipdigital.usembassy.gov/st/english/texttrans/2011/10/20111014172924su0.9650494 .html#axzz3BnMylUOo0.

59. Elizabeth Dwoskin, "Hillary Clinton's Business Legacy at the State Department," *Bloomberg Businessweek*, January 10, 2013, http://www.businessweek.com/articles/2013-01-10 /hillary-clintons-business-legacy-at-the-state-department#p1.

60. "U.S. Export Competitiveness in China: Winning the World's Fastest-Growing Market," *Viewpoint*, American Chamber of Commerce in Shanghai, September 2010, http://www .amcham-shanghai.org/ftpuploadfiles/publications/viewpoint/us_export.pdf.

61. Martin Feldstein, "The Case for a Competitive Dollar," remarks to the Economic Summit of the Stanford Institute for Economic Policy Research, March 3, 2006, http://www .nber.org/feldstein/siepr319.pdf.

62. C. Fred Bergsten, "Time for a Plaza II?," Baker Institute of Public Policy Working Paper, October, 2015.

63. James A. Baker, *Work Hard, Study . . . and Keep Out of Politics!* (New York: G. P. Putnam's Sons, 2006), 432.

64. Baker, *Work Hard, Study . . . and Keep Out of Politics!*, 433.

65. "Treasury Says It Is Negotiating on Currency in Context of TPP," *Inside U.S. Trade*, July 29, 2015, http://insidetrade.com/daily-news/treasury-says-it-negotiating-currency-con text-tpp.

66. Michael Pettis, *The Great Rebalancing: Trade, Conflict, and the Perilous Road Ahead for the World Economy* (Princeton, NJ: Princeton University Press, 2013), 214.

67. "Foreign Exchange Policies of Major Trading Partners of the United States," US Department of Treasury, Office of International Affairs, April 29, 2016, https://www .treasury.gov/resource-center/international/exchange-rate-policies/Documents/2016-4 -29%20%28FX%20Pol%20of%20Major%20Trade%20Partner%29_final.pdf.

68. C. Fred Bergsten and Joseph E. Gagnon, "Currency Manipulation, the US Economy, and the Global Economic Order," Peterson Institute for International Economics, December 2012, http://www.iie.com/publications/pb/pb12-25.pdf.

69. Joseph E. Gagnon, "Foreign Exchange Intervention since Plaza: The Need for Global Currency Rules," Baker Institute for Public Policy Working Paper, October 1, 2015, https:// bakerinstitute.org/files/9793.

70. Shanker A. Singham, "Freeing the Global Market: How to Boost the Economy by Curbing Regulatory Distortions," Council on Foreign Relations, October 2012, http://www .cfr.org/world/freeing-global-market-boost-economy-curbing-regulatory-distortions/p29123.

71. Edward Alden, "With TPP and TTIP, U.S. and EU Reassert Control over Rules of Global Trade," *World Politics Review*, December 19, 2013, http://www.worldpoliticsreview .com/articles/13454/with-tpp-and-ttip-u-s-and-eu-reassert-control-over-rules-of-global-trade.

72. Thomas Bollyky, "Better Regulation for Freer Trade," Council on Foreign Relations, June 2012, http://www.cfr.org/trade/better-regulation-freer-trade/p28508.

73. Edward Alden and Rebecca Strauss, "Curtailing the Subsidy War within the United States," Council on Foreign Relations, May 2015, http://www.cfr.org/united-states/curtailing -subsidy-war-within-united-states/p32762.

74. Tom Fairless, "Tax Probe Targets U.S. Firms," *Wall Street Journal*, June 11, 2014, http://www.wsj.com/articles/eu-to-probe-tax-affairs-of-apple-starbucks-1402476699.

75. For more elaboration, see Edward Alden, "The TTIP and 'Tax Incentives,'" Cato Institute, September 15, 2015, http://www.cato.org/publications/cato-online-forum/ttip-tax -incentives.

76. Kay Alison Wilkie et al., "The US-Peru Trade Promotion Agreement (TPA): Report of the Intergovernmental Policy Advisory Committee," Intergovernmental Policy Advisory Committee, February 1, 2006, http://www.citizen.org/documents/IGPAC_Peru_Report.pdf.

77. Dow Jones Business News, "Tesla Wants White House to Press China," August 28, 2015; Mike Ramsey, "Tesla Wants Obama Administration to Press China on Auto-Industry Rules," *Wall Street Journal*, August 28, 2015, http://www.wsj.com/articles/tesla-wants-white -house-to-press-china-on-auto-industry-rules-1440794628.

78. Andrew H. Card et al., "U.S. Trade and Investment Policy," Council on Foreign Rela- tions, September 2011, http://www.cfr.org/trade/us-trade-investment-policy/p25737, 76.

79. Card et al., "U.S. Trade and Investment Policy," 76–77.

80. Ricardo Hausmann, "The Education Myth," *Project Syndicate*, May 31, 2015, http://www.project-syndicate.org/commentary/education-economic-growth-by-ricardo-haus mann-2015-05.

81. James Bessen, "Employers Aren't Just Whining—the 'Skills Gap' Is Real," *Harvard Business Review*, August 25, 2014, https://hbr.org/2014/08/employers-arent-just-whining-the -skills-gap-is-real.

82. Robert Maxim, "No Helping Hand: Federal Worker-Retraining Policy," Council on Foreign Relations, January 2016, http://www.cfr.org/labor/no-helping-hand-federal-worker -retraining-policy/p35885.

83. Maxim, "No Helping Hand."

84. Jan Lee, "Volkswagen Launches New Auto Apprenticeship Program," TriplePundit, October 29, 2014, http://www.triplepundit.com/2014/10/volkswagen-launches-new-auto -apprenticeship-program.

85. Thomas Hilliard, "Building the American Workforce," Council on Foreign Relations, July 2013, http://www.cfr.org/united-states/building-american-workforce/p31120.

86. Hilliard, "Building the American Workforce."

87. Penny Pritzker, "U.S. Commerce Secretary Penny Pritzker Highlights Importance of Workforce Development and Skills Training at Historic Signing Ceremony between U.S. and Germany," US Department of Commerce, June 5, 2015, https://www.commerce.gov/news /secretary-speeches/2015/06/us-commerce-secretary-penny-pritzker-highlights-importance -workforce.

88. Grant D. Aldonas, Robert Z. Lawrence, and Matthew J. Slaughter, "Succeeding in the Global Economy: A New Policy Agenda for the American Worker," Financial Services Forum, June 26, 2007, http://www.hks.harvard.edu/fs/rlawrence/Final%20Report.pdf.

89. Robert Z. Lawrence and Robert E. Litan, *Saving Free Trade: A Pragmatic Approach* (Washington, DC: Brookings Institution, 1986).

90. See Robert B. Zoellick and Matthew J. Slaughter, "A Bipartisan Work Plan: Helping America to Work," Council on Foreign Relations, Policy Innovation Memorandum No. 52, January 2015, http://www.cfr.org/labor/bipartisan-work-plan-helping-america-work/p35888.

91. Sparks and Waits, "Making Our Future."

92. "Fact Sheet: The Investing in Manufacturing Communities Partnership," US Department of Commerce, April 17, 2013, https://www.commerce.gov/news/fact-sheets/2013/04 /fact-sheet-investing-manufacturing-communities-partnership.

93. "U.S. Secretary of Commerce Penny Pritzker Announces Designation of 12 New Manufacturing Communities under the Investing in Manufacturing Communities Partnership Program," US Economic Development Administration, July 8, 2015, http://www.eda .gov/news/press-releases/2015/07/08/imcp.htm.

94. Heidi Crebo-Rediker, "Infrastructure Finance in America—How We Get Smarter," Council on Foreign Relations, March 2014, http://www.cfr.org/united-states/infrastructure -finance-america-we-get-smarter/p32597.

95. "Recommendations of the Build America Investment Initiative Interagency Working Group," US Department of the Treasury, http://www.treasury.gov/resource-center/economic -policy/Documents/Build%20America%20Recommendation%20Report%201-1515%20 FOR%20PUBLICATION.pdf.

96. Scott Thomasson, "Encouraging U.S. Infrastructure Investment," Council on Foreign Relations, April 2012, http://www.cfr.org/infrastructure/encouraging-us-infrastructure -investment/p27771.

97. See Vivek Wadhwa and Edward Alden, "America's Reinvention Is Helping It Leap Further ahead of the World," *Washington Post*, November 2, 2015, https://www.washington post.com/news/innovations/wp/2015/11/02/americas-reinvention-is-helping-it-leap-further -ahead-of-the-world.

98. Edward Alden and Rebecca Strauss, *How America Stacks Up: Economic Competitiveness and U.S. Policy* (New York: Council on Foreign Relations, February 2016).

99. See Edward Alden and Rebecca Strauss, "The US Should Fix Immigration and Patents or Kiss Its Innovation Edge Goodbye," *Quartz*, October 29, 2015, http://www.cfr.org/united -states/us-should-fix-immigration-patents-kiss-its-innovation-edge-goodbye/p37205.

Index

adjustment, 26–28
Advanced Technology Program, 149
AFL-CIO. *See* American Federation of
  Labor and Congress of Industrial
  Organizations
Airbus, 49–51
aircraft, 156–57; competitive new
  companies for, 51; European Union and,
  49–51; subsidies of, 49–51; trade rule
  enforcement for, 49–51
Alabama, 18
American Apprenticeship Fund, 199
American Competitiveness Initiative, 131,
  149
American Federation of Labor and Congress
  of Industrial Organizations (AFL-CIO),
  80; China labor standards confronted
  by, 101; on multinational corporations,
  13; on TPP, 82; on trade adjustment
  assistance, 118–19
American Recovery and Reinvestment Act
  of 2009, 122
American Society of Civil Engineers
  (ASCE), 129, 145
Apple, 93, 157
ASCE. *See* American Society of Civil
  Engineers
Atkinson, Rob, 157, 180, 186, 195

Austin, Kenneth, 60–61
autarky, 1, 2
automobiles: China and, 40–42; Japan
  import of, 36–37
Autor, David, 114–15

Baker, James, 68–69, 190
Balance Agriculture with Industry, 178–79
Barshefsky, Charlene, 38, 40–41
Battle Hymn of the Tiger Mother (Chua), 127
beggar-thy-neighbor, 16, 29, 61
Bergsten, Fred, 56, 60, 73; on currency
  manipulation, 191; on currency
  misalignment, 76–78; "The
  International Economy and American
  Business" by, 107; on offshore
  investment, 102; on trade adjustment
  assistance, 107, 113, 126; on *The United
  States in a Changing World Economy*, 15;
  on US competitiveness, 137
Biemiller, Andrew, 81, 89
bilateral investment treaties (BITs), 102–3,
  194
Blecker, Robert, 161–62
Blinder, Alan, 156
Boeing, 49–51
Border Industrialization Program, Mexico,
  81

bottoms-up strategy, 177–78, 183
Brady, Nicholas, 74
Bretton Woods economic system, 9–10, 59, 62
broadband, 147
Buffalo, 171–73
Buffalo Billion, 172–73
Build America Investment Initiative, 201
Burke, James, 87. *See also* Burke-Hartke bill
Burke-Hartke bill, 86, 92; business lobby and, 87–91; import quota under, 88; imports and multinational taxation in, 88; unions and, 87–91
Burns, Arthur, 67
Bush, George H. W.: competitiveness initiatives by, 138; on currency manipulation by China, 74; on education competitiveness, 141–42; on Japan, 36
Bush, George W.: American Competitiveness Initiative by, 131, 149; on currency manipulation by China, 61; on earnings stripping, 96; on education reform, 142–43; fast-track approval for, 54; Invest in America by, 91–92; Select USA and, 187; TAA under, 121–22; on tax havens, 104; on US innovation, 149
business: competition of countries compared with, 155–56; competitiveness of US for, 8; import competition results for, 80; labor interests and, 79–80; local-serving and export-serving, 180; on NAFTA and TPP, 82; offshore investment by, 80–82; on value of US currency, 67–68. *See also* lobby, business
business, small, 133, 139–40, 150
Business Roundtable and the Emergency Committee for American Trade (ECAT), 87, 90

CAFTA. *See* Central American Free Trade Agreement
Camp, Dave, 96–97
capital mobility, 2–3, 3–4
Carter, Jimmy: currency manipulation under, 66; Japan and, 36, 107; TAA in budget of, 120–21

Caterpillar: competitiveness theories and, 158–60; location incentives for, 160; offshore investment and, 159–60; on overvalued US currency, 67–68; Plaza Accord and, 159; wages and competitiveness of, 169
Cato Institute, 124
CEA. *See* Council of Economic Advisers
Central American Free Trade Agreement (CAFTA), 54, 94, 101
Chamber of Commerce, 87–88
China: comparative advantage with, 38–39; competitiveness and, 30, 39–40, 127–28, 161; consumption tax in, 42; currency manipulation by, 61, 64, 72–75, 191–92; currency value of, 57, 64, 72–75; exports and, 38–43; IMF and, 72, 74–75; imports and, 31, 38–39, 40–42, 114–15; job loss and imports from, 31; market distortions by, 43–44; petition on labor standards in, 101; steel subsidies by, 42–43; subsidies in, 40–43; technology transfer in, 39–40; television industry and, 110; trade deficit with, 30, 38–39; WTO and, 27–28, 30, 33, 38–44, 51
Chua, Amy, 127
CIEP. *See* White House Council on International Economic Policy
Clinton, Bill: on Airbus, 50; on China WTO membership, 38; on civilian R&D, 148–49; currency policy under, 70–72; on education reform, 142; exports and, 22–24; fast-track approval for, 54; industry-specific negotiations by, 36; Japan and, 21, 71; on NAFTA, 22; on NAFTA, labor and environment, 99; TAA under, 121; on tax havens, 103–4; trade conditions under, 70–71; on US competitiveness, 138–39
Clinton, Hillary, 188–89
Cold War, 24
Commission on Foreign Economic Policy, 116–17
Commission on Industrial Competitiveness, 135–36
Common Core, 143

comparative advantage, 25, 30, 38–39
competition: business lobby advocacy for,
133; business results of import, 80; of
countries and businesses compared,
155–56; in open economy, 4; sectors
vulnerable to international, 156–57;
technology and import, 5; US presidents
on, 128. *See also* investment competition
The Competitive Advantage of Nations
(Porter), 164
competitive dollar, 76, 189–92
competitive economies, 92
competitiveness, 6, 135–36; bottoms-up
strategy of, 177–78, 183; of China, 30,
39–40, 127–28, 161; Congressional
Caucus on, 137; European Economic
Community and, 12; Germany and, 30,
161; of Japan, 11–12, 30; wages and,
97–98, 168–69, 183
competitiveness, assessment of, 160; foreign
investment flows and, 162–63; global
rankings and, 163–64; productivity and,
164–65; trade balances and, 161–62
competitiveness, economic strategy for: in
Buffalo, 172–73; competitive dollar as,
189–92; cost competition as, 184–86;
enforcement strategies in, 195–97;
export competition as, 188–89; federal
support for state and local, 182–83;
investment competition as, 186–88;
market distortion reduction as, 192–95;
National Research Council on, 130;
Race to the Top and, 143, 199–201;
second chance for, 202; by state and
local governments, 173–83, 197; worker
focus as, 197–99
competitiveness, theories of: Caterpillar
and, 158–60; cost and productivity
based, 165–70; countries and, 153–58,
165–67; governments and economists
on, 154–55; sports, countries, and, 154
competitiveness, US, 8, 11–13; Commission
on Industrial Competitiveness on,
135–36; cost and, 182–83; domestic
challenges of, 127–30; education and,
132, 140–44; of infrastructure, 144–47;
innovation and, 147–51; movement

for, 130, 134–40; national strategy
for, 130–34, 151–52; policy needed
for, 16; Reagan and, 67–70, 135–36;
Republicans, Democrats and, 133,
138–40, 170, 175; US presidents on,
131–32, 138–40, 152
Competitiveness Policy Council, 137
Congress, US: on currency manipulation,
70, 73; fast-track approval by, 54;
protectionism in, 68; US Export-Import
Bank shut down by, 19
Congressional Caucus on Competitiveness,
137
consumer goods, 29
Cook, Tim, 93
corporations, 7, 93–96, 184–85. *See also*
multinational corporations
cost: of adjustment, 26–28; competitiveness
theories and, 165–70; economic
competitiveness strategy and, 184–86;
federal regulations and, 185–86; taxes and,
184–85; US competitiveness and, 182–83
Council of Economic Advisers (CEA),
66–67, 135
Council on Competitiveness, 136–37
Council on Foreign Relations, 31, 148
Council on Jobs and Competitiveness, 132,
152
Crebo-Rediker, Heidi, 201
Cuomo, Andrew, 172–73
currency, 9–10; China value of, 57, 64,
72–75; Clinton, B., policy for, 70–72;
foreign exchange reserves nationality
of, 211n9; global balance of, 58–65;
institutional system for exchange of, 59;
Japan and, 56, 63–64, 66; misalignment
of, 76–78; Nixon policy for, 61–63;
Reagan policy for, 65–70; unfair
exchange provisions for, 55
currency, value of US, 25, 59, 63, 189–92;
Federal Reserve on, 60, 65; Plaza Accord
and, 69–70, 213n56; Reagan on, 61,
66; trade, deficit and, 55–58; trade
results of exaggerated, 64–65, 211n25;
unemployment and, 68; US businesses
on, 67–68. *See also* competitive dollar;
strong dollar

currency manipulation, 54–55; under
Carter, 66; by China, 61, 64, 72–75,
191–92; definition of, 56; IMF and, 56,
190; Korea, Taiwan and, 74; regulation
of, 56–57, 190–92; results of, 57,
60–61, 75; surplus nations incentives
for, 58–59; TPP and, 190; trade deficit
and, 60–61; US government on, 59–61,
70, 73

Day of Empire (Chua), 127
deferral, 95–96
deficit: currency manipulation results for
US, 60–61; currency value and, 55–58,
63; of infrastructure, 200; of Reagan
federal budget, 66–67; recession results
for, 162; TAA and budget, 121; of US
trade, 161–62. *See also* trade deficit,
US
Democrats, 133, 170, 175
Denmark, 126
developmental state, 34
Dillon, Douglas, 95
disability, 112–13
Dorn, David, 114–15

earmarking, 146
earnings stripping, 96
Easton, 35
ECAT. *See* Business Roundtable and the
Emergency Committee for American
Trade
economics: competitiveness theories
and, 154–55. *See also* Bretton Woods
economic system; competitiveness,
economic strategy for; Council of
Economic Advisers; European Economic
Community; Organization for Economic
Cooperation and Development; Peterson
Institute for International Economics;
White House Council on International
Economic Policy; World Economic
Forum
economic statecraft, 188–89
economy: competitive, 92; open, 4. *See also*
global economy; "The International
Economy and American Business";

*The United States in a Changing World
Economy*
economy, US, 3, 70–71
education, 128–29; job market success
and, 140–41; reform of, 133, 142–44;
retraining and, 113, 114, 123–25; US
competitiveness and, 132, 140–44; US
presidents and governors on, 141–43;
wealth results for, 143–44; of workforce,
125, 197–99
Eisenhower, Dwight D., 79, 116–17
Emergency Committee for American Trade,
13
Empire State Development Corporation,
173
entrepreneurship, 157, 181–82
environment, 99–100
European Commission, 194
European Economic Community, 12, 88
European unemployment programs, 126
European Union: aircraft dispute with,
49–51; GATT, aircraft, and, 50; market
distortions and, 193–94
European Union (EU), 49–51, 194
Evergreen Solar, 40
exchange, currency: institutional system for
rates of, 59; nationality of reserves for,
211n9; unfair provisions for, 55
Export-Import Bank, US, 19, 133
exports, 1–2; China and, 38–43; Clinton,
B., administration on, 22–24;
competition strategy for, 188–89;
currency value results for, 64–65,
211n25; Germany promotion of, 189;
local-serving contrasted with, 180;
semiconductors as, 49
Ezell, Stephen, 180, 186, 195

fabless companies, 44, 49
fast-track mechanism, 54
FDI. *See* foreign direct investment
Federal Reserve, 60, 65–66
Feldstein, Martin, 67, 76, 189, 213n56
Five Rivers Electronic Innovations, 110
Ford, 123–24
foreign direct investment (FDI), 162–63
foreign exchange reserves, 211n9

foreign investment flows, 162–63. *See also* global investment; offshore investment

foreign tax credit, 95

France, 166–67

free trade, 8; Israel agreement for bilateral, 27; Kennedy on, 111; protectionism debate with, 4; Putin and, 27; TAA as encouragement for, 116. *See also* trade

Friedman, Thomas, 133

Gagnon, Joe, 60, 191

Gallois, Louis, 167

Garten, Jeffrey, 27

GATT. *See* General Agreement on Tariffs and Trade

GDP. *See* gross domestic product

General Agreement on Tariffs and Trade (GATT), 28–29; EU aircraft dispute and, 50; Japan and, 34–36, 114

Generalized System of Preferences (GSP), 99–100

General Motors (GM), 41, 157

Gephardt, Richard, 131

Germany: competitiveness and, 30, 161; export promotion by, 189; US Treasury on, 75–76

Global Competitiveness Report (WEF), 163–64

global economy: currency imbalance in, 58–65; job and wage effects of, 3–6. *See also* "The International Economy and American Business"; trade; *The United States in a Changing World Economy*

global investment: competitive economies and, 92; US government and, 19–20, 102; US presidents on attracting, 91–92; US states and cities attracting, 18–20, 92, 104, 173–78. *See also* offshore investment

globalization, 8–9, 115–16

global rankings, 163–64

global rules, 20, 102–5

GM. *See* General Motors

gold convertibility, 9–10

Gordon, Robert, 165

government: on competitiveness theories, 154–55; on currency manipulation, 59–

61, 70, 73; federal support for state and local, 182–83; global investment and, 18–20, 102; R&D funded by, 148–50; small, 139–40; state and local, 18–20, 92, 104, 173–83, 197

governors: on education, 141–43. *See also* National Governors Association

Graham, Lindsay, 74

Greeneville, Tennessee, 109–10

greenfield investment, 163

Greenhouse Compact, 179–80

Greenspan, Alan, 60

gross domestic product, 2

gross national product, 2

GSP. *See* Generalized System of Preferences

Guatemala, 100–101

Guidelines for Multinational Enterprises, 103

Hanson, Gordon, 114–15

Harper, Edwin, 134–35

Hartke, Vance, 87. *See also* Burke-Hartke bill

Harvard Business School, 97

Hashimoto, Ryutaro, 23

Hecksher, Eli, 111

Henning, Randall, 60, 72–74

Heritage Foundation, 124, 149

high-technology: deficit with China in, 39; government funded R&D for, 148, 150; trade and, 30

Hlatshwayo, Sandile, 31

Hoover, Herbert, 97

Hughes, Kent, 89, 130–31

human rights, 99

Humphrey, Hubert, 117

IGPAC. *See* Intergovernmental Policy Advisory Committee on Trade

ILO. *See* International Labor Organization

IMD. *See* Institute for Management Development

IMF. *See* International Monetary Fund

import competition, 114–15

imports, 3; beggar-thy-neighbor and, 29; under Burke-Hartke bill, 88; China and, 31, 38–39, 40–42, 114–15; Japan and,

21–24, 34–37, 46–48, 107–8; 1960s
    business results of, 80; semiconductors
    as, 46, 48; SolarCity and tariff on, 172;
    technology and competition of, 5; US
    need for, 1–2
income, median family, 7
income inequality, 7
inflation, 65–66
infrastructure, 129, 134; for broadband,
    147; deficit of, 200; earmarking, tax
    and, 146; National Infrastructure Bank
    and, 146; Rebuild America Fund for,
    139; in United Kingdom, 147; US
    competitiveness of, 144–47
innovation, US, 147; military and, 148;
    R&D and, 201; US presidents on,
    149–50
Institute for Management Development
    (IMD), 163–64
Intel, 48, 186
intelligence, 187–88
Interagency Trade Enforcement Center
    (ITEC), 44, 195–96
interest rates, 65
Intergovernmental Policy Advisory
    Committee on Trade (IGPAC), 194–95
international burden sharing, 24–26
"The International Economy and American
    Business" (Bergsten), 107
International Labor Organization (ILO),
    97, 99
International Monetary Fund (IMF),
    55; China and, 72, 74–75; currency
    manipulation and, 56, 190; currency
    misalignment recommendations for,
    77–77; TPP and, 190; on wage
    competition, 98
International Trade and Investment Task
    Force of the Business Roundtable, 68
inversions, 94
Invest in America, 91–92
Investing in Manufacturing Communities
    Partnership, 200
Invest in the U.S.A., 91
investment, 166–67. See also foreign
    investment flows; global investment;
    offshore investment

investment competition, 186–88. See also
    location incentives
Israel, 27
ITEC. See Interagency Trade Enforcement
    Center

Jager, Elizabeth, 81
Japan: auto imports in, 36–37; Clinton, B.,
    and, 21, 71; competitiveness of, 11–12,
    30; currency and, 56, 63–64, 66; GATT,
    imports and, 34–36, 114; imports and,
    21–24, 34–37, 46–48, 107–8; overview
    of trade in, 33–34; semiconductor trade
    with, 46–49; tariff on imports from,
    21–24, 36, 47–48; technology transfer
    to, 46; television industry and, 107–9;
    TPP and, 37; trade deficit with, 22–23,
    29–30; United States–Japan Trade
    Facilitation Committee with, 36
Jensen, Brad, 156
jobs: China imports and lost, 31; education
    and success of, 140–41; entrepreneurship
    and, 157; global economy results for,
    3–6; import competition results for,
    114–15; for lower-skilled Americans,
    114; with multinational corporations,
    84–86; multinational corporations and,
    158; offshore investment results for,
    84–86; trade agreement results for,
    30–32. See also unemployment
Jobs and Competitiveness Council, 132,
    152
Johnson, Chalmers, 34
Johnson, Lyndon B., 118–19
Judis, John, 87, 90

Kantor, Mickey, 21, 23–24, 36
Katz, Lawrence, 7
Kendall, Donald, 90, 113
Kennedy, John F.: on deferrals, 95–96; on
    free trade, 111; Invest in the U.S.A. by,
    91; TAA and, 110–11, 117–18; Trade
    Adjustment Act of 1954 by, 117–18;
    Trade Expansion Act of 1962 by, 14,
    80, 111
Kennedy Round, 28. See also General
    Agreement on Tariffs and Trade

Keohane, Robert, 27, 28
Kissinger, Henry, 10, 15
Korea, 74
Krugman, Paul, 98–99, 155

labor: business and interests of, 79–80; OECD ranking of market for, 125; offshore investment, wages and, 97–101. *See also* unions
labor mobility, 2–4
labor standards: in China, 101; environment and, 99–100; in Guatemala and Peru, 100–101; OPIC and, 99; TPP and, 100
Lawrence, Robert, 31, 57
Lego model of production, 83
level playing field, 28–33
Levin, Carl, 93
Levin, Sander, 37
Lew, Jacob, 55, 60
Lincoln, Edward, 37–38
Lipsey, Robert, 84–85
lobby, business: Burke-Hartke bill and, 87–91; competition advocacy by, 133; on earnings stripping, 96; offshore research funded by, 90–91
location incentives: for multinational corporations, 102–3, 160, 186; site location industry and, 180–81; state and local governments and, 104, 173–82; in US trade agreements and BITs, 103. *See also* investment competition
Louvre Accord, 69
Lufthansa Technik, 187

Magaziner, Ira, 179–80
Magnavox, 107–10
Mandelbaum, Michael, 133
manufacturing, US: offshore investment and, 88; R&D and, 151; under Reagan, 67–70; undervalued Chinese currency results for, 75. *See also* National Association of Manufacturers
Manufacturing Extension Partnerships, 149
market distortions, 32–33; by China, 43–44; European Union and, 193–94; reduction of, 192–95; in TPP, 52. *See also* subsidies

market interventions: Federal Reserve and, 65–66; by Treasury Department, 66, 72–74. *See also* currency manipulation
Massachusetts Institute of Technology (MIT), 83
Mathematica Policy Research, 121, 124–25
McDonald, David J., 116
Meany, George, 80
Merkel, Angela, 189
Mexico, 98, 109–10
middle class. *See* income, median family
Milanovic, Branko, 29
military, 148
military, US, 45–46, 148
milling industry, 171
minimum wage, 89
Ministry of International Trade and Industry (MITI), 34, 46, 48
Mississippi, 178–79
Mississippi Industrial Act of 1936, 178–79
MIT. *See* Massachusetts Institute of Technology
MITI. *See* Ministry of International Trade and Industry
MITI and the Japanese Miracle (Johnson), 34
monopolies, 156
Morgan, Lee, 68
Morristown, Tennessee, 107–8
multinational corporations, 82; Burke-Hartke Bill and, 86–92; jobs in US and abroad with, 84–86; location incentives for, 102–3, 160, 186; offshore investment by, 83–86; rules for, 20, 102–5; unions on, 13; in *The United States in a Changing World Economy*, 13, 86–87; US jobs and, 158; wages in US with, 85–86. *See also* corporations

NAFTA. *See* North American Free Trade Agreement
National Academy of Sciences (NAS), 128–29
National Association of Manufacturers, 68, 87, 117–18
National Competitiveness Act, 149
National Export Initiative (NEI), 188–89

National Governors Association, 182, 200

national infrastructure bank, 146

National Network for Manufacturing Innovation, 150

National Research Council, 130

national savings rate, 34

A Nation at Risk (NAS), 128

NCLB. *See* No Child Left Behind

NEI. *See* National Export Initiative

New Deal, 113–14

Nike, 18–19

Nixon, Richard, 9–10; Burke-Hartke bill and, 91; currency policy of, 61–63; import tariff by, 62; TAA under, 119–20; on trade adjustment assistance, 119–20; on unemployment insurance, 119; on *The United States in a Changing World Economy*, 14–15

No Child Left Behind (NCLB), 142–44

North American Free Trade Agreement (NAFTA): Clinton, B., on, 22, 99; Mexico wage results of, 98; Obama on, 53; union-business conflict over, 82; US trade deficit and, 31

Nye, Joseph, 28

Obama, Barack: American Apprenticeship Fund under, 199; on education reform, 143–44; on infrastructure, 146; on labor standards in Guatemala, 101; on level playing field, 28; on NAFTA, 53; NEI and, 188; Race to the Top and, 143, 200; Select USA by, 92; TAA under, 122; on tax reform, 96–97; on TPP, 6, 32, 53–55, 100; on TPP, labor and environment, 100; trade adjustment assistance under, 122; Trade Enforcement Center created by, 44; unemployment insurance under, 122; on US competitiveness, 131–32, 140, 152; on US innovation, 150; on wage insurance, 199

OECD. *See* Organization for Economic Cooperation and Development

offshore investment, 79, 105; Burke-Hartke Bill and, 86–92; by business, 80–82; business lobby research of, 90–91;

Caterpillar and, 159–60; global rules for, 102–5; job and wage results of, 84–86; by multinational corporations, 83–86; by RCA, 80; of R&D, 150–51; tax for, 88–89, 93–97, 103–5; unions and, 13, 81–82, 88–91; US manufacturing and, 88; wages, labor standards and, 97–101. *See also* global investment

Ohlin, Bertil, 111

Omnibus Trade and Competitiveness Act of 1988, 73–74; China labor standards petition and, 101; Competitiveness Policy Council mandated by, 137

O'Neill, Paul, 104

open economy, 4

open market, US, 24

OPIC. *See* Overseas Private Investment Corporation

Organization for Economic Cooperation and Development (OECD), 7; on international tax policies, 103–4; US education ranking by, 141; US foreign investment ranking by, 92; US labor market policy ranking by, 125

Organization for International Investment, 96

Our Kids: The American Dream in Crisis (Putnam), 8

outsourcing. *See* offshore investment

Overseas Private Investment Corporation (OPIC), 91, 99

Panama Canal, 147

Paul, Rand, 93

Perot, Ross, 82

Perry, Rick, 178

Peru, 100

Peterson, Peter George, 17–18. *See also The United States in a Changing World Economy*

Peterson Institute for International Economics, 60

Philips Consumer Electronics of the Netherlands, 109–10

Pisano, Gary, 8, 151

Plaza Accord: Caterpillar and, 159; Reagan and, 64, 69–70, 159; US currency value and, 69–70, 213n56

poaching, 178, 181
Porter, Michael, 131, 135; on attractiveness of investment, 166; *The Competitive Advantage of Nations* by, 164
Portland, Oregon, 18–19, 174
Portman, Rob, 54–55
presidents, US: on attracting global investment, 91–92; on competition, 128; on education, 141–43; on US competitiveness, 131–32, 138–40, 152; on US innovation, 149–50. *See also specific presidents*
Prestowitz, Clyde, 35
production, Lego model of, 83
productivity, 98, 164–70
protectionism, 25, 62; free trade debate with, 4; in House and Senate in 1985, 68; in 2016 presidential election, 26
Puerto Rico, 187
Putin, Vladimir, 27
Putnam, Robert, 8

Qualcomm, 44, 49

Race to the Top, 143, 199–201
Randall Commission, 116–17
Rawlings, 35
RCA, 80
R&D. *See* research and development
Reagan, Ronald, 6; currency policy of, 65–70; on currency value, 61, 66; industry-specific negotiations by, 36; Japanese import tariff under, 22, 47–48; on labor standards in GSP, 99; Plaza Accord and, 64, 69–70, 159; on Small Business Innovation Research Act, 149–50; TAA and, 113, 120–21, 124; on US competitiveness, 135–36
Rebuild America Fund, 139
recession, 162
Regan, Donald, 66
regulations, federal, 185–86
Reich, Robert, 131
religious rights, 99
Rendell, Ed, 127–128
renewable energy, 156

Republicans: on R&D, 149–50; small business and, 133, 139–40; small government and, 139–40; state and local competitiveness and, 175; Tea Party and, 140; US competitiveness and, 133, 138–40, 170
research and development (R&D), 152; government funded, 148–50; for high-technology, 148, 150; military funded, 148; offshoring of, 150–51; Republicans on government funded, 149–50; for small businesses, 150; US innovation and, 201
retraining, 113, 123–25; of displaced Ford workers, 123; in US and abroad, 114. *See also* education
Rhode Island, 178–79
rise of the rest, 11–13
Rising above the Gathering Storm (NAS), 128–29
Robinson, David, 178
Romer, Christina, 71
Rubin, Robert, 71
Ruttenberg, Stanley, 81

SBIR. *See* Small Business Innovation Research
security interests, 27–28
Select USA, 92, 187
self-initiated trade enforcement, 196–97
semiconductors, 176–77; China tax rebate for, 44; Japan, trade rule enforcement and, 46–49; SolarCity and, 172; US military and, 45–46
Senate, 68
Senate Permanent Subcommittee on Investigations, US, 93
Shaiken, Harley, 98
Sharp, 46
Shih, Willy, 8, 151
Silevo, 172–73
Singham, Shanker, 32
site location industry, 180–81
Small Business Innovation Research (SBIR), 201
Small Business Innovation Research Act, 149–50

SolarCity, 172, 173
solar energy, 40
Solomon, Anthony, 68
South Carolina, 18
Spence, Michael, 31
Sperling, Gene, 158
sports, 154
Stabenow, Debbie, 54–55
Startup-NY, 181
steel, 42–43
strong dollar, 57–59, 61, 64–65, 67–68, 71, 189–90. *See also* currency, value of US
Structural Impediments Initiative, 36
Subpart F, 96
subsidies: of aircraft, 49–51; BITs and rules for, 194; in China, 40–43; European Union and, 49–51, 194; of industry by states, 178–79; of solar energy in China, 40; in TPP, 52
Sullivan, Martin, 94, 104
Summers, Larry, 38, 71
surplus nations, 58–59
"Survey of Current Business" (1961), 1

TAA. *See* trade adjustment assistance
Taiwan, 74
tariff: currency manipulation and, 57; on Japanese imports, 21–24, 36, 47–48; Nixon import surcharge, 62
Tariff Commission, 118–19
tariffs, 88
tax, 184; China semiconductor rebate of, 44; on consumption in China, 42; of corporations, 93–96, 184–85; foreign credit for, 95; infrastructure and gas, 146; for offshore investments, 88–89, 93–97, 103–5; state and local competitiveness and, 177, 181; on US Treasury securities and bonds, 67; value-added, 12, 185
tax avoidance, 93
tax havens, 93–94, 103–4
tax reform, 96–97
teachers, 144
Tea Party Republicans, 140
technology, 4–5, 138

technology transfer, 102–3; in China, 39–40; in Japan joint ventures, 46; unions on, 89
television industry: China and, 110; in Greeneville, Tennessee, 109–10; Japan and, 107–9; Mexico and, 109–10; TAA requests in, 107–8, 110
Tennessee, 18, 107–10
tiger mother, 127
Tokyo Round. *See* General Agreement on Tariffs and Trade
TPP. *See* Trans-Pacific Partnership
trade, 6, 26, 52; consumer goods results of, 29; currency value and, 55–58; currency value results for, 64–65, 67, 211n25; high-technology and, 30; Japan overview of, 33–34; 1990s conditions of, 70–71; practices of various countries, 17; security interests and, 27–28; United States–Japan Trade Facilitation Committee for, 36; US share of international, 3. *See also* free trade
Trade Act, 1974, 99
Trade Act, 1988, 73–74, 101, 137
Trade Adjustment Act of 1954, 117–18
trade adjustment assistance (TAA), 197; budget deficit and, 121; Carter on, 120–21; from Clinton, B., to Obama, 121–22; Eisenhower on, 116–17; European unemployment programs and, 126; as free trade encouragement, 116; from Johnson to Nixon, 118–20; Kennedy and, 110–11, 117–18; for losers of globalization, 115–16; National Association of Manufacturers on, 117–18; Reagan and, 113, 120–21, 124; research on outcomes for, 124–25; retraining and, 113–14, 123–25; Tariff Commission on, 118–19; television industry and, 107–8, 110; in Trade Expansion Act of 1962, 14, 111; unemployment, disability and, 112–13, 117; unions on, 118–20; in *The United States in a Changing World Economy*, 13–14, 112, 202
trade agreements, US, 28–32, 54
trade balances, 161–62

trade deficit, US: with China, 30, 38–39; with Japan, 22–23, 29–30, 37; NAFTA and, 31

Trade Expansion Act of 1962, 80; adjustment assistance in, 14, 111

trade policy, US, 16–17, 27–31, 37–39

Trade Representative, US (USTR), 40, 42–43, 194–96

trade rule enforcement, 44–45; for aircraft industry, 49–51; priorities of, 196; resources for, 195–96; self-initiated, 196–97; for semiconductors, 46–49; state and locally initiated, 197; by WTO, 33, 44, 50–51

trade-to-GDP ratio, 2

Trading Places (Prestowitz), 35

Transatlantic Trade and Investment Partnership (TTIP), 16, 52, 53–54, 193–94

Trans-Pacific Partnership (TPP), 16; currency manipulation and, 190; Japan and, 37; labor standards and, 100; Obama on, 6, 32, 53–55, 100; security interests in, 27; subsidies and market distortion in, 52; union-business conflict over, 82

Treasury, US, 58, 69; on currency manipulation, 70, 73; on Germany, 75–76; market interventions by, 66, 72–74; tax on bonds and securities of, 67

Trumka, Richard, 82

TTIP. *See* Transatlantic Trade and Investment Partnership

UI. *See* unemployment insurance

unemployment: currency manipulation results for, 60–61; European programs for, 126; TAA and, 112–13, 116–17; US currency value and, 68. *See also* jobs

unemployment insurance (UI), 113–14, 119, 122

unions: Burke-Hartke bill and, 87–91; on infrastructure, 145; on multinational corporations, 13; on NAFTA, 82; offshore investment and, 13, 81–82, 88–91; religious rights, human rights and,

99; on TAA, 118–20; on technology transfer, 89; on TPP, 82

United Kingdom, 147

United States–Japan Trade Facilitation Committee, 36

The United States in a Changing World Economy (Peterson), 9–10, 20, 60, 175; on currency and global balance, 58–59; on international burden sharing, 24–26; on multinational corporations, 13, 86–87; reception of, 14–15; on trade adjustment, 13–14, 112, 202; on US competitiveness, 11–13, 129–30

Uruguay Round. *See* General Agreement on Tariffs and Trade

USTR. *See* Trade Representative, US

value-added tax (VAT), 12, 185

VAT. *See* value-added tax

Volcker, Paul, 62, 68; on currency value, 63; interest rates raised by, 65

Volvo, 18

wage insurance, 122, 199

wages: Caterpillar competitiveness and, 169; competitiveness and, 97–98, 168–69, 183; global economy results for, 3–4, 6; import competition results for, 114–15; labor standards, offshore investment and, 97–101; of lower-skilled Americans, 114; minimum, 89; with multinational corporations, 85–86; trade agreement results for, 30–32

wealth, 143–44

We Build Green Cities, 174

WEF. *See* World Economic Forum

welfare, TAA and, 112–13, 116–17

White House Council on Competitiveness, 138

White House Council on International Economic Policy (CIEP), 10–15

Wilson, Charles E., 79

Wilson, Woodrow, 97

Wolff, Alan, 37

workforce development, 125, 197–99. *See also* education

World Bank, 92

World Competitiveness Yearbook (IMD), 163–64

World Economic Forum (WEF), 132, 153; *Global Competitiveness Report* by, 163–64; on US infrastructure, 144

World Trade Organization (WTO), 5, 16, 23; China and, 27–28, 30, 33, 38–44, 51; on currency manipulation, 56; currency misalignment recommendations for, 77; EU aircraft dispute and, 49–51; rule enforcement by, 33, 44, 50–51; on VAT, 185

Wright, Jim, 130–31

WTO. *See* World Trade Organization

Young, John, 138; Commission on Industrial Competitiveness and, 135–36; on competitiveness, 6; on competitiveness and wages, 168–69; Council on Competitiveness and, 136–37

Zoellick, Robert, 38

About the Author

Edward Alden is the Bernard L. Schwartz senior fellow at the Council on Foreign Relations in Washington, DC, and the former Washington bureau chief for the *Financial Times*. He is the author of *The Closing of the American Border: Terrorism, Immigration, and Security Since 9/11*, which was named a finalist for the J. Anthony Lukas Book Prize for non-fiction. The judges called the book "a masterful job of comprehensive reporting, fair-minded analysis, and structurally sound argumentation." He has written extensively about the US response to globalization, focusing particularly on international trade and immigration. He was the co-project director for the Council's *Independent Task Force on U.S. Trade and Investment Policy* (2011), co-chaired by former White House chief of staff Andrew Card and former Senate majority leader Thomas Daschle. He also directed the *Independent Task Force on U.S. Immigration Policy* (2009), which was co-chaired by former Florida governor Jeb Bush and former White House chief of staff Thomas F. (Mack) McLarty. Most recently, he was co-author of a book-length assessment of US economic competitiveness titled *How America Stacks Up: Economic Competitiveness and U.S. Policy*. He has testified to Congress numerous times, and has written for a wide range of publications including the *New York Times*, the *Wall Street Journal*, the *Washington Post*, and *Foreign Affairs*. He holds degrees from the University of California, Berkeley, and the University of British Columbia.